THE PARADIGM DIALOG

Edited by
Egon G. Guba

THE PARADIGM DIALOG

*Sponsored by Phi Delta Kappa International and
The School of Education, Indiana University*

SAGE Publications
International Educational and Professional Publisher
Newbury Park London New Delhi

For information address:

SAGE Publications, Inc.
2455 Teller Road
Newbury Park, California 91320
E-mail: order@sagepub.com

SAGE Publications Ltd.
6 Bonhill Street
London EC2A 4PU
United Kingdom

SAGE Publications India Pvt. Ltd.
M-32 Market
Greater Kailash I
New Delhi 110 048 India

Printed in the United States of America

Library of Congress Cataloging-in-Publication Data

The Paradigm dialog / Egon G. Guba, editor.
        p. cm.
        "Sponsored by Phi Delta Kappa International and the School of
Education, Indiana University."
        Includes bibliographical references and index.
        ISBN 0-8039-3822-5. — ISBN 0-8039-3823-3 (pbk.)
        1. Social sciences—Methodology—Congresses. 2. Paradigms (Social
sciences)—Congresses. I. Guba, Egon G.
H61.P29 1990
300—dc20   90-43947
                                                                CIP

        98 99 00 01 11 10 9 8

Sage Production Editor: Judith L. Hunter

Contents

Foreword

This book is about options for inquiry: options among the paradigms—basic belief systems—that have emerged as successors to conventional positivism. Three options are explored in this book: *postpositivism*, on the shoulders of whose proponents the mantles of succession *and* of hegemony appear to have fallen, and two brash and sometimes contentious contendors, *critical theory* and *constructivism*. Although all three alternatives reject positivism, they make very different diagnoses of its problems and, therefore, offer very different remedies. United in what they oppose, they are nevertheless divided, sometimes sharply, on what they espouse.

Appreciation of this state of affairs served as stimulus for the "Alternative Paradigms Conference" held in San Francisco, March 25 and 26, 1989, under the sponsorship of Phi Delta Kappa International and the Indiana University School of Education. The purpose of this conference was *not* to crown the new queen of paradigms but to clarify the rival alternatives that have emerged. Attempts at clarification lead inevitably to the identification of certain salient issues, whose exploration was the second purpose of the conference. Finally, the conference was intended to legitimate the two contenders not now enjoying hegemony, by demonstrating that their positions are at least as reasonable and useful as those of either positivism or postpositivism.

The conference was organized to facilitate the achievement of these ends. As it opened on Saturday morning, three keynoters presented papers intended to set forth the basic systems of beliefs undergirding the three emergent paradigms. Each of the speakers was well known as an advocate of his or her particular position: Denis Phillips, Stanford University, for postpositivism; Thomas Popkewitz, University of Wisconsin, for critical theory; and Yvonna Lincoln, Vanderbilt University, for constructivism. On both Saturday afternoon and Sunday morning, eight concurrent sessions were held in which eight issue areas were examined. Each issue was addressed by a speaker whose charge was to assess the interpretation that advocates of each of the three paradigms might make of it. Critiques of *their* papers were then made by eight "critic/respondents," following which participants engaged in questions and discussion. Participants were thus enabled to attend two issue presentations of their choice, one on each half day. These issues, the speakers, and the critic respondents were as follows:

(1) *Accommodation.* Must choices, however hard, be made among these paradigms, or is it possible that they might be brought into some complementary or ecumenical posture?

Speaker: William Firestone, Rutgers University
Critic/Respondent: Thomas Skrtic, University of Kansas

(2) *Ethics.* Do the several paradigms raise ethical issues unique to their own philosophical postures? Or is there one set of ethical problems that *all* paradigms face?

Speaker: Louis Smith, Washington University, St. Louis
Critic/Respondent: Ernest House, University of Chicago

(3) *Goodness criteria.* Is it possible to derive a set of goodness criteria equally applicable to all paradigms? What evidence of quality would (should) be considered appropriate for each paradigm?

Speaker: John Smith, University of Northern Iowa
Critic/Respondent: Catherine Marshall, Vanderbilt University

(4) *Implementation.* What is the relation of research and practice? How can the findings of inquiry be put to use?

Speakers: Judith Green and Susanne Chandler, Ohio State University
Critic/Respondent: David Crandall, Regional Laboratory for Educational
    Improvement, Northeast and Isles

(5) *Knowledge accumulation.* Is knowledge accumulated in similar ways within the several paradigms? Is the concept of knowledge accumulation appropriate to each? What is the role of theory and of the literature in this accumulation process?

Speaker: Jennifer Greene, Cornell University
Critic/Respondent: Margaret LeCompte, Private Consultant

(6) *Methodology.* Is methodology independent of paradigmatic considerations? Do paradigms imply methodologies?

Speaker: Thomas Schwandt, Indiana University (then Northern Illinois
University)
Critic/Respondent: Gail McCutcheon, Ohio State University

(7) *Training*. Does a shift from paradigm to paradigm imply more
than mere training or retraining in the newly appropriate inquiry
skills? Is resocialization required? Is training controlled by adherents
of the paradigm having hegemony?

Speaker: Shulamit Reinharz, Brandeis University
Critic/Respondent: Jeri Nowakowski, North Central Regional Educational
Laboratory (then Northern Illinois University)

(8) *Values*. What role do values play in inquiry? If inquiry is not
value free, is not all inquiry ideological? Does the admission that
values play a role open the door to the use of inquiry as an instrument
of social reformation at the expense of its role as generator of knowledge?

Speaker: Patricia Lather, Ohio State University
Critic/Respondent: Madeleine Grumet, Brooklyn College

The conference had several additional features. Elliot Eisner, Stanford University, in the role of dinner speaker but bringing a much
more serious message than is usual on such occasions, addressed the
audience on "the meaning of alternative paradigms for practice."
Alan Peshkin, University of Illinois, served as "postnoter," providing
an ethnographic perspective on "what happened here" based on early
reading of all papers, telephone conversations with many of the
presenters, and on-site observations of many sessions and interviews
with a variety of participants. His paper, "Tales from the Rear," is both
amusing and insightful as a record of what transpired.

Three additional groups of eight persons each, termed *chairs, recorders*, and *auditors*, performed other vital functions for the eight issue
sessions. The chairs introduced speakers, managed the sessions, and
led the discussions. The recorders kept track of what transpired
during the question/discussion portions of the sessions; because each
issue session was presented twice, their reports (edited by recorder
chair Thomas Gregory, Indiana University) combine the comments
and observations made in *both* sessions. The *auditors* (for want of a

better name) were effectively "listening posts"; although auditors were assigned to specific issue sessions, they were asked to listen for any suggestions made by anyone at any time about next steps that might be taken to build on the conference experience and to capitalize on the momentum that had built up. Their individual reports are combined into one overall statement prepared by auditor chair Harbans Bhola, Indiana University.

All these papers and reports are contained in this book, together with this Foreword and introductory and concluding chapters. A glance at the Contents will show how the conference format is reflected in these pages. But whether the aims of the conference have been satisfactorily achieved is a matter not so easily determined; that judgment must necessarily be left to the reader. There was no effort to control the content of the several papers; each speaker was at liberty to make whatever interpretation of the assignment that pleased him or her. When bright people are asked to do creative work, it is not surprising when they produce something that varies considerably from what had been imagined by the asker. Give people a creative task to do and they will be creative about the way they do it. The reader should, therefore, not expect, nor will he or she find, papers that adhere strictly to the outline above. But he or she *will* find papers that are imaginative, insightful, provocative, and, yes, evocative as well. Their call will be hard to resist; their message hard to ignore.

It is also the case that their message is uneven, tentative, and formative. In the process of negotiating the contents to be included in this book, a considerable debate arose over whether the book should, finally, be "authentic," as one of the participants put it, or "sanitized"—a "best" book possible. A book that attempts to capture authentically what the state of mind of the many participants was as they prepared their papers will necessarily reflect their sophistication and commitment but also their intellectual doubts and their conflicts. It cannot be a well-articulated book, nor will the opinions expressed always be in agreement—even among those who profess to adhere to the same paradigm (or those who think the whole paradigm issue is trumped up and meaningless). No doubt, many of the participants have altered their own conceptions as a result of their conference experience, so that the opinions they expressed there might not be identical to those they would express now, given the opportunity to rewrite their papers. On the other hand, a book that aimed for "best book" status would include those rewritten versions and quite possibly might have seen some of the papers eliminated altogether. But it seemed to me as editor, and to many others whom I consulted, that the authentic book, while undoubtedly conceptually weaker and less coherent than a sanitized book would be, nevertheless would more accurately reflect the state of affairs abroad in the land as professionals come to grips with the paradigm problem. We felt it more important to allow the indecision, the conflict, and the contradiction to show than to paper it over with massively edited and reworked papers.

It is important, we think, for everyone—and in particular, those younger professionals and students for whom the paradigm issue may be particularly relevant—to understand that there are still few answers but many questions; indeed, we believe that such a posture is vital to continuing progress and growth. We invite the reader to approach these papers with the openness that is possible only when there are still matters to be resolved. We invite the reader also to enter into their resolution with enthusiasm—to participate to the fullest extent possible in the ongoing debate. However the reader may feel on that score, it must be obvious that no words and no book can capture the excitement that the participants felt in their participation. There was joy in discovering that there were others of like mind. There was joy in the ways that people found to connect—intellectually, emotionally, socially. There was joy in the often heated discussions, the challenges, the compromises, the moves toward consensus—or toward agreement to continue to disagree. Quite probably the full impact of the conference on those who were there will be neither fully understood nor appreciated for months to come. It was, in that word of the 1960s, a *happening*. It is likely that, if asked, each of the 255 persons taking part—presenters and participants—would give a very different view of what occurred. But it is equally likely that each of those 255 people would agree that the conference made a major impact on them, one not soon to be forgotten.

It is usual to acknowledge indebtedness to the people who have contributed to an event in significant ways. It is clear that this conference could not have been planned and implemented without help from a large number of people. I must first of all thank my former chairperson in the Department of Counseling and Educational Psychology, School of Education, Indiana University, DeWayne Kurpius, who initially proposed that such a conference be held. Howard Mehlinger, Dean of the Indiana School of Education, encouraged us to go ahead, lending both his counsel and his material support. I received an enthusiastic welcome from Phillip Harris, Director of Professional Development for Phi Delta Kappa, the international honorary fraternity in education, when I proposed PDK sponsorship. PDK took complete responsibility for all logistical and fiscal aspects of the conference, relieving me of that terrible burden. His staff, including, in the early days, Duane Richards, and, later, Polly Pershing and Enid Richards, performed the most difficult tasks with equanimity and grace. My own secretary at Indiana University, Coral Mulinix, ventured well beyond the call of duty in providing both logistical and moral support. To all of them I shall be forever grateful.

Others helped with more substantive tasks. I have already mentioned the names of the speakers and the chairs of the auditor and recorder groups. To that list must be added

- members of an ad hoc advisory committee at Indiana University who read and commented on early drafts of the conference proposal: Harbans Bhola, Jesse Goodman, Samuel Guskin, Jerome Harste, Robert Heinrich, Anna Ochoa, Melinda Swenson, and Richard Pugh
- conference discussion leaders: Thomas Barone, Northern Kentucky University; Robert Covert, University of Virginia; William Foster, University of San Diego; Valerie Janesick, Gallaudet University; James Pearsol, The Ohio State University; Leslie Roman, Louisiana State University; Jonas Soltis, Teachers College, Columbia University; and Melinda Swenson, Indiana University
- conference recorders: Ann Austin, Vanderbilt University; Judy Barford, Community School District 1, Charleston, Illinois; John Beck, United Paperworkers International Union; Marion Lundy Dobbert, University of Minnesota; Corrine Glesne, University of Vermont; Judith Preissle Goetz, University of Georgia; Thomas Gregory, Indiana University; and Lous Heshusius, York University
- conference auditors: Harbans Bhola, Indiana University; Marie Brennan, University of Wisconsin; Robert Donmoyer, The Ohio State University; Edward Halpern, AT&T Bell Labs; Les McLean, Ontario Institute for the Study of Education and the University of Toronto; Judith Meloy, Castleton State College (then Consultant for Program Evaluation, Connecticut State Department of Education); Rodman Webb, University of Florida; and David Williams, Brigham Young University

To each of them I say a heartfelt word of "thanks."

Egon G. Guba

PART I

Setting the Stage

Part I, Setting the Stage, consists of but a single chapter. Essentially this chapter reprises the substantive portion of the original conference proposal, setting out what, in my opinion, are the parameters of each of the three paradigms that were considered: postpositivism, critical theory, and constructivism. In that sense Part I sets the stage for all the chapters that follow.

The reader will quickly see, however, that *my* construction of what constituted the paradigm parameters, and of the emergent issues, was not necessarily shared by other participants. It is likely that readers of this volume will not share them either. Nevertheless, this construction did serve as a common point of reference, and, whether it was reinforced or rejected by individual presenters, it served a useful purpose as a kind of moving target.

I invite the reader to compare my constructions with those developed by the three keynoters (Part II), because their task, as proponents of the paradigm each presented, was to flesh out the form and substance of these three alternatives. In the case of the issue papers (Part III), it is interesting to note how the individual speakers differ among themselves, with the keynoters, and with this Part I construction. The differences are instructive and form the basis for any continuing dialectic.

[1]

The Alternative Paradigm Dialog

EGON C. GUBA

It is not surprising that most persons asked to define the term *paradigm* are unable to offer any clear statement of its meaning. I say it is not surprising because Thomas Kuhn, the person most responsible for bringing that concept into our collective awareness, has himself used the term in no fewer than 21 different ways, if Masterman (1970) can be believed. Some persons view that lack of clear definition as an unfortunate state of affairs. But I believe that it is important to leave the term in such a problematic limbo, because it is then possible to reshape it as our understanding of its many implications improves. Having the term *not* cast in stone is intellectually useful. Thus I will use the term in this chapter only in its most common or generic sense: a basic set of beliefs that guides action, whether of the everyday garden variety or action taken in connection with a disciplined inquiry. Refinement of that definition can be made by each reader while progressing through the book.

In this opening chapter I propose to outline what I take to be the salient differences between traditional positivism, on the one hand, and the three paradigms that have emerged to challenge (replace? parallel?) it on the other. Of course, I have my own preference among them; it would be remiss of me not to acknowledge that preference at once. It is *constructivism*. One immediate consequence is that I recognize that what I am about to say is *my own construction*, not necessarily an *objective* (whatever that may be) analysis. Indeed, as we shall see, constructivists not only abjure objectivity but celebrate subjectivity. The reader should not, therefore, read this chapter in the mistaken notion that it represents gospel or even a widely agreed to position. I offer it as *one* way to understand the paradigm issue. I should also point out that constructivists are relativists (a position that, I contend, can be well defended; see Guba, 1990); hence it is quite possible for me to entertain *any* construction (including, of course, a paradigm) that is proposed by reasonable and well-intentioned persons. The reader should never forget that the only alternative to relativism is absolutism. As a relativist, I will not reject any construction out of hand.

Generating Inquiry Paradigms

There are many paradigms that we use in guiding our actions: the adversarial paradigm that guides the legal system, the judgmental paradigm that guides the selection of Olympic winners, the religious paradigms that guide spiritual and moral life, and many others. Our concern here, however, is with *those paradigms that guide disciplined inquiry.* Historically there have been many such (Guba & Lincoln, 1989; Lincoln & Guba, 1985), but since the time of Descartes (1596-1650), inquirers have tended to focus on what, in its latter-day version, came to be known as positivism. Nevertheless, all these past paradigms, as well as the emergent contenders, can be characterized by the way their proponents respond to three basic questions, which can be characterized as the *ontological*, the *epistemological*, and the *methodological* questions. The questions are these:

(1) *Ontological*: What is the nature of the "knowable"? Or, what is the nature of "reality"?
(2) *Epistemological*: What is the nature of the relationship between the knower (the inquirer) and the known (or knowable)?
(3) *Methodological*: How should the inquirer go about finding out knowledge?

The answers that are given to these questions may be termed, as sets, the basic belief systems or *paradigms* that might be adopted. They are the starting points or givens that determine what inquiry is and how it is to be practiced. They cannot be proven or disproven in any foundational sense; if that *were* possible there would be no doubt about how to practice inquiry. But all such belief systems or paradigms are *human constructions,* and hence subject to all the errors and foibles that inevitably accompany human endeavors.

There are certainly many different ways to answer these questions. Descartes, obsessed with the idea that he might be gulled into believing something not true, searched for a sure foundation. (Indeed, his legendary pronouncement, "I think, therefore I am," was the only proposition that he felt that he could propose without himself immediately doubting it.) His overriding concern for certain knowledge has come to be called *Cartesian anxiety,* a *dis*-ease that is still reflected in the positivist (and postpositivist) search to find out "how things really are" and "how things really work."

The Basic Beliefs of Positivism

The phrases "how things *really* are" and "how things *really* work" are ontological creeds. The basic belief system of positivism is rooted in a *realist* ontology, that is, the belief that there exists a reality *out there,* driven by immutable natural laws. The business of science is to discover the "true" nature of reality and how it "truly" works. The ultimate aim of science is to *predict and control* natural phenomena.

Once committed to a realist ontology, the positivist is constrained to practice an *objectivist* epistemology. If there is a real world operating according to natural laws, then the inquirer must behave in ways that put questions directly to nature and allow nature to answer back directly. The inquirer, so to speak, must stand behind a thick wall of one-way glass, observing nature as "she does her thing." Objectivity is the "Archimedean point" (Archimedes is said to have boasted that, given a long enough lever and a place whereon to stand, he could move the earth) that permits the inquirer to wrest nature's secrets without altering them in any way.

But how can that be done, given the possibility of inquirer bias, on the one hand, and nature's propensity to confound, on the other? The positivist's answer: by the use of a manipulative methodology that controls for both, and empirical methods that place the point of decision with nature rather than with the inquirer. The most appropriate methodology is thus *empirical experimentalism,* or as close an approximation thereto as can be managed.

The basic belief system (paradigm) of conventional (positivist) inquiry can thus be summarized as follows:

Ontology: Realist—reality exists "out there" and is driven by immutable natural laws and mechanisms. Knowledge of these entities, laws, and mechanisms is conventionally summarized in the form of time- and context-free generalizations. Some of these latter generalizations take the form of cause-effect laws.

Epistemology: Dualist/objectivist—it is both possible and essential for the inquirer to adopt a distant, noninteractive posture. Values and other biasing and confounding factors are thereby automatically excluded from influencing the outcomes.

Methodology: Experimental/manipulative—questions and/or hypotheses are stated in advance in propositional form and subjected to empirical tests (falsification) under carefully controlled conditions.

There are many ways in which this belief system can be undermined. Each of the three emergent paradigms raises its own objections and proposes its own solutions. I will examine each in turn.

The Basic Beliefs of Postpositivism

Postpositivism is best characterized as a modified version of positivism. Having assessed the damage that positivism has incurred, postpositivists struggle to limit that damage as well as to adjust to it. Prediction and control continue to be the aim.

Ontologically, postpositivism moves from what is now recognized as a "naive" realist posture to one often termed *critical realism*. The essence of this position is that, although a real world driven by real natural causes exists, it is impossible for humans truly to perceive it with their imperfect sensory and intellective mechanisms (Cook & Campbell, 1979, p. 29). Inquirers need to be critical about their work precisely because of those human frailties. But, although one can never be sure that ultimate truth has been uncovered, there can be no doubt that reality is "out there." Realism remains the central concept.

Epistemologically, postpositivism recognizes the absurdity of assuming that it is possible for a human inquirer to step outside the pale of humanness while conducting inquiry. Work in the "hard" sciences has aptly demonstrated that "findings" emerge from the *interaction* of inquirer and inquired into, as shown by, say, the Heisenberg Uncertainty Principle and the Bohr Complementarity Principle (Hesse, 1980; Zukav, 1979). To overcome these problems postpositivists counsel a modified objectivity, hewing to objectivity as a "regulatory ideal" but recognizing that it cannot be achieved in any absolute sense. It *can* be achieved *reasonably closely*, by striving to be as neutral as possible; by "coming clean" about one's own predispositions (as did I in the early paragraphs of this chapter) so that the reader can make whatever adjustments to the proffered interpretations of findings that seem appropriate; by relying on "critical tradition," that is, requiring the reports of any inquiry to be consistent with the existing scholarly tradition of the field; and by subjecting every inquiry to the judgment of peers in the "critical community," that is, the editors and referees of journals as well as their readers. Of course, the latter two requirements also make it virtually impossible for new paradigms to assert themselves, an advantage not lost on the power brokers who protect and defend the (new) hegemony of postpositivism.

Methodologically, postpositivism provides two responses to emergent challenges. First, in the interest of conforming to the commitment to critical realism and modified subjectivity, emphasis is placed on *critical multiplism* (Cook, 1985), which might most usefully be thought of as a form of elaborated triangulation (Denzin, 1978). If human sensory and intellective mechanisms cannot be relied upon, it is essential that the "findings" of an inquiry be based on as many sources—of data, investigators, theories, and methods—as possible. Further, if objectivity can never be entirely attained, relying on many different sources makes it less likely that distorted interpretations will be made.

Second, and perhaps more important, postpositivism recognizes that many imbalances have been allowed to emerge in the zeal for achieving realistic, objective inquiry. A major part of the postpositivist agenda has been devoted to identifying these imbalances and proposing ways of redressing them. It is believed that, if they can be redressed, positivism, in its new postpositivist clothes, can be made useful once again. There are four imbalances; of course, not all postpositivists would agree that all exist and certainly not that they are equally critical.

(1) *The imbalance between rigor and relevance.* In more traditional terms this is the inescapable trade-off between internal and external validity. The greater the control established to achieve internal validity, the less the generalizability of the findings, for, in the final analysis,

laboratory results are generalizable only to another laboratory. The imbalance, created by excessive emphasis on context-stripping controls, is redressed by carrying out inquiry in more *natural* settings. The reader should note that the term *naturalistic* inquiry, often used in the past to denote what, in this book, is called *constructivist* inquiry, is *not* equivalent to this postpositivist proposal; the term *naturalistic* is identified with a *paradigm*, while the term *natural* is identified with a *methodology*, the *doing* part of a paradigm.

(2) *The imbalance between precision and richness.* Precision is critical to a science that defines its major goal to be prediction and control. That the press for precision should lead to an overemphasis on quantitative methods—that epitome of precision—is not surprising, particularly in view of the impressive array of mathematical and statistical methods that are available. This imbalance is redressed by including more qualitative methods. The reader should again note the confusion engendered by this use of the term *qualitative methods* (or, if one chooses, ethnographic, phenomenological, or case study methods). The term *qualitative* is a methods-level term, not a paradigm-level term. The call for qualitative methods is by itself *not* a call for a paradigm shift.

(3) *The imbalance between elegance and applicability.* The press to predict and control places great emphasis on the statement of formal theories—and preferably, broadly based, reductionistic ("grand") theories. The development and testing of these theories characterize much of scientific activity. But such grand theories, while abetting generalizability, often are not found to "fit" or "work" (Glaser & Strauss, 1967) in local contexts. Locality and specificity are incommensurable with generalizability. This imbalance is redressed by "grounding" theory in local circumstances, that is, conducting the inquiry so that theory is the *product* rather than the *precursor* of the inquiry.

(4) *The imbalance between discovery and verification.* Discovery, that is, the process by which a priori theories and their implied questions and hypotheses emerge, is not a formal part of the conventional paradigm. Discovery is merely a precursor rather than an integral part of the scientific process, whose purpose is solely *verification* (falsification). But this position is immediately seen to be absurd when one considers that most of the important advances of science have been made via the creative discovery route rather than by the more mundane and plodding verification route. Clearly both processes are necessary; it is not only unfair but also extremely shortsighted to reserve the mantle

of science only for verifiers. This imbalance is redressed by defining a *continuum* of inquiry, which ranges from "pure" discovery at one end to "pure" verification at the other. The reader should note that the earlier tendency to relegate paradigms other than postpositivism to the discovery end has been replaced with a more ecumenical stance that seems to recognize that both processes can go on in all paradigms. But it should be clear that making this adjustment has nothing to do with paradigm differences; it simply recognizes that positivism, if not postpositivism, made an error in its earlier assessment.

We may note then that the basic belief system of postpositivism differs very little from that of positivism. We may summarize the stances as follows:

Ontology: *Critical realist*—reality exists but can never be fully apprehended. It is driven by natural laws that can be only incompletely understood.

Epistemology: *Modified objectivist*—objectivity remains a regulatory ideal, but it can only be approximated, with special emphasis placed on external guardians such as the critical tradition and the critical community.

Methodology: *Modified experimental/manipulative*—emphasize critical multiplism. Redress imbalances by doing inquiry in more natural settings, using more qualitative methods, depending more on grounded theory, and reintroducing discovery into the inquiry process.

The Basic Beliefs of Critical Theory

The label *critical theory* is no doubt inadequate to encompass all the alternatives that can be swept into this category of paradigm. A more appropriate label would be "ideologically oriented inquiry," including neo-Marxism, materialism, feminism, Freireism, participatory inquiry, and other similar movements as well as critical theory itself. These perspectives are properly placed together, however, because they converge in rejecting the claim of value freedom made by positivists (and largely continuing to be made by postpositivists).

Because they are human constructions, paradigms inevitably reflect the values of their human constructors. They enter into inquiry at choice points such as the problem selected for study, the paradigm within which to study it, the instruments and the analytic modes used, and the interpretations, conclusions, and recommendations made.

Nature cannot be seen as it "really is" or "really works" except through a value window.

If values *do* enter into every inquiry, then the question immediately arises as to what values and whose values shall govern. If the findings of studies can vary depending on the values chosen, then the choice of a *particular* value system tends to empower and enfranchise certain persons while disempowering and disenfranchising others. Inquiry thereby becomes a *political act*.

Given that counterclaim, one might expect critical theorists (ideologists) to reject a realist posture. For if there is a real state of affairs, then it seems unreasonable to argue that value positions that inquirers might take could influence it. Moreover, a *real* reality requires an objective epistemological approach to uncover it—as positivists and postpositivists have claimed all along. But, for whatever reason, critical theorists (ideologists) have elected to believe in an objective reality—as the phrase commonly used by them, "false consciousness," readily demonstrates (because it implies that there is a "true consciousness" somewhere "out there," or, more likely, possessed by the inquirer or some better-informed elite). The task of inquiry is, by definition, to raise people (the oppressed) to a level of "true consciousness." Once they appreciate how oppressed they are, they can act to *transform* the world. The close parallel between *transforming* the world and *predicting and controlling* it should not be lost.

Thus there appears to be a logical disjunction: a *realist* (but probably with the postpositivists, a critical realist) ontology coupled with a *subjectivist* epistemology—subjectivist because inquiry acts are intimately related to the values of the inquirer. The move to a subjectivist epistemology no doubt represents a forward step, but, so long as that epistemology is enlisted in the service of a realist ontology, it seems to lose much of its force.

At the *methodological* level, critical theorists (ideologists) seem more consistent. If the aim of inquiry is to transform the (real) world by raising the consciousness of participants so that they are energized and facilitated toward transformation, then something other than a manipulative, interventionist methodology is required. Critical theorists (ideologists) take a dialogic approach that seeks to eliminate false consciousness and rally participants around a common (true?) point of view. In this process, features of the real world are apprehended and judgments are made about which of them can be altered. The result of effective, concerted action is transformation.

Given this view, we may summarize the basic belief system of the critical theory (ideological) paradigm as follows:

Ontology: *critical realist,* as in the case of postpositivism
Epistemology: *subjectivist,* in the sense that values mediate inquiry
Methodology: *dialogic, transformative;* eliminate false consciousness and energize and facilitate transformation

The Basic Beliefs of Constructivism

It is my belief that proponents of both the postpositivist and the critical theory (ideological) paradigms feel that there can be an accommodation between their positions and, indeed, with conventional positivism. Constructivists, on the other hand, feel that the positivist (and postpositivist) paradigms are badly flawed and must be entirely replaced. Among the more telling arguments are these (Guba & Lincoln, 1989; Lincoln & Guba, 1985):

(1) *The theory ladenness of facts.* If empirical tests are to be valid as arbiters of propositions (hypotheses and questions) put to nature by inquirers, then it is essential that theoretical and observational languages be independent. The "facts" that are collected must be *independent* of the propositional (theoretical) statements. But philosophers of science now uniformly believe that facts *are* facts only *within* some theoretical framework (Hesse, 1980). Thus the basis for discovering "how things really are" and "really work" is lost. "Reality" exists only in the context of a mental framework (construct) for thinking about it.

(2) *The underdetermination of theory.* No theory can ever be fully tested because of the problem of induction. Observing one million white swans does not provide indisputable evidence for the assertion, "All swans are white." There are always a large number of theories that can, in principle, "explain" a given body of "facts." Thus no unequivocal explanation is ever possible. There can be many constructions, and there is no foundational way to choose among them. "Reality" can be "seen" only through a window of theory, whether implicit or explicit.

(3) *The value ladenness of facts.* Constructivists concur with the ideological argument that inquiry cannot be value free. If "reality" can be seen only through a theory window, it can equally be seen only through a value window. Many constructions are possible.

(4) *The interactive nature of the inquirer/inquired-into dyad.* Even post-positivists have conceded that objectivity is not possible; the results of an inquiry are always shaped by the *interaction* of inquirer and inquired into. There is no Archimedean point. And if there is such an intimate interconnectedness in the physical sciences, how much more likely is it that the results of social inquiry are similarly shaped? This problem of interaction is devastating to both positivism and post-positivism. First, it renders the distinction between ontology and epistemology obsolete; what can be known and the individual who comes to know it are fused into a coherent whole. Further, it makes the findings of an inquiry not a report of what is "out there" but the residue of a process that *literally creates them.* Finally, it depicts knowledge as the outcome or consequence of *human* activity; knowledge is a *human construction*, never certifiable as ultimately true but problematic and ever changing.

Given this critique, it is apparent why constructivists feel that an entirely new paradigm is needed. *Ontologically*, if there are always many interpretations that can be made in any inquiry, and if there is no foundational process by which the ultimate truth or falsity of these several constructions can be determined, there is no alternative but to take a position of *relativism*. Relativism is the key to openness and the continuing search for ever more informed and sophisticated constructions. Realities are multiple, and they exist in people's minds.

Epistemologically, the constructivist chooses to take a *subjectivist* position. Subjectivity is not only forced on us by the human condition (as the postpositivist might admit) but because it is the only means of unlocking the constructions held by individuals. If realities exist only in respondents' minds, subjective interaction seems to be the only way to access them.

Methodologically, the constructivist proceeds in ways that aim to identify the variety of constructions that exist and bring them into as much consensus as possible. This process has two aspects: hermeneutics and dialectics. The hermeneutic aspect consists in depicting individual constructions as accurately as possible, while the dialectic aspect consists of comparing and contrasting these existing individual (including the inquirer's) constructions so that each respondent must confront the constructions of others and come to terms with them. The hermeneutic/dialectic methodology aims to produce as informed and sophisticated a construction (or, more likely, constructions) as possible. Simultaneously the methodology aims to keep

channels of communication open so that information and sophistication can be continuously improved. Constructivism thus intends
neither to predict and control the "real" world nor to transform it but
to *reconstruct* the "world" at the only point at which it exists: in the
minds of constructors. It is the mind that is to be transformed, not the
"real" world.

We may thus summarize the constructivist belief system as follows
(retaining the threefold organization for the sake of contrast despite
having argued that, in constructivism, the ontology/epistemology
distinction is obliterated):

Ontology: *Relativist*—realities exist in the form of multiple mental constructions, socially and experientially based, local and specific,
dependent for their form and content on the persons who hold
them.

Epistemology: *Subjectivist*—inquirer and inquired into are fused into a single
(monistic) entity. Findings are literally the creation of the
process of interaction between the two.

Methodology: *Hermeneutic, dialectic*—individual constructions are elicited
and refined hermeneutically, and compared and contrasted
dialectically, with the aim of generating one (or a few) constructions on which there is substantial consensus.

What is the Paradigm Dialog About?

I must stress again that what have been outlined on the preceding
pages are *my* constructions about the nature of four paradigms—conventional positivism and three contenders for its "crown": postpositivism, critical theory (ideology), and constructivism. We are,
nationally and internationally, engaged in a major debate about which
of these is to be preferred. It is my own position that a struggle for
primacy is irrelevant. As a constructivist I can confidently assert that
none of these four is *the* paradigm of choice. Each is an alternative that
deserves, on its merits (and I have no doubt that all are meritorious),
to be considered. The dialog is not to determine which paradigm is,
finally, to win out. Rather, it is to take us to another level at which *all*
of these paradigms will be replaced by yet another paradigm whose
outlines we can see now but dimly, if at all. That new paradigm will
not be a closer approximation to truth; it will simply be more informed
and sophisticated than those we are now entertaining. The reader is
invited to enter into that dialog as she or he reads the following pages.

PART II

Points of View

Part II, Points of View, sets the stage for the dialog that follows in the remainder of the book. Four papers are included: the three keynote addresses and the dinner address.

The keynoters described in ways each thought most appropriate the three alternative paradigms that have emerged in recent decades. Denis Phillips sets out the *postpositivist* position, electing to deal first with an assessment of the current states of affairs that brought positivism into question, and following with a discussion of certain "myths" that he feels represent misunderstandings of postpositivism. Thomas Popkewitz begins with a discussion of certain principles underlying the *critical* position and follows with six questions that he believes spell out the implications of that position for inquiry. Yvonna Lincoln ends the paradigm presentation with a Proustian retrospective of her intellectual journey through *constructivism*, pointing out what she believes are its implications for selected problem areas.

Elliot Eisner's address did not come at the point at which I have placed it in this volume, that is, as part of the plenary session devoted to delineating the alternative paradigms. I inserted it here, nevertheless, because I believe it is a superlative statement about what it means to make a paradigm shift, and it creates a splendid context for what follows.

[2]

Postpositivistic Science
Myths and Realities

It is arguable that recent advances in the philosophical understanding of science have vindicated many of John Dewey's views on the matter. Scientific reason is not marked off from other forms of human intellectual endeavor as a sort of model of perfection that these lesser activities must always strive (unsuccessfully) to mimic. Rather, science embodies exactly the same types of fallible reasoning as is found elsewhere—it is just that scientists do, a little more self-consciously and in a more controlled way, what all effective thinkers do. As Dewey pointed out, he believed strongly that intellectual inquiry,

> in spite of the diverse subjects to which it applies, and the consequent diversity of its special techniques has a common structure or pattern: that this common structure is applied both in common sense and science. (Dewey, 1966, p. 101)

Recent work has shown that scientists, like workers in other areas, are in the business of providing reasonable justifications for their assertions, but nothing they do can make these assertions absolutely safe from criticism and potential overthrow. (There are no absolute justifications, hence the somewhat misleading name sometimes given to recent epistemology—"nonjustificationist." This is misleading because it suggests that, if there are no *absolute* justifications, there are no justifications at all!) It is salutary to remember that Dewey pre-

AUTHOR'S NOTE: Helpful comments have been provided by Harvey Siegel and Debby Kerdeman.

ferred not to use the term *truth* but, instead, the term *warranted assertibility*, and he recognized that different types of assertions required different warrants. Furthermore, this change of language highlighted the fact that a warrant is not forever; today's warrant can be rescinded tomorrow, following further inquiry.

None of this means that science is *unbelievable*, or that "anything goes" or "anything may be accepted," or that "there is no justification at all for scientific claims," or that "there are no standards by which the truth or adequacy (or both) of a piece of science can be judged." It simply means that no longer can it be claimed there are any *absolutely* authoritative foundations upon which scientific knowledge is based (hence the other title often given to contemporary epistemology—"nonfoundationalistic"). The fact is that mány of our beliefs are warranted by rather weighty bodies of evidence and argument, and so we are justified in holding them; but they are not *absolutely* unchallengeable.

This view of science fits comfortably with what every experienced action researcher and evaluator of social programs has come to understand about his or her own work; these are, par excellence, fields of "the believable," of building the "good case," but where even the best of cases can be challenged or reanalyzed or reinterpreted. Nothing is more suspicious in the field of evaluation than a report that is presented with the implication that it has the status of "holy writ." Researchers in the "pure" sciences, and in the more laboratory-oriented of the social and human sciences, now have to accept that good science is a blood brother if not a sibling to what transpires in these messier and more open-ended fields of endeavor.

What happened in philosophy of science to build this new and modest view? Or, alternatively, what destroyed the older view?

An Outline of Recent Developments

The new view of science could not get off the ground until the foundations of the dominant older view, positivism, had been shown to be untenable. The role that had been ascribed to observation—that it was both the rock-bottom foundation of science and, at the same time, the final arbiter of what could be believed—was reevaluated; and the relation between scientific theories and evidence was shown to be more complex than had been thought. The related view that science grows by steady accumulation of findings and theories was challenged by the work of Thomas Kuhn and subsequent scholars such as Lakatos and Feyerabend. Obviously these matters are too complex to discuss in full, but a few of the crucial issues can be highlighted.

Observation

It is clear (to all except some mystics) that, if the aim of science is to establish bodies of knowledge about the world, then somewhere in the process of doing science the world must be studied or observed. But it has been recognized for many decades that the positivistic and operationalistic view that all theoretical terms of science must be reducible to (i.e., definable in terms of) observational language is quixotic. The status of operationalism in the behavioral sciences was a hot issue in the decade immediately following World War II, and there were international symposia on the matter. A consensus was reached (except, of course, for a few diehards—an old story): If the positivist/operationalist view were to be accepted, it would have a chilling effect on theorizing about unobservable mechanisms such as the subatomic events that have won Nobel prizes for so many physicists. Carl Hempel, a somewhat "lapsed" logical positivist, drew (in his postpositivist years) the following enticing picture that makes absurd the operationalist notion that concepts can each be reduced to a set of observation statements:

> Scientific systematization requires the establishment of diverse connections, by laws or theoretical principles, between different aspects of the empirical world, which are characterized by scientific concepts. Thus, the concepts of science are the knots in a network of systematic interrelationships in which laws and theoretical principles form the threads. . . . The more threads that converge upon, or issue from, a conceptual knot, the stronger will be its systematizing role, or its systematic import. (Hempel, 1966, p. 94)

Thus the point was driven home that the theoretical concepts of science have meanings that transcend definition in observational terms, and it was realized that, if this were not the case, science would have trouble in growing and extending into new areas.

There is another issue about the role of observation. It has often been held that observation is the "neutral court" that adjudicates between rival scientific claims; together with this has usually gone the belief that science is actually built upon the foundation of indubitable observation. (The operationalist thesis discussed before concerned the *status* of theoretical concepts, not their *origin*. That is, according to the operationalist view, theoretical concepts had the status of being short-hand summaries of observation statements, no matter how these theoretical concepts happened to have originated.) The crucial work that challenged the view that observation is the "theory-neutral" basis on which science is erected was that of N. R. Hanson, where *Patterns of Discovery* (1958) has become a classic. Hanson was not the first to say the things that he said; Wittgenstein used the key illustration that Hanson used, and even Dewey made much the same point. But it was Hanson's work that fired most imaginations.

Hanson's theories may be stated in one sentence: "The theory, hypothesis, or background knowledge held by an observer can influence in a major way what is observed." Or, as he put it in a nice aphorism, "There is more to seeing than meets the eyeball" (Hanson, 1958, p. 7). In other words, observation is theory laden—it is not a theory-neutral foundation. Thus, in a famous psychological experiment, sliders were made from cards selected from a normal deck, and these were projected for very short periods onto a screen in front of observers. All were correctly identified, except for a trick slide that had the color altered (for example, it might be a black four of diamonds). Most commonly this slide was *seen* as a blur or else as a black suit (spades or clubs). A Hansonian interpretation is that there is an interaction between the visual stimulus and the observers' background knowledge ("diamonds are red"), so the final result is that a blur is observed.

Subsequent writers have drawn a variety of conclusions from Hanson's work; for instance, many have taken it as supporting relativism—"there is no such thing as objective truth, for what observers take to be true depends upon the framework of knowledge and assumptions they bring with them." Sometimes an example is given that comes from Hanson himself: He imagined the astronomers Tycho Brahe and Kepler watching the dawn together; because they had different frameworks, one would see the sun moving above the horizon, while the other would see the earth rotating away to reveal the sun! However, a closer reading of Hanson provides no succor for such extravagant relativism, for he explicitly acknowledged that *both* astronomers would agree that what they actually *observed* during the dawn was the sun increasing its relative distance above the Earth's eastern horizon (Hanson, 1958, p. 23); but, of course, they would insist on talking about what they had observed in different terms. This acknowledgment is evidence that Hanson realized people with different frameworks nevertheless can have some views—or can hold some data—in common, and these things can serve as the basis for further discussion and clarification of their respective positions. Thus there is little comfort here for relativists.

A less extreme interpretation then is that, while we must be aware of the role played by our preconceptions in influencing our observations, and while we have to abandon the view that observation is "neutral" or theory free, there is nothing in Hanson that forces us to the conclusion that we cannot decide between rival claims and cannot arrive at consensus about which viewpoint (or which observations) seem to be most trustworthy under the prevailing circumstances. Israel Scheffler (1967, p. 44) put it well:

> There is no evidence for a general incapacity to learn from contrary observations, no proof of a pre-established harmony between what we believe and what we see.... Our categorizations and expectations guide by orienting us selectively toward the future; they set us, in particular, to perceive in certain ways and not in others. Yet they do not blind us to the unforeseen. They allow us to recognize what fails to match anticipation.

Theory and Evidence

Over the past few decades, it has become increasingly clear that scientific theories are "underdetermined" by nature; that is, whatever evidence is available (or possibly could be available) about nature, it is never sufficient to rule out the possibility that a much better theory might be devised to account for the phenomena that our presently accepted theory also explains. Or, to put it another way, a variety of rival theories or hypotheses can always be constructed that are equally compatible with whatever finite body of evidence is currently available. (An implication of this, of course, is that we can never be

certain that the particular theory we have accepted is the correct one!)
There are several developments that are worthy of brief comment.[1]

The first point is illustrated by Nelson Goodman's notorious example of "grue and bleen" (Goodman, 1973), although it should be noted
that Goodman made slightly different use of this case. A large amount
of observational evidence has accumulated over the ages concerning
the color of emeralds; all that have been studied have been found to
be green. It might be supposed then that this amounts to irrefutable
evidence for the hypothesis "all emeralds are green." But the *very same*
evidence also supports the hypothesis that "all emeralds are grue"
(where *grue* is the name of a property such that an object is green up
to a certain date, for instance, the year 2000, and blue thereafter). The
fanciful nature of this example is beside the point; it nicely illustrates
the underdetermination of theory by available evidence, for it shows
that a general theory ("emeralds are green," that is, "always have
been, and always will be") necessarily goes beyond the finite evidence
that is available ("the finite number of emeralds observed to date have
been green"), thus leaving open the possibility that some ingenious
scientist will come up with an alternative explanation for the very
same finite set of data.

A related issue concerns what happens when new evidence turns
up necessitating the making of some accommodatory change in whatever theory is currently the favored one. Postpositivists now generally
recognize that there is *no one specific change* that is *necessitated*. Different
scientists may change different portions of the theory—they are free
to use their professional judgment and their creativity. It would be a
mistake to interpret this as indicating that scientific theories are a
matter of mere whim or individual taste; to stress that judgment is
required is *not* to throw away all standards. Rather, it is to stress that
decisions cannot be made using some mechanical procedure.

This point is often made in terms of the "Duhem-Quine" thesis.
Scientific theories, indeed vast areas of science, are interrelated; the
image of science as a huge fishnet is a predominant one in much recent
writing. It is this network as a whole, rather than little portions of it,
that has to withstand the test of dealing with whatever evidence is
gathered. It might appear that some piece of recalcitrant data offers a
serious challenge to one particular section of the net, but the threat
cannot be localized in this way—one scientist may react to the data
by altering the "obvious" portion of the net, while others might want

to preserve this piece and so might advocate changing some other portion of the net to accommodate the new information. Once again scientists must use their professional judgment; decisions about how to modify theories cannot be made mechanically.

It might even be the case that, when some counterevidence turns up, scientists might decide to make no accommodatory changes at all—a course of action (or, rather, a course of inaction) that receives the blessing of the new philosophy of science. For one thing, it might well be the case that one of the auxiliary assumptions is faulty. Many such assumptions have to be made in any piece of scientific work. For example, in doing laboratory work, the auxiliary assumption is often made that the chemical samples being used were pure, or that there were no unplanned temperature fluctuations, or that the psychological tests being used were reliable, or that an observer was unbiased, and so on. Scientists can blame one or another of these rather than accept the counterevidence at face value and thereby be forced to change their net.

On the other hand, scientists might simply ignore the counterevidence in the hope that "something will eventually turn up to explain it." It was a traditional tenet of methodology that a scientist must abandon a theory, no matter how attractive it might appear, once some counterevidence became available. It turns out, however, that there are good reasons to suppose that it can be quite rational to adhere to the theory even under these adverse conditions. Paul Feyerabend (1970, pp. 21-22) has been the most forceful writer on this and related issues:

> The idea of a method that contains firm, unchanging, and absolutely binding principles for conducting the business of science gets into considerable difficulty when confronted with the results of historical research. We find, then, that there is not a single rule, however plausible, and however firmly grounded in epistemology, that is not violated at some time or other. It becomes evident that such violations are not accidental events. . . . On the contrary, we see they are necessary for progress.

Imre Lakatos (1972) devised his "methodology of scientific research programs" in an attempt to gauge when changes made in an ongoing research tradition are progressive or degenerative.

Scientific Change

Perhaps the most famous feature of the new philosophy of science, however, is its focus upon dynamics. The process of scientific change has come under increasing investigation since Kuhn's work on scientific revolutions popularized the notion of "paradigm clashes." Science is not static. Theories come and theories go, new data accumulate, and old findings are interpreted in new ways. Involved in all this is the question of the *rationality* of change—what justifies scientists in throwing out old ideas and accepting new ones? There has been much debate, but little consensus, among the postpositivists— witness the work of Kuhn (1970), Popper (1968a), Lakatos (1972), Feyerabend (1970), Toulmin (1970a, 1970b), Laudan (1977), and Newton-Smith (1981). It will suffice to quote a brief passage from Popper to illustrate this major theme in the new postpositivist philosophy:

> I assert that continued growth is essential to the rational and empirical character of scientific knowledge; that if science ceases to grow it must lose that character. It is the way of its growth which makes science rational and empirical; the way, that is, in which scientists discriminate between available theories and choose the better one. (Popper, 1968a, p. 215)

Questions and Answers

There are some who have drawn a dangerous moral from the developments just outlined. Science has fallen from its pedestal; if no knowledge can be totally and unchallengeably justified, then nothing can be disbarred. We have embarked on the rocky road to relativism. But it is possible to retain a hopeful outlook, and even to relish the challenge that this new picture of science presents. It is here that we can obtain succor from the fields of evaluation and action research. People here do not lose heart, yet they are faced with a reality that (we now realize) closely parallels that of "pure" scientists; and some even thrive on the uncertainties of their field. Seekers after enlightenment in any field do the best that they can; they honestly seek evidence, they critically scrutinize it, they are open to alternative viewpoints, they take criticism seriously and try to profit from it, they play their hunches, they stick to their guns, but they also have a sense of when it is time to quit. It may be a dirty, hard, and uncertain game, but it is the only game in town.

Although, to me, this seems a modest, nondoctrinaire, unsurprising, and eminently reasonable position, there are many who feel uneasy and who continue to raise questions about it. So it might be fruitful to grapple with some of these directly.

Question 1. In what sense is the new position, which has been outlined above, "postpositivistic"? Isn't it merely a weaker form of positivism in disguise? (The position certainly shares some features in common with positivism.) It may have come *after* positivism, and that is the chief reason for calling it *post*positivism.

Answer. In no sense is the new philosophy of science—broad and ill defined though it is—closely akin to positivism (or, more especially, to the most notorious form of positivism, logical positivism). Logical positivism became discredited in the years immediately following the end of World War II; few if any philosophers these days subscribe to its core tenet, the "verifiability criterion of meaning," according to which a statement is meaningful only if it is verifiable in terms of sense experience (excepting logico-mathematical propositions).[2] As was pointed out earlier, one of the serious problems associated with the use of this principle in science was that it made theoretical terms meaningless. The fact is that many theoretical entities cannot be verified in terms of sense experience; neither can laws be confirmed absolutely (for they make universal claims that cannot be verified); but there are few today who would want to argue positivistically that the discourse of subatomic particle physicists or of black-hole theorists is meaningless!

A historical note might be helpful here. In the opening sentences of a paper written in 1956, when positivism was in its death throes, the major logical positivist Rudolf Carnap said that one of his main topics was going to be

> the problem of a criterion of significance for the theoretical language, i.e., exact conditions which terms and sentences of the theoretical language must fulfill in order to have a positive function for the explanation and prediction of observable events and thus to be acceptable as empirically meaningful. (Carnap, 1956, p. 38)

Carnap indicated his optimism (not shared by many others in the mid-1950s) that he would still be able to draw the line that "separates the scientifically meaningful from the meaningless" (Carnap, 1956, p. 40). A few years later, in the same publication series, Grover Maxwell wrote what must be considered the majority antipositivist opinion:

> That anyone today should seriously contend that the entities referred to by scientific theories are only convenient fictions, or that talk about such entities is translatable without remainder into talk about sense contents or everyday physical objects . . . strike(s) me as so incongruous with the scientific and rational attitude and practice that I feel this paper should turn out to be a demolition of straw men. (Maxwell, 1962, p. 3)

Question 2. Aren't contemporary postpositivists clinging to an old and outmoded realist paradigm?

Answer. The question embodies a serious confusion. The *old positivist view* was antirealist; as explained in the previous answer, the logical positivists (on the whole) denied the reality of theoretical entities, and indeed claimed that talk of such entities was literally meaningless. Modern realism is not a carryover from positivism but is a recent postpositivistic development. Furthermore, there is little consensus within the philosophical community; whether or not realism is viable is a hotly debated topic—there are many contemporary philosophers for it, but there are many against it.[3] There is even controversy about the precise definition of realism; Arthur Fine (1987, p. 359) has written:

> Given the diverse array of philosophical positions that have sought the "realist" label, it is probably not possible to give a sketch of realism that will encompass them all. Indeed, it may be hopeless to try, even, to capture the essential features of realism.

Question 3. Well, old or new, many influential postpositivists are realists. Aren't they overlooking the fact that multiple realities exist, and aren't they overlooking the well-known fact that each society *constructs* its own reality? If you accept these two points, you cannot be a realist! Egon Guba has written that educational researchers (if not all social researchers) are studying phenomena that are

> *social* in nature. There is no need to posit a natural state-of-affairs and a natural set of laws for phenomena that are socially invented—I shall say socially constructed—in people's minds. I suggest . . . an ontology that is relativist in nature. It begins with the premise that all social realities

are constructed and shared through well-understood socialization processes. It is this socialized sharing that gives these constructions their apparent reality. (Guba, in press)

Answer. There are several important issues here, some of which were touched upon in the earlier discussion. In the first place, this question seems inspired by an extreme reading of Kuhn—the view that all of us are trapped within a paradigm and that we cannot converse rationally with those in other paradigms because our beliefs are incommensurable. Even the later Kuhn—the Kuhn of *The Essential Tension* (1977) or of the "Postscript" to the second edition of *The Structure of Scientific Revolutions* (1970)—did not accept this extreme relativism. Furthermore, such relativism seems contradicted by everyday experience within science. Freudians do understand—but, of course, disagree with—Skinnerians, and neo-Marxist social scientists understand colleagues of more conservative bent, and vice versa. The point is that paradigms (if one accepts this controversial notion[4]) serve as lenses, not as blinders.

Second, there is a confusion here between, on the one hand, the fact that different people and different societies have different views about what is real (a fact that seems undeniable) and, on the other hand, the issue of whether or not we can know which of these views is the correct one (or, indeed, whether there is a correct one at all). The relativist is committed to the view that *all* such differing (and contradictory) views are correct (or could be correct at one time), whereas the realist is committed to the view that at best only one view can be right (of course, all views might have portions that are sound or all might be wrong.)[5]

To make this a little more precise: Suppose that one social group believes that "X is the case," and another group believes that "not X is the case." The realist holds that *both* of these views cannot *be* correct, although, of course, some people *believe* one or the other of these to be true—it is the case either that X, or that not-X, but not both. (The realist does not have to believe that we can always *settle* which of these views, X or not-X, is true; the issue is whether both or at best only one *can* be true.) The relativist has to hold that there are multiple realities—that reality is (or could be) both X and not-X—for, if the relativist does not hold this position, then his or her position dissolves into the realist position. Stated thus boldly, it can be seen that the relativist case here hinges on obscuring the distinction between "what people believe to be true" and "what really is true, whether or not we can determine this truth at the moment."[6]

Third, it is important to note that there are several quite different issues concerning realism, which the neophyte tends to run together, causing a great deal of confusion. The issue discussed directly above concerns whether, and in what sense, multiple realities exist; the opponents of realists here can be correctly labeled as relativists. A different issue was discussed earlier: The point in contention was whether or not theoretical entities (such as those postulated in the theories of particle physics, or in Chomskian linguistics, or in theories in cognitive psychology) can be said to be real; here the opponents of realists are properly labeled as antirealists. It is crucial to note that these antirealists are in no sense relativists. Thus it is a serious flaw in scholarship to claim that, because, in contemporary philosophy of science, there is much debate about the viability of realism, relativism thereby takes on more respectable status. The current debates in philosophy of science are between realists and antirealists, not between realists and relativists (Leplin, 1984; Siegel, 1987).

Finally, this third question raises the very important matter of the social construction of reality. Certainly there is nothing in postpositivism per se that requires denying that societies determine many of the things that are *believed* to be real by their members. Thus an "exotic" society may define certain spirits as being real, and the members of that society may accept them as real and act accordingly. A similar thing certainly happens in our own society, and not just with spirits. All a postpositivist would want to insist upon is that these matters can be open to research: We can inquire into the beliefs of a society, how they came about, what their effects are, and what the status is of the evidence that is offered in support of the truth of the beliefs. And we can get these matters right or wrong—we can describe these beliefs correctly or incorrectly, or we can be right or make mistakes about their origins or their effects. It simply does not follow from the fact of the social construction of reality that scientific inquiry becomes impossible or that we have to become relativists. It does not follow from the fact that a tribe of headhunters socially determines its own beliefs (i.e., the things the members of that group *believe* to be real) that we thereby have to *accept* those beliefs as *true*. What is true—if we have done our research properly—is that we have accurately determined that the members of the tribe do *believe* in their realities. But that is a different issue, which raises no problem of principle at all for postpositivists. (In a similar vein, it is clear that Freudians believe in the reality of the id and superego and the rest, and they act as if these are realities; but their believing in these things does not make them real.)

It is worth noting that, for decades, postpositivists have accepted this notion of "the social construction of reality." Thus Sir Karl Popper, one of the major postpositivists (it is relevant to note that he claimed to have been the person who killed positivism), stressed that his philosophy "assumes a physical world in which we act," although he added that we may not know very much about it. But, crucially, he stressed it was also necessary to "assume a social world, populated by other people, about whose goals we know something (often not very much), and, furthermore, social institutions. These social institutions determine the peculiarly social character of our social environment" (Popper, 1976, p. 103). Popper includes laws and customs among "institutions."

Question 4. Given the acceptance by postpositivists of Hanson's thesis concerning the theory ladenness of perception, and given the general nonfoundationalist tenor that nothing can be considered as absolutely certain, and so forth, does it not follow that postpositivists have to abandon the notion of objectivity? Hasn't it been stripped of any meaning that it might have had?

Answer. Certainly not! The notion of objectivity, like the notion of truth, is a regulative ideal that underlies all inquiry (Phillips, in press). If we abandon such notions, it is not sensible to make inquiries at all. For if a sloppy inquiry is as acceptable as a careful one, and if an inquiry that is careless about evidence is as acceptable as an inquiry that has taken pains to be precise and unbiased, then there is no need to inquire—we might as well accept, without further fuss, any old view that tickles our fancy.

Now, it *is* true that the objectivity of an inquiry does not guarantee its truth—as was shown earlier, *nothing* can guarantee that we have reached the truth. Perhaps an analogy will help to clarify matters: Consider two firms who manufacture radios; one is proud of its workmanship and backs its products with a strong guarantee; the other firm is after a quick profit, practices shoddy workmanship, and does not offer any warranty to the buyer. A consumer would be unwise to purchase the latter's product, but nevertheless it is clearly understood that the first firm's guarantee does not absolutely mean that the radio will not break down. The fact that this situation exists is not taken by consumers as invalidating the notion of a warranty, nor is it seen as making each purchase equally wise. And the very same situation exists in science.

The Popperian account of objectivity is widely, though not universally, accepted by postpositivists. The following sentences capture the essence of his approach:

> What may be described as scientific objectivity is based solely upon a critical tradition which, despite resistance, often makes it possible to criticize a dominant dogma. To put it another way, the objectivity of science is not a matter of the individual scientists but rather the social result of their mutual criticism, of the friendly-hostile division of labour among scientists, of their co-operation and also of their competition. For this reason, it depends, in part, upon a number of social and political circumstances which make criticism possible. (Popper, 1976, p. 95)

Conclusion

It can be seen from the foregoing discussion that postpositivism is a broad, complex, and dynamic approach to understanding the nature of science. There is little unanimity on important issues among its "adherents" (if people can be said to adhere to so amorphous a position)—but this is a healthy feature and not a weakness. Paul Feyerabend (1968, p. 33) wrote, a quarter- century ago, that unanimity of opinion may be fitting for some church, or for the followers of a tyrant, but it is most unfitting for science.

The danger to postpositivism comes not from internal dissension but from outside—from those who draw false, and often oversimple, conclusions from some of the very same developments that have produced postpositivism itself.

Notes

1. Many of the following issues are discussed at greater length in Phillips (1987b).

2. For more details on the complicated demise of positivism, see Phillips (1983).

3. A leading postpositivist antirealist is Bas van Fraassen (1980). His *grounds* for antirealism are not those of the logical positivists.

4. It is far from clear that the notion of paradigms as developed by Kuhn is sustainable; see the books by Phillips, Newton-Smith, and Siegel quoted elsewhere in this chapter.

5. It must be stressed that this point holds only for views that are contradictory or opposing, such as "there is an X" and "there is not X." If the views are orthogonal, that is, noncontradictory, there is no problem with them both being true—"there is an X" and "there is a Y" present no problems.

6. There are many other problems with relativism; see, for example, Siegel (1987).

[3]

Whose Future? Whose Past?
Notes on Critical Theory and Methodology

THOMAS S. POPKEWITZ

In writing about a critical science, one of the three paradigms explored in this book, I draw upon and clarify particular elements of a broad epistemological field that has developed in Europe and later in the United States since the middle of the nineteenth century. I call this tradition *critical* to focus upon the conceptualization of educational problems as part of the social, political, cultural, and economic patterns by which schooling is formed. A critical science gives reference to schooling as a socially constructed enterprise that contains continual contradictions: There are the noble dreams and hopes about creating a better and more equal society while, at the same time, social differentiations maintain unequal power relations and subtle forms of social regulation. A critical *science*, in turn, gives reference to a systematic inquiry (scholarship, or *wissenshaft*) that focuses upon the contradictions of educational practice. That inquiry, however, is not solely that of empirical investigation. There is a recognition of the interaction between the empirical tasks (that is, attention given to the ongoing events and phenomena of the world in which we live) and the concepts, theories, and insights that form simultaneously through interchanges with philosophy, history, the arts, other disciplines, and social practice.

AUTHOR'S NOTE: This chapter was written while at the Swedish Collegium for Advanced Study in the Social Sciences, Uppsala. I would like to acknowledge my gratitude to colleagues there and at other institutions who shared their time to talk with me about the ideas of this chapter. These include Ingrid Carlgren, Aant Elzinga, Tomas Englund, Sigbrit Franke-Wikberg, Sverker Lindblad, Lief Ostman, and Cark Anders Säfström.

To probe the character of a critical science in education is to bring the theme of the socially constructed character of knowledge into questions about methodology. Throughout the discussion, I will consider the rules and standards of educational research as historically formed and tied to particular social values and political relations that are often hidden through the rituals and rhetoric of science itself. I will do this by focusing on two meanings of *critical*, the role of history and values in science and, in the last section, the relation of science to the problem of social improvement and progress.

What Is Critical About a Critical Science?

There are at least two senses to *critical* that are of importance to this discussion. First is the internal criticism that comes from analytical questioning of argument and method. There is a focus upon theoretical reasoning and the proper procedures for selecting, collecting, and evaluating empirical data. It stresses the logical consistency in arguments, procedures, and language. Continual cross-examinations and rigorous scrutiny of data are its hallmarks.

But to say that the rules of argument are important does not imply that rules of argument are always the same in different times and places. In different intellectual traditions, there are different ways of constructing arguments. We could compare the writing of behaviorialism in psychology with the narratives of history and anthropology to consider different rules that can be applied for defining evidence and constructing a reasoned argument. The differences in the rules of writing portray different assumptions about knowledge and truth: The American Psychological Association emphasizes the cumulative quality of knowledge through placing references into the text; the historical community, in contrast, places greater emphasis upon footnotes to locate where information is found and for criticism and discussion of references to occur (see Bazerman, 1987).

These differences in presentation are partly explained by the "nature" of the problem and the data that each discipline considers. The differences are also understood through the social purposes of the discipline as methods and concepts historically develop. The legacy of late nineteenth-century and early twentieth-century psychology, such as found in the work of G. Stanley Hall and Edward Thorndike, is related to the importance given to individualization, the belief in useful knowledge that is interrelated with institutional developments found in schools, social welfare agencies, and the military. More will be said about this later.

A second meaning of *critical* can be drawn from these differences to reformulate the issue of logic. Logic involves not just a formal organization and internal criteria of scrutiny but also particular forms of reasoning that give focus to skepticism toward social institutions and a conception of reality that ties ideas, thought, and language to social and historical conditions. *Critical*, in this second sense, considers the conditions of social regulation, unequal distribution, and power. It is most visibly articulated in Marx's concern with the alienation produced with the division of labor in capitalism, Weber's focus on rationalization and bureaucratization, and Durkheim's discussion of the breakdown of the collective organization of culture. Recent social criticism has sought, in various ways, to respond to the constitutive questions posed by these nineteenth- and early twentieth-century writers. The Frankfurt School's Critical Theory, the French structuralists and literary poststructuralism, the sociology of knowledge, cultural Marxism, and feminist theory are contemporary tribal views that vie for the authority to speak for a critical science.[1] As this tradition is carried into educational research, its purpose has been to explore the conflict and tensions of schooling as a socially constructed institution. Let me explore this briefly.

The formation of schooling carried a worldwide hope for the school to fulfill the ideals of individualism and democracy for all in society (Boli, 1989; Kaestle, 1983). At the same time, differentiations of race, gender, class, ethnicity, and religion were brought into the everyday interactions and pedagogical patterns of schooling. An early twentieth-century redesigning of American school mathematics or the creation of new subjects such as "social studies" responded, in the first situation, to assumed different destinations of children and, in the second case, to a desire to provide education for Blacks and American Indians that would make their conditions more humane (Lybarger, 1987; Stanic, 1987).

Learning and teaching, as well, have social implications that are more than the measurement of achievement or the mastery of concepts. Schooling is an institution whose pedagogy and patterns of conduct are continually related to larger issues of social production and reproduction.[2] In this context, pedagogical practice is a form of social regulation in which particular social knowledge is selected and cast for children to guide their everyday lives; yet the social differentiations in the larger society make school knowledge not equally accessible or equally available for all who come to school. Further, the construction of school processes and knowledge contain codes of ethics and notions of civility and discipline that are to govern personal and public lives.

A critical science is concerned with ways in which social, cultural, and economic conditions produce a certain selectivity in the processes of teaching and the organization of curriculum. It involves a continual skepticism toward the commonplaces and socially accepted conventions of schooling, realizing that social practices contain contradictions in which there are continually issues of power domination. The science of schooling is to inquire into the relations of the conditions and organization of schooling, as continually bound to processes of production and reproduction in society. The relationships, however, are not linear in fashion but shaped through debate and struggle as pedagogical practices are constructed.[3] Important to the debates in the critical sciences are different conceptions of power. For some, priority is given to certain structural relations in the constructions of schooling, such as class, ethnicity, or gender. A different position remains sensitive to these concepts but focuses on how power is circulated through the relation of knowledge to the construction of identity.

It is in the contradictions of schooling that we can talk about the work of educational sciences as one of inversion: The construction of more appropriate social conditions involves making history fragile. A science of schooling explores the constraints and restraints of school affairs, thus poking holes in the causality that confronts us in daily life and that limits our possibilities. Human possibility, it is believed, occurs through understanding how the boundaries and structures are formed through struggle rather than as given as an inevitable and unalterable present.

There is a point of debate within those who practice a critical science about the relation of researchers to social movements. One strand argues that the partisan role of science makes it an obligation to pursue those commitments through active participation in political movements (see Ginsburg, 1988; Giroux & McLaren, 1986). Ginsburg, for example, argues that *critical* is not only an intellectual involvement in the production of ideas but entails a direct and explicit involvement in efforts to transform current social relations. A different stance is taken here; social scientists are partisans in the forming of social agendas through the practices of science, but that involvement is not necessarily the same issue as that of praxis and the making of strategic choices in political contexts (see, e.g., Cherryholmes, 1988). There is also a distinction here between Anglo-Saxon and Continental traditions of social science that has to be historically considered. (I discuss this more fully in Popkewitz, 1984, and in the manuscript on which I am current working.)

History and the Study of School Life

The epistemological commitment to a study of schooling is also a commitment to a certain self-reflection about the rules and standards of the work of science. A critical stance is to reconstruct a science of education by making history an integral part of the study of methodology. Social values, struggles, and interest influence the questions, concepts, and strategies of educational science. Words of scientific standards, such as *adequacy, values,* or *rigor,* are not logical artifacts independent of social affairs but are concepts formed and reformed in a dynamic world of institutional arrangements, linguistic conventions, and contested priorities. There is no individuality in science without communal rules. There is no personal knowledge in any absolute sense or practices that are not bound to the cultural conditions and social circumstances.

I use the notion of history not as a chronology of events or in mere deference to context. History is to acknowledge the present as a heritage not only of physical goods but also of social forms and knowledge. The analytic procedures of theory development or the statistical procedures for data analysis, for example, are a part of more general institutional developments that made abstract knowledge a valued form for organizing social affairs in the nineteenth and twentieth centuries. The reason of the present, therefore, should be seen in relation to its past.

Six themes frame the discussion considering the meaning of *critical* in the practices of a science of education: (a) Certain institutional conditions and practices of educational sciences make the distinctions between methodology, methods, and procedures into technical problems, obscuring the historical problem of scientific epistemology; (b) standards and rules of science are a form of reasoning that is always bound in time and space; (c) the dichotomy between *objective* and *subjective* is misleading and obscuring of research practices; (d) the production of knowledge is the production of values; (e) there are social interests in the claims for disinterest; and (f) when thinking about science as guiding the future, there is the irony that science is inevitably about the past. The limitation of what science can offer also sets limits on what should be sold to people in positions of power and powerlessness.

(1) *Procedures, methods, and methodology of science.* The commonsense practices of educational research tend to remove social and historical concerns from problems of the construction of procedures and rules for research. This separation is found most often in graduate programs that require students to take particular courses in "methods" or methodology that are, at root, programs concerned with the procedures of collecting and analyzing data. These courses are typically concerned with ways of collecting information: constructing survey instruments, interview procedures, observational techniques, and coding procedures and, more recently, the use of computer-generated data analysis. These activities are important to scientific practices, but it would be in error to understand them in a context devoid of the problems of study or the concepts that are employed in research. The history of science has provided strong evidence that the procedures of statistics, interviews, or observation strategies do not stand alone but are part of a matrix of curiosities, questions, and social practices that, in their entirety, constitute the scientific enterprise.

It is in this matrix of research that methods of study can be properly discussed. Methods are formed from exemplars, given in science, but are reworked through the interrelation of questions, concepts, and procedures as curiosities are directed to empirical phenomena. In the physical sciences, one learns how to use the machinery of the laboratory as the part of a whole: The questions at hand, the concepts brought to bear upon the investigation, and the particular contextual variations contain ambiguities and complexities that researchers work through to shape and fashion their methods of inquiry. There is no scientific method, rather methods related to the particular study being undertaken. Methods of science emerge from a complex process in which the conduct of study occurs.

Methodology, in this context, is concerned with the relations of the various parts of study with the production of findings. Methodology is concerned with the moral order (the rules, values, and priorities given to social conditions and individual action) presupposed in the practices of science. It is the study of what is defined as legitimate knowledge and how that knowledge is obtained and ordered.

Conventional ways of talking about science that conflate methods and procedures provide little understanding of the underlying matrix of assumptions, dispositions, questions, concepts, and procedures that interrelate in the production of knowledge. It is this sense of paradigm that is most provocative in the work of Thomas Kuhn (1970). But to accept Kuhn's notion of science would be to view the production of knowledge as solely one of the conflict of ideas without locating the practices of science within its social conditions (see Lecourt, 1975; Manicas, 1987; Tiles, 1984).

To distinguish among the three layers of scientific practice helps in understanding that a strictly logical approach to science makes the choices seem procedural. To study scientific methods and intellectual traditions is to consider the relation of rules in historical conditions. A philosophy of science is also its history—how various types of questions are formed in intellectual traditions *and* institutional conditions, that is, how different sets of questions of study emerge as a part of an intellectual tradition. Further, there is a need to explore how questions are determined by, and determine methods in, the production of knowledge. What seems logical about inquiry is made so because of systems of meanings and relations that make "things" seem reasonable and plausible. The practices of statistics or field approaches are not independent skills but exist within general sets of questions and assumptions that provide conditions and purpose to inquiry.

As an example, consider the turmoil in political science during the early 1970s. Two important studies of the problem of governing gave completely different answers about who rules. C. Wright Mills's (1956) *The Power Elite* studied the interrelation of social, business, and governmental elites, identifying how they were connected in subtle but important ways. Mills argued that there was an interlocking institutional arrangement among educational institutions, government, and business in the production of power in society. In contrast, Robert Dahl's (1961) study of *Who Rules* traced the changing background patterns of politicians to changing demography. He defined the process of governing as organized around changing pluralistic interests, arguing that there was no center of power.

Some people asked how two such bright people could come to such different conclusions. The answer had little to do with traditional questions of procedural rigor or bias, for both studies have withstood severe scrutiny. One way to think about an answer is to consider the paradigmatic assumptions by which the studies were conducted. The way in which concepts of power were defined within intellectual traditions (Mills worked within the sociology of knowledge and Dahl from behavioralism) interrelated with the manner in which the techniques of study were brought into and related to the purposes and conceptions of inquiry. Each tradition of inquiry presupposed certain dispositions toward the patterns of the world that were "built into" the methods and concepts of study.

I can summarize the previous discussion in the following manner: Powerful institutional practices support and sustain a belief that educational sciences are only to address procedural problems in defining strategies of research. The organization of science is separated from social movements, historical conditions, or political interests, except in terms of a technical issue to control bias and prejudice. In contrast, if we "see" these procedures as historical constructions, the procedural stance is inadequate. A more adequate approach to purposes and boundaries is explored by considering certain commonplaces of educational research: the separation of objective and subjective in research, the separation of social values from scientific values, and the perception of scientists as disinterested observers. Proceeding in this manner, I intend to reformulate the purpose and rules of a science of schooling related to the critical tradition.

(2) *Redefining the standards and rules of science as a logic in historical context.* I would like to pursue the meaning of *logic* as a way of moving closer to the sets of relations and standards that are important to a critical science. Conventional "wisdom" is that logic is a universally valid process that continually clarifies and redefines what knowledge is, introducing science as a cumulative and progressive development. I want to argue, instead, that the logic of science changes in a manner that is not necessarily cumulative. It occurs as breaks and ruptures in practices and ideas in social transformation. In the fifteenth century, the study of logic was to uncover the rules of the mind through the study of grammar and speech, for the laws of the mind were seen as a microcosm of the larger laws of the world given by God (Durkheim, 1977). Today, logic has a very different set of meanings. Rules of

science give reference to the empirical, rather than to the social, status of the speaker or to the authority of God (Gouldner, 1979). Language is seen as having cross-contextual validity in that its rules transcend the particular and the idiosyncratic.

The changing of logic as scientific practice can be explored in the study of professions. There is no universal concept to assign to the word *profession*. Rather, it entails shifting concepts within different historical settings. In the early nineteenth century, professions were implicitly tied to the American schools' purpose in educating children in the moral precepts of Christianity. Teacher education aimed to have teachers express their sincerity and empathy with Christian values. Teacher seminars were constructed to enable a "professing" of one's religious conviction, to commit to vocations to affirm one's calling. Science was the search for methods to introduce moral and religious values.

Profession in the reform movement of the past decade has very different sets of concepts and epistemologies. Moral and ethical convictions of the 1800s are replaced with knowledge that ties the expert to practices associated with rational planning. In contemporary U.S. society, *profession* assumes an ideological quality that provides occupations with social and cultural authority.

The tying of logic to reason and social history can also be pursued by noting the various roles of psychology in educational research. Although historical considerations could be applied to other disciplines in education, including the development of critical sciences in the United States, my purpose in choosing psychology is its central location in educational research.

Psychology was the only social science to emerge solely within the university, first as a subdiscipline of philosophy and then as a separate discipline in the late nineteenth century. The challenge of psychology was twofold. It was to replace philosophy in a religious crisis about the mind/body split produced by the materialism of Darwin. Psychology was also tied to the emerging schools, with behaviorism dominating through its experimentation, testing, and measurement, which were seen as plausible responses to issues of administering schools.

The invention of behavioral psychology needs to be understood in relation to institutional conditions. The experimentation procedures developed in Leipzig by Wilhelm Wundt were part of the background discussion in the formation of American psychology (O'Donnell,

1985). Although Wundt's experimentation was to focus on human purpose and the objective conditions in which the mind is formed, the American psychologists took a narrower concern with attitudes, attributes, and skills. What Americans saw in the laboratory of Wundt was the study of psychological processes through individual case descriptions about what people thought. American psychology redefined the problem of individualism to consider statistical distributions and group experimentation that would identify population characteristics. (I am reminded here of the first American translation of the Soviet psychologist, Lev Vygotsky. Although Vygotsky sought to develop a Marxist psychology after the Soviet revolution, the English translator left out all references to Marx because they were considered irrelevant.)

The shift in procedures had little to do with the issue of scientific progress or knowledge accumulation. The approaches to American psychology were related to demands for collective data about aggregates of students going to schools. The "audiences" who provided resources were instrumental to the paths taken as science rather than to any "inherent" quality in either the knowledge gained or the scientific approaches used (Danziger, 1987). Historians of psychology have suggested that the particular methods were more related to the utilitarian pursuits in the field of education than to a more general concern with science (Napoli, 1981; O'Donnell, 1985).

The relation of methods of psychology to institutional conditions can help us focus upon certain issues raised about research practices. First, questions about what procedures exist for data collection/analysis are part of the *social* field of science. The ordering of data in psychology had to do with the types of knowledge that were appropriate for professional development, legitimacy, and resources. Second, ontology and epistemology are undifferentiated in the practical world of science. What is to be known and the means of knowing are intertwined and influence each other. Third, what is deemed as adequate knowledge and its development are not necessarily related to what has been previously accumulated through empirical investigations. I can remember the efforts made in secondary (meta) statistical analysis of empirical research, which only result in so much variation in the concepts, sampling, and analysis that straightforward comparisons were not possible.

From this initial discussion, I want to consider the logic of science as a problem of a social epistemology. What is accepted as procedures, concepts, rules, and investigation is not "natural" or inevitable to research but is made reasonable within institutional settings and social interests. A critical science is concerned with how these rules are socially constructed, responding to and a part of the relations and power arrangements in which science is practiced.

(3) *If I have nice thoughts, will the world become nicer too? The poverty of the dichotomies of subjective and objective.* I will continue the theme of reason and thought as part of their historical and social context but will recast it in relation to discussions about objective or subjective knowledge. I interpret a central debate in philosophy and social science as concerned with this relation.

First, I would accept a modified realist view that there are real objects in the world (see Manicas & Rosenberg, 1985). We do pass through doorways and can hurt our knees if we fall off a bicycle and hit the pavement. Things occupy physical space and time. Yet, once that is said, I still have to take a modified view of realism and, therefore, of objectivity. To say that there are trees is also to recognize that *tree* is an arbitrary name that assumes particular and possibly different meanings as it is placed within symbolic fields. There is a difference in speaking about trees in a school curriculum between a scientist concerned with the environmental issues of tropical forests and ozone layers and a literary description of lovers in a forest. Our categories and distinctions assume significance because of the ways in which they are positioned within language and as that language is made part of the rules and standards of social practice itself. In this sense, there is no essential or "basic" meaning to a word but continual processes by which words are given meaning.

The arbitrary and situationally derived meaning of words has important consequences when approaching a central dualism of research, the separation of *objective* and *subjective*. These two words are made into oppositions that I believe are misleading, obscuring, and often mystifying. *Objective* has nothing to do with external laws or a "nature" to be discovered or verified. Rather, it is to consider the *socially* formed patterns that impinge upon our daily life as unquestioned and seemingly natural boundaries; and, at the same time, because these conditions are historically formed through human struggles, the patterns are dynamic and changing. *Subjective*, in contrast, directs attention to what is occurring in the minds of people, such as the dispositions, sensitivities, and awarenesses that people have in their daily lives.

Once these two words are posed in relation to the phenomena of the world, it is not easy to tease out what is one's individuality and what is formed by unseen and unacknowledged rules that act as horizons for individual reason. Feminist scholarship, among others, has explored the interrelation of family structure, economic transformations, and political forms in defining women, men, and their participation in civic and political affairs (see, e.g., Pateman, 1988b; Weedon, 1987). Although there are reasoned arguments to give value to caring and nurturing in human relations, feminist scholarship has made us aware about the problem of "naturalizing" such characteristics by recognizing that these "womanly" traits were part of the social transformation of the bourgeois home and workplace. Social historians of schooling help us understand that teachers' talk about curriculum, methods, or management of classrooms is not *merely* teachers' talk but words that express complex social relations that are brought into the discursive patterns of schooling through historical processes (see, e.g., Hamilton, 1989). Two collateral issues about research methods emerge from the consideration of the interplay of object/subject. One is the distinction of hard and soft data. We often think that statistics is objective, providing *hard* data that can be trusted. *Soft* data—empathy, open interviews, and introspection—are to be viewed with suspicion. The use of statistics, however, is no better or worse than the questions and methods that underlie the research and the social processes in which the research is used. One needs only to construct a survey to understand how such surveys contain patterns of selection, omission, and dispositions toward the social world. The distinction of *hard* and *soft* also has a gendered quality that cannot be ignored in research and among researchers.

A second collateral issue is the movement to develop field methods to illuminate the actual words, language, and patterns of interactions. Here, the real is considered as the situated thoughts, language, and particular practices of people. The argument is that surveys do not enable researchers to understand the intent and purpose of people as they communicate; it considers qualitative methods as providing an approach that gets to the basic or underlying values, meanings, and interpretations. This second approach naturalizes the present by assuming that there is an essence or reality to be discovered. The view that there is a grounded theory has to be rejected.[4] Reasoning is itself a part of a historical process; the data of perceptions, attitudes and belief need to be continually placed in social and cultural horizons.

In this sense, a critical science assumes that there is no psychology of schooling without a corresponding sociology and concern with history. While talking about voice, empowerment, and personal autonomy is ideologically potent in contemporary rhetoric, the complexity of the interrelation of objective conditions and subjectivity is less straightforward and more profound than can be captured in a language of dichotomies.

(4) *Can there be a disinterested science among interested social scientists?* The rejection of a notion of *objective* as describing the essential properties of a real world also entails a rejection of the belief that the scientist is a disinterested observer. The belief in disinterest is related to the idea that the most appropriate knowledge is "purely" descriptive explanations of how things work. Such knowledge could be used by any groups or interests in society as they seek to understand social affairs (see Easton, 1957). Max Weber, the German sociologist, spoke about a value-free professoriat. He was concerned with university lecturers and their providing different arguments for a problem. He did not assert a value-free science. As the German idea was brought to America, it became the idea of disinterest that contained different meanings and purposes from those found in Europe.

The idea of disinterest became part of the social science debates as the professions were organized during the Progressive era reforms (1880-1920). Disinterest is a political strategy.

The notion of disinterest was given definition in relation to institutional issues. Certain economists, political scientists, and sociologists who were to dominate the professional organizations expressed concern about a reformist scholarship tied to Christian social ethics and socialist causes. It was feared by university presidents that business leaders who supported the university would react against social scientists' involvement in social protests. It was argued that professional debate should be limited to professional meetings and journals. Undue publicity would undermine professional claims of expertise as the internal conflicts about purpose and values were brought into the public discussion. An outcome was a professional ethics that stressed an empiricism without professional involvement in political agitation.

The notion of disinterest emerges in this debate (Furner, 1975; Silva & Slaughter, 1984). It was tied to a particular type of empiricism that was thought necessary to provide social scientists with a secure position in the university, resources for occupational development in an expanding state and economy, and jobs for the new scientists produced by the emerging graduate schools around the nation. The notion of disinterest was to deny the professoriat legitimacy to act toward social amelioration except in an expert role.

It is interesting to note that the social scientists emerge as part of nineteenth-century movements for social amelioration, and that heritage continues in today's educational reform practices. The appearance of disinterest is easy to maintain when values and dispositions appear to be consensually agreed upon or so dominate that there seems no reason to scrutinize the concepts and theories that are used. Many of the early social scientists took for granted dominant social, cultural, and religious values that they thought should be promulgated. Today, much educational research focuses upon functional relations between teaching and learning and school organizational characteristics while structuring out of consideration the conflict of values in schooling. The functualist obscures the relation between research concepts and strategies and the social values of reform that are being maintained (see Popkewitz, 1984).

At best, disinterest can mean a disciplined and systematic approach to investigation in which one "plays" with different interpretations. But this play always occurs within boundaries, as there are presuppositions, paradigmatic assumptions, and social fields in which practice occurs.[5] Disinterest cannot mean lack of commitment or ideas that have no social location or consequences.

To this point, I have pursued assumptions of a critical science by probing certain beliefs, social values, and interests that are embedded within the practices of educational sciences. I have proceeded in this manner to place the methodological categories and distinctions of educational science in a historical confrontation with those of the social formation of institutions. At the same time, the discussion has sought to reconstruct the rules of research as a problem of engaging in relating history to epistemology. A science of schooling is one that involves complex social, philosophical, political, and historical questions that are intertwined with the practices of science itself.

(5) *The production of knowledge is the production of values.* Social science knowledge is a part of the production, administration, and ideological spheres in society. One way to think about the multiple values that are continually embedded in inquiry is to focus upon two roles of social sciences even though they are contradictory.

One is a civil service function in planning. Often this relates to state practices, such as found in reform movements and evaluations of inputs and outputs of school activities. Much of what can be considered within positivist research is a part of that structured relation to collect information and rationally guide and administer state programs. Second, and at the same time, social science can provide a critical voice of social consciousness. It takes a skeptical attitude toward the public rhetoric, taken-for-granted patterns, and daily practices found in schools. In considering these different affiliations and social purposes, there has been debate about whether scientists are part of a new technical class in society or whether they are an important stratum in the production/reproduction of class and cultural relations.

In whatever role social scientists adopt, the discourse of social science helps to establish boundaries by which strategies for reform and innovation are to occur. The organization of data posits assumptions about society, such as that the world should be considered as in equilibrium or in conflict or people as rational or irrational. The categories of schooling frame and carry assumptions about what is to be argued;[6] this can be illustrated by juxtaposing the categories of *learning* and *work* as a lens for studying classroom practices. Each word provides a different point of entrance for thinking, seeing, talking, and feeling about schooling.

The legacy of positivism has dulled our senses to these issues of values by focusing upon rules and procedures of science, defining the world as asocial and ahistorical. Taxonomic and hierarchic schemes are created that assume that the sum of the parts equals the whole. Change is a sequential and hierarchic arrangement of discrete elements. A consequence is fragmented notions of causation. The minuscule is made important and social life trivialized.[7] The positivism that I speak about is not necessarily a philosophical position but one concerning the folklore, reconstructions, and training in educational sciences. The development of American behaviorism and empiricism, for example, occurred in ways that were independent of the work being done by the logical positivist; only later was there some interaction.

Another way to consider values is by considering the procedures of inquiry. The use of statistics and case studies can help us focus more clearly on this issue.

We tend to think of statistics as producing a sophisticated science because it is thought that the only values are in the numbers themselves. The discussion, however, ignores the debates in mathematics about what visions are appropriate for exploring both natural and social worlds (see e.g., Crutchfield, Farmer, Packard, & Shaw, 1986; Ralston, 1986). Further, there is a selective memory that has lost sight of the origin of "statistic" as a science of the state that was to guide modern governments as they began to organize social reforms.[8] Demographic data provided information about social welfare and amelioration.

But more particular to educational sciences are the social values that are in its techniques. The situation is not unidirectional. Statistics have enabled an expansion of phenomena to be examined not previously available, therefore, enlarging the problems studied. At the same time, when statistical measures are constructed, they are always embedded in a system of social values and interests. Let me give two examples.

Factor analysis was derived from factor psychology. It divided the mind into separate spheres that were thought to exist independently of the other but that could be correlated. This view of the mind has long been in disrepute and is no longer given serious thought, yet the technique is still in use. We can consider as well the work of Karl Pearson dealing with group tendencies. It is plausible to relate the direction of his mathematics to his concern with proving the collective superiority of the White race as Britain expanded its colonial empire.

The development of case studies that define social life as a negotiated order provide another set of values that can be read in contradictory ways. Sociology and anthropology introduced approaches to consider the dynamic qualities of people's interactions and language that are not amenable to behavioral methods. But the "deep" description of interactions is also related to the problems of the social management of micro levels in modern states. The methods provide new methods of supervision, observation, and control of individuals as intimate thoughts and feelings are opened to public scrutiny (Foucault, 1978; Martin, Gutman, & Hutton, 1988).

The plausibility of case studies entails a consideration of the American social context in the Depression years of the 1930s and again in the aftermath of the struggles in the 1960s. When other parts of social life become more remote and complex, case studies have a symbolic potency in establishing the importance of one's immediate encounters and power in defining situations (see Popkewitz, 1984, chap. 4). As symbolic canopies, they provide a linguistic structure that emphasizes a negotiated order and participation in a community. In doing so, the prior assumptions and historical conditions in which the interactions occurred are taken for granted.

Although we can identify prior assumptions in the procedures of science, it is not sufficient to talk about values. We have to know how procedures are used in relation to the methods of study. Earlier I spoke of words as having meaning only as they are established in relation to other words and in context. The social implications of techniques also entail rational thinking. Statistics can have different implications: They can be used to produce efficiency and effectiveness in administrative reforms; they can also provide understanding about differentiated cultural dispositions among different class positions and the unequal distribution of wealth. In a similar manner, we need to consider ethnographies. Tom James (1986), a historian, has described how anthropologists worked with progressive educators in Navaho communities. Their task was to create strategies to produce acceptance of federal land use policy during the 1930s. A few of the anthropologists, however, felt moral indignation at the conditions they found and testified in Congress for reform.

From this brief discussion, we can see that procedures and techniques are not the only elements of research subjected to values. Values are in all layers of science. The issue is not to rid science of them or to identify bias for purposes of control. Such control is a chimera that has long been recognized in positivism, hermeneutics, and critical sciences. The problem is to consider the contradictions that interact at all levels of the practice of science. It is also to recognize that the commonsense approach that defines values as distinct and separable from the procedural concerns of science has its own poverty by decontextualizing the way choices are made and the priorities formed.

As part of a critical science concerned with educational research, questions are asked: What social and cultural conditions make plausible the forms of analysis that dominate the educational sciences? How is it that certain forms and styles have come to dominate psychology, sociology, and anthropology in education? What social debates, and by whom, give support to the manner in which the standards and rules of inquiry are adopted and revised? And how have these standards changed over time and in relation to what social transformations?

(6) *Whose future is it anyway? Science as the study of the past.* Let me pose the issue about the usefulness of educational paradigms as a question about what a science can do and cannot do: Any social science is *inevitably about the past.* Epistemologically, social science is

a dialect of language about what *has* happened. Although we like to think of our generalizations as about the present, generalizations are constrained because they are constructions that occur after the events.

There is also a political question when we assume social science is about the present, educational reform, or future social progress. When we adopt a belief that knowledge is about prediction and administration, we have left science and its relation to the empirical world to move into the realm of ideology and social control. The rituals of science become a rhetorical form that is to convince others that what is being done to them is in their own interest.

I say this because I can find no evidence that social science has anything to say qua science about the future, but it does have methods for understanding the boundaries that exist in the past. This is not to say that science cannot help us in the choices we make but that is often in a negative voice. To borrow partially from Karl Popper, science does not verify but refutes. Science can help to understand what choices not to make, such as in eliminating fluorocarbons, controlling the deforestation in the Amazon, or limiting the use of intelligence testing. But in the policy arena, the findings of science are part of a public debate that is rarely that of evidence alone. The determination of futures is not reserved for particular elites and experts who claim a sacred knowledge.

Before ending this discussion about past, futures, and science, there is an important caveat. Science is about the future in an indirect way, but not because it can predict and control. The categories organize phenomena in a manner that sensitizes us toward certain possibilities and, at the same time, filters out others. Implicit in practices then are ways in which people are to challenge the world and locate themselves in its ongoing relations. This role of science and scientists in the ongoing construction of the world needs continual attention.

Some Concluding Thoughts

The major charge of the conference from which the chapters in this book have been drawn was not to determine "who is right about science" but to search for differences and distinctions that can lead to more fruitful practices. In this context, I have considered the values and methodology within an epistemological field that I associate with "critical." I have argued that our traditional ways of organizing the work of social science as objective/subjective, rigor/relevant, and discovery/verification obscures more than it illuminates.

Central was a placing of debates about methods and truth in a social and historical context. In different ways, I have argued against a notion of knowledge accumulation as a reification of the social and historical conditions in which knowledge is produced and transformed. Although we need to understand what others have said and done before us, it is not just a problem of "adding on" knowledge. It is a complex process of interpretation and analysis that considers how the social forms, knowledge, and struggles of those before us are a part of the present.

One might raise the question, at the end of this short foray into paradigms: What does a critical science have to recommend as a tradition for the study of schooling? I believe that its various strands provide the most elaborate theoretical discussions of the problems of schooling as a socially constructed institution in a world of inequalities. It offers a way to reassert history, value, and ethical choice into the knowledge that we have about social practice. It enables us to understand that freedom and autonomy are never absolutes but always practices within patterns of constraints and restraints, with a purpose of an educational science to poke holes in the seeming causality of social life.

The methods of a critical science are also a cross-checking mechanism on the hubris of intellectuals and power relations that underlie the formation of knowledge itself. For example, much current research accepts the logic and reasoning found in schooling, arguing that researchers and policymakers need to respect teachers' talk. Yet, the style of argument in teaching cannot be taken for granted. It presupposes the particular cultural competence found in schooling, with its interpretive stances and cognitive frames. To evoke images of stages of development, children's "nature," or teachers' reasoning is to engage in conversations that are organized within particular historical settings that are presupposed in the conversations. The words and their assumptions cannot be taken for granted but are part of the problem of the sciences of schooling.

To consider language and thought as existing in historically produced contexts is not to deny that there are agents. Nor is to adopt a philosophical position of extreme relativism, a stance that the earlier discussion of schooling would rule out. Rather, it is to relativize issues of methodology by making them historical issues that tie the practices of science to those of power and control in society.

One of the questions posed in the formulation of the conference and subsequent book is whether it is possible that the various paradigms discussed here can find any room for accommodation. I have a practical and a "theoretical" answer to this question. Practically, there is accommodation that occurs through the hiring practices in universities and in the scholarly debates.

If we focus upon paradigms as social epistemologies, then we cannot nor do we want to homogenize the distinction and have accommodation. The importance of the divergence is epitomized in the papers from this conference. If we read them not only as giving us information but as ways of expressing relations in the world, we can understand some of the fundamental issues that underlie the "modernity" of the world in which we live. As Habermas (1971) argued, there are different human interests in social science, and these contain different dispositions toward the world and how we challenge it. The argumentation, debate, and cross-fertilization concerning these interests have a dual quality, which makes for a more serious debate about the work and knowledge of science. It also enables a certain humility as we are continually made aware of the precarious quality of our knowledge and agendas.

Yet for me, the practice of science in all the paradigms needs to be reconstructed with a strong sense of its social epistemology, that is, the interrelation of science with the historical conditions in which it works. Without this, science becomes procedural, technical, and one-dimensional. Here, I guess, I leave the pluralism. To include a disciplined sense of history into methodology and methods introduces strong questions about ethics, morality, and politics. It rejects "seeing" the discrete events, whether bound to "qualitative" or "quantitative" techniques, in isolation from the relation of events to historical formations. In that manner, neopositivism and hermeneutic traditions have to be reconstructed. History becomes a part of the analysis and logic of a science as the researched, research, and researcher are interrelated.

A final comment about understanding scientific practices. The three traditions entail a continual debate and struggles about who has the authority to control the signs of science. In the relations among the various traditions, there occur changing boundaries and conceptual relations (see Manicas, 1987; Toulmin, 1972). One cannot adequately consider positivism without also focusing upon the debates on critical sciences and hermeneutics. At the same time, alternative and oppositional traditions are defined within a horizon of positivism that dominates American culture and science. It is in the interactions and boundaries among the competing traditions that we can locate the practices of science and an adequate study of paradigms.

Notes

1. For those who wish to explore some of the nuances among these different approaches to study, see Beechey and Donald (1985), Bourdieu (1977), Dreyfus and Rabinow (1983), Foucault (1980), Giddens (1987), Habermas (1971, 1984, 1987), Jay (1973), Mannheim (1936), Pateman (1988), Weedon (1987), and Williams (1977).

2. Important to the debates in the critical sciences are different conceptions of power and its implications. For some, priority is given to certain structural relations in the constructions of schooling, such as class, ethnicity, or gender. A different position rejects the argument about privileged concepts and focuses upon how power is circulated to produce subjugation.

3. I think that the reader should be aware that my background is pedagogy; my department is one called "curriculum and instruction." I might take a different position here if I were located in a sociology department or educational foundation, such as British researchers who are interested in similar concerns but housed in sociology departments.

4. In a recent report, a researcher treated a teacher's comments about stages of development and teaching as management as a way of talking about pedagogical reasoning and action. What is ignored is how that language of stages and management came into schooling as a form of social regulation of women teachers, how that language has been incorporated into the "natural" setting of teaching in a manner that makes issues of control and power invisible.

5. I have begged the issue of change only because that will involve another discussion about structured relations.

6. I discuss this in Popkewitz (1984).

7. While a methodological individualism is contained in the empiricism that dominates behaviorism and cognitive psychology and most American sociology, it has been severely critiqued as an untenable philosophical and methodological position (see Udehn, 1987).

8. *Statisik* was initiated in seventeenth-century Germany and as political arithmetic in Britain. In the ancien régime, the French civil service provided information about aspects of society essential to direct the affairs of state. Initially, it did not imply that such information need be quantitative (Clark, 1973, p. 27).

[4]

The Making of a Constructivist
A Remembrance of Transformations Past

YVONNA S. LINCOLN

Ours is a time of crisis and deep ferment—not only politically but intellectually: older school doctrines and entrenched philosophical positions are crumbling or being swept aside and replaced by more flexible and unconventional vistas. In the Anglo-American context, the sway of logical positivism—focused on scientific epistemology—has largely come to an end. (Dallmayr, 1985, p. 411)

As careful readers may have noticed while they perused the history of science literature, there are vastly different definitions of positivism, depending on whom one reads and what his or her original sources might have been (Harre, 1981; Hesse, 1980). I attribute this less to failure to communicate among the positivists (or historians of science) than to something that I shall use as a springboard for this chapter: the highly individual nature of the paradigm-building process and the focus on several elements of a paradigm to the exclusion of others. Since the constructivists have lived with singularly sharp criticism, it has not always been their luxury to be selective about focal elements. Nevertheless, the idea that fooling around with a new paradigm is an intensely personal process, evolving from not only intellectual but also personal, social, and possibly political transformation seems a persuasive and compelling path to take.

In part, I wish to focus on the more recent past, although, of course, the early years were equally important. The early arguments have been available for criticism, for examination, for comparison, and for use by others for some time. That the paradigm revolution is here is a given. Bernstein (1976, p. xii) has observed that the initial impression one has in reading through the literature in and about the social disciplines during the past decade or so is that of sheer chaos. Everything appears to be "up for grabs." There is little or no consensus—except by members of the same school or subschool—about what are the well-established results, the proper research procedures, the important results, the important problems, or even the most promising theoretical approaches to the study of society and politics. There are claims and counterclaims.

I have argued Bernstein's point in many other places (Guba & Lincoln, 1981, 1987, 1989; Lincoln, 1985, 1989; Lincoln & Guba, 1985). That the new paradigm's final shape is not yet fixed is also fairly apparent, although I've been attempting to do my part in the hammering process. Critics of constructivist (or naturalistic or ethnographic) inquiry have aided and abetted this cause by pointed criticism of various aspects of the paradigm.

As any good biography begins with the "early years," I'll begin with mine. Please consider what follows next as the childhood reminiscences.

The Early Years of Naturalism

It is handy to think of my intellectual development in terms of early years, an adolescence, and a more mature period. The early years remind me now of the credo of many small business owners: "If I'd known what I was in for, I'd never have started this!" Egon and I rejected conventional inquiry on three basic grounds: its posture on reality, its stance on the knower-known relationship, and its stance on the possibility of generalization. This seemed to us most appropriate when we considered the special case of evaluation (as one form of disciplined inquiry). On a regular basis, we confronted endless political problems dealing with multiple constructions of the same evaluand. It also became clearer and clearer that knower and known not only could *not* remain distanced and separated in the process of evaluation but probably *should* not. And, finally, we began to doubt seriously the possibility of generalization from one site to the next because of contextual factors (Guba & Lincoln, 1981). We had been "brought up" to believe that what is unknown or unusual to us will be explained or accounted for by natural sciences in general (e.g., physics, chemistry and biology) and *by the methods they employ in particular.* This natural scientific approach makes a number of assumptions, the three most crucial . . . being that: (a) the phenomenon under study . . . must be observable . . .; (b) the phenomenon must be measurable . . .; and (c) the phenomenon must be such that it is possible for more than one observer to agree on its existence and characteristics. (Valle & King, 1978, p. 4, emphases added)

In this world that we have nearly all inherited,

the priority is given to the measurement perspective, and, in order for something to be measured, only its tangible aspects can be apprehended, and thus the *indices itself of a phenomenon become more important than the phenomenon.* (Giorgi, 1970, p. 291, emphases added)

From our rejection of conventional assumptions associated with logical positivism, we derived three axioms, and from them a number of what we first called "derivative postures" (Guba & Lincoln, 1981) and later called "implications," because they were implied by accepting the axioms. They included qualitative rather than quantitative methods as the preferred (though not exclusive) techniques for data collection and analysis; relevance rather than rigor as the quality criterion; grounded rather than a priori theory; changes in the nature of the causal questions asked and thought possible to answer; expansion of the knowledge types utilizable from propositional to propositional *and tacit*; an expansionist rather than reductionist stance toward the inquiry; a presumption of the human inquirer as the major although not necessarily only form of instrumentation; an emergent rather than preordinate design strategy; a selection rather than intervention style as focus for the inquiry; a natural, in situ rather than laboratory context for the research; a variable rather than invariant "treatment" mode; patterns as opposed to variables as the analytic unit (Kaplan, 1964); and invited interference—an invitational and participatory mode—as opposed to control in the exercise of the research (Guba & Lincoln, 1981, p. 65).

But as soon as our first work went to press, we were disturbed by things that we had said, or taken for granted. Most particularly, two things that we had taken for granted began to trouble us and our critics: First, we began to understand that traditional and conventional assumptions regarding causality were axiomatic statements themselves. Should causality not, therefore, also be a parallel axiom for us? We were, after all, playing the Lobachevskian geometry game: turning conventional axioms on their heads and trying to determine whether or not they made sense. From that moment on, we began to talk about a fourth axiom.

Second, the question of what role values played in inquiry also troubled us. Increasingly, we became attuned to a powerful assumption that we had earlier missed, to wit, that inquiry not only could but should be value free. We began to understand that "science" demanded that scientists stand outside of time and context, and, indeed, outside of themselves as persons, in order to deliver research results that stood apart from human values. The purpose of such a stance was clearly, at least for the social sciences, the rendering of judgments regarding appropriate social strategies for the solution of human ills. Only if research results were free of human values, and, therefore, free of bias, prejudice, or individual stakes, could social action be taken that was neutral with respect to political partisanship. But how could humans stand outside of themselves, even in the research process? We were beginning to understand, especially from the feminists, critical theorists, and neo-Marxists, that the research process itself was a political endeavor, with some groups and research models favored over others, with some definitions of problems more acceptable than others, with avenues to funding and support clearly discriminatory (Keller, 1985).

Given our concerns, we finally realized that two items that we had earlier believed to be merely postures, or implications, of the first three axioms were themselves axioms. When we understood this, we realized that there were five axioms, at least as we originally constructed the paradigm.

A Thorny Problem, a Turbulent Summer

At about that time, a challenge arose from a strange source. The editors of education journals were interested in seeing naturalistic case studies appear in print, but they were at a loss as to how to judge the rigor of those studies, and their reviewers were no better off. After his participation in a conference to deal with these issues, Egon took

up the express intellectual task of the development of a set of criteria
for judging the process of naturalistic inquiries. The result of that
self-imposed task was a set of criteria for judging whether or not
any given inquiry was *methodologically* and *analytically* sound (Guba,
1981). The criteria, called "trustworthiness" criteria to distinguish
them from the criteria of "rigor" that were applicable to the conventional paradigm, paralleled the standard criteria of internal validity,
external validity, reliability, and objectivity but were framed in a very
different manner. These parallel or trustworthiness criteria, criteria of
credibility, transferability, dependability, and confirmability, could
not establish quality with the confidence and assurance that the older
rigor criteria did, Egon said, but were nevertheless useful. Somehow,
over the years, we have continued to make modest claims for those
criteria, never realizing that uncertainty, flux, and transformation,
hallmarks of the paradigm itself, meant that certainty would never be
possible and would always preclude the certitude and presumed
rectitude of conventional rigor criteria. The two of us discussed this
work often, but in retrospect—and this is a retrospective and, therefore, reconstructed logic—we were too modest.

We were also only half right.

What Egon had developed was, in fact, a set of criteria that, as our
loyal critic John K. Smith pointed out, were parallel, or *foundational*,
criteria. That is, they had their foundation in concerns indigenous to
the conventional, or positivist, paradigm. If we did not have the
conventional paradigm, would we not develop criteria indigenous to
naturalism, to phenomenology, or to constructivism?

Of course, John was right. We asked ourselves, can you ever "forget" what has gone before you, what you knew—stand outside of
your historical self? Of course not, but it might well be possible to
imagine oneself outside of one's own history and at least try to think
about the question. The answers took more than two years to develop,
and we're not certain that they're finished even now. But Egon and I
took two different tacks, finally, and managed to come up with some
interesting answers. This is more or less what happened:

We first thought about what might come out of a naturalistic and
responsive inquiry that would not, or should not, or could not evolve
from a conventional one. These forms of knowing and action we
called "authenticity criteria" to distinguish them from the methodological process criteria that we had designated as "trustworthiness"

criteria. They included "states of being," particularly for respondents, participants, and stakeholders, which were not expected (or warranted) in conventional inquiry, and one additional criterion, which recognized and attended to the need for such inquiries to express multiple, socially constructed, and often conflicting realities. The latter we termed *fairness*, and judgments were made on the achievement of this criterion in much the same way that labor negotiators and mediators determine fairness in bargaining sessions.

The "states of being" represented something much more subtle. They related both to (a) levels of understanding and sophistication and to (b) the enhanced ability of participants and stakeholders to take action during and after an inquiry and to negotiate on behalf of themselves and their own interests in the political arena. Those "states-of-being" criteria included *ontological authenticity*, or the heightened awareness of one's own constructions and assumptions, manifest and unspoken; *educative authenticity*, or the increased awareness and appreciation (although not necessarily the acceptance) of the constructions of other stakeholders; *catalytic authenticity*, a criterion that is judged by the prompt to action generated by inquiry efforts; and *tactical authenticity*, the ability to take action, to engage the political arena on behalf of oneself or one's referent stakeholder or participant group (Lincoln & Guba, 1986a).

In that intuitive way in which some intellectual tasks proceed, it was only later that we realized the powerful implications of designing and adopting new criteria for trustworthiness. In particular, the distinction between process and data struck us. For instance, the conventional inquirer's assertion that "the data speak for themselves" was erroneous. In conventional inquiry, actually, the *methods* attest to the strength of the conclusions. And in parallel fashion, in constructivist fashion, the data are what speak for themselves. For example, in evaluation (as one form of disciplined inquiry), data are confirmable, but the "test of the pudding" is in the enhanced sophistication of stakeholders and in the comprehension of avenues of action. Likewise, in research, data are likewise confirmable, by reference to original field notes, and the "test of the pudding" is increased understanding as a form of knowledge. In conventional inquiry, pure process leads to pure results. In constructivist inquiry, process is only one means of determining the utility, responsibility, and fidelity of the inquiry. Action and understanding were other components of the judgments regarding the goodness of any given inquiry.

We weren't finished yet, however.

Increasingly, we had come to understand—largely through our able, curious, and harrying students—that there were other judgments to be made about naturalistic or constructivist inquiries. Baldly put, could the methodological strategy be good, could the inquirer be an honest and faithful servant to the inquiry question and still turn out a *product* that fell short of the mark? The answer, of course, was yes. We needed criteria by which we might judge *products*—most typically, a case study rather than a conventional scientific, technical report. We began again, this time taking as our model the study of fiction as a narrative form, and the work of a student, Nancy Zeller (1987), who had training in this area and who sought to explore what judgments about fiction might tell us about compelling narrative.

Building on Zeller's work, and deriving our own criteria from judgments made about case studies which students prepared in various classes for us, we were able to propose a set of criteria which seemed to us appropriate for naturalistic or constructivist inquiries. These criteria were, like the authenticity criteria, *nonfoundational*, because they rested not on conventional inquiry's requirements for research reports but, instead, grew from the concerns of this particular paradigm. The constructivist paradigm, it should be recalled, had as its central focus not the abstraction (reduction) or the approximation (modeling) of a single reality but the presentation of multiple, holistic, competing, and often conflictual realities of multiple stakeholders and research participants (including the inquirer's). Further, in the presentation of those multiple realities (social constructions), a vicarious, déjà vu experience should be created in the reader. This vicarious experience, in addition to providing certain technical help to other researchers (e.g., in the presentation of thick description, which enables judgments regarding transferability to be made), should aid the reader in understanding the nuances and subtleties of conflict and agreement in *this place and at this time*. Further, the written report should demonstrate the passion, the commitment, and the involvement of the inquirer with his or her coparticipants in the inquiry.

Because those things needed to be apparent from the case study, we developed a set of criteria that were responsive to the paradigm itself (or, more precisely, to the *product* of the paradigm). *Axiomatic criteria* are those criteria that display resonance with constructivist (naturalistic) inquiry. *Rhetorical criteria* are those criteria relating to the "form and structure, or the presentational characteristics" of the written document issuing from a naturalistic inquiry (Lincoln & Guba, 1988, p. 8), and include power and elegance, creativity, openness and prob- lematic qualities, independence, the writer's emotional and intellec- tual commitment to the case itself, social courage, and egalitarianism.

Action criteria "mean the ability of the case study to evoke and facilitate action on the part of readers," or the "power of such an inquiry to enable those whom it affects directly or indirectly to take action on their circumstances or environments." This is essentially an *empowerment criterion* (Lincoln & Guba, 1988, p. 19). The *application or transferability criterion* refers to the "extent to which the case study facilitates the drawing of inferences by the reader that may have applicability in his or her own context or situation" (Lincoln & Guba, 1988, pp. 20-21).

Now, nobody—least of all me—would argue that the last word has been written on criteria for adequacy of case studies as reports or on trustworthiness or authenticity issues. But our critics and students had clearly pushed us far beyond where we—or I—ever expected to go.

The Middle Years:
Experimentation and Excursions

My own observation has been that those careers that can be read as straight lines reflect a single-mindedness that is more akin to narrow- ness and parochiality than it is to great determination in purpose. Some of the more interesting academic lives I've observed tend to be those that are, in part, committed to explore a line of inquiry and, at the same time, are open to interesting side-street excursions. I'd like to think I'd been big on side streets, conceptually intriguing tangents, and occasionally swerving down "the road less traveled." Thus, in the middle of what might be termed systematic development of new-par- adigm inquiry, I took some side roads. And because they tell the reader something about how "problems" occur to inquirers, they are worth some discussion here.

The first tangent occurred when Egon and I were team-teaching a class in program evaluation at the University of Kansas. During the course of one discussion, Egon asserted that, of course, the flowchart for naturalistic inquiry would be the same as that for conventional inquiry, save that the terms—the labels in the boxes—would be dif- ferent. That assertion was challenged both by me and by the students in the class, who were determined that such could not be the case. The group of students retired for two days to figure out how the "flow" of naturalistic inquiry might be pictorially represented to demonstrate its difference and distinction from conventional inquiry. What they "drew" shocked and stunned us into a major intellectual exploration of methodological, or strategic, differences between conventional and naturalistic inquiry, and we elaborated on it extensively. A graphics artist connected with the Center for Public Affairs at the university drew up a fine set of models for us, and we took it upon ourselves to work out the question of whether or not inquiry paradigms imply inquiry methodologies (by which we meant, overall design strategy).

The question was important because a number of our critics had been charging that *procedurally* naturalistic inquiry was *not* different from conventional inquiry and that the major difference between paradigms lay in the rather heavier reliance on qualitative methods demanded by naturalism. We argued, and I think successfully, that switching paradigms meant switching strategy in rather dramatic ways, and we provided the "models" to demonstrate how and in what ways (Guba & Lincoln, 1988a).

It might have been years before we tumbled to that problem without the insistence of my students. Sometimes, problems are presented fortuitously; the point is, you explore them when and where you find them, if you find them interesting.

A second side-street incident will show you what I mean. I'd read a number of classic works in program evaluation and, over the years, had begun to be troubled by the ongoing reference of evaluation experts to "evaluation research," to "policy analysis research," or, worse yet, to "policy analysis evaluation research." My hunch was that this language and terminology took hold because major avenues of funding were opening up in evaluation of social action programs and education, and researchers who went after such money were feeling pressure to justify such work as "research" on their own campuses. Evaluation work has never been as highly regarded as research work, especially with promotion and tenure committees, and those who undertook the former needed to connect their work directly to either basic or applied research. But the careless blending of such terms irritated me.

The more I thought about the problem, the more it occurred to me that there were different *categories* of what Cronbach and Suppes (1969, p. 16) had called "disciplined inquiry," inquiry that "has a texture that displays the raw materials entering the argument and the logical processes by which they were compressed and rearranged to make the conclusion credible." Further, different forms of inquiry ought to lead to different end products, have different expected outcomes, address different audiences, and perhaps employ different strategies in arriving at outcomes.

It was not until I began to chart out differences between research, evaluation, and policy analysis that I realized someone should have argued much sooner that these three activities were actually different *forms* of disciplined inquiry. Hence it made no sense to refer to "evaluation research," save as research *on* evaluation methods or models. Likewise, it made no sense to talk of "policy analysis evaluation" or of "policy analysis research." Research, evaluation, and policy analysis were different inquiry processes, and sorting them out—an interesting intellectual and practical problem—was one of the more fascinating things I've done in the last several years (Lincoln & Guba, 1986b). The important thing about this work, other than its less-than-apparent centrality to new-paradigm research, is the way in which it occurred: as a nagging irritant, a "something" that was wrong but that resided, until I began to grapple with it explicitly, in the tacit domain.

A third side street will demonstrate another way in which problems occur to inquirers. Egon and I had been commissioned to put together an informal workshop with a highly talented group of special educators at the New England Regional Resource Center (NERRC). We gathered oceanside in Maine to discuss problems they were having in providing services to state departments of education throughout New England. During the course of the conversation, someone asked whether the ethical implications of naturalistic inquiry were the same as for positivist inquiry. I did my usual number when someone asks me a question to which I haven't a clue: I made it up as I went along. No, I said, the ethical implications of naturalistic inquiry went far beyond those of conventional positivist inquiry, which are by and large embodied in our federal laws on privacy, confidentiality, harm to research subjects, and informed consent. And I went on to suggest ways in which I thought contemporary federal law failed to take account of new-paradigm research. Fortunately for me, someone with a lap-top computer took all of this down. That provided me with notes to mull over and a chance to think about what I'd so rashly said.

After the workshop, Egon and I went to work on a proposal for the American Educational Research Association, the purpose of which was to have a paper accepted that would force us to write on the area of ethical issues in constructivism. The result of acceptance was a paper that not only criticized current law on research ethics (aided and abetted by criticism from the positivist camp) but that also outlined special problems with ethics in naturalistic inquiry (Guba & Lincoln, 1989; Lincoln & Guba, 1987, 1989).

By this time, things were starting to be really fun. Our critics were less and less successful at ruining our days, and we were just beginning to understand that we'd hit on something very, very important, something that was part and parcel of a changing worldview in Western society—something that would change the face of research profoundly over the years. It would have applications throughout the academic disciplines and the formal structure of knowledge (Lincoln, 1989b) and had already altered the face of the hard sciences (Zukav, 1979). I felt profoundly the changes implicit in committing oneself to a radical critique of social science: the sense of being an outlaw, a conscientious objector, a civilly disobedient academic.

Clearly, I still didn't appreciate the extent of the problem.

The Rites of Passage

We began to reformulate the axioms. Rather than stating them as we had, initially, in five parts, we began to talk about the ontology, the epistemology, and the methodology of naturalistic, or constructivist, inquiry. In their new form, they went like this:

(1) The ontological axiom states that reality is a social, and, therefore, multiple, construction; that there is no single tangible, fragmentable reality on to which science can converge; that reality exists rather as a set of holistic and meaning-bounded constructions that are both intra- and interpersonally conflictual and dialectic in nature; that, whereas the positivist construction of reality is realist in orientation, the constructivist is relativist; that, whereas the aim of positivist science is to expose and articulate immutable natural laws (for both the social and the natural world), usually expressed as generalizations, and usually in the form of cause-and-effect relationships, the aim of constructivist science is to create idiographic knowledge, usually expressed in the form of pattern theories, or webs of mutual and plausible influence expressed as working hypotheses, or temporary, time- and place-bound knowledge.

Table 4.1 Contrasts Between the Postpositivist, Critical Theory, and Constructivist Paradigms

Question	Paradigm		
	Postpositivist	*Critical Theory*	*Constructivist*
Ontology	Realist	Realist	Relativist
Epistemology	Dualist, objectivist	Interactive, subjectivist	Interactive, subjectivist
Methodology	Interventionist	Participative	Hermeneutic, dialectic

(2) The epistemological position of constructivist inquiry dictates that the positivist subject-object dualism and objectivism be replaced by an interactive monism; that the interactivity between researcher and researched be recognized and utilized in the teaching and learning process between the two; and that the values that inhere in the research process—in the choice of a problem, the choice of an overall design strategy, the choice of the setting, and the decision to honor and present the values that inhere in the site(s)—be explicated and explored as a part of both initial and final research processes and products.

(3) Methodologically, constructivism demands that inquiry be moved out of the laboratory and into natural contexts, where organizational processes create naturally occurring experiments, dictates that methods designed to capture realities holistically, to discern meaning implicit in human activity, and to be congenial to the human-as-instrument be employed; that such methods are typically, although not exclusively, qualitative rather than quantitative; that designs for such inquiries can never be fully articulated until after the inquiry has been declared complete, because the design must emerge as salient issues emerge from research respondents and coparticipants; that theory must arise from the data rather than preceding them; and that the method must be hermeneutic and dialectic, focusing on the social processes of construction, reconstruction, and elaboration, and must be concerned with conflict as well as consensus.

These two paradigms—positivism (or postpositivism) and constructivism—along with critical theory can best be contrasted in the manner shown in Table 4.1.

My colleagues' chapters discuss the other two traditions more extensively, but I believe this table captures the major domains of difference between the competing paradigms on axiomatic or philosophical grounds.

The table has a number of meanings, all of which are important for the debate surrounding paradigm allegiance.

Implications, Paradigmatic and Personal

The interpretive phenomenon. First and foremost, it means an "interpretive turn" (Bloland, 1989), or what Bernstein (1983, p. 30) called "a recovery of the hermeneutical dimension, with its thematic emphasis on understanding and interpretation." Bernstein (1983, p. 31) notes:

> There is, however, a much stronger and much more consequential sense than Kuhn's notion of a "sensitive reading" in which the hermeneutical dimension of science has been recovered. In the critique of naive and even of sophisticated forms of logical positivism and empiricism; in the questioning of the claims of the primacy of the hypothetical-deductive model of explanation; in the questioning of the sharp dichotomy that has been made between observation and theory (or observation and theoretical language); in the insistence on the underdetermination of theory by fact; and in the exploration of the ways in which all description and observation are theory-impregnated, we find claims and arguments that are consonant with those that have been at the very heart hermeneutics, especially as the discipline has been discussed from the nineteenth century to the present.

The divorce of science from its contemporary raw empiricist base, and its realliance with judgment, discernment, understanding, and interpretation as necessary elements of the scientific process, has been slowly formalized over the twentieth century. Bernstein calls this "the shift from a model of rationality that searches for determinate rules which can serve as necessary and sufficient conditions, to a model of practical rationality that emphasizes the role of *exemplars* and judgmental interpretation" (Bernstein, 1983, p. 57, emphasis in original). The significance of this shift is that it presupposes a reliance on tacit as well as propositional knowledge (a major implication of constructivist inquiry) and acknowledges, with feminist critics of science and philosophers, that *"the teaching of method is nothing other than the teaching of a certain kind of history"* (MacIntyre, cited in Bernstein, 1983, p. 57, emphasis in original).

Thus science, in returning to the hermeneutical tradition, openly acknowledges its own social construction, its roots as a historically derived and practiced process, not devoid of values but firmly committed to the legitimacy and authority of ruling scientific interests.

The interpretive turn in itself has implications for what we understand and know about the world. The (false) certitude of logical positivism, its quiet determinism, are being replaced by less certain forms of knowing and, therefore, more attendant anxiety about knowledge (Bloland, 1989). The "persistent claim that it is science and science alone that is the measure of reality, knowledge and truth" (Bernstein, 1983, p. 46) has been replaced by the claim that reality is socially constructed (Berger & Luckmann, 1973; Harding & Hintikka, 1983), that knowledge is problematic and contested (Lather, 1988a), and that truth is locally and politically situated (Popkewitz, 1984). The implications of this relativity of knowledge are sufficiently unnerving to provoke even inquirers persuaded to constructivism to ask whether we can't have both—ideographic knowledge and generalizable knowledge—much as British chemists asked Lavoisier, the discoverer of oxygen, how he accounted for phlogiston, the mystical element that oxygen replaced (McCann, 1978).

Giving up certitude has been far more difficult than giving up other aspects of the paradigm. Two other aspects, the switch from rigor to relevance and the adoption of qualitative methods, have proceeded much more rapidly and thoroughly than anyone could have guessed. But empiricists cannot part with that need for definitive, concrete, orderly, and certain knowledge, knowledge of a sort that constructivists believe is impossible to achieve—more about knowledge later.

Paradigm pervasiveness. For me, second, the paradigm shift has meant that a quotation that I used years ago is truer than I ever knew. I cited Michael Patton (1975, p. 9) as having said that a paradigm is

> a world view, a general perspective, a way of breaking down the complexity of the real world [sic] . . . paradigms are deeply embedded in the socialization of adherents and practitioners telling them what is important, what is legitimate, what is reasonable. Paradigms are normative; they tell the practitioner what to do without the necessity of long existential or epistemological considerations.

At the time, I failed to realize just how pervasive, how ineluctable, paradigms really were. It was not until challenges began to come in from the field—challenges on criteria, on more criteria, on ethics, on values—that I realized that laying out the ontological, epistemological, and methodological boundaries was just the easy beginning—there's more.

The adoption of a paradigm literally permeates every act even tangentially associated with inquiry, such that any consideration even remotely attached to inquiry processes demands rethinking to bring decisions into line with the worldview embodied in the paradigm itself.

The immediate realization is that accommodation between paradigms is impossible. The rules for action, for process, for discourse, for what is considered knowledge and truth, are so vastly different that, although procedurally we may appear to be undertaking the same search, in fact, we are led to vastly diverse, disparate, distinctive, and typically antithetical ends.

Although accommodation may be possible in terms of what we will allow to be published and disseminated, accommodation between and among paradigms on axiomatic grounds is simply not possible. The socialization processes associated with each paradigm are sufficiently divergent, and the emotional and political commitments so high, that a mix-and-match strategy, at either the axiomatic or the practical level, is likely to produce little more than internal dissonance in the research process, a form of discursive incoherence that renders the findings useless for both camps.

The thoroughly *universal* nature of any paradigm eventually forces the choice between one view or the other. The intrapsychic need for coherence, order, and logic demands that an individual behave in ways that are as congruent and as nonconflicting as possible. Paradigms are ubiquitous entities, permeating and dictating choices even when we are unconscious of their influence in that process. Thus we have to make a commitment as inquirers to one or the other and behave in a fashion congruent with its dictates until we choose another system. To do otherwise is not only to commit paradigmatic perjury, it is to invite psychological disaster.

Subtheoretical implications. There are other implications just beginning to be explored. Those are what I shall call, using the term *theory* loosely, *subtheoretical implications.* By this, I mean whole arenas of inquiry that are affected by paradigm choice. The arenas of which I speak form inquiry lines for philosophers and historians of science, and no discussion here could do them justice. But it turns out, as I have discovered to my horror, that each arena is profoundly affected by paradigm, or worldview, or choice, such that rethinking one's paradigm commitment means giving time to thought about these things also. They include values; ethics; knowledge accumulation, or models of knowing; scientific discourse; and training issues (i.e., how do we socialize prospective adherents to a paradigm, particularly one that is not the dominant paradigm?).

Questions regarding these arenas will likely consume my maturity as a researcher, and so I shall cover what little I know about them in order to provide some sense of the ways in which they affect inquiry, legitimacy, and hegemony:

Values. It is now becoming quite clear that inquiry does not have to be openly ideological (Lather, 1988a) in order to be value bound. In fact, some would argue (Beardsley, 1980) that inquiry that purports to be value free is probably the most insidious form of inquiry available, because its inherent but unexamined values influence policy without ever being scrutinized themselves. Increasingly, however, even traditional and conventional scientists are calling for an examination of the values that undergird inquiry (Bahm, 1971; Baumrind, 1979). Other more nonconventional scientists—feminists (Bleier, 1986; Keller, 1985), critical theorists (Popkewitz, 1984), and others (Reason & Rowan, 1981)—have called attention to the role that values, under multiple guises and in varied forms, play in inquiry. It seems clear, given criticism from all quarters, that only the most intransigent or the most naive scientist still clings to the idea that inquiry can, or should, be value free. The tidal wave of criticism of this concept (Bernstein, 1983) places it squarely into the *history* of science, not in its contemporary formulations.

Ethics. To admit that values play a role in inquiry, to abjure the objectivity criterion, is to call into question the entire system of ethics that governs inquiry and researcher-researched relations. In the process, it becomes clear that current regulations, standards, and laws that govern the research enterprise are helpful but wholly inadequate (Lincoln & Guba, 1989). Laws that address informed consent, protection of human subjects, privacy and confidentiality, and the use of deception, particularly, were developed in support of the dominant paradigm. They rest on assumptions that undergird that paradigm and, therefore, ill serve emergent-paradigm inquiry.

No paradigm is without ethical problems, but the problems that plague constructivism are radically different from those that engage the attention of conventional postpositivist researchers. The emphasis on face-to-face interaction, on faithfully representing multiple, constructed, and often conflicting realities, and on maintaining privacy and anonymity while utilizing extensive word-for-word, natural language quotations in case studies as well as the case studies in general are all problems typically faced by the emergent-paradigm inquirer (Guba & Lincoln, 1989; Lincoln & Guba, 1989).

In addition, questions of *process* become singularly critical in new-paradigm inquiry. By questions of process, I mean questions that direct our attention to just how we behave, both as inquirers and toward our respondents and coparticipants in the inquiry process. Heron (1981) makes the argument exceptionally well. He contends that, if we see ourselves (as scientists) as independent humans who exercise rights and control over our own lives with direction, dignity, freedom, and agency, do we have the right to treat others in a lesser manner? But the granting of rights of dignity, agency, freedom, and independence to our respondents creates a situation where our own, often specialized, knowledge is nevertheless *only one form of knowledge that is available.* Our education puts us in a privileged position with respect to formal knowledge, but it does not grant us rights beyond those that are granted to all free human beings. Thus our demeanor both toward our work and toward those who provide us the means to conduct our work—our respondents—must undergo profound alteration. The *invitational* aspects of this form of inquiry are often considered entirely too ideological to have a place within mainstream science. It's better, such critics would say, to leave such inquiry to liberation theologists, Freierian critical theorists, and neo-Marxists. In fact, however, what we have is not a carbon copy of nonmainstream, or "ideological," social science but a mainstream rethinking of the role the social sciences play in everyday, ordinary life (Baumrind, 1985) and the legitimate roles our respondents should be playing in framing the agendas for social research (Lather, 1988a). Criticism of researcher roles vis-à-vis respondents comes from traditional science as well as from emergent inquiry almost equally often.

We have not yet begun to think through an entire ethical system that supports constructivist inquiry. But its political implications are being felt in many places. Soon gone, it is to be hoped, are the days when a well-known researcher can stand in front of an audience at a major professional association and assert that determining facts is best left to scientists and not to research "subjects," who "don't know a fact from a bag of popcorn" (Boruch, 1986). When the "stuff" of science is constructions of reality, rather than "facts" determined by scientists, we will have moved to a social science in which respondents have as strong a voice as the priesthood of science.

Knowledge accumulation and models of knowledge. The question often is directed either to me or to Egon: "Well, if all we have is social constructions of reality, then how do we do what science demands that we do, and accumulate knowledge about our natural or social world?" I think the answer to that question is one that I keep giving but about which I know less than I should (although, please notice, I don't think anyone knows any more about it than I do).

Conventionally, we have operated on an accumulation, or aggregationist, model of knowledge: knowledge as hierarchy, taxonomy, or pyramid. Knowledge is conceived as a series of building blocks, and we are trying to construct a Tower of Babel, which, when done, will lead us to heaven. But this pyramid model of knowledge is simply another construction, and perhaps not the most serviceable one at this period of time. It is quite possible that knowledge is more *circular* or *amoebalike*, or that knowledge exists in *clumps* of understanding, with different kinds of knowledge taking different shapes. We desperately need new models of knowledge and knowledge accumulation.

We simply do not have the metaphors we need yet for conceiving of knowledge in any other way but hierarchic, pyramidal, or taxonomic. But we could use images that enlarge and enrich our understanding of how we know and how we organize what we know. There is no doubt that some of our knowledge may effectively be organized in the way in which conventional science directs, but it is equally clear that other forms of knowledge may be organized and stored in very different patterns. And we do not have a language for talking about those patterns yet.

It may be the case that, if some forms of knowledge exist in clumps, or in nonhierarchic organization, we ought to be talking not about "building blocks of science" but about extended sophistication, or the artistic and expressive process of creatively conjoining elements in ways that are fresh and new. We ought to think of bridging, as a means of linking two bodies of knowledge or understanding, or of synthesizing, as a way of combining hitherto uncombined elements, or of some other linkage processes. As I said, we have no models for scientific knowledge that account for nonhierarchic learning, and we may have to borrow from the poet, the artist, the madman, the mystic.

Discourse. Slowly but surely, it has dawned on me—as it has dawned on others—that the discourse of science supports and reinforces a way of looking at the world that is antithetical to naturalistic or constructivist inquiry. It is also, parenthetically, destructive of human dignity and agency. The language of science, described by Firestone (1987) as a "stripped-down, cooled-out," value-neutral form of discourse, is itself a model of detachment and presumed objectivity. It separates the knower from the known and places science squarely in the domain of distanced disinterestedness. Its very remoteness and passive voice place a barrier between researcher and researched that strategies for ensuring validity could not achieve alone. Popkewitz noted this in the preface to his *Paradigm and Ideology in Educational Research* (1984, pp. vii-viii) when he observed that one

> social dimension of research . . . is the social and cultural location of our research activities. We can think of social science as *dialects of language which provide heuristic fictions for supposing the world is this way or that way.* These fictions or theories are *made to seem neutral by the conventions of science which decontextualizes language and makes knowledge seem transcendent.* (emphases added)

Popkewitz goes on to observe what linguists and anthropologists have known for some time, but what we have ignored in studies of science (particularly social science) as a historical creation: that "to adopt a language for structuring existence is to give organization to the ways in which the existence is to be changed. . . . The languages of science contain thought, ideas, and values, as well as 'mere' descriptions" (Popkewitz, 1984, pp. 52-53).

To play the same Lobachevskian game with discourse that we played with the earlier axioms of naturalistic inquiry (Lincoln & Guba, 1985), we can turn the assumptions of discourse upside down trying to understand what a reversal of rules might mean. For instance, leaving behind a language that reflects an intended subject-object dualism, we could search for a language that displays *connectedness*. Leaving behind a (meaningless) objectivity, we could aim for a language that reflects *intense interaction* and *interactivity*. Rather than an uncontested language of "fact," we could begin using a language and linguistic forms that reflect the *dialectical and problematic nature of human existence*, a language that shows power, persuasion, arenas of bias, values, conflict, construction, and reconstruction. We could try to avoid the distancing of conventional science by adopting a language that demonstrates *emotional and social commitment* on the part of the inquirer. We could find a form for our work that avoids the dispassionate tone of traditional, conventional science in favor of the language of *energy and passion*. We could, in short, abandon the role of dispassionate observer in favor of the role of passionate participant.

The tone of our inquiries will change radically. Nor should we be, as I have been, ashamed to be called "passionate" or "polemic" or "argumentative." All of those labels, I now understand, reflect the increasing involvement and passion I find in my work. They should reflect the involvement with and commitment to inquiry experienced by other constructivists. We have deluded ourselves that the discourse of constructivism could resemble the discourse of other science, and I and others were wrong. To array the arguments of emergent-paradigm science in the raiments of conventional science is to do new-paradigm inquiry an injustice. We cannot just change the forms and interactions; we have to alter the way in which we discuss those new forms and relationships. The discourse of constructivist inquiry must be recontextualized in such a way as to make it apparent that science and knowledge are not transcendent but, instead, another set of "heuristic fictions" for meaning-making in our world.

The language of the "rape model" of research (Reinharz, 1978), or of force and violence (Easlea, 1986), needs to be replaced with the language of trust, sharing, cooperation, teaching, and learning—a "lover model" of research (Reinharz, 1978) or the "neighborly" concept of community (Savage, 1988). The *moral dimensions* of social research enterprises are of necessity brought to the fore in this language.

To paraphrase a contemporary television ad, "This is not your father's scientific discourse!" But we do need to know more about it. And we haven't begun to think about such a language or what we might agree it should look like.

Training. I have often told questioners that research training programs should be two-tracked, with training in conventional and emergent-paradigm inquiry models, followed by training in quantitative and qualitative methods both, completed with computer applications for both quantitative and qualitative data.

But with what I have intuitively come to understand about the pervasiveness of the paradigm we use to conduct inquiry, I now think that training in multiple paradigms (at least in more than a historical sense) is training for schizophrenia. If we want to change new researchers' paradigms, we must do more than legitimate those paradigms in the inquiry outlets, such as journals. We have to train people in them, intensively. We probably ought not to be dividing their attention with other than historical accounts of conventional science. We probably ought to recognize the profound commitments people make to worldviews and create centers where such training can go on, much as there are centers where psychologists can train to be Freudians, or Jungians, or Adlerians, or places to train conventional dentists, or Crozat dentists, and the like. Dual training, in retrospect, only diminishes the attention that is focused on the intent of inquiry. I once offered such a "parallel" training program model to the critical conventionalists in my audiences. I wouldn't do so now.

A Retrospective

So where does that leave us now? More specifically, where does that leave me now? Feeling a bit foolish, I suppose, because I thought 1985 and *Naturalistic Inquiry* would do it for positivism, naturalism, and inquiry in general and for good. Clearly, there are areas that have not even occurred to me or to us yet, and much systematic work and thinking has yet to be done.

It looks as though both middle and old age will be spent exploring the questions raised in my mind and the paradigm's early adulthood.

Note

1. With all due respect to Proust, whose madeleines provided such a flood of memories.

[5]

The Meaning of Alternative
Paradigms for Practice

ELLIOT W. EISNER

Although it's nice for academics to chew on epistemological questions and to debate normative and methodological issues, the aim of scholarship in education is not disinterested knowledge—even if there were such a creature—but the improvement of schooling. It is appropriate, therefore, to ask about the practical ramifications of the new models of mind, method, and knowledge we are so fond of discussing. I intend to do just that. I will address four areas in which the new paradigms can have significant implications: First, I want to discuss the conceptual implications of alternative paradigms; second, their implications for practice; third, their implications for policy; and, fourth, their normative implications.

I know, as you do, that no set of categories, dimensions, aspects, or features of a world as interactive as schooling can be neatly separated into the areas I have just enumerated. But you also know, as I do, that analysis requires separation, even if the parts are part fiction. Consider, therefore, the analysis that I am going to provide as analysis—a way of highlighting different aspects of a complex whole. I address each aspect separately because language itself is a diachronic, not a synchronic, medium. I bracket in order to illuminate and write in parts because I write rather than paint.

Conceptual Implications

Let's consider first the conceptual implications of alternative paradigms. By *alternative paradigms,* I refer to those ideational structures that portray humans as beings who generate different forms through which they hope to understand and represent the world they inhabit and who believe that the different forms they use to understand and represent that world should be appraised by criteria appropriate to the form. Further, these paradigms hold that "truth" is ultimately a kind of mirage that in principle cannot be achieved because the worlds we know are those crafted by us and because we cannot uncouple mind and matter to know the world as it "really" is (Goodman, 1978). By *alternative paradigms*, I refer to views of mind and knowledge that reject the idea that there is only one single epistemology and that there is an epistemological supreme court that can be appealed to to settle all issues concerning Truth.

One set of conceptual implications of alternative paradigms is a broader view of knowledge, a cultural view of mind (Cole, 1985), a multiple view of intelligence (Gardner, 1983), and a constructive view of cognition. Let's consider each in its turn.

By definition, the introduction of alternative paradigms for inquiry undermines the tacit but widely held belief that there is only one dependable way to know, something vaguely called "the scientific method." Acquiring a critical consciousness of method or knowledge is unlikely when a particular paradigm is so dominant that it has no competitors. What is pervasive often goes unexamined. When alternatives are suppressed or unavailable, we tend to accept what is accepted. When this occurs, we are in a poor position to know what we have. From this perspective, the emergence of alternative paradigms provides platforms from which to examine unexamined assumptions; in effect, their presence forces us to present our position, to defend it, and, therefore, to understand it better.

If this were the only contribution that alternative paradigms made to our conceptual life, it would be of profound importance. Professionally socialized doctoral students in schools of education are often unable to question the premises upon which accepted research methods rest. We usually do not encourage them to consider alternatives— or haven't until quite recently. The reasons for this neglect are many, but things are changing. The growing interest in alternative paradigms makes problematic the belief that one epistemology fits all or that nonscientific modes of inquiry are permissible only as reconnaissance efforts; if you "really" want to know, you need to conduct an experiment.[1] One conceptual consequence of alternative paradigms in education is their salutary effect on the research community. We are now less parochial than we once were.

The emergence of a broader and pluralistic view of knowledge can also contribute to a less dogmatic view in our schools of what it means "to know." Cognitive pluralism makes it more likely that students will understand that propositions, a necessary feature of scientific inquiry, are not by any means the only forms through which we come to understand the world. Poetry and literature, for example, were invented to say what words can never say and, through what they say, we can come to understand what we cannot state. Science, Dewey reminds us, states meaning (Dewey, 1934). Art expresses it. The meanings we are able to construct are influenced by the cultural tools we know how to use and the materials upon which we act. With the emergence of the new paradigms, "coming to know" in the school curriculum can take on a wider meaning. In the process, we are more likely to recognize the epistemic functions of fields we now dismiss as essentially "affective."[2]

Another conceptual consequence of alternative paradigms is a warming toward the idea that mind itself is a cultural achievement (Cole, 1985; Eisner, 1982). Everyone knows what a culture is—it is a place for growing things, and schools are places for growing minds (Cole, 1985). The curricula we offer and the teaching methods we employ are means for creating minds. It is in this sense that the curriculum is a mind-altering device (Bernstein, 1971) and the school a culture for growing minds. As this conception of mind takes root in our conceptual life, it creates an optimism for education for it emphasizes the possibilities of schooling, its capacity to make a difference in the kind of minds that students can come to own. The kind of culture we create in schools, the forms of thinking we cultivate, the forms of representation we make available (Eisner, 1982), the recognition of the relationship between what we give students an opportunity to learn and the content of their experience is intimately related to a conception of inquiry that regards humans as creators of knowledge and makers of mind. Given this conception, we are more likely to cease seeking a fixed, measurable mental entity given at birth and seek instead to do what we can to grow minds as best we can.

Because alternative paradigms engender a pluralistic conception of knowledge, they share a family resemblance to what Gardner (1983) calls multiple intelligences. Intelligence is often conceptualized as something largely uninfluenced by culture, something biologically given. After all, what self-respecting psychometrician would choose to spend his or her time measuring what is fugitive or fleeting? The real task is to get at what is basic, what is enduring, what is fixed (Jensen, 1969).

But when one entertains the notions of multiple ways of knowing and a cultural view of mind, it is not difficult to entertain the idea that intelligence itself is not one but many, that people cope with important problems in ways that depend on the kind of problem the problem is. Intelligence is, in this view, related to different kinds of action, which in turn is related to the kind of problem, task, or material one acts upon.

In addition to the implications that alternative paradigms have for our view of knowledge, mind, and intelligence, alternative paradigms also influence our conception of cognition. *Cognition*, a term that refers to the process through which the organism becomes aware (Statt, 1981), has often been identified with linguistically mediated thought. To *cognize* is, for many, to think in language. Indeed, some writers believe no other form of conceptual thought is possible (Schaff, 1973). Thinking and the use of language, for them, are synonymous. As our views of knowledge expand and our conceptions of the varieties of intelligence grow, it becomes increasingly difficult to restrict cognition to linguistically mediated thought. Thinking and knowing are mediated by any kind of experiential content the senses generate. Language, severed from semantics, is without meaning, and although images do not accompany every thought carried by language, our language refers to referents we are able to experience, recall, or imagine. Whether we are talking about unicorns, quarks, infinity, or apples, our cognitive life depends upon experience (Eisner, 1988). Cognition is wider than words, and the forms through which our cognition is given public status are as diverse as the social forms of representation we use in culture to convey meaning. As Polanyi (1962) put it, "We know more than we can tell." Again, once we seek a pluralistic universe, we find differences we previously did not cognize; that is, we *re*-cognize the world and that world includes cognition itself.

Finally, with respect to the conceptual implications of alternative paradigms, I want to reiterate what I only touched upon earlier; the newfound appreciation of the epistemic functions of the subject matters of schooling. I refer here to our growing understanding that the forms of representation used in fields like art, poetry, literature, film, theater, and history, as well as those used in the natural and social sciences, were invented to convey meaning that would not take the impress of forms other than those employed: We are able to exemplify in art, for example, what words cannot articulate, and we are able to describe in words what we cannot exemplify (Goodman, 1978). We are able to convey through analogy, prosody, innuendo, and metaphor what escapes the precision of literal language (Langer, 1957). Forms of representation are functionally unique resources. The newfound appreciation of their contributions to cognition have potentially profound implications for curriculum, that mind-altering device I described earlier.

Implications for Practice

Given the conceptual shifts I have described, what might be their implications for the second of the four areas I wish to address, their implications for educational practice? One is that there is likely to be greater parity across the fields students study. By *parity*, I mean that literature, the visual arts, music, history, theater, and dance, as well as mathematics and science, would be recognized as cognitive in character, requiring intelligence and providing insight, understanding, and experience worth having. At present, this is clearly not the case, Some fields—the arts, for example—are marginalized in education. Some fields are regarded as "more cognitive" than others. Some fields are acknowledged by college admissions committees who count the grades secured by students in these areas when calculating GPA.[3] Other fields, such as the arts, regardless of the brilliance with which a student works in them, are simply discounted. As our epistemologies widen, the potential for rescuing curriculum from a hierarchy that reflects a more or less Platonic conception of knowledge and cognition increases. In short, the privileged place of a limited array of fields of study in our schools would give way to a more ecumenical and broadly arrayed set of curricular options.

Evidence of such a shift in curriculum would be displayed in that most telling indicator of our educational priorities—the way we allocate time to what we teach. Time allocation would reflect both a parity among fields and what Gardner (1983) calls individual proclivities. There would be less effort to put all children through the narrow eye of the same needle. Its details would also manifest themselves in our notion of what constitutes a core set of studies for all—what I refer to as a kind of *culturally referenced* curriculum balance and what individual students could elect without penalty, a kind of *personally referenced* curriculum balance. The general point here is that changes that take deep root in our conception of mind, knowledge, and intelligence can have very significant practical implications for what we teach.

What is taught is only one aspect of the practical consequences of new paradigms for education. How we organize what we teach is another.

School curricula, particularly at the middle and high school levels, are organized into what Basil Bernstein (1971) calls a "classification code." Subject fields have strongly bounded contours and are insular and essentially independent of each other. In addition, these subject fields are taught mainly through text and other propositional forms. As our understanding and appreciation for multiple ways of knowing grows, there is greater likelihood that a more synthetic, integrated curriculum will be developed. Within a curricular form that relates field to field, the use of multiple forms of representation is more likely. To illustrate the point, consider how a unit on slavery prior to the Civil War might be taught (Epstein, 1989).

Students could, as they do now, rely mainly on textbooks to learn about the past. Yet, given the assumptions in the new paradigms, the textbook would be replaced or at least enhanced with films like *Roots*, with the music of the slaves, with the reading of their stories, their "folksay," with the food they ate; in short, students would encounter a wide range of curricular resources that serve epistemic ends to help them understand the life and times of the slaves prior to the Civil War. Hopefully, what becomes recognized in research circles will get reflected in curricular practice. The literal text is only one means through which the lives of others can be understood. Indeed, the novel may be a more powerful vehicle for transporting adolescents to Alabama, Mississippi, and Kentucky in the 1850s than a textbook rendition of the facts of the period.

Another implication of alternative paradigms for educational practice pertains to educational research and evaluation. We are already seeing in the field several vivid practical consequences of the appearance of the new kid on the block. We are debating issues and exploring methods that did not show a glimmer 20 years ago. The sacred cow has become a bit more profane. There is greater tolerance, even affection in some circles, for new ways to study educational practice and to assess its outcomes. We have new journals devoted to alternative paradigms,[4] more articles are appearing in learned journals that push deliberation a bit further, and conferences like the one on which this book is based and like the conference "Qualitative Inquiry in Education" that was held at Stanford in June 1988, are providing further legitimation. We have a qualitative special interest group in AERA that is not only alive and well but growing.[5]

But beyond these concrete practical manifestations of the new paradigms, we are inventing new ways to conduct research and creating new forms and methods with which to do educational evaluation. Whether it's Lincoln and Guba's (1985) naturalistic inquiry, Parlett and Hamilton's (1977) illuminative evaluation, Stake's (1975) responsive evaluation, or my own (Eisner, 1985) educational connoisseurship and criticism, efforts are being made to weave a finer and wider net through which the processes and outcomes of educational practice can be understood and appraised. To be sure, we do not have the technical logic that has been developed for conventional approaches to research and evaluation. Furthermore, I do not believe we will ever create the kind of algorithms that are useful in treating quantitatively rendered data, but we have learned that there is more than one way to parse reality, and, with more refined approaches for describing, interpreting, and appraising the educational worlds we care about, greater confidence in methods that elude the security of rule will, I believe, develop. As the new paradigms really take hold, it will be increasingly recognized that Aristotle was correct when he said in his *Ethics*:

> Our discussion will be adequate if it has as much clearness as the subject-matter admits of, for precision is not to be sought for alike in all discussions, any more than in all the products of the crafts ... for it is the mark of an educated man to look for precision in each class of things just so far as the nature of the subject admits; it is evidently equally foolish to accept probable reasoning from a mathematician and to demand from a rhetorician scientific proofs. (McKeon, 1941, p. 936)

Although we can argue with Aristotle about the meaning of precision—metaphor, for some things, may be more precise than measurement—the point of his statement is surely on the mark. Different forms require different expectations: Aristotle's biological interests served him well in matters epistemological.

It is difficult to imagine a more potent lever for changing the priorities of schools than the evaluative methods we employ. What we count counts. What we measure matters. What we test, we teach. After all, adaptation is a primary form of survival, and our appetite for assessment requires forms of adaptation in teaching that make survival possible. That is what it means to be accountable. Teachers and school administrators are expected to provide an account in forms that, for many, miss what they care about the most. The promise of new paradigms resides in their potential to provide methods and approaches that are both more equitable and closer to the values practitioners cherish.

In my experience, very few teachers value the tests they are required to administer to their students. They resent being held accountable through methods that they believe neglect what they feel is most important about their own teaching. With the new epistemology and new methods, we may be able to affect schools through assessment procedures that are more congruent with the educational values that I believe most teachers embrace. Should such consequences occur, it would be no small victory.

Thus far I have addressed two potential implications of the new paradigms for practice. One of these was their conceptual implications—the way they shift our way of thinking about knowledge, mind, intelligence, and cognition. The other was their implications for practice itself. Here I spoke of their consequences for curriculum content, for curricular form, and for the way in which we evaluate practice and we conduct research. Now I want to move up a notch and focus on the implications of the new paradigms for educational policy and then for our educational norms, that is, for what we hope to achieve in our schools.

Implications for Policy

Policy is a set of ideas reflecting certain values and beliefs that are created to guide decision making. The policies we form about education in general and about its components such as teaching and evaluation both constrain and stimulate practice. They constrain practice because policies legitimatize particular directions and values. They stimulate for the same reasons they constrain: Policies tell the educational world the direction decisions should take. For example, a school district policy that expects teachers to prepare a lesson plan each day so that the principal of a school can inspect it tells teachers something about how teaching is viewed and the importance of intentionality in their work. Policy that requires teachers to specify in behavioral terms the objectives toward which they aim articulates further what "the district" believes competent teachers do. Policy that requires that all teachers be evaluated once a year with an "objective" observation schedule by three appraisers independently observing a single 45-minute lesson conveys to those evaluated a tacit, if not explicit, epistemology and its application to the teaching process. Policy that publishes in local newspapers the achievement test scores of students on standardized tests on a school-by-grade basis reveals a set of values about what really counts in that school district and inevitably influences what teachers are likely to attend to in their classrooms.

The examples are endless and I do not want to perseverate. The point is that educational policy is shaped by beliefs about the kind of knowledge one can trust and the kinds of methods one can use to get such knowledge.

In contrast, consider the ways in which the new paradigms might influence how we think about policy pertaining to teaching. One potential consequence of the new paradigms is the way they encourage us to consider the sources of action. In conventional paradigms, action is idealized as a premeditated, goal-directed, cybernetically driven system. To act rationally, you have to have specific goals; the goals, in turn, determine the means you are to employ; the means you employ are then to be evaluated by their effects to determine the congruence between prespecified goals and the behavior of students. If the fit is not good enough, a new cycle is implemented.

What we have here is a recursive system, a means-ends model of rational behavior. Indeed, we have a very tidy world. As new paradigms have emerged in our educational discourse, our understanding of the sources of action in teaching has become less tidy and the role of intuition and qualitative thinking more salient. Body knowledge, as Johnson (1987) puts it, or reflectivity, as Schoen (1983) describes it, or craft, as Tom (1984) regards it, or artistry, as I think about it (Eisner, 1983), have become a part of the way people think about teaching. The industrial model born of Taylorism (Callahan, 1962) and implemented in new garb in the 1970s and 1980s has become less attractive. There is a greater tendency these days to talk about reflective practitioners and clinical supervision (Sergiovanni, 1983) and collaborative teaching. Although there is still plenty of appetite in the 108,000 American schools for formulaic approaches to the teaching act—the six steps to successful teaching—the picture today is more approximately complex than it was a few years ago.

The new paradigms have altered our conception of the sources of action, and we are recognizing that goals cannot always be specified; some are even difficult to articulate. We are recognizing that intuition is not some mystical process emanating from some Muse but the immediate grasp of field forces, of being able to read immediately the structure of the field in which one acts (Arnheim, 1985), a feat wonderfully performed by a Larry Bird, or an Isaiah Thomas, and that the teacher's *sense* of what is needed, what is right here and now, are critical aspects of skilled teaching. In short, new paradigms that acknowledge the several ways in which humans think and know have loosened the corset that a narrow conception of human rationality imposes upon our conception of competent teaching.

The new paradigms make it more difficult to entertain the desiderata of teacher-proof curricula, or the use of a check-off observation schedule for evaluating teaching, or a Betty Crocker recipe for advancing teaching effectiveness. The new paradigms, I believe, contribute to more generous and more realistic educational policy affecting how teachers are to function. The longer-term consequences of such a policy are yet to come, but one place they might emerge is in the teacher's role in educational research.

The conventional role for research in education is built upon a paradigm that assigns to the specialist the job of studying teaching and learning in order to identify variables that have predictable effects on students. Once these variables are identified, the results of the research are published in journals and shared through in-service programs for teachers. The idea is that, once teachers learn about these studies, they will act upon their results in their own classrooms, that is, they will use what has been discovered by university researchers to do "what works" in their schools (U.S. Department of Education, 1986).

This model is itself modeled after research in agriculture. The agronomist and the botanist do the basic research, the agricultural-extension agent carries the findings to the farmers, the farmers implement what the extension agent has provided, and, seven months later, a larger crop is harvested, all thanks to basic research. I know that this description is something of a caricature, but I also know that in its essentials it is the way we have proceeded. The t test, invented by William Gosset, was first used to determine the effect of fertilizer on the growth of corn.

What this paradigm has meant for research policy is a top-down orientation: Researchers create knowledge and pass it down to teachers. The knowledge that is transmitted is propositional and statistical in form. From such material the teacher—at least the really professional teacher—is to do things differently, and better.

The new paradigms advance another view. Although there is a place for conventional approaches, there is a difference between the kind of knowledge a teacher needs in a particular context and the abstracted generalizations found in learned journals or provided by in-service programs for teachers.[6] Teachers, some such as John Elliott (1986) in England and Mike Atkin (1989) in the United States argue, need themselves to conduct research. It's called action research. It's important that they do so, they argue, because the kind of knowledge secured by those on the inside, working in local contexts and needing to act upon what they know, differs in fundamental ways from the kind that will get an assent from three referees reviewing a manuscript submitted for publication to a learned journal. Research, given the new paradigms, is not likely to be the sole preserve of the university academic. At the very least, it will be a collaborative effort in which professors and teachers have parity.

Furthermore, what research yields is not to be regarded as dependable prescriptions for action but as analogues to increase the quality of teachers' deliberations. As Cronbach (1975) put it, it's to help practitioners use their heads. This is a significantly different view of the use of research. No longer are researchers in the business of sending to the social world information about cause-and-effect relations that ultimately direct action, instead, they provide ideas that can be creatively shaped by teachers in their own situations. This aspiration is at once more modest and more complex. It is more modest because it relieves researchers from the burden of finding the Holy Grail. It is more complex because it recognizes the need for creative rationality in teaching. It expands teaching rather than reducing it to rule. In the process, it confers professional status to the teacher. Behavioral prescriptions might work for bank tellers and airline attendants but they cannot work for teachers in schools concerned with education.

Alternative Paradigms and Educational Aims

I turn now to the fourth and final consideration on my agenda: the implications of the new paradigms for what we hope our schools will achieve. I suspect that the educational values implicit in the features of the new paradigms that I have described are not especially difficult to discern, but, to make them explicit, I address them here and now.

When one operates on the belief that there is one way to validate knowledge, it is not a long step to the belief that students should learn that knowledge. In other words, the primary mission of the school is to see to it that the transmission of knowledge occurs and that students get it right.

Knowledge transmission also means that knowledge not only can be discovered, it can be packaged and stored and transported and tested. In short, it has a life of its own. Furthermore, if there is a canonized body of knowledge, it seems reasonable that it be specified and transmitted to all students (except perhaps to those thought to be incapable of assimilating it; those unfortunates can always work with their hands). Because the same body of knowledge is to be transmitted to all, the same standards should be applied to all and the same criteria should be used to determine who graduates and who does not. The aim, whether intended or not, explicit or implicit, is to standardize curriculum and assessment and to diminish variability among students. Everyone is to have an equal (more or less) share in the same cultural legacy.

It takes no huge imagination to recognize that the recent efforts to specify the content of cultural literacy (Hirsch, 1987), to develop a common curriculum, and to apply standardized "quality indicators" in schools participates mightily in the paradigm I have just described.

The new paradigms, yet again, provide more complex views of educational ends and make educational evaluation a much more daunting enterprise. You will recall that, when I was discussing the meaning of the new paradigms for practice, particularly for curriculum, I said that there were two kinds of curricular balance, a culturally referenced balance and an individually referenced balance. Culturally referenced balance encourages a common array of curriculum content for all students. I do believe that virtually all students ought to have *some* common program of education. An individually referenced balance fosters the development of those aptitudes, proclivities, and interests that individual students wish to pursue; in short, it fosters productive idiosyncracy. Given the new paradigms' acknowledgment of multiple intelligences and its recognition of parity across subject matters, it would be inconsistent to hold that all students should have nothing but a common educational diet and be assessed by the same set of standardized measures. The good school, given the values that permeate the new paradigms, would aim at increasing individual differences, not reducing them. The good school would seek to increase variance in performance, not to attenuate it.[7]

Such ambitions are, of course, at odds with prevailing lore about effective schools. Yet what the new paradigms imply for educational ends is productive diversity. They acknowledge and value different ways of learning and diverse forms of thinking. Once schools liberate themselves from the idea that the course to be run must be the same for all, and that the goals of that course should be, in the name of equity, common, schools become free to recognize differences as social as well as personal virtues. Educational equity should not be confused with a one-size-fits-all model of practice.

I said earlier that the problem of assessing such a program is daunting. It is. Commensurability simplifies life. One set of goals operationalized within a state or district examination that can be hermetically sealed and optically scored to yield numbers from which stanines can be computed really does simplify educational life. I know, after sitting on admissions committees at Stanford's School of Education for over 20 years, how seductively simple it is to focus on GRE scores and how difficult and time-consuming it is to interpret a student's statement of purpose or even transcripts. When we seriously promote individual differences, we will find it difficult to use the same set of measures to determine what has been achieved. When we care about the journey and the students' experience, as well as the destinations at which they arrive, a fixed multiple-choice test is unlikely to be particularly relevant. When we recognize that learning about culturally rich periods of life requires multiple sources of data, multiple forms of representation, and the use of multiple intelligences, we are inclined to eschew single outcomes. Statistical comparisons may be relevant for some outcomes but surely not for the ones we are likely to care about the most.

Resistances to Change

I would like to conclude with the acknowledgment that the implications for practice I have described are riddled with optimism. My private hope is that the thought can be the parent of the deed. The kinds of practices I have described are, on the whole, more a description of aspiration than a description of fact. So I leave you with questions—questions that ratchet the problem up to what might be considered a political level.

What are the resistances to the kinds of changes I have described? What functions are now served by the forms of practice that now pervade our schools?[8] What makes it so difficult to diversify our programs of study, to alter the structure of our schools, and to use the approaches to research and evaluation in our schools that so many of us have pioneered? These questions invite us to examine what I have called the politics of method (Eisner, 1988).

So let me end with another hope. It is the hope that Egon, maybe with our encouragement and help, will be willing to organize another conference next year, one that examines the politics of method and the possibilities of change in our schools. If he does, I know that I, along with all of you, will be among the first in line for tickets.

Notes

1. In some circles, qualitative research is thought to provide no basis for establishing causal relationships. Experiments are considered the paradigm procedure for securing causal knowledge, and qualitative research is considered an essentially exploratory activity until one can secure "hard" data.

2. The distinction between feeling and knowing is deeply ingrained in Western culture. It is also deeply rooted in our educational culture. Relatively few theoreticians dealing with epistemological issues in education underscore the importance of feeling as a source of knowing. The result is a marginalization of subjects deemed "affective." The arts are the first to be assigned to such residual categories. The result, in my view, is a profound misunderstanding of the sources of knowledge.

3. My own institution, Stanford University, does not include grades that students receive in the fine arts in high school when calculating their grade point average for admission to Stanford. This policy is both a symbolic and a practical reminder of the marginality of the arts and the parochial conception of knowledge that still pervades universities.

4. See, for example, the *International Journal for Qualitative Studies in Education*.

5. Membership in the qualitative interest group in AERA has more than doubled since its inception in 1986.

6. In-service programs operate on the assumption that experienced teachers are well served by listening to professors of education and others teach them, in settings removed from the school, how to perform in their own classrooms. This is akin to a basketball coach providing advice to a team he has never seen play.

7. Sir Herbert Read, British aesthetician, poet, and critic, wrote in *Education Through Art* (1943) that there were two principles that could guide education. One was to make children into what they are not. The other was to help children become what they are. He opted for the latter, stating that fascist societies try to do the former. Self-realization, he believed, was a primary educational goal. Furthermore, when individual differences are cultivated and fostered, the quality of the society itself is increased because of productive diversity. Given Read's observation, one that I share, bringing all children to the same place would be a liability, not an asset, in education.

8. This question has, of course, been raised by many critics of schooling. See, for example, Michael Apple, *Education and Power* (1982), and the works of Henry Giroux.

PART III

The Need for Dialog: Issues and Interpretations

Part III, The Need for Dialog: Issues and Interpretations, is in many ways the heart of the book. As I noted in the Foreword, the three keynote presentations were followed by eight simultaneous sessions (repeated on each of the two conference days so that conferees had the option of two sessions to attend), each addressed to a major issue that seems to spring up whenever paradigm differences are discussed. These by no means exhaust the range of issues that might have been explored, but they seemed to me and to a variety of persons that I consulted as those that could most profitably be addressed at this time.

The eight issues, treated in Chapters 6-29, are (in alphabetical order), *accommodation, ethics, goodness criteria, implementation, knowledge accumulation, methodology, training,* and *values.* These terms are all problematic, of course, as is the whole concept of *paradigm.* Obviously it is my hope that the papers presented and the discussion that took place in each session represent useful steps in their unfolding definition.

Each of the eight issue areas is divided into three parts. The first part is the paper prepared by the initial speaker; the second is the response prepared by the critic/respondent; and the third part is the summary of the ensuing discussions (combining the two session replications) prepared by the recorder.

ACCOMMODATION

[6]

Accommodation
Toward a Paradigm-Praxis Dialectic

WILLIAM A. FIRESTONE

There are more things in heaven and earth, Horatio, Than are dreamt of in your philosophy.
(Hamlet, Act I, Scene iv)

My task is to help achieve some accommodation among paradigms of inquiry that many believe to be incommensurable. I come to this task from a particular perspective. Unlike several of the authors in this book, I am not so much a philosopher of science as a practitioner—that is, a researcher. In the course of my work, I have to reconcile the nitty-gritty problems of collecting data in a recalcitrant world and of making sense of them within the canons of various methodological paradigms. The nature of my work puts me squarely on the fence between the postpositivist and constructivist paradigms so some of the decisions I make are more "kosher" than others to the people on either side. On the other hand, while they are arguing that paradigms cannot be accommodated, I am in fact doing it.

That two of the paradigms can be accommodated is demonstrated by the fact that I do so. Whether they can be accommodated legitimately depends on one's stance on the nature of paradigms and the relationship between philosophical principles and research practice. Those who argue that paradigms are incompatible view them as systems of rules that are largely deductive. Higher-order theoretical principles about the nature of the world (ontology) and how one knows it (epistemology) govern the conduct of research. My first task is to suggest alternative conceptions of paradigms. One approach is to view paradigms as cultures; another is to suggest that the relationship between principles and practice should not be unidirectional but dialectical.

Once the possibility of more interplay between research and principles is established, two divisive issues are addressed. First, the implications of the divergent assumptions about reality of the postpositivist and constructivist paradigms are explored. Next, the significance of the critical paradigm's political/value challenges is examined.

Paradigms and Practice

It may be useful to begin discussion of a relatively abstract topic with a personal story. Sometime in 1986 I read Smith and Heshusius's (1986) piece on closing down the debate over qualitative and quantitative methods. They argued that qualitative and quantitative methods simply could not be combined. Moreover, there was no room for debate; it was time to move on to other issues. The article was frustrating because it argued that I could not do what I and a number of colleagues had done extensively. I had conducted studies that combined survey and interview data (Firestone & Wilson, 1983) and was aware of a rich literature that goes beyond debates about whether to combine methods to discussions of how it should be done (Rossman & Wilson, 1985; Smith & Louis, 1982).

It turned out that I had misinterpreted Smith and Heshusius (1986, p. 8), who found the problems of combining *"specific individual procedures . . . relatively uninteresting"* (emphasis in original). The issue was at a much higher conceptual level of paradigms. To put it baldly, paradigmatic assumptions determine research strategy. According to Lincoln (this volume): "The adoption of a paradigm literally permeates every act even tangentially associated with inquiry, such that any consideration even remotely attached to inquiry processes demands rethinking to bring decisions into line with the worldview embodied in the paradigm itself." Researchers must either assume that

- there is a real world out there that one can know more or less well and where one could explain relationships among phenomena and attempt to generalize from one situation to another, or
- it is pointless to worry about whether there is a real world so one should concentrate on reporting and clarifying people's interpretations about what is happening in specific settings.

The first position is positivist; the second is constructivist; there is no middle ground between the two. Moreover, the primacy of paradigmatic assumptions creates incompatibility according both to Lincoln and to Smith and Heshusius.

This did not help me a lot. I had described parents' beliefs and perspectives about schooling and used them to explain the demise of parent-run schools in the 1960s and 1970s (Firestone, 1976). On several occasions, I have described teachers' interpretations of planned change efforts, explained those interpretations in terms of larger social-political forces, and used those interpretations as a partial explanation of program implementation (Firestone, 1980; Rossman, Corbett, & Firestone, 1988). In addition, I have studied teacher commitment—a highly etic concept to be sure, but we did explore what teachers became committed to—and tried to identify school and district characteristics that explained levels of commitment (Firestone & Rosenblum, 1988).

Even at a more conceptual level then I was combining the "uncombinable." My efforts to explain beliefs and interpretations and use those beliefs to explain other phenomena took me out of the constructivist camp, but my more positivistically oriented survey-research colleagues found me a strange bedfellow indeed.

My own resolution of how I can do the undoable begins with a consideration of the concept of paradigm. Although recognizing that paradigms contain a good deal of tacit knowledge, Lincoln (with her colleague Egon Guba) has devoted a great deal of energy formalizing them, especially the constructivist one, as systems of prescriptive rules. Her recounting of her intellectual odyssey is replete with formulations and reformulations of "axioms," "postulates," and "criteria."

Yet, there is another way of thinking about paradigms. In his original popularization of the term, Kuhn (1970, p. 43) observes:

Close historical investigation of a given specialty at a given time discloses a set of recurrent and quasi-standard illustrations of various theories in

their conceptual, observational, and instrumental applications. These
are the community's paradigms, revealed in its textbooks, lectures, and
laboratory exercises. By studying them and by practicing with them, the
members of the corresponding community learn their trade.

This passage illustrates two important points. The first is the emphasis
on specialties. His examples include Aristotle's analysis of motion,
Ptolemy's computations of planetary position, and Maxwell's mathe-
matization of the electromagnetic field (Kuhn, 1970, p. 23). Educational research examples might include the process-product approach
to studying teaching, which is now being challenged by a more
cognitively oriented program. Initially, at least, paradigms were not
intended to be broad approaches to all social science inquiry as they
are currently formulated in this book.

The second is the emphasis on illustrations or exemplars. Kuhn
goes on to state that "the search for rules [is] both much more difficult
and less satisfying than the search for paradigms" (Kuhn, 1970, p. 43)
and that people can agree on the existence of a paradigm without
agreeing on its rationalized form. It would seem that paradigms are
more analogous to cultures than to philosophical systems. Culture is
"socially shared and transmitted knowledge of what is, and what
ought to be, symbolized in act and artifact" (Wilson, 1971, p. 90).
Although substantial portions of the cultural knowledge of a paradigm resist formulation, the textbooks, exemplars, and training programs are among the acts and artifacts that symbolize it and facilitate
its transmission to the next generation.

This cultural analogy has important implications for the relationship of paradigms to practice. For instance, however difficult it is for
someone steeped in a culture to imagine doing things differently, the
whole thrust of anthropology has been to illustrate the variety of
behavior. Moreover, this variation is socially determined. If paradigms are cultural constructs then, each may have its own logic, but
that logic is not necessarily compelling. "Compulsion" in such cases
comes from the social processes that reinforce the culture/paradigm.

So far I have not argued anything that those who see paradigms as
incompatible cannot agree with, but the idea of culture implies both
competition and change. Cultures are most effective in shaping behavior when their adherents cannot imagine any other way to behave
(Eliade, 1959). As soon as alternatives become available, deviance and
cultural conflict can occur as new ideas challenge the old. Such

challenges can take gradual or dramatic forms. As ideas move across cultural (paradigmatic) boundaries, either rapid and evolutionary or slower, additive change may occur (Wallace, 1970).

The more dramatic, conflict-ridden evolutionary changes are akin to Kuhn's paradigm shifts. Yet, even dramatic transformations usually draw upon the dominant culture that is under attack. Shils (1968) has discussed how revolutionary ideologies build upon ideas in the larger society. Similarly, Giddens (1976) points out that even fairly radical paradigm transformations do not necessitate a total change of thought. Although Einsteinian physics replaced that of Newton, the former actually built on the latter.

Dramatic paradigm shifts are not the only form of change in cultures or science. Cultural borrowing and intermingling lead to phenomena like cargo cults, Franglais, and research that combines postpositivist and constructivist assumptions. In a world as pluralistic as educational research, studies that combine practices from different paradigms (cultures) will be extremely common. Moreover, just as cultural diffusion leads to creativity, cross-paradigm research can be extremely fruitful.

Cultural change can also result from noncultural phenomena like shifts in the economy and the polity. Culture is conservative, changing slowly in response to these other phenomena, but it does change. The same is true of paradigms in the Kuhn formulation. Certain observations that do not fit create a paradigm conflict. The old guard resists and seeks explanations within the existing paradigm, but eventually phlogiston theories and the like are overthrown. This feedback of observation onto paradigms is exactly what is ruled out by more recent philosophical formulations of paradigms.

One could conceivably cut through this argument by dropping the term *paradigm* and argue that there are alternative philosophically correct ways to conduct inquiry that can be formulated as constructivist and postpositivist approaches. Each of these is legitimate, but they are incompatible. This position too has its opponents. Howe (1988, p. 16) calls this the " 'queen science' " position that "pass(es) judgment on the legitimacy of knowledge claims of scientists from some privileged vantage point. Because the queen science view entails that philosophy can be abstracted from actual practice, it follows that philosophical theory has little guidance to provide regarding practice." In other words, a philosophy that sets itself above the practice of inquiry and criticizes from on high may cut itself off too much to be useful. Howe contrasts this queen science view with a "pragmatic" one that allows for interaction between the philosophy and the practice of science (see also Giarelli, 1988). The pragmatic perspective allows philosophy to criticize what researchers do but also requires that it respond to researcher challenges. Thus, when a way is found to usefully combine practices that are incompatible on the basis of first principles, the first principles must be reexamined.

Seeds of this pragmatic view can actually be found in both paradigms. Phillips (this volume) links the demise of logical positivism to the rise of particle physics. Sense data were not regulatory when some of the greatest minds of the generation were generating theories and observations about entities that could never be directly apprehended.

Lincoln's (this volume) constructivism raises more problems because she explicitly rejects a dialectical relationship between first principles and practice. Yet, it is difficult to understand how she can embrace multiple, socially constructed realities and advocate an inductive approach to research and still be so dogmatically deductive on the relationship between philosophical principles and the conduct of inquiry. Moreover, one of the roots of constructivism—or at least a fellow traveler—is symbolic interactionism. A key concept of this perspective is the idea of the negotiated social order (Strauss, Schatzman, Ehrlich, Bucher, & Sabshin, 1963). The central notion here is that rules are made up and defined by people in particular contexts as they go about their daily lives. This notion is surely compatible with the idea that researchers contribute to the definition of paradigmatic rules through the conduct of research.

Both the paradigm-as-culture analogy and the pragmatic view allow for a dialectical relationship between philosophy and the practice of research where neither side dictates to the other. To understand the implications of such a general position, it is necessary to turn to more specific issues.

Research and Reality

The debate about how assumptions about reality shape research is framed by Lincoln's and Phillips's chapters (this volume), which represent constructivist and postpositivist paradigms. A close comparison identifies areas of agreement on basic starting points and disagreement about ontological assumptions. Prescriptions for action overlap more than has previously been described. Moreover, a comparison of these positions with recent methodological thinking suggests that in practice things are more complicated, and there are more decisions to be made (and more in-between options) than a comparison of paradigmatic statements would suggest.

Comparing Paradigms

Both postpositivism and constructivism reject logical positivism and certain knowledge. Thus Lincoln (this volume) asserts that "the (false) certitude of logical positivism, its quiet determinism, are being replaced by less certain forms of knowing" while Phillips (this volume) agrees that "recent work has shown that scientists, like workers in other areas, are in the business of providing reasonable justifications for their assertions, but nothing they do can make these assertions absolutely safe from criticism and potential overthrow." Arguments about why uncertainty is unavoidable agree on two related points. First, sensory data do not govern what is known; we can theorize (with varying levels of certainty) about things we cannot see, touch, feel, and so on. Second, observations are not independent of the observer. What one looks for and, to some extent, what one sees depends upon one's theories, biases, habits, and so on. Often theory shapes observation rather than being a purely independent test of it.

The two paradigms differ substantially on how to deal with the problem of uncertainty. Phillips's postpositivism clings to the notion of truth as a regulative ideal that can be approximated to varying extents. Elsewhere he quotes Popper who likens truth to a mountaintop that is difficult to attain. It is often difficult to know when one has really gotten to the highest peak, but it is still there (Phillips, in press). Although one cannot know when truth has been achieved, the warrant for assertions about it can be assessed. The firmest warrants come from *objective* inquiry—that is, inquiry that follows the procedures of good research in the field. Objective inquiry may be "wrong," but it is at least free from gross defects, which should add to one's comfort.

By contrast, Lincoln (this volume) rejects the idea of any truth independent of the knower, concluding that "reality is a social, and, therefore multiple, construction; that there is no single, tangible, fragmentable reality onto which science can converge." If reality is socially constructed, then objectivity is impossible, and probably unnecessary; one's reality is shaped by one's values. Notice, however, the difference in emphasis on the treatment of objectivity. Lincoln stresses that values cannot be avoided. Although Phillips avoids taking the value issue on directly, he emphasizes the importance of procedure. If technically adequate procedures are employed, presumably the range of disagreement among those with different values can be reduced (never eliminated; there is no certainty). This point is unimportant to Lincoln because she has rejected the idea of a single truth on which people seek agreement.

It is interesting that the disagreement about the social construction of reality is one of degree. For Lincoln, this point is central: All truth is socially constructed. Moreover, her position is intentionally relativistic: the realities of all groups are to be accepted nonjudgmentally. Phillips acknowledges that people do develop beliefs, interpretations, and accounts of the world and that those accounts differ. This is part of the truth about the world, not something that undermines his vision about it. From his viewpoint, the warrants for these accounts can be assessed; some are more adequate than others. Presumably, although he does not say so directly, one can also seek explanations for those accounts.

Given these different views of the world, the researcher's task is quite different in these two paradigms. To Phillips, research leads to theories that are nets created by the researcher. Concepts are the knots that hold the net together. The strings of the nets are the relationships among the concepts. Causal relationships are not ruled out. Implicitly, theories are largely etic, developed with concepts coming from the researcher, and analytic. Explanations for concepts are possible. In addition to constructing theories, researchers do the empirical work necessary to assess the warrants for various theories.

Lincoln's position is that researchers are not in the business of developing and verifying (or falsifying) their own theories: "The constructivist paradigm . . . had as its central focus not the abstraction (reduction) or the approximation (modeling) of a single reality but the presentation of multiple, holistic, competing and often conflictual realities of multiple stakeholders" (Lincoln, this volume). The researcher's task then is nonjudgmental recording, although the researcher's own perspective is as valid (no more, no less) as that of anyone else in the social situation. Concepts are emic, coming from the language of those studied. Presumably, explanations offered by the researched are presentable as part of the socially constructed reality, but researcher explanations are rejected because they put the researcher outside the frameworks of those studied.

There is an important caveat to this position. Although general explanations are rejected, researchers can develop "working hypotheses" about why things work the way they do in a particular place. Explanation, and perhaps etic concepts as well, are allowed to reappear, albeit in an extremely tentative form.

The two paradigms also differ on who judges the adequacy of a research product. For Phillips, evidence is critical for determining the warrant for a theory. It comes from procedures that are well conducted and well designed, but not everyone has the knowledge to decide on the adequacy of procedures. That is the province of the specialists (Phillips, in press). Moreover, Phillips expects specialists to rigorously criticize all warrants. This is not the tyranny of the elite over the masses but an internally competitive process that rules out error. At first glance, "evidence" would seem to be a meaningless concept for Lincoln with her multiple realities. Yet, there is still a question about whether the interpretation of a particular individual or group is adequately represented. This is accomplished in two ways. The representation is fed back to the researched, who then become the arbiters of adequacy. In addition, there are some procedures—like length of engagement in the field and maintenance of an audit trail—that can be checked by other specialists (Lincoln & Guba, 1985).

Finally, the two positions appear to differ on the legitimacy of generalizing from results. Phillips does not address this point directly. It would be consistent with his other positions, however, to conclude that no generalization can be made with certainty but that adequacy of any given generalization depends on the procedures on which it is based, and those procedures must be judged by specialists. Lincoln rejects the notion of generalization. When multiple realities rule, each situation is unique or at least the extent to which guidance can be drawn from one situation and applied to another cannot be assessed at the end of the study. Instead, it is replaced by the concept of "transferability," which is not assessed by the researcher but by the reader. The information that permits the reader to assess transferability is a thick description of the situation studied with all its particularities.

Strangely enough, these two paradigms agree at the most basic level about the impossibility of certainty. They differ most substantially about how to cope with the problem at the grandest ontological level: single truth versus multiple, socially constructed truth. However, as one moves to the more operational level, the differences are not incompatibilities but ones of degree and emphasis, the kind of differences that suggest a reassessment of ontological assumptions rather than junking fruitful approaches to research. Consider:

- Both paradigms allow for the social construction of reality although they differ on the extent of social construction.
- Both paradigms allow for the recording of local interpretations and beliefs and even for researcher theorizing about what takes place although they differ on which should take primacy.
- Both paradigms allow for some specialist judgment on the adequacy of research although the constructivist position gives more attention to the judgments of the research subjects.
- Both paradigms are nervous about generalizing from a specific situation, but both seek ways to permit findings, conclusions, or accounts from one situation to be applied in another.

An examination of how researchers deal with some of these same issues in practice actually muddies the waters more, but it also shows the variety of practical compromises that are made, suggesting again the need to rethink ontological principles.

Research Methods

The complexity of the research process can be illustrated by looking at both a general framework and a particular problem. The general framework is McGrath's (1982) analysis of the "dilemmatics" of research. In part, he argues that in designing a study the research seeks to maximize three criteria: generalizability of findings, precision and control in measurement, and existential realism of what is studied. Unfortunately, the three cannot be maximized simultaneously, placing the researcher in the midst of a three-horned dilemma.

Any criterion can be maximized but only at the expense of the other two. Thus the classical ethnography is extremely strong on existential realism but at the expense of both generality and precision. The classical experiment is an especially good way to increase precision but at the expense of both realism and generality. Finally, the sample survey is the means of choice to increase generality but it reduces both precision and realism. Compromises are possible. For instance, one can increase the realism of an experiment by creating an experimental simulation or by moving experiments out of the laboratory and into the field, but only at the loss of some control and—according to McGrath—by minimizing generalizability.

This framework illustrates two useful points. First, there are a series of things that Lincoln links together as positivism—Phillips does not because he stays in the philosophical heights and avoids methodological specifics—that do not fit very well together. She links both generalization and precision to positivism (Lincoln, this volume; see also Lincoln & Guba, 1985). Operationally, their relationship is at best uneasy. McGrath gives examples of some compromises—judgment tasks in certain fields of psychology—but these work only at the risk of reducing both criteria. Second, there are compromise positions between these positivist criteria and the ultimate constructivist one, existential realism.

Compromises and fusions are also apparent when one looks at the problem of generalizability. From the reader's view, the problem is probably best stated by Lincoln and Guba (1985), rather than conventional methodologists, as follows: "How does one know that the results of a study are applicable in another situation?" In fact, three strategies or tactics have been employed to add credence to the judgment of applicability. The classic strategy, as McGrath points out, is the sample survey with a random sample drawn from a larger population. However, sampling has two problems. First, one typically wants to generalize beyond the population technically sampled to some even larger population—such as from a random sample of schools in Iowa to the nation at large. Second, sample predictions are accurate, all other things being equal. Yet, as a number of people have pointed out, those other things are rarely equal when one applies a finding in a specific situation. Thus what is accurate on average may not be applicable here.

Some experimental psychologists are remarkably cavalier about sampling—as the age-old practice of running experiments on freshman psychology majors illustrates. Instead, they rely on the second strategy: replication (Keiss & Bloomquist, 1985). Strong arguments have been made for applying the same strategy to qualitative research (Yin, 1984). Confidence in the original study is increased when it is repeated and results are similar. More replications increase confidence, but there are several other criteria. The greater the theoretically significant differences among the situations where replications take place, the more the similarity of replications with the population of interest; and the fewer the unique attributes of the replications, the greater the confidence in the conclusion (Kennedy, 1979).

Lincoln and Guba's (1985) thick description is a third strategy, but the critical element of this strategy is that the decision about applicability is made by the reader. The researcher's job is to provide the contextual information to permit such a judgment. Although largely qualitative, the idea of providing information for the reader can be applied to other kinds of research and need not come just in the form of prose, as is often implied by the term *thick description*. Sometimes the critical information is not program or cultural description but demographic or cost data. Thus, to understand the applicability of a program evaluation, one must know not only about program implementation but also about the background of the students in the program and the level of funding. For that reason, it may be better to refer to this strategy as "contextualizing," meaning providing the reader with the background information needed to make an informed decision.

Contextualizing is not uniquely constructivist. In a discussion that begins on a very positivist note, Kennedy (1979) anticipates Lincoln and Guba's work by several years. She notes the similarities between generalizing from case studies in social science and applying legal precedents as well as learning from clinical treatments in medicine and psychology. She further suggests that the applicability of one case to another situation depends partly on information provided in the case—the concrete description that helps one identify similarities—but also on the values of the person making the link to the new situation.

At some level, these strategies can be complementary. An obvious example is when a reader in San Francisco must decide whether to apply findings from the survey study in Iowa mentioned previously. The logic of applying survey results to a different population is remarkably similar to that used when applying a case study. One must make judgments on the basis of contextual similarity. Technically, the study tells one that the results generalize well to Iowa. To apply them in San Francisco, one has to be sure that relevant conditions are similar. Because "thick description" of the two states is rarely provided, one normally relies on common knowledge and common sense. If the study were of student responses to a new mathematics curriculum, the larger numbers of Asian and Hispanic students in San

Francisco might raise serious questions about the applicability of results.

To push the example a bit further, if one redid the research in San Francisco, both works could be treated as surveys for the specific populations from which samples were drawn but as replication with regard to the larger world. Further replications in Oakland, Quebec, and elsewhere would increase confidence in the utility of the study, but a person considering applying these studies in Sri Lanka would still have to consider the similarities and differences between her own context and those where the replications took place.

To summarize, the generalizability or applicability problem arises with all forms of social research. Surveys, experiments, and qualitative studies have their own special ways of dealing with the problem, none of which are perfectly adequate but all of which add confidence to conclusions. Moreover, these strategies not only can be but actually are combined, although often in very informal ways. In some sense, the contextualizing strategy is the most general; every reader does it when assessing any study. Lincoln and Guba's thick description is only a special case of the larger phenomenon. This is another complexity of the research process that is not well captured by the constructivist-postpositivist distinction.

Research and Politics

Critical theory's challenge to postpositivism asserts that the latter position ignores the role of values in social research. Phillips's chapter offers little guidance here because the world *value* never appears. Nevertheless, there are values implicit in his postpositivist perspective. These are the regulative ideals of truth and objectivity. Although not fully attainable, such ideals are the goals toward which social scientists should strive. Although Phillips's discussion of these ideals is rigorously analytic, others give examples of the passion required by the search for truth. For instance, Weber (1962, p. 569), in "Science as a Vocation," contends that "whoever lacks the capacity to put on blinders, so to speak, and to come up to the idea that the fate of his soul depends upon whether or not he makes the correct conjecture at this passage of this manuscript may well stay away from science." Thus the central value of positivism is the search for (unattainable) truth.

How then does this search for truth relate to practical activity in the political world? Here again, it is useful to turn to Weber (1962). This grandparent of modern constructivism states the positivist position for separation quite eloquently:

> To talk a practical political stand is one thing, and to analyze political structures and party positions is another. When speaking in a political meeting about democracy, one does not hide one's personal standpoint; indeed to come out clearly and take a stand is one's damned duty. . . . It would be an outrage, however, to use words in this fashion in a lecture or in the lecture room. If, for instance, "democracy" is under discussion, one considers its various forms, analyzes them in the way they function, determines what results for the conditions of life the one form has as compared with the other. . . . One can only demand of the teacher that he have the intellectual integrity to see that it is one thing to state facts, to determine mathematical or logical relations or the internal structure of cultural values, while it is another thing to answer questions of the *value* of culture and its individual contents and the question of how one should act in the cultural community and in political associations. These are quite heterogeneous problems. (Weber, 1962, pp. 579-580)

The position taken is that social facts and political values are different kinds of phenomena. One can even analyze values as facts, but to infuse one's values on the analysis is to take advantage of one's position and create a source of error. The warrant for the analysis is in jeopardy because of the analyst's bias. Moreover, the purpose of research is to get the analysis as right or at least as strongly warrantable as possible. Action in the political world is separated from scientific activity as such although an individual may engage in both.

The Manifest Challenge

Critical theory challenges the separation of research and political activity at two levels. At the manifest level, it has been argued that critical theory is not just for understanding the world but for acting in it.

Fay (1987) develops a four-part prototype for a critical theory with (a) a theory of false consciousness describing how a group's self-understandings are false or incoherent and contribute to that group's victimization, (b) a theory of crisis that specifies the conditions under which reduction of false consciousness is possible, (c) a theory of education that prescribes how to enlighten and overcome false consciousness, and (d) a theory of transformative action that clarifies the social conditions that must be changed to accomplish the group's liberation. This is more than the causal explanation sought by positivists or the constructivist's faithful rendition of perspectives. It includes beliefs—false consciousness, which it rejects as an image of the world—and "objective" social characteristics that are used to explain those beliefs. However, it goes well beyond explanation to a prescription of what should be done to change things. Thus it includes, as a fifth element, a normative theory of how the world should be when oppressive social structures are removed.

Fay's prototype points out that research can have political utility and suggests the need for a typology for political "uses" of research. Through such a typology, one can explore the question as to whether there is a necessary relationship between research and use. Roughly speaking, research can be used:

(1) For *value-free understanding*: The researcher has no larger political intent. The purpose is to understand and explain the social world.

(2) For *social control*: Here the researcher works with those in power in order to subjugate or otherwise control the "masses." The assumption here is of a divided society in conflict.

(3) For *social engineering*: Here the researcher works with those in power to help improve the underprivileged. Here again, a divided society is assumed, but the purpose of the state is to improve the welfare of the people.

(4) To *advocate the underprivileged to the powerful*: While the social engineers work within the government, advocates are outside the system, closer to the people they serve. The powerful are assumed to be ignorant or moderately uncaring but not callous or cruel. Better policies will result from better knowledge provided by researchers.

(5) To *educate the underprivileged*: This is part of Fay's critical position. It assumes that liberation is in the hands of the people, not the powerful, but that first false consciousness must be overcome through research and education. Liberation may be achieved through either individual or collective action.

(6) To *organize the revolution*: This position assumes that the existing social structure must be changed through collective action by those outside the system. The researcher's task is to clarify where changes are needed and how to accomplish them.

	Value Free	Social Control	Social Engineering	Advocacy	Education	Revolution
Positivism	X	X	X	X	X	X
Constructivism	X		X	X	X	
Critical Theory					X	X

Figure 6.1. Paradigms and Political Positions

Within this framework, it is clear that the last two positions are critical ones. Positivism has historically been associated with the first three positions. The failure to treat political issues in Phillips's chapter suggests the value-free position. There is also a long tradition of using social research for social control. As Popkewitz (this volume) points out, the field of statistics began not as a subset of mathematics but as the collection of information for the rulers on the internal condition of the state. Finally, it should not be forgotten that the first positivist, Auguste Compte, took an engineering view that saw research as promoting social improvement with scientists as the high priests of the new order (Turner & Beeghley, 1981). Moreover, a good deal of the American social research of the 1960s and 1970s was intended to ameliorate the condition of various minority groups. The relationship of constructivism to this framework is unclear.

With further consideration, a more complex relationship between paradigms and political positions becomes apparent and is summarized in Figure 6.1. The very neutrality of positivism and its failure to speak to political issues allows it to be associated with any position. All of these positions would benefit, albeit in different ways, from the development of strongly warranted theories and observations about the nature of the social order, although the preferred theories and observations would differ. Positivist research has been used for conservative agendas to argue against busing for desegregation (Coleman, Kelly, & Moore, 1975) and for more radical analyses of class structure (Wright, 1978). Constructivism can also be used for a variety of purposes. Although Lincoln sees its interest in the perspectives of others as requiring advocacy for the downtrodden, the recognition of multiple realities requires honoring the views of those in power as well. There are fairly clear historic precedents for the value-free position within anthropology. Boas it seems was primarily concerned with recording the stories and artifacts of the Kwakiutl (Wax, 1971), and Malinowski's diaries indicate no love for the people he so thoroughly analyzed (Malinowski, 1967). Although some constructivists would reject the idea of social engineering on the grounds that it implies a "real" world in which the powers that be can manipulate social facts, the rise of ethnographic evaluation illustrates that qualitative methods can provide information that is useful to civil servants. Thus constructivist social engineering is possible. It would seem that the relativism of constructivism only rules out the revolutionary and social control positions that require clearly siding with one group against the other.

The real point of this kind of analysis is to suggest that, where research paradigms are based on beliefs about ontology, decisions on political issues require additional assumptions. As a result, most paradigms (the exception being critical theory) can coincide with a variety of political positions.

The Challenge of Latent Politicization

The problem of mixing research and politics intentionally is much more straightforward than the latent politicization of research. To critical theorists like Popkewitz, value neutrality is impossible because social research is historically situated in particular cultures and responds to specific political issues, however indirectly. Social theory uses the language of everyday conversation. It responds to and attempts to interpret changes under way in the larger society. Thus Toennies's (1957) distinction between *gemeinschaft* and *gesellschaft*, Weber's (Gerth & Mills, 1946) notion of bureaucracy, and Durkheim's (1951) analysis of anomie were all attempts to make sense out of the modernization and dislocation of late-nineteenth-century European society. More recently, feminist studies reflect (and contribute to) changes in gender roles in the larger society.

Even research methods reflect assumptions about the individual, society, and the world (Popkewitz, 1984). Thus conventional statistical techniques are based on Euclidean geometry with its linear conceptions of time and space. They also force one into a mode of analysis that separates unities into discrete identifiable parts. Qualitative methods reestablish the ideas of community, individual activism, and a negotiated social order.

Habermas has linked the three paradigms discussed here to different cognitive interests. Positivism is based on a technical interest that facilitates control and instrumental action. Constructivism is based on a practical interest in understanding the meaning of social action. Critical theory has an emancipatory interest in reducing the distortions that stem from the contradictions between the first two interests (Bredo & Feinberg, 1982a).

A good deal of Popkewitz's work has been to sort out more specifically how interests, usually at a larger cultural level rather than in a short-term self-interest sense, shape research. He concludes that a disinterested social science is not possible because social scientists cannot separate their work from their lives and contexts.

The effects of cultural themes and political-economic interests on the development of research is not accounted for by postpositivism, but these effects do not nullify that position. Once one acknowledges that observations are theory laden, the door is open for a wide range of background factors to affect research. Phillips refers to studies of perception to describe how fairly low-level knowledge, for instance, of the colors and shapes of the symbols for card suits affects one's ability to "see" cards, but there are more relevant examples for our purposes. For instance, the issues deemed worthy of research are determined in part by what research funding is available. Moreover, social researchers are well aware of what are generally defined as social problems. They describe their studies in language that links powerfully to those definitions (Gusfield, 1976). These definitions are part of the culture of researchers. Coleman (1989) has recently described how those norms determine what researchers choose to study, the reception of studies that deviate from those norms, and the penalties paid by those who conduct such deviant studies. Finally, extensive studies of the social organization of science have been conducted using rather positivist methodologies (e.g., Crane, 1976). Thus postpositivism and critical theory are not incompatible. The problem is how to put them together.

Toward Accommodation

The key to accommodation among paradigms is rejection of the "queen science" viewpoint that philosophical first principles must determine methodology. Once one begins to look at what researchers do, the walls between paradigms start to break down. In practice, researchers use a variety of imperfect approaches to enhance the credibility of their arguments that require complex trade-offs among precision, generalization, and existential reality. The complexity of the choices that must be made and the advantages of combining approaches suggests that the correspondence-relativism distinction does not fully capture the problems researchers face. Moreover, these choices are made in a complex social world and are, therefore, shaped by a variety of political and cultural factors.

Accommodations among paradigms must be made at both the personal and the institutional level. My personal accommodation is fairly complex and difficult to capture in a few closing paragraphs. My own search is for "interesting knowledge." Sometimes such knowledge is quite similar to the postpositivist notion that "truth" is something worth searching for but not likely to be found, at least not with certainty. The major justification for the research enterprise is that we have the time and the skills to develop approximations of the truth that have a firmer warrant than common sense. In other situations, I am happy to settle for the generation of ideas that make sense out of the world even if they cannot be "proved" per se. Sometimes a good metaphor can be very helpful.

When searching for the truth, the postpositivist program, at least at the level of detail set out by Phillips, offers little guidance as to how to proceed. The quantitative methodologists have a lot more guidance to offer, but there are many situations where other methods are called for (Patton, 1980). The constructivists' idea of socially constructed reality is very helpful in this search for truth if one drops its mandatory relativism. Sometimes, as when one is examining the culture of a particular group, the "truth" at issue clearly is constructed. At other times, it is not. For instance, there is such a thing as a real birth rate although any measure of it is a social construction. Recognizing that research itself is a social process helps one understand the limits to the undertaking.

I deal with the political values in research in two ways. One is to treat them as a "threat to validity." Researcher bias is something that must always be guarded against. Critical theory's contribution in this sense is to point out the extent to which it appears not only in study design but also in the formulation of the problem. The more complex issue is the "knowledge for what" problem—who should benefit from the research that is undertaken. How knowledge is used and how it is generated are at least partly separable. Moreover, knowledge use is rarely controlled by the researcher, as Albert Einstein found out to his dismay. Still, it seems to me that paradigms deal with what research is about—what questions are asked and what constitutes a reasonable answer. The question of legitimate use goes beyond what is normally meant by paradigms and what I can deal with here.

Because personal accommodations will differ, an institutional accommodation is perhaps most important. Here I think the growing pluralism in education is especially healthy. In a world where there is no certainty, debate among divergent viewpoints is particularly necessary. As Popkewitz suggests, it helps to clarify the issues and generates a necessary humility about what we can accomplish. It must be recognized, however, that the debate has to be structured along two dimensions. The first is among advocates of different paradigms; the second is between those who spend the bulk of their time thinking about paradigms and those who concentrate on doing research. Understanding of research practice helps to keep discussions of principles grounded in reality (whatever that is).

[7]

Social Accommodation
Toward a Dialogical
Discourse in Educational Inquiry

THOMAS M. SKRTIC

In the preceding chapter in this volume, William Firestone identifies his task as "[helping to] achieve some accommodation among paradigms of inquiry that many believe to be incommensurable." My task is to comment on the manner in which he approaches his task and the degree to which I believe he has accomplished it. I begin by developing several ideas about paradigms and accommodation, which I subsequently use to frame and analyze Firestone's arguments and, where I can, to comment on the larger debate in educational inquiry. My conclusion is that Firestone not only fails to accomplish his task but he, like the field of educational inquiry itself, has chosen the wrong task. Finally, as a counter to Firestone's call for paradigmatic accommodation through dialectical pragmatics, I make a brief case for social accommodation through dialogical discourse.

Paradigms and Modern Social Knowledge

For the past three decades, the concept of a paradigm has been associated most often with Kuhn's (1962, 1970) analysis of scientific progress. Although the notion of a *paradigm* was the central concept in Kuhn's analysis, he was neither clear nor consistent about what he meant by it. Masterman (1970) noted more than 20 different uses of the term in Kuhn's (1962) original work, which she reduced to three types of paradigms—metaphysical, sociological, and construct. The metaphysical paradigm is the broadest unit of consensus within a given science; a total worldview, gestalt, or *weltanschauung* that subsumes and defines the sociological and construct paradigms. Kuhn used *paradigm* in this sense in the first edition of *The Structure of Scientific Revolutions* (1962) to refer to a way of seeing, a perceptual organizer that defines which entities exist (and which do not) and how they behave. The sociological paradigm is what Kuhn referred to in his 1962 edition as a concrete set of habits or a universally accepted scientific achievement and, in his 1970 edition, as "the concrete puzzle solutions which, when employed as models or examples, can replace explicit rules as a basis for the solution of the remaining puzzles of normal science" (1970, p. 175). Finally, the *construct paradigm* is Kuhn's narrowest use of the term. According to Masterman, it refers to specific tools, instruments, and procedures for producing and collecting data.

Although Kuhn reserved his notion of paradigms (and paradigm shifts) exclusively for the physical sciences, Masterman (1970) extended it to the social sciences by distinguishing among sciences according to their paradigmatic status. According to Masterman, the physical sciences are single paradigm sciences, a situation in which there is broad consensus on a particular paradigm within the scientific community. The social sciences, however, are multiple paradigm sciences, a situation in which several viable paradigms compete unsuccessfully for dominance within a scientific community.

Burrell and Morgan (1979; also see, Ritzer, 1980) conceptualized the multiple paradigms of the social sciences in terms of the relationship between two dimensions of metatheoretical assumptions about the nature of science and of society. The extremes of their nature of science, or objectivism-subjectivism, dimension are logical positivism, the dominant position in the West, and German idealism. The extreme points on their nature of society, or order-conflict, dimension are sociology of regulation, the dominant position in the West which assumes an orderly, cohesive world characterized by unity and integration, and sociology of radical change, which assumes a conflictual, exploitive world characterized by modes of domination and contradiction.

When Burrell and Morgan's science and society dimensions are counterposed orthogonally, they produce four metatheoretical or metaphysical paradigms of modern social scientific thought: the functionalist or, for present purposes, postpositivist paradigm (objective-order), which has been the dominant paradigm in the West; the interpretivist or constructivist paradigm (subjective-order); the radical humanist paradigm (subjective-conflict), which is the metatheoretical grounding for critical theory; and the radical structuralist paradigm (objective-conflict), which is the grounding for various forms of conflict theory and, at best, is underrepresented in the educational inquiry discourse (see below). The particular combination of metatheoretical assumptions explicitly or, as is most often the case, implicitly defines the metaphysical paradigm, which, in turn, defines the sociological paradigm of methodological assumptions and the construct paradigm of research practices (Burrell & Morgan, 1979; Ritzer, 1980). Each paradigm represents a mutually exclusive view of the social world and how it might be investigated because each one rests on an incommensurable set of metatheoretical assumptions about the nature of social science itself (Bernstein, 1983; Burrell & Morgan, 1979; Ritzer, 1980; Rorty, 1979). Each paradigm produces a unique form of knowledge; each is a historically situated way of seeing.

The multiple paradigm state in the social sciences means that Kuhnian paradigm shifts such as those in the physical sciences are conceptually impossible, because there is simply no dominant paradigm to be overthrown. Nevertheless, the corresponding and, in many ways, more significant development in the social disciplines has been the emergence of postmodernism, which represents a move beyond the four-paradigm matrix of modern knowledge itself (see Bernstein, 1983; Lyotard, 1984; Rorty, 1979; Schwartz & Ogilvy, 1979). Although at present postmodernism is a relatively vague conception, two versions of it can be distinguished: the more radical or Continental form (e.g., Derrida, 1982; Foucault, 1980), which at best is incredulous toward the paradigms of modern social knowledge per se (see Lyotard, 1984), and the progressive liberal or American form (e.g., Bernstein, 1983; Rorty, 1979), which reappropriates American pragmatism and thus conditionally accepts modernism as a starting point for an emancipatory critical discourse (see Antonio, 1989).

Framing the Debate in Educational Inquiry

Using these ideas, we can frame Firestone's argument and the larger debate in educational inquiry in terms of four broad paradigms of modern social scientific thought. Each of these metaphysical paradigms provides a unique way to view education, and each one subsumes and defines a corresponding set of methodological assumptions about matters such as the nature of truth and causality, the relationship between subject and object, and the role of values in inquiry. In turn, and according to their own logic, these methodological assumptions define a particular set of research tools and practices for producing and collecting data. When each paradigm is applied to education, it produces a different type of knowledge according to the value assumptions inherent in the paradigm and its corresponding methodological assumptions and research practices.

Because social science and educational inquiry thus conceived are multiple paradigm endeavors, and because there is no set of independent criteria for adjudicating the issue of the best paradigm (Rorty, 1979), a great deal of time is spent debating the question of the correct paradigm (Ritzer, 1980). In educational inquiry, the quest for the "best" paradigm, which dominated the so-called "quantitative-qualitative" debate, seems to have evolved into a debate over whether two of the paradigms, postpositivism and constructivism, can be accommodated. This has produced two camps, the "compatibilists" (e.g., Firestone, this volume; Howe, 1988) and the "incompatibilists" (e.g., Lincoln & Guba, 1985; Smith & Heshusius, 1986), who take opposite sides on the issue of whether inquiry paradigms can and should be accommodated.

Given the introductory discussion, we can see that the incompatibilists have the stronger case, a case I hope to strengthen in my critique of Firestone's chapter and extend somewhat in my concluding comments. At this point, however, I can use the framework to make a few comments about the larger debate. First, I can reinforce the incompatibilist's point that the issue of compatibility exists not at the level of research practices (Guba, 1987; Lincoln, this volume; Smith & Heshusius, 1986), but at the higher conceptual levels of methodological and metatheoretical assumptions. The "quantitative-qualitative" distinction is superficial because it emphasizes type of data at the expense of type of knowledge produced. For example, in the case of postpositivism and constructivism, the difference is between empirical (i.e., etic, researcher-driven) and interpretive (i.e., emic, participant-driven) knowledge, both of which can be based on either quantitative or qualitative data (see, e.g., Lincoln & Guba, 1985; Yin, 1984).

I can also note that the major shortcoming of the contemporary debate in educational inquiry is that it is only half a debate. Although it is ostensibly a debate over the proper posture for social science, it has largely ignored the *social* in social science because it has excluded the two paradigms that question the nature of society. Although the inclusion of critical theory in the debate (e.g., Popkewitz, this volume; Sirotnik & Oakes, in press) gives one version of radical humanism a voice, the debate will remain incomplete until radical structuralism is included. The final and most important point, however, is that, to be progressive and emancipatory, the entire debate must be raised to the postmodern level of discourse, a topic I will return to after considering Firestone's case for accommodation.

Can and Should Paradigms of Inquiry Be Accommodated?

Firestone's argument for accommodation is based on two claims: that paradigms of inquiry *can* be accommodated and that paradigms of inquiry *should* be accommodated. His first claim is built on three warrants, the first two of which, framed in the language of my introductory discussion, are that

(1) paradigms of inquiry can be accommodated at the construct level of research practices because he and others have done it and

(2) paradigms of inquiry can be accommodated at the sociological level of methodological assumptions because he has done it.

And because Firestone recognizes that whether these paradigms can be accommodated legitimately depends on one's stance on the nature of paradigms and the relationship between paradigmatic assumptions and research practices, his third warrant is that

(3) paradigms of inquiry can be accommodated at the metaphysical level of metatheoretical assumptions *if* they are conceptualized as inductive cultures, rather than deductive philosophical systems, *and* the relationship between metatheoretical assumptions and research practices is conceptualized as a dialectical process rather than a process in which metatheoretical assumptions dictate research practice.

Firestone's second claim—that paradigms of inquiry *should* be accommodated—rests on one final warrant:

(1) Paradigmatic assumptions should be accommodated at the metaphysical, sociological, and construct levels because they are superseded in importance by political assumptions about how research findings should be used.

Can Paradigms of Inquiry Be Accommodated?

Firestone's first warrant is based upon two pieces of evidence: an example of his own research in which he "combined survey and interview data" (Firestone & Wilson, 1983; Firestone, this volume) and the fact that others (Rossman & Wilson, 1985; Smith & Louis, 1982) have actually developed procedures to "combine [qualitative and quantitative] methods" (Firestone, this volume). He presents this evidence to counter his interpretation of Smith and Heshusius's (1986) claim that "qualitative and quantitative methods simply [cannot] be combined" (Firestone, this volume).

However, after rereading Smith and Heshusius, Firestone realized that he had misinterpreted their position: They not only had conceded the point that specific quantitative and qualitative research practices can be used in a single study but had also characterized the question of whether this is possible as "relatively uninteresting" (Smith & Heshusius, 1986, p. 8). Firestone realized that the incompatibility claim of Smith and Heshusius, as well as that of Lincoln (this volume) had to be addressed at the higher conceptual level of methodological assumptions.

Firestone addresses the higher level of methodological assumptions by providing additional examples of his research as evidence that "even at a more conceptual level . . . [he] was combining the 'uncombinable' " (Firestone, this volume). In these studies, Firestone and his colleagues (Firestone, 1976, 1980; Firestone & Rosenblum, 1988; Rossman, Corbett, & Firestone, 1988) *described* the beliefs, perspectives, interpretations, and/or commitments of parents or teachers and used them to *explain* the outcomes of various planned change efforts. Given the way he counterposes description and explanation in these examples, Firestone implies that carrying out these acts within a single study demonstrates that paradigms of inquiry can be accommodated at the sociological level of methodological assumptions.

Firestone's third warrant for his first claim is that paradigms of inquiry can be accommodated at the metaphysical level of meta-theoretical assumptions if the deductive notion of paradigm as a philosophical system of rules is recast in terms of the inductive notion of a paradigm as a culture that is dialectically adaptable. His first line of argument to support this warrant is based on his interpretation of Kuhn (1970, p. 43), whom he quotes as follows:

> Close historical investigation of a given specialty at a given time discloses a set of recurrent and quasi-standard illustrations of various theories in their conceptual, observational, and instrumental applications. These are the community's paradigms, revealed in its textbooks, lectures, and laboratory exercises. By studying them and by practicing with them, the members of the corresponding community learn their trade.

Firestone directs our attention to two important aspects of the quotation, the first of which is the notion of specialties. Although Firestone is correct that Kuhn used the paradigm concept narrowly to refer to a given scientific specialty, and not the broader community of the physical sciences per se, the point he tries to make from this fact—that "initially . . . paradigms were not intended to be broad approaches to all social science inquiry" (Firestone, this volume)—is wrong on two counts. First, although it is true that in Kuhn's analysis each physical science specialty has its own corresponding metaphysical paradigm and that, in principle, no particular paradigm can serve as a broad approach to all physical science inquiry, all social science specialties are dominated by the same finite set of metaphysical paradigms, any of which could serve as a broad approach to all social inquiry (e.g., functionalism in the West, radical structuralism in the Soviet Union; Burrell & Morgan, 1979; Ritzer, 1980). Second, Firestone interprets the notion of specialty too narrowly relative to Kuhn's three levels of paradigms. Although Kuhn limited the realm of applicability of a particular paradigm to a given scientific specialty, he applied all three levels of paradigms to *each* such specialty (Masterman, 1970; Ritzer, 1980).

The second aspect of the Kuhn quotation that Firestone emphasizes is the notion of illustrations, which he reads as indicating that "people can agree on the existence of a paradigm without agreeing on its rationalized form." But again, Firestone misinterprets Kuhn's use of the paradigm concept. Although it is true that illustrations "can replace explicit rules . . . [for doing] normal science" (Kuhn, 1970, p. 175), these exemplars, and normal science itself, are possible only with respect to a metaphysical paradigm. Given his misreading of Kuhn, Firestone's argument that "what works" in practice alters metatheoretical assumptions does not hold.

In his second line of argument, Firestone introduces a cultural analogy to make the case that researchers develop their research practices inductively out of experience rather than on the basis of a deductive philosophical system of rules. Although he is correct in his assumption that research practitioners develop their practices on the basis of induction within a scientific culture, his argument for an inductive metaphysical paradigm over a deductive one doesn't hold because, ultimately, the scientific culture itself is premised on the implicit metatheoretical assumptions subsumed and defined by the metaphysical paradigm (see above, also Barnes, 1982; Ravetz, 1971). As Barnes (1982, p. 10) noted, "the culture is far more than the setting for scientific research; it is the research itself." Without a metaphysical paradigm acting implicitly or explicitly as a "way of seeing," the members of a scientific culture would not know what to induct from experience; indeed, without a metaphysical paradigm, there would be no scientific culture (Barnes, 1982; Ritzer, 1980).

Should Paradigms of Inquiry Be Accommodated?

Firestone's second claim is that inquiry paradigms should be accommodated because they cannot be separated from political interests. For him, paradigmatic assumptions are less important than political assumptions about how research findings are to be used. He supports this warrant with the expert opinion of several critical theorists and several illustrations of how researchers can use various inquiry paradigms to support particular political agendas.

Ultimately, Firestone argues that "postpositivism and critical theory are not incompatible" (this volume). This is so, he contends for two reasons: first, because critical theory challenges the notion of "the separation of research and political activity," and postpositivism, although it is silent on the role of values in inquiry, implicitly is premised on the regulative ideals of truth and objectivity, and, second, because "extensive studies of the social organization of science have been conducted using rather positivist methodologies (e.g., Crane, 1976)" (Firestone, this volume). Thus the problem for Firestone is not whether postpositivism and critical theory can be or should be accommodated. It is simply "how to put them together" (this volume).

I support Firestone's arguments against the notion of separating research from political and ideological interests, and I commend him for recognizing that there are bigger issues here than the accommodation of inquiry paradigms. However, given his belief in the possibility of accommodation, I fully expected an argument for a three-way accommodation among postpositivism, constructivism, and critical theory rather than merely the two-way accommodation he proposes. The implication, of course, is that constructivism is less compatible with critical theory than postpositivism. But this is not the case, particularly when we consider that critical theory and constructivism at least share the subjectivist view of social science, whereas critical theory and postpositivism hold opposing views on science and society and thus have nothing in common at all. Moreover, as a critique of ideology, and particularly the Enlightenment ideology of objective social science, critical theory rejects positivism in all its forms (e.g., Horkheimer, 1947/1974). In any event, let me proceed to my concluding argument against Firestone's call for accommodation of inquiry paradigms by referring to the last section of his chapter, "Toward Accommodation."

Social Accommodation and Dialogical Discourse

First of all, there are many assertions in Firestone's conclusion with which I can agree. For example, his position that, when one considers the politics of social inquiry, the real issue is " 'knowledge for what' . . . who should benefit from the research that is undertaken" (this volume) is particularly appealing to me. Furthermore, I agree with his assertions that "how knowledge is used and how it is generated are at least partly separable" and that "the question of legitimate use goes beyond what is normally meant by paradigms" (this volume). In addition, I am encouraged by his recognition that debate among divergent viewpoints is necessary and helpful. Where I disagree with Firestone, however, is in his belief that accommodation among divergent paradigms of inquiry is the means to progress or the proper end of such a debate. On this point, I believe that he is dead wrong.

Although he is not as direct as Howe (1988) in invoking the pragmatist tradition, Firestone relies heavily on the notion of pragmatism to support his claims that divergent paradigms of inquiry can and should be accommodated. However, both he and Howe (1988) misread the pragmatist tradition. Neither the pragmatists of the *via media*—most notably, John Dewey (1929/1984) and George H. Mead (1934/1967)—nor their contemporary appropriators (e.g., Bernstein, 1983; Rorty, 1979, 1982a) have called for an accommodation of inquiry paradigms at the methodological or metatheoretical level. Premised on antifoundationalism, the pragmatist tradition is not a voice for *paradigmatic accommodation;* it is a voice for *social accommodation* through dialogical discourse at the *meta*paradigmatic level. As Kloppenberg (1986, p. 27) noted, the philosophers of the pragmatist tradition

> did not seek synthesis by simply blending incommensurable ideas. Mediators of that sort, as Nietzsche wisely warned, "lack eyes to see the unparalleled." The philosophers of the *via media* carefully avoided fruitless attempts to reconcile the irreconcilable; they tried instead to jostle philosophy into a productive confrontation with doubt.

The general trend in the social sciences and humanities (Bernstein, 1976), as well as in educational inquiry (Soltis, 1984), has been away from objectivism and toward subjectivism, a trend, moreover, that is consistent with developments in the physical sciences and the arts as well (Schwartz & Ogilvy, 1979). But, as significant as this trend has been, the real breakthrough has been the reconceptualization of the nature of knowledge itself. Since Descartes, the general conceptualization of knowledge in philosophy and the sciences has been foundational—the idea that there is a fixed set of foundational criteria against which all knowledge claims can be judged (Bernstein, 1983). But the emergent, or actually reemergent, view is antifoundational, a conceptualization of knowledge characterized by the recognition of the importance of the perspective of the knower. This has meant that the very notion of inquiry is being recast as a form of interaction between an object of study and an observer who is conditioned to see the object in a particular way by his or her worldview or paradigm. As Morgan (1983a) noted, the common view of inquiry as a neutral, technical process is being replaced by an appreciation of inquiry as engagement—a distinctively human process through which potential knowledges are created.

Debate in the social disciplines during the modern era was premised on the foundational view of knowledge, which led to arguments over the "best" methodology for social analysis. But today, at the start of the postmodern era, the debate is moving beyond considerations of a single research methodology or paradigm. Scholars in the social sciences and the humanities are beginning to call for a dialogical discourse—an antifoundational, reflective discourse about, and appreciation of, the variety of available research logics and paradigmatic perspectives (Bernstein, 1983; Ricoeur, 1981; Rorty, 1979).

Because educational inquiry is a multiparadigmatic endeavor, and because there are no foundational criteria to judge the adequacy of any given paradigm, such a dialogical analysis in education would bring together all paradigmatic perspectives in a democratized discourse on the nature, conditions, and implications of education. A dialogical analysis incorporates the Peircian (1931-1935) theme of intersubjective communities of inquirers into a strategy analysis. It assumes that knowledge is a social product of normatively regulated intersubjective communication, that the various paradigmatic perspectives are the social constructions of communities of inquirers, which are shaped by their metatheoretical and methodological assumptions.

Although the notion of normatively regulated scientific communities has been appropriated by postempiricist philosophers of science to reconceptualize the growth of scientific knowledge (e.g., Feyerabend, 1975; Kuhn, 1970), their work has been limited to single-paradigm sciences. But because educational inquiry is a multiple-paradigm endeavor, the notion of normatively regulated scientific communities takes on a different meaning. Rather than attempting to understand the growth of knowledge as a revolutionary overthrow of one paradigm by another—as some constructivists would have it—or as the accommodation of two or more paradigms—as the compatibilists would have it—the emphasis is on the hermeneutic growth in understanding that results from being open to multiple perspectives.

Thus the point is not to accommodate or reconcile the multiple paradigms of modern social scientific thought; it is to recognize them as unique, historically situated forms of insight; to understand them and their implications; to learn to speak to them and through them; and to recognize them for what they are—ways of seeing that simultaneously reveal and conceal. The task of educational inquiry is not to reconcile these particular paradigms with one another; rather, it is to move beyond them, through dialogical discourse, to reconcile education with the ideals of democracy and social justice.

[8]

Discussion on Accommodation

ANN AUSTIN

Vanderbilt University

Levels of Accommodation

A key aspect of our early discussion was the issue of levels of accommodation. Three possible levels at which accommodation among paradigms might be achieved were identified: the *philosophical* level, the *social-community* level, and the *personal* level. At the *philosophical* level, the key questions become these: Is it possible for several paradigms to come together philosophically or must each remain separate and distinct? Must we assume one way will "win"? At the *social-community* level, the central questions are these: Can we live with each other even though we are based in different paradigms? Can we learn from each other? At the *personal* level, the important question is this: How can I as an individual researcher accommodate various paradigms?

Possible Approaches to Accommodation

A common thread running through both discussion groups was the assumptions that indeed some kind of accommodation among paradigms can be achieved. Various approaches to achieving some kind of accommodation were identified and discussed.

Dialogical Accommodation

Tom Skrtic advocated a dialogical accommodation, which could be categorized as accommodation at the philosophical level. A dialogical accommodation is based on the notion that the social sciences are multiparadigmatic sciences, characterized by several viable paradigms and no single dominant paradigm. A dialogical accommodation involves recognizing and learning to speak to and through the various paradigms, using them for what they are—that is, just paradigms. One uses paradigms to accommodate social and educational reality; thus one should choose a particular paradigm as the framework for a given project based on its implications for society and the kind of knowledge it produces.

This approach to accommodation generated considerable discussion and interpretation. Some participants interpreted it to mean that we do not have to really accommodate paradigms but that we can just take up and use a different paradigm if the one we have been using, for some reason, does not work. Various participants had different concerns with this stance. Some argued, for example, that one's paradigm is like a religion; it is very hard to deny, to take on and off at will. Others argued that movement across paradigms could lead one to lose an anchor in any world. Also, one could be an amateur in every paradigm. A second kind of response to Skrtic's dialogical accommodation was the assertion that it is not easy for any one researcher to move between paradigms, for the reasons enumerated above. However, one researcher could recognize and appreciate each paradigm for what it offers. A third response to dialogical accommodation was the argument that such a view is not really accommodation at all.

General Respect

Another approach to accommodation involves maintaining a general respect for what each paradigm can contribute. In terms of levels of accommodation, this approach fits at the social-community level and involves evaluating each paradigm in terms of how it can solve such educational problems as low school achievement and high dropout rates. Additionally, this kind of accommodation leads to the recognition that each paradigm has made some valuable contributions. The interpretists' work, for example, has brought attention to the needs of various groups in our society, while the critical theorists have focused on power relations and class issues. In sum, accommodation defined as general respect involves understanding the key contribution and issues of each paradigm, appreciating the views of scholars who subscribe to different paradigms and one's own, and letting all paradigms try to improve educational problems. It is not necessary for one researcher to wear all glasses, but each researcher should appreciate others' views. Appreciation, not antagonism, should characterize the interactions between proponents of different paradigms, according to this approach to accommodation.

Personal Accommodation

The third approach to accommodation that was advanced by some discussants was personal accommodation in one's own work as a researcher. Those suggesting this approach argue that researchers essentially try to make sense of the world and should let the various paradigms inform practice to the extent they are useful. According to this approach, the methods that characterize the various paradigms can be combined by a researcher in order to solve particular problems and answer particular questions. This kind of accommodation can be achieved if the focus is on the dialectic between theory and practice. What works and is useful in practice can and should inform the paradigms.

Questions and Concerns

In addition to our focus on levels of and approaches to accommodation, the discussion highlighted a few questions of relevance to the conference. First, have some paradigms been ignored in terms of the structure of the conference? If accommodation is an important topic, should not proponents of additional paradigms be included (e.g., religious thinkers, Marxist thinkers)? Second, should not practitioners as well as university scholars be involved in such conferences and discussions?

ETHICS

[9]

Ethics, Field Studies, and the
Paradigm Crisis

LOUIS M. SMITH

In this chapter, paradigm crisis is an interpretation of the epistemological point raised most forcefully by Kuhn (1970), who writes of
"scientific revolutions" and the "shift in paradigms," changes in
patterns of assumptions, underlying scientific activity. The label from
the conference on which this book is based is "alternative paradigms."
In the social sciences, these patterns of assumptions have tended to
crystallize into three large worldviews for organizing and making
sense of the kind of work we do. Bernstein (1976), Bredo and Feinberg
(1982c), and Fay (1975) are reasonably consistent in speaking of positivist, interpretive, and critical traditions.

   The chapters in this volume put a twist on this with the labels
"postpositivist," "constructivist," and "critical." And it is a real and
slippery twist of ideas and labels. For instance, as I read Phillips's
chapter (this volume), his view of "postpositivism" is as far from
classical logical positivism as are the "constructivist" position of
Lincoln and the "critical" position of Popkewitz. All are postpositivist.
Gone is the logical positivist thesis upon which these several antithe-
ses arose. Phillips's chapter seems almost a claim for "the new con-

AUTHOR'S NOTE: As usual I owe thanks to my colleagues in Education and Social
Science at Washington University for helpful comments on a preliminary draft of this
chapter.

ventional wisdom." Attesting to this are his return to Dewey with such labels as "warranted assertions," his fishnet metaphor for the results of science, and his commonsense statement:

> Seekers after enlightenment in any field do the best that they can; they honestly seek evidence, they critically scrutinize it, they are open to alternative viewpoints, they take criticism seriously and try to profit from it, they play their hunches, they stick to their guns, but they also have a sense of when it is time to quit. It may be a dirty, hard, and uncertain game, but it is the only game in town. (Phillips, this volume)

Knowing anything for certain, that is, positively or absolutely, is impossible.

These epistemological words of Phillips, at this abstract, general level, are ones with which I, as a qualitative, case study, field researcher, with concerns for ethics in this chapter, can resonate. What his ideas mean when spelled out more concretely in specific institutional settings becomes a next step, a step in my experience that leads to conflict and normative stands that some kinds of inquiry (e.g., the experiment) are better than other kinds. Nonetheless, evolutions seem to be occurring within the revolutions, as Toulmin and Goodfield (1961, 1965), Toulmin (1970a, 1972), and Scriven (1956, 1958, 1959, 1966) argued earlier, and more generally.

Field studies refers to that genre of research that goes by such labels as "case studies," "qualitative research," "ethnography," and "participant observation." For some, these developments ushered in a new paradigm for educational studies. Some years ago, Smith and Pohland (1974) argued that there was no such thing as "standard participant observation," ways in which individual researchers lived in day-to-day contact with an ongoing community being studied. They presented an analysis of some of the more important differences separating scholars working in the field. A few years later, Smith (1979) argued that, for some purposes, these terms could be used as quasi synonyms. More recently, Jacob (1987) has argued that, though important patterns exist within the broader domain, differentiation of concepts and traditions is of major importance. When central concepts in a theoretical analysis have this kind of variability in meaning, the possibilities of confusion increases, as does the need for care in the language one uses in the analysis.

Ethics refers to that complex of ideals showing how individuals should relate to one another in particular situations, to principles of conduct guiding those relationships, and to the kind of reasoning one engages in when thinking about such ideals and principles. Philosophers have quarreled about all this for thousands of years (Hare, 1964, 1972; Scriven, 1966).

Putting some order into all this seems a pretty heady task. To help do this, I will discuss several classical field studies that have provoked considerable discussion regarding their ethical underpinnings. Then I will discuss a model of ethical reasoning and decision making that is drawn from some of the recent thinking about medical ethics. Medical models and metaphors have run all through social science and educational discussions and have a kind of risk that should be kept in mind. Finally, I return to see what the several paradigms have to say about the specific cases and the kind of reasoning in which we have engaged and, alternatively, what our cases and reasoning have to say about the alternative paradigms.

Controversial Cases

When terminological diversity rages, common sense and philosophy agree that concrete illustrations are helpful in promoting clarity. Consequently, I will raise several classical case studies to focus the discussion: Horowitz's (1974) account of Project Camelot, a social scientific attempt to study counterinsurgency in Third World countries: Festinger, Riecken, and Schachter's (1956/1964) study of a group that predicted the end of the world; and Humphreys' (1975) study of homosexual behavior in public park restrooms. The study of power, sex, and religion would seem to have likely possibilities for ethical discussion. Further, if "alternative paradigms" and their "crises" have any significance in field research, surely they will appear in such varied settings and problems as these.

Briefly, the substantive story of *When Prophecy Fails* (Festinger, Riecken, & Schachter, 1956/1964) is a tale of a group of people who predicted the end of the world on one December 21. Public newspapers quoted the leaders and described them, their followers, and some of the related beliefs of messages, floods, flying saucers, superior beings from another planet, and salvation for the believers. They are an interesting group for a number of reasons! The complex field research procedures were handled carefully, guided by the nature of the problem and the theory under analysis. Neither the book nor the methodological appendix mentioned any ethical issues or dilemmas. The seeking of social psychological truth overshadowed every other consideration. A strong positivistic rationale underlay their research.

The researchers made a series of procedural choices, with accompanying rationales. In discussing the impact of the addition of four supposedly "believing" members, the observers, into the group, the authors comment:

> It was an unfortunate and unavoidable set of events—we had no choice but to establish local observers in both cities where there were believers, to do it quickly, and to "push" as much as we dared to get our people well enough received so they could begin to move about in the groups, ask questions, and have a reasonable expectation of getting answers. We could not afford to have them remain peripheral members, or strangers, for very long. (Festinger, Riecken, & Schachter, 1956/1964, p. 240)

Creative? Ethical? Paradigm perspectives and ethical choices slip in. I presume Yvonna Lincoln and Tom Popkewitz would react strongly to their selection of words, "unfortunate," "unavoidable," "no choice," and "could not afford" and to the implicit connotations of naturalism involved. From my perspective, these are choices, implicit or explicit, made by the researchers. These choices are a particular resolution of the dilemma of the search for scientific truth and the ethical concerns for one's subjects (and not so incidentally for their research assistants as well).

Let me be clear on a point, making latter-day judgments on research from an earlier generation has its own kind of ethical implications. Professional historians raise strong warnings about bringing contemporary perspectives and standards to those historical periods. In the present context of this chapter, I would argue that doing science is a cultural activity and, as with all cultures, there are norms and standards about how one does things. Thirty or forty years ago, the culture of social science, at least as it existed at the University of Minnesota, made the Festinger, Riecken, and Schachter effort seem a creative instance of normal science. I dare say if we did biographies of field researchers who are over fifty years of age, the data would indicate patterns not too different from those presented here. I am arguing strongly, in conjunction I believe with Popkewitz (this volume), that the context of history, institutions, and cultures, along with individual choice and agency, are important for thinking about social science and its practices. Traditionally, positivism and constructivism make much less of the importance of history.

At its simplest level, *Tearoom Trade* (Humphreys, 1975) is a field study of male homosexual activity, *Impersonal Sex in Public Places* to follow on the book's subtitle. Humphreys, an Episcopalian minister, shed his collar, grew a beard, and assumed the participant role of lookout, "watchqueen," in a restroom in a public city park. Substantively, Humphreys pursued topics such as "rules and roles," "patterns of collective action," and "risks of the game." Our concern for ethics and alternative paradigms raises a slightly different set of issues and players. In the community being studied, fellatio is a felony. Witnessing some 200 such acts makes one something of an accomplice to crime. As a note-taking and record-keeping social scientist, one has documents that could be seriously injurious, both socially and legally, to one's subjects. Some of his subjects were "informants" and knew of the nature of the research, and some did not. One part of the study, a follow-up of the observational aspects, involved Humphreys in noting license plate numbers, obtaining, illegally, names and addresses, and then interviewing, unbeknownst to the subjects, both them and a control sample of their neighbors regarding a "health survey." Sans beard, with a haircut, suit, tie, and briefcase, he was "disguised" and unknown, once again. Ethical questions spin out in multiple directions. Would you, or should anyone, do such research? Are there parts to which you would say yea and other parts say nay? Of what help in your reasoning are your paradigmatic commitments and affiliations?

The book, *The Rise and Fall of Project Camelot* (Horowitz, 1974), is an edited volume of original documentary papers and essays written by a number of individuals. As such it carries the subtitle *Studies in the Relationship Between Social Science and Practical Politics.* It differs further in that most of the reported activity involved the funding agencies and the social science community in the initial stages of project development rather than an actualized and completed piece of social science field research, for early in its life the study was canceled by presidential order. The study had a threefold set of objectives, which Horowitz sees as both open-ended and potentially in conflict: (a) "to devise procedures for assessing the potential for internal war within national societies," (b) "to identify with increased degrees of confidence, those actions which a government might take to relieve conditions which are assessed as giving rise to a potential for internal war," and (c) "to assess the feasibility of prescribing the characteristics of a system for obtaining and using the essential information needed for doing the above two things" (Humphreys, 1975, p. 5). To say the least, such inquiry has great potential for good and evil. As field researchers, do you sign on or not for such an investigation? How do you reason through your response? Does it make a difference if you are positivist, postpositivist, constructivist, or critical theorist?

In brief, I have selected three well-known and discussed pieces of field research. At the time each was carried out, the research was argued to be important and worth doing on grounds of substance and social importance. Each as a total piece of work and each as an integrated series of research decisions raises dramatically important ethical issues. Hopefully, *Prophecy, Tearoom,* and *Camelot* will enable us to have continuing concrete examples to return to as the discussion proceeds.

Toward a Model of Ethical
Decision Making in Fieldwork

At this point, I turn from the accounts of field research to a series of interrelated issues labeled "toward a model of ethical decision making in fieldwork."

Beginning with fieldwork in the early 1960s, our study of Geoffrey's classroom (Smith & Geoffrey, 1968) started a huge reconstrual of my cognitive structure, not unlike the personal history presented by Yvonna Lincoln (this volume) in her opening remarks to the conference. Initially, this inquiry caught me explicitly in epistemological problems and forced considerable rethinking of a variety of philosophical issues I had thought about early on, as a graduate student during the early 1950s in the University of Minnesota's psychology department, under the title "rambling through the *Psychological Review*" as I had read about operational definitions and isomorphism in psychological theories. But also, and with much less awareness, the ethical problems of the social science we were practicing needed rethinking. That journey is a long one. This volume is the most recent progress report on this thinking. When one is dealing with major changes in cognitive structures, *meandering* may not be an inappropriate verb.

In this meandering, Bronowski's book *Science and Human Values* (1956/1975) became a revelation. In his view, the fundamental imperative of scientific inquiry is the search for truth, knowledge, and understanding of the world, and, some would add, toward the improvement of the human condition in that world. At their worst, those words are meaningless abstractions. At their best, they pose powerful ethical demands for the individual who wants to be a part of a community of individuals who call themselves scientists. Historically, the authority of careful observation of, and thought about, the world was to replace the varied authorities of religion, royalty, social privilege, common sense, and self-interest, rationalization, and delusion. Bronowski argued strongly that scientists would have had to invent an ethic of independence, originality, and dissent to characterize personal and interpersonal relationships, if these ideas were not scattered about already in parts of Western culture. Similarly, scientists would have had to develop values of tolerance, respect, and justice, if those too were not already a part of our culture. The dilemmas and tensions between dissent and respect, between intellectual independence and tolerance of the views of others, will not go away, according to Bronowski.

Social scientists in general and fieldworkers in particular do not have to do notorious studies such as *Prophecy, Tearoom*, or *Camelot* to know the conflicts and pressures that arise as an individual tries to understand some part of the social or educational world. Is this problem worth doing? Is it more worth doing than another? Or is it part of an in-vogue topic or one that has a high probability of funding and related resources? Do the people in the organization with whom one is working, or the people in the setting who have agreed to the study, "really" want a testimonial on the merits of the program or the institution and not any "disinterested" inquiry? If so, what are you to do? What are one's ethical commitments to the community of scientists? What are the norms of the various subcommunities within science? Do the norms nurture or constrain? Or both? At an overt level, the scientific imperative suggests some simple, basic, and important values. The alternative paradigms emphasize different aspects of these values. As the imperative works out in the practice of fieldwork, a number of different decisions arise. Each of these decisions has important ethical dimensions and implications.

When I encountered Brody's (1981) book *Ethical Decisions in Medicine*, it seemed to speak to a number of perplexing issues in a way that built upon some of the earlier reading, discussions, and reflection I had been doing. From the start, I liked the process quality, actions on a time line. Geoffrey and I had thought this was one of the major outcomes of our field study of his classroom (Smith & Geoffrey, 1968). In addition, Brody takes the perspective of the actor, another of the major outcomes of our earlier work and, not so incidentally, our partial move from an external (behavioristic?) to an internal (symbolic interactionist?) perspective on teachers and pupils—implicitly, a move from a positivist to an interpretive (constructivist?) paradigm. Furthermore, we had couched much of this growing perspective in a decision-making framework. Brody also does this explicitly. Changes or shifts in paradigms, as patterns of assumptions and worldviews, start creeping into one's thinking and discussion in the "normal" course of trying to solve particular substantive problems. I believe that that is an important generalization.

Much of the above is captured by Brody in his definition of an ethical problem as a problem that involves a real choice for an individual, a problem in which the action alternatives involve other people, and a problem that is capable of having different values placed upon the actions and their consequences. For example, do you or I as social science researchers do studies like *Tearoom Trade, Camelot,* or *Prophecy?* Such a decision is a real choice. One's paradigm must have a concept of the individual as agent, that is, capable of making and being responsible for choosing courses of action if ethical concerns are to be addressed. Logical positivism did not. Our three postpositivist alternatives do.

As Brody breaks the ethical reasoning process into sequential steps and feedback loops (Figure 9.1 presents these steps), he argues that the first of these is the perception that a moral problem exists. And this is no easy or simple issue, in spite of how it may seem initially. Now I am prone to argue that each action one takes in a research study, as it impinges upon others and as it is capable of alternative solutions, can be conceived as an ethical problem to the investigator.

The second step in Brody's conception is the listing of alternative actions available in the solution of the problem. He argues that one of the most serious problems in ethical reasoning is the limiting of options to one or two. Developing three or more options raises the

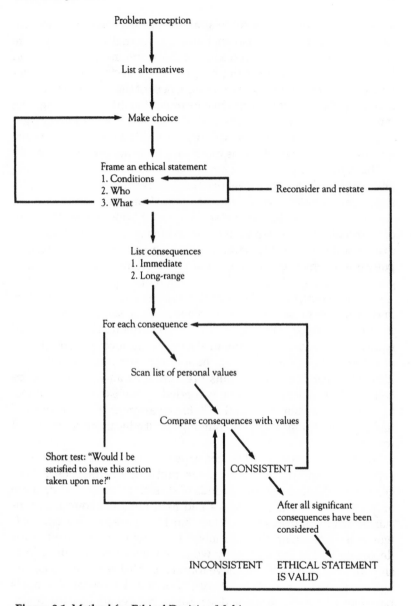

Figure 9.1. Method for Ethical Decision Making
SOURCE: Brody (1981, p. 10). Copyright Little, Brown and Company

large consideration of creativity as an intellectual component to ethical reasoning. Some of us can think up alternative options more readily than others of us. And some of those options can be more and less self-serving, and one's thinking can become clouded with rationalizations. For me, one of the consequences of these complications is a move away from simple rulelike formulas in ethical reasoning. The interrelationship of creativity, ethical decision, and rationalization deserves considerable further discussion. Critical theory with its origins in Marx and Freud seems more congruent and helpful here.

Third, Brody argues that one next makes a tentative choice among alternatives, often a "gut level reaction" to use his words. This action statement includes "who" is to do "what" under "which" circumstances. The particularities are spelled out. If I understand this item of "particularities," it demands a certain kind and level of educational discourse if not theory. Idiographic thinking and writing must accompany one's nomothetic thinking and writing. And that too is a major generalization, needing incorporation into one's paradigm. In addition, at this point, for Brody, a Kantian-type generalization now enters in (Lincoln, in press). What if everyone in these same circumstances did the same thing? What would be the consequences? The values of equity, fairness, or justice enter in at a very basic level. One might ask of the three field studies—what happens if everyone commits felonies? Or what if everyone joins organizations and pretends to be believers? Or what if everyone is funded by the Department of Defense in contradistinction to the State Department? Or vice versa? I find these questions helpful in thinking about ethical decisions in field research.

Fourth, one determines the consequences of the proposed ethical action. The empirical aspects of the problem emerge with a vengeance. Predictions run in all kinds of directions, empirical data are only partially available, guesses and assumptions abound. For instance, who could have predicted that Humphreys's *Tearoom Trade* would have brought him into intense conflict with members of his department, that the university would have withdrawn his fellowship, or even that he would have found a publisher for his research? Does one need a "realist" tenet with "warranted assertions" in one's paradigm? I believe that one does. Some, but not all, constructivists and critical theorists are realists. Brody makes a major point that both long- and short-term consequences need to be considered. And that "systemic" conceptualization, if it is that, seems very important to me. The model enlarges.

"The next step is to compare each of the consequences with one's own set of values" (Brody, 1981, p. 12). This seems to me to be a huge and difficult task. What are the values? How do the values pattern? Which are highest in priority? Which are most relevant to this problem and the particular consequences, both short and long term? For me, liberty, fraternity, and equality are very important social values at this point in the analysis. In its ultimate reaches, one asks: Is this the way I want to live my life? The philosopher R. N. Hare (1964) sees this as the fundamental idea in ethical theory, a "decision of principle." Brody presents several "short cut" suggestions in the form of questions: "Could I live with this?" And if some semblance of "no" or discomfort occurs, then one must ask, "Why does this bother me?" This is not the language of positivism. Rather, such questions require a sentient human being at the core of one's perspective.

Enlarging on this, to another very important principle of ethical reasoning, that of "dialog," I argue that each of the key issues should be discussed with others. For me, this pool of people varies from colleagues with wide social science experience to relatives and friends who have little or no social science experience. The experience, ethical assumptions, and patterns of values will be both similar and different and will help clarify slips in reasoning. This kind of give-and-take can vary from supportive to adversarial and probably should include some of both. Even a small sample of people can help one detect the grossest of the errors in ethical reasoning. The model needs a social dimension.

Brody enters another shortcut into his analysis with the question, "If I were in that person's situation, and I were like him in morally relevant ways, would I be satisfied with having this done to me?" Versions of the golden rule and Kant return again (Lincoln, in press). Suppose you were one of the tearoom trade; one of the believers in the end of the world, or a citizen in a South American country, would you want the research done at all? Would you want it conducted in the fashion it was? Tough ethical questions! And even tougher answers?

In conclusion, Brody argues, and I would agree, that making the ethical reasoning conscious and explicit is a very powerful means for improving the kind of ethical reasoning that is usually done in human affairs. The vague, the partially conscious, and the unthinking aspects of decision making have been escalated to another level. In some ways, the process seems to fit another of the recent labels of the ethics of social change, "consciousness-raising." Dialog, seeing how others with alternative views see and reason through the ethical implications, keeps one from some of the most disastrous aspects of both involvement and the attendant rationalization. Detachment, if not objectivity, is part of the contribution.

Consequentialist ethics, of the sort presented by Brody, according to May (1980), is only one of the broad general ethical theories available to researchers for help in thinking through their problems. Fieldwork as a genre of social science research has some special characteristics (Barnes, 1984; Cassell & Wax, 1980; Jacobs, 1980; Wax, 1980). Blending these additional considerations complicates and also enhances the discussion of the ethical decision-making model.

First, much of fieldwork generally and educational fieldwork in particular deals with intact groups—classrooms, schools, and communities. Most of utilitarian consequentialist ethics deals with independent or reasonably independent individuals. The individual patient or the individual subject in a laboratory experiment have a different status than a member of an intact, "natural" community. A kind of social system view and group decision making must be a part of one's thinking. Democracy, as value and process, returns.

Second, most field studies attend to processes over time as well as cross-sectional, static, frozen-in-time structures. This has implications for the amount of time one spends with one's subjects. Long-term field relationships take on their own dynamic, both intellectually and ethically. The relationship of the fieldworker to the members of the community being studied is far more complex than the one-off laboratory treatment or the survey interview or questionnaire. Participating in the events of the group—day-to-day activities, ceremonies, and rituals—involves more of the fieldworker as a person than other kinds of social science and educational research. "Being around" for long periods of time, often backstage, permits views that are more intimate, private, and unguarded. The relationship takes on a kind of depth and intensity that is not lightly put aside if one values individuals for themselves. Contracts, as a label, seem less applicable than "covenants," which carry a more sacred connotation (Cassell & Wax, 1980; May, 1980).

Third, most communities studied in field research are not homogeneous single-value entities. Divisions along age, ethnicity, class, religion, and gender, not to mention the sexual preference of the *Tearoom*, the politics of *Camelot*, and the *weltanschauung* of *Prophecy*, exist everywhere. Whose side one is on is not a rhetorical question.

Fourth, especially for those doing field research in non-Western cultures, but I would argue even for schools in Western society, the nature of field research is so different from the usual experimental approaches that many individuals, even responsible professional educators, do not understand what it is that we are trying to do and, more significantly, what it is that they are getting themselves into, that questions can be raised about how informed, informed consent is. For one who has explained and explained, and even tried Howard Becker's (1978, personal communication) tactic of putting an earlier book on the table and indicating that we hope to do something like this, concern still remains in my mind about how well one has been understood.

Fifth, field research is often "responsive" rather than "preset," as in an experiment or a survey. The changing directions, often in goals, tactics, and interpersonal relationships as the problem and methods evolve, raise difficulties with initial agreements of "informed consent" and other usual principles and procedures of ethical relationships in social research.

Sixth, power relationships run through all of one's contacts in the field. And that power is not evenly distributed among subgroups in the setting or between the individual researcher and those groups and individuals. Some people have authority to commit organizations where others do not. Some can tell you to leave while others cannot. Some people change their views, positively or negatively, over time. The ultimate reach of this is the possibility of canceling the research itself, before it is finished. Funders do do this, as illustrated in *Camelot*. Who else has the right—the researchers, the community under investigation? The ethics of power is not well analyzed in field research. Critical theorists tend to talk more of this than others.

Finally, in reporting on results, most field reports deal in narratives, stories, and portraits. The particular is honored in dramatic presentation. Means and standard deviations and correlations are not present to mask the individual lives of Tom and Suzie and Mary. Anonymity works reasonably well for those outside of the situation but less so for readers inside. And those insider relationships continue on through time. Another year of teaching occurs, colleagues are still in the rooms up and down the hall, the principal remains, the superintendent continues to occupy a desk in the central office, and school board elections will be next April as usual. Empirically, it is simple, but, ethically, it is a nightmare of concern and complexity that demands the best of one's reasoning abilities.

One might ask: What does this add up to for our inquiry into the paradigm crisis and the ethics of field research? Barnes (1984), in his trenchant analysis, answers by making the basic point that "ethical and political compromise" is intrinsic to the process of social research. For him, the "conventional model of ethical purity," as stated or implied in organizational and professional ethical codes, is inapplicable. His dilemmas and compromises reflect much of what I have been saying: "choice of topic and social field," "commitment versus impartiality," "scientist or citizen," "frankness or concealment," and "disseminating knowledge and preserving ignorance." For me these dilemmas imply, as I have indicated, the need for a model of ethical decision making that both raises the researcher's consciousness and helps him or her think through the multitude of specific questions as decisions are made. Also it means that dialog is escalated into a position of prime importance. One has to talk, seemingly never-endingly, with one's "collegial subjects," the participants in their many forms, as one inquires and builds the kind of educational community in which one wants to live. It is time-consuming. It is frustrating. It is creative. It is exhausting. But it also is immensely satisfying as well.

I believe that these issues are part of what May (1980) and Cassell and Wax (1980) and others mean when they reach for the conceptual label "covenantal ethics." They seem to be responding to May's (1980, p. 363) observation:

Utilitarianism seems to defy what common sense associates with ethics: principles that have a categorical force irrespective of results. A deontological ethic (derived from the Greek term of duty) orients less to goods or harms produced by action than to those principles of right and wrong that should categorically restrain it.

It suggests also the broader sets of ties, beyond being advocate or adversary for a particular group, the ties that bind the researcher to the public, to students, and to colleagues in one's discipline. These too are significant relationships. But I also want a model of ethical reasoning that not only includes these ideas but also helps me think through the problems. Variants of critical theory accent a position closer to covenants than other paradigm alternatives. The dialog expands and continues.

Paradigms and Crises

"Paradigms" dramatically entered the social science literature 25 years ago with the initial publication of Thomas Kuhn's *The Structure of Scientific Revolutions* (1962). As Kuhn commented in a later essay, his concerns within the history of science had from the beginnings "a totally unanticipated fascination with the reconstruction of old scientific ideas and of the processes by which they were transformed to more recent ones" (Kuhn, 1984, p. 31). His equation of scientific revolutions with shifts in the broader framework of assumptions and beliefs and the equation of normal science with the incremental changes in particular scientific theories has stirred considerable controversy. In philosophy, for me, Michael Scriven's comments have always carried vividness, acid, and relevance regarding the issues of paradigms under discussion in this conference. His view of positivism, "The Vienna Circle or *Wiener Kreis* was a band of cutthroats that went after the fat burghers of Continental metaphysics who had become intolerably inbred and pompously verbose. . . . It performed a tracheotomy that made it possible for philosophy to breathe again" (Scriven, 1969, p. 165). Do the current postpositivist alternative paradigms offer us the freedom—the breathing room, on the one hand, and, on the other, the communal responsibility, a set of ethical ideals and guidelines—to act responsibly?

Within social science and educational inquiry, the rise of qualitative research and evaluation has engendered arguments as to whether a paradigm shift is under way (Hamilton, McDonald, King, Jenkins, & Parlett, 1977). In part, also, a malaise over the less than powerful outcomes of their research, among a number of eminent positivistic social scientists, contributed to the concern (e.g., Cronbach, 1957, 1975; Gergen 1973, 1982). Something larger than simple epistemological adjustments to current theory and its assumptions seemed in the wind. The multiple domains of social discontent in the 1960s (civil rights, Vietnam, the women's movement, the decline of colonialism, ecological issues) engendered a legitimacy to the radicalization of the ways in which social scientists thought about the world. Valuational and ethical issues vied with epistemological issues.

The implications ripple in multiple directions. First and foremost is the neglect, or defining out, of values and value statements in most positivistic and interpretive discussions. In my view and the view of others (Peters, 1965; Tom, 1984), education is a value-oriented intellectual discipline. The critical theorists have the edge here.

A second demand necessary for a discussion of ethics is that the theory must deal, or at least be open to being coordinated with, the particularities of social action from the perspective of the actors in the setting. The constructivists seem to have a more direct focus on this point.

A related point is the need for a theory that can account for the actions of the researcher in the same terms as the action of the subjects. The internal world of the researcher must be relatable to the internal world of the practitioner if ethical reasoning is to have full generality. To have a decision-making framework for thinking about one's research design and decisions and to use another theory for the action of one's subjects seems to indicate a lack of generality and power for one's substantive theory. The constructionists and the critical theorists seem to capture this best, although Phillips's (in press) version of postpositivism seems not alien to this need.

Implicit in the discussion of the several controversial cases of field studies were principles of protection of the rights of human subjects, that is, the research should not harm the subjects. These principles have been codified under the labels of "anonymity," "informed consent," and "dialog". Most social scientists doing field research, as they juxtapose the search for "truth" or approximations of it—the predominate scientific value—also argue that the individuals involved should not be harmed by the research process itself. One simple and powerful way to protect subjects is to code all proper names. One cost of such a procedure is that citizens of the community, for instance, do not have any basis for directly improving school and classroom situations based on the research. Nor do individuals who are "doing a good job" have a chance for being identified and applauded or rewarded. Further, such coding moves the inquirer toward a more context-free kind of science, and toward a view that seems more congruent with one of the dimensions of an earlier positivistic paradigm. Action research, another variant of field research, does less anonymizing.

Another ethical procedure, informed consent, is often handled bureaucratically by initial discussions of the nature of the project and consent of the participants. Sometimes this involves a written sign-off by the participants. Argument can be made as to whether participants "really understand" the nature of field research at that point in time. Issues arise over the degree to which school authorities—principals, superintendents, or school boards—can give permission for research with teachers or pupils. Later, as accounts are written, who has the power to read, critique, and make suggestions? And of what force are the suggestions? Is it possible for minority accounts to be appended to or integrated into the final reports? Or is the better procedure to allow situations to be open to multiple researchers with alternative perspectives and agendas and a gradually accumulating integration of evidence and theory and recommendations? Are the alternative paradigms open to creative, reasoned, and mutually agreeable variations? Judgment is a necessity.

Finally, a brief comment about the form of metatheoretical or paradigmatic presentation made by Phillips, Lincoln, and Popkewitz seems in order. I was surprised by the informality, the commonsense quality of Phillips's presentation. I had a feeling that Clifford Geertz (1973, 1983) might have written much of it. "Blurred genres" and "common sense as a cultural system" seemed not too distant, even though these are Geertz's labels from his interpretive, "thick description" perspective. This is a major change from traditional discussions of positivism. For me, Phillips's label "postpositivism" is a misnomer, for all three alternatives are "postpositivist." In contrast, the axiomatic quality and appeals of Lincoln's presentation fostered images of the hypothetico-deductive systems of Clark Hull, the behavioristic learning psychologist of my graduate student days. I liked then the castle-like intellectual structures he was trying to build. The formalism had its own kind of clarity, but more recently the more pragmatic metatheory of Toulmin (1972) seems more congruent with my experience and more useful in the inquiry I want to do. Lincoln is solving problems other than ones that seemed important for me as I tried to think about issues in ethics. Something is amiss, for someone, such as I, who saw himself in an interpretive camp. Finally, the Popkewitz major interpretation that science as conceptualized and practiced must always be seen in its historical and institutionalized setting seems now a part of verbalized current conventional wisdom even though not of research practice. As this chapter attests, I am sympathetic to much of critical theory, but I also feel he makes me look at my experience through the medium of a foreign language.

Most significantly, it is the variability, and sometimes outspoken conflict, among proponents *within* each of these broad intellectual movements that have rendered the labels of postpositivism, constructivism, and critical theory less useful to me now than they were a half dozen years or so ago. Perhaps the revolution has occurred, and more room exists for the alternative methods and problems a number of us have wanted to work on and think about. I am left a bit surprised at my reaction. Now, I believe that the significant underlying component ideas need to be isolated and reconstructed into new patterns and new labels need to be created.

As part of this conclusion, I had wanted to develop a personal "preferred option," although not the only one that might be construed, among various elements of field research, to provide another perspective to raise regarding the interplay of ethics, field research, and alternative paradigms. Time and space do not permit. In that vignette, problems would arise from what Atkin (1973) called "practice oriented inquiry" in contrast to discipline-oriented inquiry. Grounded theory would be generated, to use Glaser and Strauss's (1967) labels. The preferred strategy would involve a variant of "action research" as Elliott (1986) and his colleagues have developed it and institutionalized in CARN (the Classroom Action Research Network). It would embody a kind of "practical reasoning" that we observed in the Milford School District (Smith, Kleine, Prunty, & Dwyer, 1986, p. 236). That introduces values and an orientation different from our traditional concerns with "description and analysis" of school programs, processes, and structures. I would seek a kind of explanation that Kaplan (1964) calls "pattern explanation," a contrast with nomothetic-deductive explanation. Finally, I would argue, in alignment with Schaefer (1967), for "the school as a center of inquiry" staffed with "scholar teachers." This scenario adds up to a large and serious agenda for the interplay of ethics, fieldwork, and the paradigm crisis, one not without its own limitations and risks but one looking for a paradigmatic alternative.

Summary

Some years ago, in language that seems "old-fashioned," Bronowski (1975, p. 6) made a case that the practice of science as "the habit of truth" implicitly demanded a set of values "which science would have had to invent afresh if man had not otherwise known them: the values which make up 'The Sense of Human Dignity.' " Because science is done by a community, "The society of scientists must be a democracy" (pp. 62-63). I see this as an extension, from epistemology to ethics, of Kaplan's (1964) autonomy of science perspective. It is central to the argument I have made.

I have tried to illustrate with some drama, the issues, broad and narrow, with an appeal to three classical field studies, *Tearoom Trade*, *Camelot*, and *Prophecy*. The nitty-gritty of particular cases seems to me to be very important for thinking about paradigms and ethics in fieldwork.

The overall argument I am making for an ethics of educational and social science inquiry is that the participants in the studies we do must also be made a part of our community, or, perhaps better stated, we need to become a part of their community. And there are larger communities beyond these. Each decision we make in our research needs to consider such larger communities. Intellectually, our "paradigms" must be large enough to include such considerations.

Further, I have argued for a modified or contextualized consequentialist ethics on the pragmatic grounds that it helps me think through the multitude of day-to-day ethical problems in doing field research. The tests along the way, suggested by Brody (1981), seem to combine some of the Kantian "deontological" ethical perspective.

Strangely perhaps, at the concrete level I was reaching for, I found, in the explication of the unique and particular characteristics of fieldwork, more ethical substance and implications than I found in the discussions of alternative paradigms. Perhaps with the seeming consensus that the earlier "logical positivism" of the Vienna Circle is now a strawman, at least at the abstract level, if not in the actions and judgments of many educational researchers, the differences, within postpositivism, within constructivism, and within critical theory are greater than the differences among them. Internal arguments abound in each camp. No purity exists. Incommensurability is not the problem. At this point in time, I believe that arguments over the concrete application of each paradigmatic position(s) are more fruitful than arguments at the more abstract level. Or perhaps a pluralism is now really possible? Maybe the paradigm revolution has come and gone, a new synthesis is in the offing, and it is time for most of us to return to inquiry on significant but specific substantive, methodological, and ethical problems, of which there are many in education and schooling?

[10]

An Ethics of Qualitative Field Studies

ERNEST R. HOUSE

Ethics are best talked about in specific, concrete situations. So, mostly agreeing with Lou Smith's reflections and using his examples, I want to suggest a few succinct principles of ethics for qualitative field studies. The reason one must talk about particulars in ethical cases is that there are a thousand factors that can make a difference in particular situations, this complexity of the world being one of the primary reasons we have resorted to qualitative studies to begin with. This same worldly complexity obtains for ethical considerations. However, just because we cannot prescribe normative action for all situations does not mean there are not certain considerations and principles that arise time and time again, even though their resolution may be different each time, depending upon circumstances.

I want to advance three basic principles—the principles of mutual respect, of noncoercion and nonmanipulation, and of support for democratic values and institutions. These by no means exhaust the potentially relevant moral principles but I believe they cover a vast number of the cases we encounter. The mutual respect principle is well stated by John Rawls in *A Theory of Justice* (1971, pp. 337-338):

> Mutual respect is shown in several ways: in our willingness to see the situation of others from their point of view, from the perspective of their conception of the good, and in our being prepared to give reasons for our actions whenever the interests of others are materially affected. . . . Thus to respect another as a moral person is to try to understand his aims

AUTHOR'S NOTE: Sandra Mathison, Margaret Eisenhart, and Kenneth Howe contributed useful comments to earlier drafts of this chapter.

and interests from his standpoint and to present him with considerations
that enable him to accept the constraints on his conduct.

This is how we should treat participants in our studies as well as each
other.

The people we deal with are not always so well treated by us. We
do not always respect their reasons for doing things enough to find
out what those reasons are. Respecting their reasons does not mean
that we agree with them but that we note, record, and study what their
reasons for their actions are, and seriously consider the strong possibility that people have good reasons for doing what they do, even
when they are wrong. I might also add that in Rawls's theory, self-
esteem is a vital part of people's conception of their own good. I
endorse this notion and assert that we should not be doing anything
knowingly to damage anyone's self-esteem. For example, in my study
of Jesse Jackson's PUSH-Excel program, I went through my interviews line by line and removed quotes from people that might make
them look foolish or put them in a bad light, and that were not critical
to the happenings in the book—even for people I did not like or agree
with (House, 1988). Most of these damaging quotations were easy to
remove without detracting from the main themes of the book.[1]

Lack of respect for people in the study is usually reflected in the
narrative of the work. The reader can detect condescension in the
author's attitude and a feeling of superiority, often revealed in irony.
It is one thing to use these techniques with one's colleagues, who can
argue back, and quite another to employ these literary devices against
the defenseless. I find this lack of respect evident even in highly
regarded works. For example, there are passages in Whyte's (1955)
Street Corner Society that reflect an attitude of superiority to the Italian
community he studied, while, on the other hand, Liebow's (1967)
Tally's Corner, a study of desperately indigent Black men, is uniformly
respectful of the shattered lives these men lead and never seems to
indulge itself in this fashion. A reader might find slippage in my own
work in this regard, irony being difficult for some of us to resist. Of
course, it is also possible to have irony without disrespect.

As to one of Smith's primary examples, Humphreys' (1975) *Tearoom
Trade*, although I have not read the full study, I suspect that closely
observing the intimate sex acts of others without their knowledge
displays a lack of respect for those people. One would have to read
the entire study to see exactly what the author did, what he said, and

how he reported it to reach a conclusive judgment. Whether he violated the self-respect and self-esteem of the people he observed depends on the details of the study, as is so often the case.

The second ethical principle is that of noncoercion and non-manipulation.[2] Coercion, the application of force or threats to secure compliance, is clearly forbidden. Coercion is not a common problem in field studies, although I may be wrong about this. I confess to an uneasy feeling that somewhere out there with the Salvadoran death squads is an American sociologist collecting data. Whether compliance is gained through legitimate authority rather than through illegitimate access is sometimes difficult to determine for the researcher as well as for the reader. Do people cooperate because they want to or because their boss told them they must? Sometimes the line is difficult to draw.

Nonmanipulation is even more difficult to determine. I take both coercion and manipulation to be relevant when people are cooperating in a study contrary to their own interests. That is, there is a conflict of interests such that participants may be damaging themselves through cooperation and hence should not be forced to comply. Manipulation is more insidious than coercion because participants do not realize that their interests are at risk. Sometimes the researcher convinces participants to cooperate when the researcher knows they may be in jeopardy, or people believe that cooperation is in their best interests but are quite mistaken (as indeed the researcher may be).

Presumably, the practice of informing participants what the study is about and securing explicit written cooperation, as required by our human subjects procedures, is directed at informing people so they cannot be manipulated. However admirable such procedures may be, the acquiescence of participants is not enough to protect their interests. Participants simply may not know that they might be damaged by the study. James Agee and Walker Evans's (1941) classic book *Let Us Now Praise Famous Men* is an example. Journalists Agee and Evans lived with sharecropper families in Alabama in the summer of 1936, recording the poverty of their lives in meticulous detail based upon their friendship with the sharecroppers, who liked the journalists very much. The tenant families took them in and had no idea what Agee and Evans were up to. While Agee lured the family out of the house, Evans took photographs of their extremely poor personal possessions, unknown to their hosts. These stark photographs, and Agee's extremely intimate narratives about these families, naming them by name, were published in 1941. The first these impoverished families knew about the book was after publication when some outsider mentioned it to them.

Although Agee and Evan's goal was admirable—to display the extreme poverty of these southern sharecroppers families so that the government might do something about it—and although both the photos and the narrative are so artful as to constitute a literary classic, I believe that this study violates the principle of nonmanipulation. And a recent television documentary interviewing the family members still alive 50 years after the study revealed that some of these people felt themselves betrayed as well. Even though well intentioned and quite respectful of the families themselves, and hence not violating the principle of mutual respect, I believe this study was unethical in its manipulation.

There is no question about the manipulation involved in Festinger, Riecken, and Shachter's (1956/1964) *When Prophecy Fails.* The researchers invented "visions" to present to the religious cult being studied in order to gain acceptance, and these visions influenced the events that followed. As Smith noted, the methodological appendix to the book reveals not the slightest concern by the researchers that their behavior was unethical or immoral, not the slightest hint. The researchers' sole concern was that their manipulation might have damaged the findings of the study by influencing events. *When Prophecy Fails* violates not only the principle of nonmanipulation but the principle of mutual respect as well. The researchers clearly had no respect for these religious cultists.

The third and most contentious ethical principle is the duty to uphold democratic values and institutions.[3] We live in a democratic society and have an obligation to support the democratic values of that society. Foremost among these are equality and liberty. Project Camelot (Horowitz, 1974), in studying how central governments might suppress popular revolts, violated this principle—and the principles of mutual respect, noncoercion, and nonmanipulation as well, a triple play of unethical conduct. Most of us would agree that we should support democratic institutions and values while operating in this society, but the case is less clear for other societies; I will not attempt to defend this principle outside the democracies. Nonetheless, I note in passing that social science is not and cannot be value free in any society, and supporting democratic values that work against oppression and subjugation extends across national boundaries. Bride-burning seems to me to be wrong no matter how disappointed the groom is in the dowry settlement.

The lack of democratic values is evident not only in individual studies but in the studies taken as a whole. Consider all the studies we have discussed—Project Camelot, *Tearoom Trade, When Prophecy Fails, Street Corner Society, Tally's Corner,* and *Let Us Now Praise Famous Men.* All these studies are of marginal, indigent, deviant, lower-socioeconomic groups—those without power. Are these simply people who cannot defend themselves against being studied? Where are the ethnographies of corporate boardrooms, high government officials, upper-class life? What would happen if researchers manufactured stories to gain entry to a corporate boardroom? In general, we seem to study those low in the power structure. Only their behavior is subject to scrutiny, and, if information is power, these studies act against the powerless and the marginal. That this strong bias should pass without notice is an indication of the tenuous place social justice holds in our practice. When we can investigate all levels of power equally, we shall have achieved a much stronger ethical practice.

All the ethical principles delineated are for individuals and are what Rawls calls natural duties, duties that are required for ethical behavior regardless of what else one does and regardless of social institutions.[4] In addition to natural duties, there are also obligations that one incurs by voluntarily entering into cooperative enterprises with others. For example, if one agrees to act as an evaluator, one incurs the obligation of fairness. Evaluation is a particular social arrangement that one enters voluntarily, and thus one incurs an obligation to be fair, which usually means living up to the terms of an explicit contract or agreement. I have discussed the principle of fairness in detail elsewhere and note that, if one conducts evaluations, one must be fair in addition to meeting the other principles (House, 1980).

There are also principles of justice that apply to social institutions rather than to individuals, but these are not the topic of our discussion. If one follows the ethical principles explicated to their logical conclusion, then one might be led to "action research," as Smith has been, or as he puts it, with the researcher becoming part of the community of the participants in the study. Becoming part of the community does not solve all ethical problems, however. What if that community is oppressive, unjust, and unfair?

Finally, what do the three paradigmatic perspectives presented earlier have to contribute to ethical consideration in our field? None of the three perspectives delineated—postpositivism, constructivism, or critical theory—is adequate by itself. Nor do these three perspectives exhaust the possibilities for a metatheoretic basis for our field. However, rather than criticize the shortcomings of each of these approaches, I prefer to focus on the positive contribution each offers. First, an ethics of qualitative field studies should focus on the words, ideals, and aims of the participants in the study, as the principle of mutual respect suggests. Lincoln's "constructivist" perspective provides such a focus. Second, an ethics of field studies should attend to the social and historical context of the study as critiqued by the values of democracy and justice. And this is what critical theory as espoused by Popkewitz does. Finally, an ethics of qualitative field study should be realist and nonrelativist, as Phillips's postpositivism chapter suggests. There is a right and a wrong, a true and a false.

In summary, an ethics of qualitative field study should be based upon a realist, nonrelativist theory that focuses upon the words, actions, and deeds of the participants and attends to the justice and democratic character of social institutions as those institutions have shaped and have been shaped historically. If this sounds too much like "business as usual," then let me say that I would judge a substantial proportion of our studies to be deficient on the basis of at least one of these ethical principles.

Notes

1. Margaret Eisenhart (personal communication) notes that removing such material is not always so easy and that sometimes such material is central to the main argument; true enough. One way of dealing with this is through giving participants the right to censure material about themselves, though this is a bit further than I would go. See Simons (1987) for a recent explication of this approach.

2. Ken Howe (personal communication) notes that noncoercion and nonmanipulation might well be regarded as derived from the mutual respect principle. I agree but state these as separate principles to stress their importance.

3. Although support of these values and institutions seems bland on the surface, discussing these values in detail in actual studies quickly results in controversy. Did one interview the dissidents in the setting? Where are the interests and opinions of the disadvantaged represented? Did the study help the powerful more than the powerless?

4. There are other natural duties, such as mutual aid, but I think these are less relevant to our studies. Sandra Mathison (personal communication) has suggested the principle of reciprocity of benefit. This principle requires that, if the researcher benefits from the study, and the researcher almost always does one way or another, then the participants should benefit from their participation as well, though not necessarily in the same fashion as the researchers. For example, one of the family members from *Let Us Now Praise Famous Men* asked why the families, because they were so poor, did not share in royalties from the book. A little money would have meant a lot to them. For all their social concern, Agee and Evans did not see fit to share their profits. I believe Mathison is correct about this principle but it is so far advanced beyond our current ethical thinking that I do not foresee its application in the near future. The distinction is this: I would call violations of the principles of mutual respect, noncoercion, and nonmanipulation as well as of the support of democratic institutions unethical behavior. But I would not label as unethical a situation in which the participants were not benefited. This judgment indicates where we stand in our current ethical sensibilities. We expect and are allowed to expect to benefit from our study of others without their benefiting as well.

[11]

Discussion on Ethics

THOMAS B. GREGORY

Indiana University

The two ethics sessions of the conference on which this book is based were full of questions, some sweeping, some intensely personal, some easily answered, some seemingly unanswerable. The sessions were also full of dilemmas, the many ways we personally confront the ethics of what we do in our work. And, of course, there were the inevitable themes, the recurring ideas that affect many elements of the ethical framework in which we function.

How does one summarize the six hours of rich discussion of ethical issues that have occurred these past two days? One could attempt it by listing the 20 or 30 questions that dotted our discussions, very few of which had ready answers, questions like: Who owns the data? You? Your funding source? Your institution? Or those you study? Is informed consent really informed? When does ethnography become spying? Should we study illegal behavior, perhaps even encourage it by participating in it in tangential ways? Should we commit illegal acts to gain access to data or sources? Should we commit deception to do so? Should we knowingly damage individuals, for example, by revealing the racist practices of one classroom teacher, for the betterment of thousands of kids who endure institutional racism? Or is the bottom line honoring the dignity of the individual?

One also could try to convey the sense of our discussions by relating some of the personal dilemmas that have confronted members of our group. When we study a group like 13- and 14-year-old mothers—children who are having children—how should we share information with them, information about contraception or about other means of affirming life aside from giving birth to it? Do we initiate discussions of these issues with these young women because *we* value them or only when we are asked? As we grow in facility as individual researchers with ever-heightening consciousnesses, how do we handle our earlier ethical transgressions? How do we help a colleague see that her decision to publish an apologia for a misstep in a study conducted 10 years earlier is an act of academic courage, not one that should make her feel foolish?

Another way to capture the spirit of these discussions would be to summarize some broad themes that wove their way through them, themes like the struggle between power and vulnerability or the conflicts we confront between deceit and openness.

But we also talked of solutions. Certainly one should mention a few of these. We talked about building a code of ethics. Most of us thought the process of doing so would be useful. Some saw a code as a valuable protection against the unethical practices our funding sources, governmental agencies, our institutions, and even our colleagues sometimes require of us. We talked about the need not only to clarify our ethics but to raise our collective consciousness; the process of developing a code would be useful in that way too. But there was also a concern voiced that ethics occur in contexts of place and time. Could a code become procrustean?

Ernie House offered three canons—he called them ethical principles—two of which the group seemed uniformly comfortable with. The first centers on mutual respect, the age-old idea of doing unto others as you would have them do unto you. The second principle requires that we eliminate coercion and manipulation from our work, that the researcher and the researched maintain a continuing dialogue and negotiation. There should be a reciprocity of benefit in every study. When a researcher benefits, the participants should too.

GOODNESS CRITERIA

[12]

Alternative Research Paradigms and the Problem of Criteria

JOHN K. SMITH

In a paper presented for the Aquinas Lecture at Marquette University, Chisholm (1973, p. 1) noted that "the problem of the criterion seems to me to be one of the most important and one of the most difficult of all the problems of philosophy." I must note that the problem of criteria seems to me one of the most difficult and important problems facing social and educational research. He added that "I am tempted to say that one has not begun to philosophize until one has faced this problem and has recognized how unappealing, in the end, each of the possible solutions is" (p. 1). I must add that one has not seriously thought about the nature of social and educational inquiry until one has confronted the criteria issue—especially given the recent interest in alternative research paradigms.

Where I part company with Chisholm (1977, p. 134) is over the "unappealingness" of the various solutions and his concern that "the general problem of the criterion has created impasses in almost every branch of knowledge." For me, the "unappealingness" of any solution and whether impasses are a problem depend greatly on the kind of solution one hopes is possible—if, that is, there actually is a problem here in need of a solution.

The Origin and Nature of the Criteria Problem

Chisholm's (1973, p. 3) paraphrase of Montaigne (*Essays*) concisely summarizes the nature of the criteria problem:

> To know whether things really are as they seem to be, we must have a *procedure* for distinguishing appearances that are true from appearances that are false. But to know whether our procedure is a good procedure, we have to know whether it really *succeeds* in distinguishing appearances that are true from appearances that are false. And we cannot know whether it does really succeed unless we already know which appearances are *true* and which ones are *false*. And so we are caught in a circle.

For philosophers this circle invokes the standard epistemological questions: "What can we really know about the world?" (Chisholm, 1973, p. 4). How can we distinguish genuine knowledge from false claims to knowledge? For researchers, the same problem is generally expressed somewhat differently: What can we do so that our research will yield an accurate (objective) as opposed to a distorted (biased) depiction of reality? What criteria can we apply to distinguish valid from invalid research? These questions can be rephrased with reference to different inquiry paradigms:

> Is it possible to devise a set of goodness criteria that might apply to an inquiry regardless of the paradigm within which it was conducted? Or is it the case ... that goodness criteria are themselves generated from and legitimated by the self-same assumptions that undergird each inquiry paradigm, and hence are unique to each paradigm? (Guba, 1988, p. 16)

Both questions also ask about the kind of evidence needed to justify judgments of validity and invalidity. However, one other question is important: Are these the only alternatives or is there something in this discussion of different paradigms that means there actually is no problem (at least if *problem* is understood in an epistemological sense) in need of solution?

The Empiricist Solution and What Went Wrong

Until recently there appeared to be an acceptable solution to the criteria problem. Valid research was distinguished from invalid research in terms of the extent to which the proper procedures were properly applied. According to Bauman (1978, pp. 15-16), the founders of modern social science believed that

> social facts are "things" like all others, i.e., that they exist in their own right as real entities "out there," outside the realm of individual experience. They naturally concluded, first, that one can study social realities without necessarily looking at the process of their social production and, second, that whoever does this study with proper method and diligence will certainly arrive at the same results . . . they regarded true knowledge as, above all (if not solely), the question of method and of its systematic application.

Exactly what certain procedures were supposed to do for inquiry, and why genuine knowledge was linked to methodology, can be expressed in various ways. One common possibility is in terms of objectivity and subjectivity. By the end of the last century, the idea that the world of acts must be logically and distinctly separate from the world of values became firmly implanted (see Brecht, 1959). This separation led researchers to think of themselves as similarly divided into factual (cognitive) and evaluative (normative) sides. Thus, as researchers used their cognitive sides to search for an objective depiction of reality, they had to guard against the distorting influences of their own subjectivity. How then could research be immunized from an infection by personal values? The proper procedures, properly applied, in that they were thought neutral or unbeholden to any particular philosophical perspective, were the answer. As Kerlinger (1979, p. 264) put it, "the procedures of science are objective—and not the scientists. Scientists, like all men and women, are opinionated, dogmatic, ideological. . . . That is the very reason for insisting on procedural objectivity; to get the whole business outside of ourselves."

For empiricism a judgment about the quality of research was in effect a judgment about methodology; valid studies were procedurally correct, inept studies were procedurally flawed. This did not mean that every properly done study automatically made an important contribution to knowledge because the results still could be judged trivial and unimportant. However, it did mean that the improperly done study could not make, happenstance aside, a serious contribution to knowledge. For empiricism the proper methodology was the necessary, although not sufficient, condition for good research.

The demise of empiricism means that methodology is no longer an acceptable solution to the criteria problem. Because many of the major criticisms of empiricism appear in the chapters by Lincoln, Phillips, and Popkewitz (all this volume), only one point, directly pertinent to the supposed neutrality of methodology, need be noted.

Many people have argued effectively that methodology is not neutral. Among the more important of these critiques are Taylor's (1985) concern over the lack of univocity of statistical transformation procedures, Gadamer's (1975) point that a particular method only reveals the truth inherent in that method, MacKenzie's (1981) historical assessment of the social basis of the development of statistics, MacIntyre's (1973) discussion of the epistemological status of laypeople and that of professional social scientists, Hesse's (1980) concern that social inquiry has not achieved the goal of increasingly successful prediction and control, and Putnam's (1981) analysis of the nature of Bayesian priors as subjective degrees of belief. All of these arguments lead to the conclusion that "the hope for a formal method, capable of being isolated from actual human judgment about the content of science (that is, about the nature of the world), and from human values seems to have evaporated" (Putnam, 1981, p. 192).

Alternative Paradigms and Criteria

Obviously the discussion of alternative perspectives on inquiry has serious implications for the problem of criteria. What is equally obvious, as is apparent in what follows, is that the exact nature of these implications is not at all obvious.

Postempiricism or Postpositivism

Postempiricists have severely criticized almost every tenet of traditional empiricism (see Manicas, 1987, pp. 243-265). These criticisms pose a major problem for issues such as how to judge the validity of research and how to decide when to accept one theory in place of another. There are four related points about postempiricism that are crucial to the way it addresses the problem of criteria.

In that postempiricists argue there is no Archimedean point or absolute foundation for knowledge, they accept a nonfoundationalist epistemology. This does not mean, however, that we are condemned to a relativism of "anything goes." There are still standards, non-foundationalism notwithstanding, to prevent a "descent" to this unacceptable level. Thus any discussion of criteria from a postempiricist perspective must find a *via media* between "no absolute foundation for knowledge" and "not every knowledge claim is equally well warranted."

Second, there is a distinction made between what people believe to be true and what really is true. Inquiry can determine what people believe and how they have come to hold these beliefs. Inquirers can be right or wrong about these things; they can depict the beliefs of others and the origins of their beliefs either accurately or inaccurately. However, to determine that people believe certain things are true does not mean that others, including inquirers, must accept these beliefs as true. Examples from the physical world, such as "the belief the world is flat versus the reality that it is not," are often used to illustrate this distinction between believed true and really true.

This distinction is crucial to the postempiricist definitions of objectivity and truth. *Objectivity* is the regulative ideal that guides all inquiry, and, in the absence of this ideal, there could be no *inquiry* in any serious sense of the term. This ideal is in large measure directed at how researchers undertake and carry out their research in that it requires them to be precise, unbiased, open, honest, receptive to criticism, and so on. *Truth*, although often not defined directly by postempiricists, appears to be characterized in terms of "some form of correspondence with reality" (Trigg, 1985, p. 109). A true statement, in other words, is most often thought of as one that accurately depicts an independently existing reality.

Third, postempiricists are realists. Realism can be defined as "the view that entities exist independently of being perceived, or independently of our theories about them" (Phillips, 1987b, p. 205). This realism gives substance to both the distinction between "believed true" and "really true" and the definitions of *objectivity* and *truth*. Realism is essential for postempiricism because it poses "at least in principle, a standard by which all human societies and their beliefs can be judged: they can all have beliefs abut the world which turn out to be mistaken" (Trigg, 1985, p. 22). Without an independent reality as an external referent for knowledge, everything would turn on the mere fact of belief itself and not on "the what" that is believed in. A denial of realism makes it very difficult to understand what is meant by the terms *mistake* and *error*. Moreover, this denial makes it virtually impossible to imagine how competing claims to knowledge could be adjudicated.

Finally, the notion of the properly done study is central to post-empiricists and they hold it is possible to distinguish unbiased, open, honest, and precise research from that which is not. These standards for judging the quality of inquiry are somewhat loose and imprecise—especially when compared with the methodological rules of traditional empiricism. Yet, this imprecision notwithstanding, it is possible to determine the extent to which researchers have acted appropriately in carrying out their research. Those who have been open, honest, and unbiased, or at least more so than others, have made an undistorted or at least less distorted contact with reality and their research must be judged accordingly. It is in this sense that the research process—nonfoundationalism notwithstanding—can be protected from a relativism of anything goes. There are criteria, based on the regulative ideal of objectivity, for sorting out valid from invalid research.

What can one say about this approach to criteria? Certainly the point that researchers must be honest, open, and precise makes sense. It also appears reasonable to conclude that, if researchers adhere to these standards in a systematic, controlled, and self-conscious manner, they can accomplish a number of related goals: (a) The threat of relativism is blunted; (b) disagreements can be resolved, at least potentially and in principle if not immediately in practice, via an assessment of who has exercised the greatest care, precision, and honesty in the research; and (c) in that researchers are more systematic and self-conscious than other thinkers, their knowledge is "superior" or privileged relative to everyday commonsense knowledge.

As long as this line of thinking is applied to the observable, physical world in particular, it appears to be quite in order. The physical world does seem to have a certain independence, permanence, and "coerciveness" about it that makes it a solid referent point for judgments about objectivity, truth, and validity. There is clearly little mileage to be made by advancing the claims that the belief that the world is flat has an effect on the actual shape of the earth and that, if two inquirers disagree over the shape of the earth, further open and honest inquiry will not help resolve this dispute. However, this perspective on criteria is much more complex and problematic when it comes to the interpretation of the meanings, purposes, and interpretations people give to their own actions, the actions of others, and to events in the world around them.

Put differently, it is one thing to validate beliefs in terms of the extent to which they accurately depict an independently existing reality; it is another thing to determine that one has correctly interpreted the interpretations of others. As Larmore (1986, p. 162) puts it, especially from a postempiricist perspective, "the determination of a text's meaning must always remain the *proximate* goal of interpretation, a distinct project logically (if not temporally) prior to its use in pursuit of different *ulterior* goals, such as evaluating the truth of what it says." Thus postempiricists must develop their version of criteria in light of those situations when inquirers have presented different interpretations of the beliefs of others—for example, Leach (1969) and Spiro (1966) over the beliefs about conception of the Tully River Blacks (see Turner, 1980), Redfield (1941) and Lewis (1930) as to the nature of life in Tepoztlán (see Miner, 1952), and Mead (1961) and Freeman (1983) over who really understood the Samoans (see Patience & Smith, 1986; Rappaport, 1986).

In the case of the Tully River Blacks, the disagreement was over what these Australian aborigines believed about human reproduction. The extent to which their beliefs about conception matched how conception really occurs was a secondary issue or only the backdrop for the discussion. When framed in this way, the problem for postempiricists is to make good on the claim that they can know, at least in principle if not necessarily at any given moment in practice, who has correctly depicted the beliefs of others. This is where the idea of the properly done study becomes important (as is evident in the Mead/Freeman situation in that the latter criticized the former for her methodological failings). Presumably, an assessment of who exercised the most care and precision (bolstered by further properly done inquiry if necessary) should greatly assist in the judgment as to who has correctly interpreted the interpretation of the Tully River Blacks (allowing, of course, for the possibility that parts of both interpretations are correct or that both are incorrect).

The realism of postempiricism makes what the Tully River Blacks *really believe* the referent point for judgments about accuracy of depiction. This idea of the author's intention or meaning as the independent, external to the inquirer, referent point is essential if terms like *correct* and *objective* are to have any serious meaning, that is, a meaning that goes beyond merely the hope that a time- and place-conditioned agreement might be possible.

To redeem this approach to the interpretation of interpretations requires a move on the order of Hirsch's (1967) distinction between meaning and significance in his validation or objectivist version of hermeneutics. Hirsch (see also Betti, 1980; Larmore, 1986; Pannanberg, 1986) argues that what is actually meant by a written passage or by a verbal or physical expression stands separate from the significance that passage or expression has for the interpreter. The assessment of meaning can be undertaken in line with Popper's (1968a) ideas about falsification. The interpreter hypothesizes as to an author's meaning and is entitled to hold on to a hypothesis until such time as there is evidence to refute it (see Hirsch, 1967, pp. 165-207).

Meaning is thus a determinate entity that can be objectively depicted, whereas *significance* will vary according to the interests and purposes of any given interpreter. This distinction poses meaning as the independently existing, external referent point against which to assess whether an interpretation is right or wrong. And the author's meaning is susceptible to accurate depiction, at least in principle, via the properly done study. If one accepts this position, it makes a good deal of sense to talk about objectivity in postempiricist terms, to hold that there are standards to prevent relativism, to claim that there are reasonably clear criteria for judging inquiry, and so on.

It is not surprising that important questions can be raised about this meaning-significance split. For example, Gadamer (1975) argues that validation hermeneutics simply revives the unacceptable subject-object dualism of the empiricist theory of knowledge and, in doing so, reawakens the prospect of presuppositionless knowledge, edges back toward the fact-value dichotomy, implies that inquirers can dispense with their own values, interests, and purposes in order to objectively grasp meanings, and so on. As is discussed in greater detail in the next section, Gadamer finds all of this misguided because the idea of unprejudiced understanding is an inadequate understanding of the fundamental nature of understanding.

In any event, if one accepts Hirsch's (1967) position, it is possible that postempiricism has achieved an acceptable solution, at least conceptually, to the criteria problem. There are standards and a referent point against which to judge inquiry, resolve interpretive disputes, and prevent relativism. Although there is nothing mechanical about the situation—Hirsch (1967, pp. 202-203) cautions that these standards are always provisional—there is a way to distinguish valid from invalid research.

Constructivism

In that various ideas important to postempiricism are likewise important to constructivism, it may seem that the two perspectives have much in common. This is really not the case because constructivists more aggressively interpret these ideas and thereby address the problem of criteria much differently. There are at least three basic elements of constructivism that must be briefly noted prior to discussing these implications.

Constructivists clearly are nonfoundationalists in that they decisively reject the idea that certitude is possible. However, in contrast to postempiricists, constructivists have pushed their nonfoundationalism onto the terrain of relativism. A major reason for this difference resides in the different definition each gives to *relativism*. Rorty (1985, pp. 5-6) says there are three views associated with this term:

> The first is the view that every belief is as good as every other. The second is the view that "true" is an equivocal term, having as many meanings as there are procedures of justification. The third is the view that there is nothing to be said about either truth or rationality apart from descriptions of the familiar procedures of justification which a given society— ours—uses in one or another area of inquiry.

Postempiricists, especially as they criticize other paradigms, favor the first definition. Contructivism, given its interactive and subjectivist thrust, has adopted generally the third definition.

Constructivism is also nonrealist. Social reality is not an independent reality but is a socially, and very often multiply, constructed reality: The reality of meanings, intentions, and purposes is found in the interpretation or is established by the interpretation. Any hint of a subject-object dualism is abandoned thereby in favor of an interaction between the investigator and investigated (subject-subject relationship). The values and purposes of the interpreter are thought to influence the interpretation in a much stronger way than is acceptable to postempiricists. Thus, for constructivism, there is no independently existing reality of meanings that is susceptible to objective depiction, and there is no epistemological sense to be made of the dichotomy between meaning and significance.

Finally, both postempiricism and constructivism recognize the importance of hermeneutics. However, each perspective conceptualizes hermeneutics in markedly different ways. Postempiricism, as noted, adopts an objectivist version, with a distinction between meaning and significance; constructivism accepts a philosophical version, with a collapse of the distinction between understanding and interpretation.

For Gadamer (1975), those who see hermeneutics as a method for the objective understanding of meaning, apart from significance, make a number of fundamental mistakes. First, this objectivism perpetuates an unacceptable subject-object dualism. This dualism is an illusion because "finite, historical man always sees and understands from his standpoint in time and place; he cannot, says Gadamer, stand above the relativity of history and procure 'objectivity valid knowledge' " (Palmer, 1969, p. 178).

Gadamer (1975) develops his argument with an analysis of our relationship to works of art. To understand art the interpreter must share in a work of art in the sense that, just as the interpreter questions the work, the work questions the interpreter. The interpreter is not "detached from the work of art but is someone upon whom the work of art makes a claim. The spectator, then, is present to the work of art in the sense that he or she participates in it" (Bernstein, 1983, p. 123). Thus "the meaning of what we seek to understand comes into being only through the happening of understanding" (p. 146).

This point that art achieves presentation only through the interpreter must be extended to all understanding. Understanding is not the accurate depiction of the meaning of an expression through the properly done study because, on the contrary, "understanding must be conceived as a part of the process of the coming into being of meaning, in which the significance of all statements—those of art and those of everything else that has been transmitted—is formed and made complete" (Gadamer, 1975, p. 146).

The objectivists' second major mistake is that they remain influenced, even if not completely so, by the idea that genuine knowledge is methodologically self-conscious knowledge. For constructivism, because method only reveals what was already implicit in the method, new knowledge is not the result of the supposedly methodologically proper depiction of independently existing meanings. Rather, knowledge is the result of a dialogical process between the self-understanding person and that which is encountered—whether a text, a work of art, or the meaningful expressions of another person.

Finally, there can be no such thing as the "right" interpretation. For philosophical hermeneutics, interpretations can only be referenced to the interpreter in the sense that they result from a dialogue between the interpreter and that which is interpreted. Because meaning can only be arrived at dialogically, *correct* and *right* are not terms of accurate depiction but are expressions of agreement and commendation. Thus, for Spiro to say Leach got it wrong (or vice versa) cannot be cast as a failure of accurate depiction, it is an expression of a disagreement of interpretation based on different interests, values, and purposes.

Because constructivism finds no determinate way to justify knowledge and has accepted relativism, what does this mean for the issue of criteria? These implications can be examined in terms of Feyerabend's (1981, p. 8) ideas about different traditions and explanation by lists. He distinguishes between two major traditions as follows:

> Theoretical traditions try to replace the quasi-intuitive and only partly standardized procedures of their members by abstract models with abstract concepts and abstract relations between them and they make maximal use of these relations in their arguments. One believes that the inventions of the human mind will eventually replace the work of all our known and unknown, explicit and hidden, adaptive faculties, emotions and commonsense included, so that the whole work of creation can be built up anew, on the basis of human reason alone. . . . Defenders of *empirical traditions* deny the universal usefulness of such a procedure; they assert that there are areas where theoretical traditions *can* but *should not* be introduced for empirical as well as moral reasons.

Within theoretical traditions, explanations require abstract standards and the corresponding methodological rules; within empirical traditions (or practical traditions), explanations are based on lists. An example of this difference can be found in a comparison of introductory quantitative and qualitative research textbooks. For the former, as in the book by Ary, Jacobs, and Razavieh (1985), the discussion is organized around abstract principles and various logically derived procedures; for the latter, as in the Hammersley and Atkinson (1983) book on ethnography, topics from access and entry to field-note analysis are discussed in terms of exemplars. The former expresses a theoretical tradition of inquiry as rule bound, the latter reflects a practical tradition of inquiry by making lists.

There has been a constant desire to transform practical traditions into theoretical traditions in all areas, including that of social and educational inquiry. A practical tradition is often seen as the initial move on the road to a more secure form of inquiry (hence the old idea that interpretive inquiry generates hypotheses that must be more rigorously tested by empiricist techniques). For constructivists this is incorrect for the tradition of social inquiry because "a list is not a mistaken first step on the way to a more appropriate definition: it is the only adequate form of knowledge" (Feyerabend, 1981, p. 5).

Lists are always open-ended; they can be added to and subtracted from without serious change in the idea represented by the list. The limits for modification derive from the actual use of that list—this a practical matter that cannot be reduced to formulas or rules. As Feyerabend (1981, p. 5) notes, "There are of course limits to enrichment and change, but these limits are implicit in the use of the list; they cannot be captured in a formula; tact and not logic determine the content of a concept and the permissible changes." Moreover, one becomes part of a practical tradition not by learning rules and procedures but by immersion or by playing around with the lists and with exemplars.

These ideas of traditions and lists are central to the constructivist position on criteria. Over the last few years constructivists have discussed the process and results of inquiry in terms of lists (see, for example, the discussions of axiomatic criteria, action criteria, and so on by Guba & Lincoln, 1981, 1989; Lincoln & Guba, 1985, 1986a, 1986c). Whereas initially these lists were often thought of as the first steps on the road to a more definitive criteria, recently they have been recognized for what there actually are—an open-ended, always evolving, enumeration of possibilities that can be constantly modified through practice.

The idea of criteria as an open-ended list is related to what has been called the "interpretative turn" in social inquiry. This "turn" asks researchers to "recognize that theory-choice is a judgmental activity requiring imagination, interpretation, the weighing of alternatives, and the application of criteria that are essentially open" (Bernstein, 1983, p. 56). Thus constructivism has shifted away from "a model of rationality that searches for determinate rules which can serve as necessary and sufficient conditions, to a model of practical rationality that emphasizes the role of *exemplars* and judgmental interpretation" (p. 57).

These ideas have distinct implications for resolving interpretive differences. To make a case for an interpretation is to tell "a story with a point" (Feyerabend, 1981, p. 6), and learning to tell stories is "part of learning to get along with people" (p. 6). To the extent constructivism eschews the abstraction of the completely rational argument directed at the completely rational person, the case one makes for an interpretation—the attempts to convince another—must take into account the particular interests and purposes of the other. Just as criteria are open-ended and tested and modified through practical use, the resolution of differences among interpreters is a practical, dialogical matter.

This practical and dialogical approach to judging inquiry means that researchers must pay attention to the norms that guide the social practice of dialog and negotiation. If judgments of good research versus bad research are dialogical, then the social interaction character of these dialogs are the crucial factor. In this sense constructivism has edged quite close to the idea that the "value of cooperative human inquiry has only an ethical case, not an epistemological or metaphysical one" (Rorty, 1985, p. 6). At the core of constructivism is the regulative ideal of solidarity rather than objectivity.

As might well be expected, this position on criteria has been criticized from various directions. Two examples of these criticism must be briefly noted. For postempiricists, constructivists are not even talking about *criteria*, or for that matter *research* itself, in any serious sense of the terms. The problem is that constructivists have pushed nonfoundationalism so far that they are enmeshed in a completely unacceptable relativism—one that reduces knowledge to the level of merely belief, opinion, and/or taste. For critical theorists, as discussed in more detail in the next section, constructivism is inherently conservative in that it is unable to utilize theoretical knowledge for emancipation and empowerment. The philosophical hermeneutics of constructivism is unable to advance an objective understanding of distorted communication and ideological distortion.

Critical Theory

Although a number of the ideas common to the other two perspectives are important to critical theory, they are interpreted differently in most instances. This perspective thereby poses different considerations for the issue of criteria. At least three major points must be noted in order to illuminate these considerations.

The critical perspective holds that knowledge must be situated historically and cannot be a matter of universal and timeless abstract and abstractly related principals (nonfoundationalism). Although this does not lead to a relativism of anything goes, it does mean that knowledge, and the justifications given for knowledge claims, must be "historized." This point poses at least two further implications. First, concepts such as rigor and relevance have no fixed or timeless meaning because they cannot be delineated apart from the actual historically constrained practices of inquiry. What is known and how knowledge is obtained are mutually influencing and intertwined within a historical context. Second, what is judged as adequate knowledge is not necessarily knowledge that is supposedly cumulative or that supposedly increasingly clarifies what is known.

The second major point involves the modified realism of critical theory. Critical theory acknowledges that there are real objects out there in the world, but the qualifier *modified* means one must fully recognize that the words used to denote objects must be placed within different symbolic fields, and, accordingly, reality can take on different meanings. Although this point is in one sense similar to the realism of postempiricism and the idea of no theory-free knowledge, in another sense it is different because discourse practices are seen as more strongly constitutive of the world.

This modified realism is important for the definitions critical theory gives to *objective* and *subjective*. *Objective* is not referenced simply or directly to an external, independently existing reality but is a way to consider the dynamic and changing, historically and socially sedimented, patterns that influence our daily lives. These patterns are objective, however, in the very sense that they have been historically and socially formed through human struggles. *Subjective*, on the other hand, directs attention to what is inside people—the interests and purposes that allow them to make sense of their day-to-day lives.

These definitions lead critical theorists to reject the objectivist pretensions of both quantitative analysis and grounded theory. In the first instance, because analytical procedures are intimately tied to an inquirer's historically situated disposition toward the world, they cannot have any special epistemological privilege. In the second instance, a similar criticism is made of the idea that field methods allow an inquirer to penetrate through to the essences of everyday words, language, meanings, and intentions. The latter approach makes the erroneous assumption that there are essences or fundamental underlying realities that are necessarily expressed at this day-to-day level. In other words, people are very often unaware that they are enmeshed in patterns of distorted communication.

For critical theory there can be no such thing as objective or disinterested, as traditionally defined, inquirers and inquiry. On the contrary, the major thrust of critical theory is to reunite that which has been divided into the modern era—knowledge and practical/moral concerns. The study of society and schooling, for example, must be joined to a commitment to produce the social conditions necessary for emancipation and empowerment. Inquiry is thereby directed at both the understanding *and* the practical transformation of these conditions. If the regulative ideal for postempiricism is objectivity, and for constructivism it is solidarity, for critical theory it is the conjunction of reason and commitment or the integration of knowledge and purposeful action. The task of inquiry is to illuminate the meaning of historical processes—objective historical conditions—and bring this knowledge to the practical task of emancipation.

These points, from nonfoundationalism to the ideal of purposeful action, are related to one of the most important aspects of critical theory; that of the role assigned, and interpretation given, to hermeneutics. Moreover, it is in this area that some very important differences appear with the other two paradigms.

Critical theory has embraced a critical version of hermeneutics that seeks to uncover—that is, make transparent—the causes of distorted communication and understanding. These are the historically formed distortions that operate behind the seemingly normal, unquestioned interactions of our daily lives. The chief task of inquiry is to illuminate the contradictions the Enlightenment has brought to the formation of modern society and schooling.

The knowledge of objective historical conditions, which for social inquiry takes the form of the critique of ideology, has distinct implications for practical engagement on the side of historical truth and emancipation. As Bleicher (1980, p. 148) puts it, the idea is to render individual and social processes "transparent to the actors involved, enabling them to pursue their further development with consciousness and will—rather than remaining the end-product of a causal chain operative behind their backs." Once the objectivations of our human struggles are objectively grasped, people will understand how they are enmeshed in distorted communication, why this is the case, and how they can free themselves from this condition. For Marxists, in a more traditional sense, this means to uncover the contradictions of economic conditions and relationships; for a variety of other critical perspectives, the focus is on the ideological distortions inherent in a broad range of historically formed social and cultural conditions.

What then do these considerations mean for the task of distinguishing valid from invalid inquiry? At one level the answer is obvious; a good study is one that makes transparent the historically formed contradictions and thereby promotes emancipation and empowerment. At another level, however, the issue is much more complicated. The complicating factor is expressed by a question that originates in the Habermas (1986) and Gadamer (1986) debate: What prevents a critique of ideology from itself being ideological? Or, as Bredo and Feinberg (1982c) ask, "Is critical theory another partial theory that conceals as much as it reveals and is thereby likely to function as another self-serving ideology?"

Critical theory has generally responded to this criticism by calling upon a theory of history and/or self-reflection. Various critical hermeneuticists have argued that an understanding of both the past and present requires a universal theory of history. For example, one variation on this theme is that of the "ideal communicative community" (Bleicher, 1980, p. 151). In effect this means that "our understanding of texts and authors allows us to criticize and go beyond the 'truths' contained in them because we are in possession of a more truthful way of life" (p. 151). Or, in a second example, Habermas (1980, p. 206) expresses the situation as follows:

> It is only the formal anticipation of an idealized dialogue, as the form of life to be realized in the future, which guarantees the ultimate supporting and contra-factual agreement that already unites us; in relation to it we can criticize every factual agreement, should it be a false one, as false consciousness.

This solution to the criteria problem is far from universally accepted. Gadamer (1986), for example, has argued that this position fails to understand how every one of us, even a critical theorist, "is so little separated from the ongoing tradition . . . that he is really *himself engaged* in contributing to the growth and development of [that tradition]" (p. 286). Thus there is a definite dogmatism associated with this attempt to structure "an opposition and separation between the ongoing, natural 'tradition' and the reflective appropriation of it" (p. 286).

Habermas (1971, p. 228) makes one of the most prominent cases that self-reflection, because of its emancipatory potential, can prevent the critique of ideology from becoming itself ideological: "In self-reflection, knowledge for the sake of knowledge comes to coincide with the interest in autonomy and responsibility. For the pursuit of reflection knows itself as a movement of emancipation." For Bredo and Feinberg (1982c, p. 439), similarly, the point is this: "What can save critical theory from being used in this way [to legitimize a new set of authorities in as unquestionable a fashion as in other ideologies] is the insistence on self-reflectivity, the insistence that this theory of knowledge also be applied to those propounding or using the theory."

This position on self-reflection has been criticized from a number of different directions (see Dallmayr, 1981, pp. 246-269). There are two essential thrusts to these critiques. The first is that reflection is itself historically situated and cannot make any claim to a transcendent quality. Second, although reflection may reveal a formal interest in emancipation, it does not necessarily or automatically provide a linkage between this formal interest and actual emancipatory action. Even if one has reflectively appropriated underlying contradictions or ideological distortions, emancipation still requires active engagement (political) and choice and commitment.

To briefly summarize: If one accepts the ideals of a universal history and of self-reflection, then it is highly possible that critical inquiry can reveal our objective historical conditions: tie this knowledge to the expunging of false consciousness, distorted communication, and so on; and thereby promote emancipation and empowerment. Good research can be separated from bad research in terms of its emancipatory and empowerment possibilities because there are definite argumentative warrants to support knowledge claims. If one takes a contrary position in regard to a universal history and self-reflection then, as Ingram (1987, p. 68) notes,

> Critical theory must live disconsolately with the knowledge that its truth is ungrounded. Inherent in this situation is a contradiction insofar as the privileged status of those who proffer enlightenment to those who have fallen under the sway of ideology is itself without argumentative warrant.

Is There a Problem?

Each perspective poses an overall regulative ideal for inquiry; postempiricism-objectivity, constructivism-solidarity, and critical theory-emancipation. These regulative ideals would seem to mean, at least potentially, that each paradigm has universal and well-defined standards for judging knowledge claims. Knowledge that contributes to the realization of the particular ideal is genuine knowledge and vice versa. Moreover, it would seem possible to translate these ideals into reasonably well-established and generally agreed-upon criteria for judging research. As it turns out, this last aspect remains somewhat problematic.

The problems begin with the fact that each paradigm has dispensed with the idea of an absolutely authoritative foundation for knowledge. This nonfoundationalism greatly complicates the criteria issue. Moreover, further complications arise because each paradigm gives a different interpretation as to exactly what nonfoundationalism means for inquiry. Constructivists, in particular, gives a more aggressive interpretation to nonfoundationalism than do advocates of the other two paradigms. This situation can be illuminated by examining certain points of agreement and disagreement across the three paradigms.

There are at least three points common to these different perspectives. First, there is no possibility that a mechanical decision-making procedure can be applied to distinguish valid from invalid research. Second, methodology or procedures, in and of themselves, are not sufficient for decisions about the quality of inquiry. Finally, although only briefly noted earlier, an appeal to consistently successful prediction is not a live option in that none of the three perspectives has done very well in this area.

There are two related points over which major differences occur among the perspectives. First, although all three realize that any particular criterion can be stated and applied only loosely or imprecisely, constructivism goes further with the ideas of imprecision and looseness. Second, given that all three positions are explicitly nonfoundational, each recognizes that judgments made about inquiry have a distinct ethical and moral component. These judgments, in that they are intimately tied to the social practices of dialog and negotiation, must involve the norms governing dialog and discourse. For constructivism the norms important to our professional interactions are seen as very much the same as those important to our day-to-day interactions. As such, constructivism has pushed this implication for criteria more aggressively than has been the case for postempiricism and critical theory. And, oddly enough, this more aggressive stance leads to the possibility that the problem of criteria is actually a nonproblem—at least if *problem* is thought of in epistemological terms.

Put differently, each perspective must assess the implications for researchers of what MacIntyre (1973, p. 332) refers to as "the epistemological limitations imposed on ordinary agents." The ultimate limitation is that ordinary, day-to-day judgments as to what constitutes genuine knowledge are "adopted, held, and changed in ways that are essentially prescientific and nonscientific" (p. 332). The question is, accordingly. "Can social inquirers understand social life in a way that allows them to transcend these epistemological limitations?"

For constructivism the answer seems to be *no*. Constructivism sponsors a form of inquiry, as Rorty (1979, 1982b, 1985) would have it, that looks much like ordinary conversation. As such, the judgments made about research are like the judgments made about knowledge claims at the day-to-day level. In both cases people are expected to be reasonable in their claims, responsive to challenges to these reasons, open with others, honest, and so on. But all of these things are quite loose and imprecise as far as criteria goes and they can be applied differently at different times and in different situations. They are themselves subject to interpretation. This is why, to the extent constructivists talk about criteria, they talk about exemplars and open-ended lists that are modified, changed, and so on as they are played out within the social practices of inquiry.

Based on this thinking, from the constructivist point of view, the lack of definitive criteria, and the relativism that seems inevitable thereby, is not a problem—or at least no more of a problem than we face in our daily lives. What has not led to impasses at the lay level should not lead to impasses at the professional level. Just as the impasses arrived at in daily life are resolved in large measure because people, in the name of solidarity, fellow feeling, or whatever, desire to resolve them, so it is for professionals. Moreover, constructivists would further argue that there is nothing in this approach that exempts people from the need to present the best case possible for their claims, be open to counterreasons and criticism, take into account the feelings and dispositions of others, and so on. This is expected of people in ordinary conversation and should be expected of researchers in their conversations. But, again, it must be remembered that these "standards" are open to interpretation and reinterpretation.

Both postempiricism and critical theory seem uncomfortable with this situation and are reluctant to accept a such a direct *no* to the question of whether inquirers can transcend this epistemological limitation. For example, although postempiricism argues that researchers have much in common with other effective thinkers, they still hold to the idea that researchers approach their inquiries more systematically, self-consciously, and intensely. Critical theory poses a similar situation. The self-reflection of critical inquirers presumably goes beyond the self-reflection of ordinary agents, and this is what allows the former to realize the ideological distortions of which the latter are not necessarily or normally aware. Thus, for both perspectives, there are criteria for our professional judgments—even though they are much looser than the criteria as posed by the traditional empiricist theory of knowledge. Both maintain that there are standards for judgments about the quality of inquiry that surpass or are somehow superior to those used by ordinary people. And, if this is so, then the relativism common to our ordinary deliberations can be, if not eliminated, certainly seriously blunted, at the professional level.

What does all of this mean for the problem of criteria? Certainly it is clear that the demise of empiricism with its focus on criteria as procedures and the rise of alternative paradigms for inquiry have resulted in a fair amount of confusion over the appropriate way to judge inquiry. It would be foolish not to acknowledge that considerable thought and further elaboration are needed in this area.

This acknowledgement aside, however, I think that constructivism may be headed in the right direction. In part this is because constructivism has accepted the inevitable consequences of nonfoundationalism and the epistemological limitations that befall us as human beings. In a related sense, I must question whether the approaches taken by postempiricism and critical theory to blunt these consequences, or to get beyond these limitations, are truly up to the task. The problem is that certain concepts that each has introduced, such as *systematic, intense,* and *self-reflection,* are not now, and seem resistant to ever being translated into, relatively stable and general standards. In other words, these concepts themselves are open to the permanent possibility of interpretation and reinterpretation. The judgments researchers make as to whether someone has been more or less systematic or appropriately self-reflective are as open to interpretation and reinterpretation as the judgments they make about the quality of research. In both cases the way these things are decided, and the extent to which agreement is reached, are the result of a process of social interaction within which people play out their different interests and purposes.

In the end, the task of making judgments about inquiry is an eminently practical one whose rationality is not based on determinate rules but is a rationality that emphasizes judgmental interpretation, exemplars, and the norms that guide social discourse and agreement. Constructivism, more so than postempiricism and critical theory, realizes that this may be the only appropriate way to address the issue of criteria.

[13]

Goodness Criteria
Are They Objective or Judgment Calls?

CATHERINE MARSHALL

When I first read the conference papers on which this book is based, the wonderful exchanges among Alice, the March Hare, and the Mad Hatter came to mind.

"Then you should say what you mean," the March Hare went on.

"I do," Alice hastily replied; "at least I mean what I say—that's the same thing, you know."

"Not the same thing a bit!" said the Hatter.

"Why you might just as well say that 'I see what I eat' is the same thing as 'I eat what I see!'" (Carroll, 1915, pp. 100-101)

I often was as lost and impatient as Alice in the convoluted arguments about the nature of truth and goodness. Wouldn't it be more productive, I thought, for us to actually collect data and then argue about the persistent criteria of goodness questions. Suppose one-third went forth to study (Spradley, 1979) the hobos of San Francisco; one-third went forth to study the organization of work at the San Francisco Hilton; and the remainder studied the patterns of behavior at the annual meeting of the AERA. All would be doing field studies, in the natural setting, with an exploratory stance. So all would inevitably confront the persistent goodness questions.

Persistent Goodness Questions

Questions that arise persistently in qualitative methods classes, in doctoral committees, and on editorial boards considering qualitative methodology are these:

(1) How do I decide which is the important research question or focus?

(2) Must I become a part of the culture to truly understand it? If I do, how can I leave it and reestablish myself as an "objective" researcher?

(3) Aren't I manipulating people and altering their environment when I enter it to study it?

(4) How do I know how many cases or subjects or observations are enough?

(5) How do I know when my study is complete?

(6) How do I present my methods so that others will be convinced that what I have found is the truth?

(7) How do I prevent my values and biases from slanting the findings?

(8) Could someone else do the same things I did and get the same findings?

(9) How can I present my findings in such a way that they will be accepted and used by practitioners and policymakers?

Goodness questions (in ancient terminology: reliability, replicability, validity) are mixed with value questions (in ancient terminology: generalizability). Students get angry, frustrated, when I so frequently reply, "It depends." It's a judgment call. It depends upon your purpose, your audience, and how finely tuned you are as a research instrument. But it also depends upon the tradition, as Jacob (1988) says, or on the paradigm framing your endeavor.

Assumptions About Goodness and Truth

J. Smith (this volume) recounts the historical evolution of assumptions that affect goodness criteria. Early empiricists accepted the following:

Assumption 1. There is a knowable truth. The aim of research is to "see nature in its own terms" (Rorty, 1982b, p. 192). This assumes that there is one knowable truth that can be discovered when we use proper methods well. Under this assumption, the criterion for good-ness is the analysis of the goodness of the use of the right method. We ask questions like these: "Was the t-test the right method?" "Shouldn't he have used more participant observation and less focused inter-viewing?"

Assumption 2. Values can be excised from the research process. Here the criterion becomes the degree to which the researcher did separate "the facts" (a.k.a. *findings*) from the values (a.k.a. *interpretation, recom-mendations, implications*).

Empiricists did not worry about utility and contribution of re-search. They assumed that the scientists' work was complete when they did objective studies using proper methods. This would lead to lawlike generalizations about human nature that would assist in shaping the efforts of those who would improve society.

But empiricism has failed to deliver on its promise to provide an intellectual practical mastery of the social world (J. Smith, this vol-ume). With this failure came postempiricists' recognition that the theories and methods shape the knowledge obtained from research. So new rationales and value in research and corresponding new criteria of goodness were sought. From the critical scientist repre-sented by Popkewitz (this volume), we find:

Assumption 3. Good research must empower people by helping them to see the historical meaning of events and to place themselves, their institutions, and their roles in historical context. Researchers should help people choose how they wish to respond and reshape their present and future. Thus good research includes an analysis of past truths.

The flaws in this assumption (i.e., historical "truths" are just as subjective and relative as current "truths") lead us to examine the next assumption:

Assumption 4. Research is a process in which the researcher uncov-ers his or her own as well as others' truths. Thus good research must include a self-revelation. Only then can the researcher go forth and uncover the stories of others. This assumption leaves us again with no hope of discovering truth; we consider:

Assumption 5. Research is the process of uncovering what people believe to be true (regardless of any absolute truth). Thus good research can be objective in that it uncovers what people believe—it uncovers a variety of subjective truths. Goodness is judged by the degree to which the researcher explores the full range of beliefs and presents them clearly and objectively. Thus a statement is true if it accurately depicts beliefs (J. Smith, this volume).

Finally, we find a postpositivist version of Assumption 1:

Assumption 6. There is no such thing as an absolutely authoritative foundation of the truth but good research comes from good method properly applied. That is, good research is honest, open inquiry where the researcher searches for alternative explanations and is self-critical. Thus good research can be recognized by examining whether the researcher searched for alternative hypotheses, explored negative instances, examined biases, and so on. Sloppy research is that which starts with an idea and goes forth in the real world to gather evidence supporting the idea, without being systematic in searching for the wide range of alternative explanations and versions of truth, and without trying to be self-critical.

Most postempiricists try to avoid relativism, the "anything goes" response. They acknowledge that, although there is no one truth, there is a truth to be known about a range of beliefs at a given point in time. But there are disagreements even about that, as J. Smith (this volume) demonstrates in his discussion of the disputes over Spiro (1966) and Leach's (1969) studies of the Tully River Blacks. Disputes arise over the meaning as well as the significance of findings. These disputes are often settled by examining whether the studies were "properly done" or objective. This moves us back to discussion of what we mean by "properly done," a focus on procedures. It forces us to acknowledge again that every study has biases and presuppositions and that research involves the interpretation of the interpretations people give to their own situations (J. Smith, this volume). We are merely making a judgment when deciding whether one study is more valid than another. We have to decide whose biases were *more* correct. All of the earlier assumptions really lead to this reality: Evaluating the goodness and value of research requires a judgment call.

Judges of Goodness

The metaphor of the courtroom serves to frame judgment calls. "Adversarial evaluation" used this metaphor: Proponents of different evaluations of the same program must present their case and "duke it out"; the group with the best defense or offense is the group whose truth is to be viewed as valid. Extending this metaphor to the question of goodness in qualitative research, one then asks, What counts as a good offense or a good defense? If it were a boxing match, what would win points? If it were a court of law, what would convince the judge or jury of the goodness of one piece of research?

Would a critical scientist judge, a constructivist judge, or a post-empiricist judge have different criteria?

The conference keynote presenters implied that each paradigm has its own assumptions and goodness criteria.

For postempiricist judges, the best case is the one that can document an honest, open, and careful procedure for arriving at a description of the beliefs that people hold.

Constructivist judges are happy with descriptions of the varied and multiple realities that are socially constructed. Good data are obtained by getting inside the worlds of others. The only truths are the emic realities of insiders. Certitude is not possible, there is no correct interpretation, and there is no end to the ever-evolving interaction that reveals meaning. In the constructivist tradition, the debate over the goodness of one's interpretation is resolved by a dialogic process.

For critical theorist judges there are subjective and objective realities. Objective realities are the institutions, statuses, and roles created in history. The subjective realities are the individual's sense-making processes. And neither the objective nor the subjective realities are free of the taint of prior social manipulation. So, good research is that which uncovers those manipulations, thus empowering people to see ways to control their own destinies. Social critique, to be good, however, must have an internal self-critiquing mechanism—the researcher must, for example, avoid the patronizing stance of findings that empower the research subjects to accept the *researcher's* view of the best system. Otherwise, the researcher simply becomes a new social controller.

Common Agreements on Criteria

Suppose, instead of abstractly debating goodness, we did go forth and conduct research on the hobos, the Hilton work norms, and the functions of convention behavior. We would each have varying foci, data collection strategies, different ways of using raw data to buttress our stories, and varying stances on whether to interfere with people and settings. How would we ever decide which studies were good?

Which ones deserved publication? Which ones would speak to people in such a way that the human condition would be bettered? Which ones were most methodologically and ethically pure?

Would there be enough agreement on goodness to fend off those who would sanitize the research process and lay positivist criteria on qualitative research (Miles & Huberman, 1984)? Would we have enough agreement to be able to denounce those trying to make research researcher-proof, eliminating the biases but also the varying interpretations that come from the human research instrument (see Marshall, 1985b, for a critique of this "testing-in-context" approach)? We would also shy away from outright acceptance of "portraits" à la Lightfoot (1983). We would not accept apologies as in *Boys in White* (Becker, Geer, Hughes, & Strauss, 1961, p. 17) saying "in one sense we had no research design."

I suggest that we would agree on common criteria (although different paradigms would weight each criterion differently). Most of us in judging the goodness of qualitative studies would look for the following evidence:

(1) The method is explicated in detail so the reader can judge whether it was adequate and makes sense. An articulate rationale for the use of qualitative methods is given so that skeptics will accept the approach. The methods for attaining entry and managing role, data collection, recording, analysis, ethics, and exit are discussed. There is an auditability trail—a running record of procedures (often done in an appendix)—and there is description of how the site and sample were selected. Data collection and analysis procedures are public, not magical.

(2) Assumptions are stated. Biases are expressed, and the researcher does a kind of self-analysis for personal biases and a framework analysis for theoretical biases.

(3) The research guards against value judgments in data collection and in analysis (i.e., avoiding transgression like Whyte's, 1955, judgmental field notes about "dilapidated houses" in *Street Corner Society*).

(4) There is abundant evidence from raw data to demonstrate the connection between the presented findings and the real world, and the data are presented in readable, accessible form, perhaps aided by graphics, models, charts, and figures.

(5) The research questions are stated, and the study answers those questions and generates further questions.

(6) The relationship between this study and previous studies is explicit. Definitions of phenomena are provided, with explicit reference to previously identified phenomena, but it is clear that the research goes beyond previously established frameworks—challenging old ways of thinking.

(7) The study is reported in a manner that is accessible to other researchers, practitioners, and policymakers. It makes adequate translation of findings so that others will be able to use the findings in a timely way.

(8) Evidence is presented showing that the researcher was tolerant of ambiguity, searched for alternative explanations, checked out negative instances, and used a variety of methods to check the findings (i.e., triangulation).

(9) The report acknowledges the limitations of generalizability while assisting the readers in seeing the transferability of findings.

(10) It is clear that there was a phase of "first days in the field" in which a problem focus was generated from observation, not from library research. In other words, it is a study that is an exploration, not merely a study to find contextual data to verify old theories.

(11) Observations are made (or sampled) of a full range of activities over a full cycle of activities.

(12) Data are preserved and available for reanalysis.

(13) Methods are devised for checking data quality (e.g., informants' knowledgeability, ulterior motives, and truthfulness) and for guarding against ethnocentric explanations.

(14) In-field work analysis is documented.

(15) Meaning is elicited from cross-cultural perspectives.

(16) The researcher is careful about sensitivity of those being researched—ethical standards are maintained.

(17) People in the research setting benefit in some way (ranging from getting a free meal or an hour of sympathetic listening to being empowered to throw off their chains).

(18) Data collection strategies are the most adequate and efficient available. There is evidence that the researcher is a finely tuned research instrument, whose personal talents, experiential biases, and insights are used consciously. The researcher is careful to be self-analytical and recognize when she or he is getting subjective or going native.

(19) The study is tied into "the big picture." The researcher looks holistically at the setting to understand linkages among systems.

(20) The researcher traces the historical context to understand how institutions and roles have evolved. (For further discussion see Marshall, 1985a, 1985b.)

For each of these criteria, there are still judgment calls, cautions, limits, assumptions, and "buts." In chapters in this volume, Smith, and the conference keynote speakers, Lincoln, Popkewitz, and Phillips, are among those who have raised them. For example, how do you provide the historical context when history is socially constructed? Even if the researcher lays bare her or his theoretical and personal biases—what about the ones that are subconscious? What prevents the research from being simply explication of those biases, taking an idiosyncratic, subjective researcher's view? When abundant thick description and raw data are presented, must the reader take it on faith that they were not selected to argue a position, prove a point, or find context-laden evidence of a previously existing theory or bias? On what basis does the researcher decide which evidence to present?

How can the study be reported in a manner accessible to practitioners and policymakers when they will only hear and use research that fits within traditional ways of thinking? The only "usable knowledge" is that which fits within policymakers' "assumptive worlds" (Lindblom & Cohen, 1979; Marshall, Mitchell, & Wirt, 1989). How can one incorporate cross-cultural perspectives knowing that the practitioner does not want to read about how leadership in elementary schools compares with leadership in tribes in Borneo? How can qualitative researchers show how *One Boy's Day* (Barker & Wright, 1951) or *The Man in the Principal's Office* (Wolcott, 1973) contains transferable, if not generalizable, knowledge, in spite of the small sample? Even when the researcher has explicitly detailed the procedures—one must still ask, do the methods not shape the findings?

Even with all of these questions, caveats, limits, and "buts," we do have criteria. Criteria of goodness, like our search for knowledge, are ever evolving. One judge puts more emphasis on criterion 1 than on criterion 21. Another counts 12 heavily, throwing out studies lacking cross-cultural comparisons. Judgment calls must still be made.

Infiltrating to Construct New Realities

When editors, tenure and promotion committees, and policymakers judge qualitative research, they must know how to use postpositivist criteria, those appropriate for qualitative methods. We need to be on those boards and committees, *armed* with alternative criteria from alternative paradigms.

We also need to be articulate and passionate in advocating the importance of supporting researchers who go beyond the testing-in-context approach to explore for meaning. We need to build offensive weaponry to demonstrate the importance of postpositivist research. We must show the following:

(1) Researchers cannot avoid the ethnocentrism of their field without methods that explore beyond dominant paradigms.

(2) Many practices, policies, folk wisdoms, and accepted myths (e.g., rational bureaucracy, meritocracy) do not work, and so research methods are needed to uncover hidden meanings, the subjective interpretations, the voices of the powerless.

(3) Many dominant theories and assumptions were established inappropriately (e.g., administrative theory, decision-making theory, and career development theory evolved without incorporating women's experience; assumptions about how to manage schools were developed in times of growth and with persistent myths about the separation of education and politics). Therefore, new grounded theory (Glaser & Strauss, 1967) must be developed by *exploring* how these theories fit with a wider reality.

(4) There is great value in research on the dynamics of power, the social construction of reality, organizational myth-making, and a focus on micro-politics and language, for, as Greenfield (1985, p. 3) has said, "Language is a dialect with its own army and navy."

(5) Research can *benefit* from the intuitive and metaphorical insight of human researchers, and "to isolate one psychological function, in this case the rational from all others, is to limit the effectiveness of that function, diminish the quality of its product" (Barger & Duncan, 1982, p. 12).

(6) When we allow those who are powerful to hold all the definitions of what is good and what is useful, we can never get beyond the dominant worldviews (Noblit, 1984).

Validity, practicality, utility, credibility, and worth are socially constructed judgment calls. We need to identify and build on our common agreements so that we too are participants in that social construction.

Too often, alternative paradigmers are beaten into submission as illustrated in this vignette, borrowed from Van Maanen (1979, p. 519):

Qualitative Researcher: "Many people these days are bored with their work and are . . . "

Quantitative Researcher: "What people, how many, when do they feel this way, where do they work, what do they do, why are they bored, how long have they felt this way, what are their needs, when do they feel excited, where did they come from, what parts of their work bother them most, which . . ."

Qualitative Researcher: "Never mind."

[14]

Discussion on Criteria

LOUIS HESHUSIUS

York University

The central question around which the criteria discussion session centered was this: Do we need a list of criteria that need to be met in order to know whether the research did what it was supposed to do? Several positions were taken:

Criteria Are Not Needed

If something is good, you know it. It is a mark of naïveté to be dependent on a list of criteria to arrive at something you can trust. Such dependence is a regression into security seeking, a reverse kind of positivism. It is finding refuge once more in "method."

Criteria Are OK But Can Never Be Fixed or Descriptive

This position holds that criteria point to no more than actions you may or may not want to engage in because no criterion can ever be independent of our own construction of it. Criteria cannot be prescriptive, and one cannot know in advance which criteria one needs to meet. It is only afterward that one can know what criteria were relevant and could be met, because central to alternative inquiry is the position that one stays true to the phenomena one wishes to understand in their own context. This part of the discussion led to the question: What is it that makes us worry so intensely about criteria? Responses to this question led to the third position.

We Must Have Criteria

This position springs from several observations: First, criteria are at the heart of power relations; whoever defines the criteria has the power. Researchers should keep such power in their own hands. Second, criteria are useful in an array of practical contexts, such as when serving on dissertation committees or when reviewing proposals. Third, we need criteria to separate inquiry from fiction.

Someone then put in a word or two on behalf of fiction. The intent of the position taken here was not to make fiction similar to inquiry or vice versa but to speak in favor of fiction as a valid way to know and as a vehicle that can expand that we can attend to.

For those who feel that we must have criteria, the questions then become: Which criteria should we use? Which ones need to be met (there are too many already listed in the literature)? How can we be reasonable about the demand to meet them? *Reasonableness* in this context was defined as meeting some criteria but not all and meeting them only to some extent.

Our session's speaker, John Smith, then directed this question to those who insist that certain criteria be met: Because we all have different interpretations of the nature of the criteria and of which criteria should be met, how would you resolve the disputes over evidence that invariably will result? No answer to that question was forthcoming from our group. Instead, we acknowledged the inevitableness of the need for human dialog and agreement in solving disputes rather than reliance on criteria. The group seemed to agree that constructivists go "all the way" in this regard while the other two paradigms of inquiry featured at the conference do not. The latter hold on to the possibility of formulating independent criteria.

The Nature of Expertise

The course of the conversation prompted the question: Isn't there a regulative ideal? Isn't there something called expertise? Aren't there some who have more expertise than others? And doesn't that distinction again raise the possibility of criteria? The existence of expertise was acknowledged ("I know an expert when I see one") but the conditions of that expertise were not seen as something on which individuals could objectively decide. A decision on expertise would have to be an intersubjective, communal agreement, but on what exactly such agreement would be based was not clear. Nor were the origins of such expertise clear (once we reject the notion that expertise is merely knowing how to correctly apply methodology).

Some participants felt that the idea of an expert required one to accept the positivist's notion of a ranking system. Therefore, there would be no place in the thinking about new paradigms for experts.

The discussion on expertise and its relationship to criteria turned to the intriguing question: Why are we so uneasy about trusting "regular people" to know what is "good"? That question led us to a central issue: Once we turn our back on positivist belief in method, what sets us apart, as social scientists, from "regular people"? (No one ventured an answer.)

Another issue discussed was the need to educate those who think they need us to do research for them and whose expectations for us are based on what earlier researchers have promised to deliver (to test hypotheses, to help them to predict and engineer behavior). Now we have to tell them that we cannot perform these feats. So what shall we claim is worthwhile about our work? Suggestions ranged from playing the positivist's game, hiding intentions in order to get funding, to more gentle ones, such as making clear to our clientele and funding agencies that our research will have direct relevance for present practice (rather than predictive value), that they will get more information for their money, and once in the field (because qualitative research often uncovers unpleasant information) that we will tell them the news bit by bit.

Natural Science, Social Science, and the Arts

The last issue discussed was the relationship between the natural sciences, the social sciences, and the arts. Here questions and positions ranged widely: Can we perhaps still learn something from "them" (the natural sciences)? Should we accommodate? Are we talking about replacement? We aren't talking about replacement but we are demanding the freedom to engage in other ways of knowing. The last question raised here was this: Do we actually need to put our efforts into demarcating the natural sciences from the social sciences and from the humanities? The group seemed to conclude that we should and, moreover, that we should examine anew those disciplines that focus directly on what it means to study human behavior including those that preceded the natural sciences because the subject matter we engage in just isn't the same as that of the natural sciences.

IMPLEMENTATION

[15]

Toward a Dialog About Implementation Within a Conceptual Cycle of Inquiry

JUDITH L. GREEN
SUSANNE CHANDLER

The initial charge for this chapter focused on discussing the nature of implementation of new paradigms, specifically those referred to under the qualitative research umbrella.[1] Central to this charge was the need to consider implementation in terms of issues of acceptance of alternative paradigms. Certainly the development of any new paradigm raises questions about acceptance by different audiences (e.g., policymakers, publishers, practitioners; Kuhn, 1962).[2]

We argue, however, that qualitative research is no longer "new." Qualitative is one of the established approaches to educational research. Thus newer alternative ways of knowing (e.g., feminism, critical theory, and postmodernism) are finding easier acceptability simply because they follow those qualitative paradigms that have already been accepted. This argument is based on the fact that alternative forms of research and thus alternative ways of knowing are becoming more readily accepted in major journals.[3] In addition, qualitative studies are a regular part of educational research conferences.

We see a need to transcend the issue of acceptability facing alternative paradigms to consider the question of implementation more broadly. This exploration is needed if we are to engage in a productive conversation of practice (Yinger, 1988) across groups concerned with educational research (e.g., policymakers, practitioners, researchers). Underlying this argument is the view that implementation is not a generic process. Implementation is undertaken by people for a particular purpose in particular contexts and requires something that is implemented (e.g., purpose, theory, method, findings). Thus to have a conversation of practice that extends our knowledge about education processes, institutions, and phenomena, we need to understand issues of implementation and the differing purposes for engaging in inquiry that exist across types of educational inquirers (researchers, practitioners, and policymakers). We argue that such understandings will lay the foundation for an open conversation of practice (dialog and debate) that will move us beyond the "détente" and competition among perspectives that currently exist (see Gage, 1989, for an example of the détente/competition argument). In addition, such conversations will help us bridge the "perceived gap" among policy, theory, and practice.

Locating the Context of Use: The Cycle of Inquiry

The term *implementation* is often used in a way that assumes a "common understanding" of the word. Our theoretical grounding, however, assumes that meaning of a term depends on the context in which it is situated (e.g., Gumperz, 1982; Hymes, 1974; Mishler, 1979) as well as on the way it is used (e.g., Lakoff & Johnson, 1980; Ortony, 1979). Thus to understand what is meant by implementation involves understanding the contexts of use.

For the purpose of discussion, implementation will be situated within a cycle of inquiry that includes four contexts: the context of purpose, discovery, presentation, and implementation. By *cycle of inquiry*, we are referring to a holistic process that begins with establishing an inquiry purpose. This view of inquiry is based on cycles of activity in which people engage in a variety of actions to achieve particular purposes. Practitioners, researchers, and policymakers are all seen as inquirers who engage in activities driven by particular purposes.

From this perspective the inquiry process does not begin and end with a single research study but with a purpose that leads to a series of actions. *Inquiry* refers to any examination for the purpose of discovering information or examining particular phenomena (Heap, 1987). Inquiry may take many forms (e.g., a research study, a policy study, an exploration of practice by a practitioner, or a synthesis). This view of inquiry sees the four contexts described above as interrelated but driven by concerns and interests of differing groups of people (e.g., researchers, policymakers, and practitioners; Mitchell & Green, 1986).

The four contexts of the inquiry cycle are proposed to show issues in implementation. They are heuristic devises that reflect a wide range of activities inquirers use to make informed decisions about ways of refining, extending, or modifying practice in their own contexts. Thus, although these are common contexts for all inquirers, each context may be implemented in a variety of ways. The relationship among these contexts is based on a set of assumptions about the shifting nature of activity that enable educational researchers to complete a cycle of inquiry.

Any inquiry process should begin with a purpose and with locating a setting in which the purpose is available to be observed or accomplished. This context we label the *context of purpose*. The context of purpose varies with the role and perceived needs of the person engaging in the inquiry (e.g., researcher, practitioner, policymaker; Mitchell & Green, 1986).

Once the context of purpose has been identified and entry obtained, the observer begins collecting information and exploring the phenomenon of interest. This context we label the *context of discovery* (see Heap, 1987; Kaplan, 1964). A variety of phenomena may be explored in the context of discovery (e.g., practice, research findings, or other types of information). Discovery is not equated with research in the formal sense but with any purposeful exploration of a phenomenon.

Once information has been collected and interpretations made, the inquirer decides on the audience to be addressed (e.g., self, researchers, policymakers, community, students), what will be presented to the audience, and how the information will be presented (e.g., film, orally, journal articles, newsletters). This phase of the inquiry cycle we label the *context of presentation* (see Heap, 1987).

After the information is presented to an audience, the audience then decides on whether and how to use the information. This aspect of the inquiry process we label the *context of implementation*. If the inquirer decides to take action based on the information obtained, a new context of purpose is formed that overlaps with the context of implementation to redefine purpose and institute a new cycle of inquiry.

The cycle of inquiry then is not a set of discrete contexts linearly related by a series of overlapping and interacting contexts. It is potentially generative in nature. By conceptualizing implementation in this manner, the contexts of use for implementation are seen as more than the end point of a research project or the application of a particular set of findings. It is both a context within a cycle of inquiry (the context of implementation) and a process that occurs within and across all contexts of the cycle of inquiry. These distinctions are central to the identification of issues of implementation and will be examined further.

Implementation: Distinctions and Definitions

To establish a "common" base for exploring *implementation* within a cycle of inquiry, we begin by considering the term in a decontextualized form. Once the decontextualized definitions are established, we will return to the contexts of use to construct a situated definition appropriate to the discussion of issues of implementation of alternative ways of knowing and alternative approaches to inquiry. These definitions form an important base for a conversation of practice.

To establish boundaries for the decontextualized definition of implementation, we initially consulted a dictionary (*Webster's* 1972). We elected to begin with the dictionary definition to help us to "break" our own definitions and to revisit the issue anew.[4] *Webster's* defines *implementation* in two ways: as a process (transitive verb) and as a tool (noun).

The question that needs to be asked is which definition is appropriate given our interest in the nature of implementation within a cycle of inquiry. Within the cycle of inquiry described above, both of these definitions are useful. Each, however, addresses different aspects of the cycle. For example, if the concern is how we implement some aspect of the inquiry cycle (e.g., theory, method, paradigm, evidence from social science research), the noun (tool) definition is useful. The evidence (findings), theory, paradigm, and method become implements "adapted to facilitate a definite kind or stage of work" (*Webster's*, 1972, p. 419). Evidence, theory, method, or paradigm, therefore, become tools that can be used to accomplish a particular aspect of work at a particular point in time (e.g., engage in a research study, engage in practice informed by the research evidence). When educators speak of putting research into practice, or researchers speak of using theory to guide their research, they are referring to findings or theory as tools that serve *an instrumental function* (Kennedy, 1984). Through this use, findings become an implement for informing practice, and theory becomes an implement for orienting research (Green, 1990; Green & Collins, in press).

The need to consider implementation as a process as well as a tool, and the existence of different types of tools (theory, method, paradigms, and findings), suggests the need to explore how tools are implemented within and across the various contexts of a cycle of inquiry. Before we can explore the process(es) of implementation, we need to define *process*.

Webster's (1972, p. 419) defines *process* as "a series of actions or operations conducing to an end." Thus the process of implementation can be viewed as a set of actions that contribute to a particular end at a particular point in the inquiry cycle. By referring to implementation as a process, we are indicating that whoever is involved in this process will engage in a series of "concrete measures" to ensure fulfillment of practical effect of the phenomena or object (e.g., theory, paradigm, method, findings) being implemented. The exact nature of this process will be determined by the purpose for which the inquiry was undertaken as well as the needs of the individual inquirer or person initiating the inquiry.

This definition extends the "tool" definition and provides a general understanding of the process of implementation. To understand how this process occurs and what is involved within and across the various contexts of the inquiry cycle, however, we must ask a series of questions: How does one carry out the process? Who is involved? Who gives practical effect to what? What is implemented? Who ensures the fulfillment by concrete measures? Where do these actions take place? What are the conditions surrounding the actions? When do these actions occur? What are the expected outcomes of the process of implementing?

Consideration of these questions provides a means of making visible the nature of the inquiry process and a means of conceptualizing the implementation process. To define *implementation* in its contexts of use, therefore, requires a conceptual approach that considers the purposes of the inquiry, not merely an instrumental one (Kennedy, 1984).

Conceptualizing Implementation in the Context of Use

To extend the definition of *implementation* as "tool" and "process" to educational inquiry, we need to return to the conceptualization of the cycle of inquiry begun above. Thus we extend our understanding of the cycle by exploring the role of people within the cycle and the different contexts of inquiry. This exploration provides a means of distinguishing between instrumental functions related to implementation (as a tool) and process of implementation. In addition, the exploration illustrates how the purpose of the inquiry leads the person engaging in the inquiry to focus on different aspects of a phenomenon, to take specific actions, and to use information in particular ways.

We argue that these distinctions of purpose and value are often invisible in most dialog across groups of inquirers and lead to miscommunication and a "perceived" gap. By understanding the different purposes and the resultant actions, we can explore areas of common interest, understanding, and direction as well as locate areas of difference during a conversation of practice.

The Context of Purpose

By beginning with the purpose and suggesting that it is a context rather than a stated goal, we lay the foundation for understanding the various purposes different types of inquirers have. For example, a researcher's purpose may not be the same as a practitioner's purpose or a policymaker's. The researcher may be concerned with understanding the nature of a phenomenon (e.g., literacy at home and school). At the point of the study the researcher may not be concerned with the implications of the research for practice but concerned with generating baseline information for future work. For this researcher the concern for application occurs at a later stage and may involve a series of studies before moving to the context of presentation (e.g., publishing) and/or context of implementation (e.g., application to classroom practice).

The practitioner and the policymaker, on the other hand, have different needs and concerns at the initial phase of inquiry and a different audience for the work. The purposes of these groups are thus driven by differing value systems and needs. These differences lead each type of inquirer to configure the inquiry process in particular ways and to act in ways that permit each to achieve particular goals and meet particular needs (Mitchell & Green, 1986). In addition, each inquirer brings specific knowledge to the process that influences what the question will be, what will be implemented, how the inquiry process will be implemented, the ways in which evidence from inquiry will be interpreted, and how interactions with others involved in similar processes will occur. Understanding these differences is essential if we are to develop a productive conversation of practice.

Another aspect of the context of purpose is a context of practice or setting in which educational practitioners (e.g., teachers, students, administrators, support personnel, parents, policymakers, researchers) engage in practices that affect learners either directly or indirectly. It is within and about a context of practice that questions for inquiry are generally posed by members of each group (e.g., researchers, practitioners, policymakers). The existence of differing purposes suggests that, even when all groups wish to examine the same context of practice (e.g., classroom instruction), the types of inquiry undertaken will differ as will the purposes of the inquiry. For example, policymakers may identify classroom practices as the context of practice they seek to explore in order to lay a foundation for improvement of practice. The policymaker will often turn to an exploration of the literature or to a particular body of literature that reflects a philosophical or commitment-based belief about effective practice to determine what is effective.

The teachers, however, are concerned with their students and how to improve the opportunities and learning for individual students in their classrooms. The teacher, therefore, will engage in a different type of inquiry that may consider the literature in the field but will also permit exploration of the phenomenon as it applies to students in the classroom. The nature of the inquiry among these two groups differs as does the nature of the processes of implementation that will be undertaken and the values guiding the research.

In these examples the purpose of an inquiry process entailed particular contexts of practice that reflected different contexts of purpose. By viewing the context of purpose and of practice as interrelated, we can begin to examine the purposes and resultant practices of different groups. By distinguishing among these various contexts of practice by purpose during the conversation of practice, we can see instances when the goals, purposes, and practices of the groups involved in the conversation overlap and instances when they differ. In this way, we can assess the contribution of each group and explore ways of bridging perceived gaps among practice, theory, and policy.

This discussion has focused on differences among groups of inquirers. A similar case can be made for differences within groups. Not all researchers have the same purpose. Not all teachers have the same needs. Thus the variability within groups with respect to the context of purpose and the context of practice must also be considered so that a conversation of practice within groups can occur in productive ways.

The Context of Discovery

The context of discovery is defined by the set of actions that lead to the discovery of information that will be used to answer the initial questions and to raise new questions. As suggested above, the discovery does not mean research but rather the more general phenomenon of inquiry.

Inquiry is a general term that suggests a disposition to engage in various forms of discovery and observation to obtain information. The exact nature of the inquiry process depends on a series of factors, including the person seeking to "discover" information, the purpose of the inquiry, the type of information needed, the way the person perceives the world, the beliefs the person holds about what "counts" as knowledge, the way the person conceives of the phenomenon under study, the approaches the person has in her or his repertoire, and the audience the person wishes to address.

The context of discovery thus comprises a complex set of factors that combine in particular ways to make visible particular types of information. The overriding purpose of this context is inquiry into particular phenomena. This goal may be realized through "research" in one of its many forms or in some other form of inquiry (e.g., synthesis, conceptualization).

One of the invisible dimensions of this context that is ignored in most definitions of inquiry is the existence of others with whom the inquirer interact. In most contexts of discovery, the inquirer does not act alone. The inquirer interacts with others in a context of practice to explore the phenomenon of interest. Such interactions influence just how the discovery process will develop as well as what can be known. Consider, for example, a context of practice for a particular teacher. This context is influenced by many people (e.g., teachers, students, parents). Each of these groups may provide information, or fail to provide information, to an inquirer. If a researcher enters this context to inquire into instructional practices, the researcher must depend on those in the ordinary context of practice to cooperate.

The type of access to information that the researcher has may depend on how the researcher is perceived. In a study of curriculum in three seventh-grade reading classes, for example, Chandler (described in Zaharlick & Green, in press) found that students would not provide their actual views until they had determined that the teacher and the researcher "liked" each other. The students assumed that, because the researcher and teacher did not talk during class, they did not like each other. Once the teacher and researcher began interacting in front of the students, the students provided different information to Chandler about the curricular expectations and practices of this classroom. A similar discussion of trust and access to "insider" knowledge is reported by Bussis, Chittenden, and Amarel (1976). They found that it took eight to ten hours of interview time with a teacher to get "below the surface curriculum" to the teacher's actual curriculum.

Viewed in this way, inquiry within the process of discovery is an interactive and dynamic process. In addition, what occurs in this context is influenced by the context of purpose that frames the inquiry as well as by the perceived purpose and interpretation of actions of those being "studied." Thus what is available to be "discovered" may not be evident on the surface.

The Context of Presentation

The context of presentation (Heap, 1987) occurs after a context of discovery and involves presenting the information obtained from the context of discovery to others interested in this information or deemed in need of the information. This context is not simply one of publishing all of the findings but one involving identifying what is "news" to a particular audience and then presenting this information in a way that makes the information accessible (Heap, 1987). Thus, in the context of presentation, the inquirer must have a "sense of audience" if the information is to be understood and accepted.

Presentation may take many forms. It may be *formal* (e.g., a written, spoken, or visual presentation) or *informal* (e.g., discussing findings with a colleague). Regardless of its specific nature, the presenter must know the "audience" and understand what they will "count" as evidence and how they expect to have the information presented. In other words, the presenter must understand language of the group to which the information is to be presented, and the groups' ways of perceiving the world, and then determine how the new information can be of use to this group.

Another way to view this process is to see presentation as a need to understand what an audience needs to understand about the information, because one of the best predictors of comprehension is prior knowledge. As Lakoff and Johnson (1980) point out, our conceptual system is metaphorical in nature and we understand new concepts in light of old. In addition, they argue that the metaphors we hold are visible in the ways in which we use language to communicate information. Therefore, if new information is to be understood, it must fit within our conceptual system.

The task of the presenter then is to understand what metaphors an audience holds and find ways to make the information accessible to that particular audience while maintaining the integrity of her or his own approach. This may require the researcher to present the information in ways that build on the audiences' knowledge rather than simply presenting the researcher's way of knowing. Presentation, here, is not simply writing a clear report but involves understanding the cultural expectations of the audience, the prior knowledge of the audience, and then presenting the information in ways that are culturally compatible with the expectations of the audience.

The Context of Implementation

The final context is the context of implementation. This context involves issues of acceptance of information and the actions of those who use the information to inform practice. In this context, the principal actor is the practitioner or policymaker who seeks information that will enable her or him to make decisions about ways of informing practice in a particular context. In other words, the person in the context of implementation asks what concrete measures must be taken to ensure the appropriate implementation of the information.

The above description of the cycles of inquiry is based on a view of inquiry as a process that is situated in a particular group and that serves particular purposes. Inquiry, therefore, is not the purview of one group but a process available and used by a variety of groups for a variety of purposes. Inquiry is a dynamic and interactive process in which information at any point may influence what is understood and what occurs at other points.

Implementation decisions within the inquiry process are based on what the inquirer sees, believes, and interprets throughout the inquiry cycle. In addition, at each point in the inquiry cycle, there is an audience that must addressed whether the issue is question generation, discovery processes, presentation of information, or implementation of findings. From this, the inquiry cycle is seen as a holistic process that begins with a question generated in or about a context of practice and continues through to implementation of information generated by the context of discovery and made available in the context of presentation.

Framing a Conversation of Practice

In the model of inquiry presented above, all members of the educational enterprise are seen as potential inquirers. Inquiry is viewed as a conceptually based process that depends on the person, the purpose of the study, the way people view the phenomena, the background knowledge of the inquirer, the beliefs about inquiry held by the inquirer, and the way in which the inquirer conceptualizes and implements the inquiry process. Underlying this perspective is a model of knowledge generation that is constructive in nature. Knowledge is not discovered and then transmitted to an audience. Rather, knowledge is interpreted and then integrated into the audiences' ways of perceiving, believing, acting, and evaluating everyday life in the context of practice.

Underlying this view of inquiry is a *situated model of inquiry* that is conceptual in nature. The difference between this model and the more dominant instrument model is found in the ways in which the movement from research to practice is defined. In an instrumental approach, there is a differentiation of task and purpose for the researcher and the consumer (e.g., practitioner or policymaker). The product of the discovery process is generally viewed as evidence upon which consumers may act. The evidence is assumed to be directly applicable to the consumers' context of practice. Underlying this way of conceptualizing the inquiry cycle is a transmission of knowledge model. Researchers "discover" the relationships between theory and practice and factors that support and/or constrain practice being implemented appropriately or well. The practitioners or policymakers "receive" these "findings" and "implement" them to inform or improve practice. There is an assumed *direct link* or *linear relationship* between the researcher's inquiry cycle and the implementation of findings.

The instrumental model sees outcomes of research as tools and does not provide a means of conceptualizing the role and resultant actions of those using the information. This conceptualization of the inquiry process ignores several factors. First, the assumed differentiation of roles and the linear nature of the process ignore the fact that each person involved in educational inquiry has a theory about the nature of practice and a patterned way of viewing and engaging in practice. That is, each person or group has a set of questions about practice, a need or purpose for exploring or informing practice, and a way of acting. An instrumental model assumes a direct line and compatibility between perspectives of the different inquirers as well as an assumed hierarchy about whose information counts. This assumption is problematic and is one of the principal reasons for the frame clash between research, policy, and practice so often referred to in the education literature as the gap between research and practice.

The *situated model of inquiry* described above begins with an assumption that each group will engage in inquiry in a particular way, have differing purposes, present information in particular ways to differing groups, and value particular types of information. The situated model is based on the premise that, to have a conversation of practice, issues of situation (context) must be understood as they influence the needs and action of different inquirers as well as the outcomes of the inquiry cycle.

The discussion of implementation presented above must be viewed as a beginning of a process of understanding. The definitions and discussion of the situated nature of implementation as a process that occurs within and across the contexts of a general process of inquiry must be viewed as a move toward a conceptualization of this complex phenomenon. To complete this process of conceptualization, an ongoing dialog and a debate among those who are engaged in the educational inquiry will be needed. This dialog and debate must occur both across groups of inquirers as well as within groups. Researchers, practitioners, and policymakers need to develop strategies for engaging in a dialog about practice as will researchers of differing perspectives and practitioners and policymakers with differing perspectives, goals, and positions. In other words, all educators need to develop a conversation of practice (e.g., Green, 1990; Green & Collins, in press; Yinger, 1988).

One of the topics that will need to be subjected to dialog and debate within this conversation of practice is the issue of implementation. A clearer understanding of what is involved in implementing theory, method, paradigm, and findings needs to be developed across programs of inquiry. By understanding who implements what, in what ways, and for what purposes, we will be better able to determine the contribution of different ways of engaging in inquiry to our understanding of educational phenomena. Although the dialog and debate may need to focus on what each paradigm permits us to explore and understand, the conversation of practice must ultimately focus on developing more complete understanding of specific phenomena within and across different contexts of practice.

Recent work on multiple perspective analysis of educational phenomena indicates that such a conversation is possible. Green and Harker (1988) present a series of studies in which a multiple perspective approach to education inquiry was used to explore particular sets of data. What these studies show is that, by conceptually combining approaches to inquiry, a more complex understanding of a phenomenon is obtained (Green & Harker, 1988). Rather than viewing the different groups as competing, a conversation of practice can enable us to develop systematic understandings of the complexity of educational phenomena.

Although the conversation about phenomena is important and the information that will result from such dialog is promising, the mere identification of elements of a phenomenon does not ensure that it will be used to inform practice. Central to this conversation is an understanding of audience and the ways in which audience expectations, goals, beliefs, prior knowledge, and perceptions influence what can be known and what is accepted as of value. The conversation of practice must thus include a conversation about ways of thinking about and using evidence from the contexts of discovery and presentation. This conversation will lay the foundation for inquiries into the factors that support and/or constrain the use of evidence from social science research by those in the context of practice. Such a conversation will enable us to begin to eliminate the gap between policy, research, and practice. It will also enable us to develop new understandings of the needs, roles, and expectations of the various participants in an inquiry cycle. What can result from this dialog are strategies of implementation that extend our current knowledge and understanding of educational phenomena as well as ways of moving beyond the détente that currently exists within and across groups and paradigms.

Notes

1. The use of the label *qualitative research umbrella* is a heuristic device. Under this umbrella are a variety of perspectives, including interpretive perspectives (e.g., phenomenology, hermeneutics, ethnography, symbolic interactionism, ethnomethodology, sociolinguistics), feminism, critical theory, and postmodernism. Qualitative research, therefore, is a general category to facilitate the discussion of implementation that transcends a particular paradigm.

2. The order of presentation of these different groups of inquirers is rotated throughout this chapter. No indication of hierarchy is intended by the order of presentation. Each group is seen as having its own purposes and activities that contribute to the nature of the educational enterprise in specific ways. Each group is viewed as making unique contributions that need to be understood and accepted if we are to bridge the perceived gap among research, practice, and policy.

3. We find that alternative research approaches appear in most major educational research journals. For example, the board of directors of the *Reading Research Quarterly* required a statement addressing how those applying for editorship of the journal would ensure publication of research representing multiple perspectives on reading and literacy. This requirement represents a major shift in editorial policy for this research journal. Finally, journals currently exist that are committed to publishing qualitative studies of education (e.g., *Qualitative Studies in Education* and the *Anthropology and Education Quarterly*). Another example is the *American Educational Research Journal* under the editorship of Virginia Richardson at the University of Arizona.

4. The process of "breaking open" a term can also be referred to as deconstruction within the qualitative research approach. (For discussions of this process, see Lather, 1989a, and Caputo, 1987.)

[16]

Peering at Paradigms Through the Prism of Practice Improvement

DAVID P. CRANDALL

Implementation is a relatively meaningless concept when examined in the absence of any context, as Green and Chandler (this volume) point out. Without something to implement and "clients" with whom to implement, the discussion runs the risk of remaining overly abstract and somewhat vacuous. To provide substance to our exploration, we could focus on one of two possible charges within the context of the "Alternative Paradigms Conference." The first is to focus on the implementation of a particular alternative inquiry paradigm: What would be required to undertake such an implementation effort? Who would be involved at what stages? What factors would need to be considered? What process(es) would be followed? How would you know if you succeeded? But such a charge is not entirely true to the spirit of the conference. Collectively, we are searching not for "the" paradigm but for a better understanding of a range of alternatives. In addition, the "paradigm implementation process" may well end up looking more like a conversation—or the product of a long philosophical journey—involving a variety of processes that few would recognize as a typical (or realistic) implementation effort.

An alternative to examining the implementation of a particular paradigm—one that should be of equal interest regardless of the paradigm espoused by the keynote speakers—is to focus on implementation of the *outputs* from any paradigm of inquiry. Presumably all of us, regardless of our view of the world and the process of inquiry we employ within it, hope that what we learn can somehow make some tangible difference in an important aspect of our life or work.

For me, the primary arena of attention is improvement of teaching and learning in the K-12 educational enterprise. As a result of this emphasis, this chapter is primarily focused on implementation at the school level. Although expanding the perspectives of our academic colleagues (i.e., implementing the notion of alternative paradigms) is important as well, I suggest concentrating on one set of actors—building-level practitioners—to explore implementation issues initially, acknowledging that implementation in the worlds of higher education and R&D might look somewhat different.

Given this focus, Green and Chandler (this volume) have identified some important and useful conceptual clarifications. Their paper moves us forward in distinguishing between an "instrument-focused" definition of implementation and what they, and I, consider to be the much more useful "process" approach. Similarly, I embrace their (apparent) identification of four characteristics of implementation: that there is (a) a set of actions (b) undertaken deliberately (c) by an actor—I would say "actors"—(d) toward some end. I would emphasize more strongly than Green and Chandler the importance of this final aspect—that implementation should be aimed at achieving some end, normally some identifiable changes in behaviors. From our pragmatic stance, implementation is concerned with ultimately bringing about such changes. Hence, it is on this aspect that I want to focus at least part of our attention.

One of the more valuable contributions of Green and Chandler is in the latter portion of their chapter, where they discuss conceptual and instrumental models of inquiry. But this is also where I suspect there are areas of disagreement. We regret that they did not explore these issues further and provide additional thinking to which I could respond.

Their view, it appears, rests on a model of knowledge generation that is constructivist in nature. Although I would not necessarily disagree that this may be a more productive approach to inquiry, I would argue that the challenge is to identify implementation processes that are equally effective regardless of the paradigm of inquiry. I find myself in the unusual position of arguing against the more organic approach to inquiry implied by Green and Chandler and instead urging a more pragmatic approach that allows "implementation" to be separated from any one inquiry paradigm.

I concede my discomfort with arguing the feasibility of such a position, even if simply for the purpose of exploring these issues in greater detail. But, as we discuss in the following few pages, my hope is to identify ways that the implementation process can serve as a bridge between paradigms or as a "translator" between inquirer and practitioner, when the two are not the same, which is the more common scenario. That is, I am interested in identifying ways that the outputs from a paradigm can be effectively "translated" so that they are appropriately implemented (in the eyes of the "knowledge generators"), that is, used by practitioners and policymakers who do not embrace—nor perhaps even fully understand—the paradigm from which they were generated.

This is not to argue that proponents of each inquiry paradigm might not want to develop an implementation step within its inquiry loop that is consistent with its methods, beliefs, assumptions, and so forth. There clearly is much to be said for the coherence of such an approach. But in this response to Green and Chandler, my interest is in pursuing with our colleagues the feasibility of developing a more generic process that "transcends" any one paradigm, so to speak, and empowers people—practitioners, policymakers, researchers, and others—to communicate effectively across paradigms and to understand and apply one anothers' findings in appropriate ways. We agree with Denis Phillips (this volume) that only an extreme interpretation of Kuhn would suggest the impossibility of such cross-paradigm discourse and that indeed paradigms "serve as lenses, not a blinders." It is likely, however, that we would place more faith—or express more concern—about the distortions these lenses may cause than would Phillips.

It is striking to hear the subtle—and not so subtle—distinctions that have been made as the keynote authors describe their alternative paradigms for inquiry—or the "lenses" they look through in exploring the world. Our work focuses on attempting to bridge the gap between research and practice, always with an eye on school reality. Thus we are continuously pushed to imagine how distinctions such as those articulated by the keynoters play out in practice—and if those who are in fact playing them out are aware of what they are doing or would recognize the particular paradigm within which they are operating. Although I agree with Yvonna Lincoln (this volume) that a "mix-and-match" approach to paradigms within the academic community is not likely to be the norm, I am less convinced that this is the case for the practice and policy communities. The thinking that has been devoted to developing the alternative paradigms presented here is enormous. But it seems likely that people who have not engaged in this process are living contentedly with any number of internal inconsistencies that they neither recognize nor even particularly value within their context and priorities.

Our experience suggests that it is unrealistic to expect most practitioners and policymakers to consciously articulate or embrace any particular paradigm. Although I would not deny that we all have been touched (perhaps unknowingly) by dominant paradigms (for example, a Newtonian view of the world), it seems quite unlikely that many school people have spent substantial time contemplating the ontological, epistemological, and methodological distinctions outlined by Lincoln and others. It simply isn't how most people in schools function.

Some colleagues of ours involved in a recent restructuring effort have made an interesting comparison among those of us in the R&D business, higher education, and schools. In the R&D world, our general form of operation can be characterized as something similar to "Look-Learn-Do"; in higher education, it is more similar to "Learn-Look-Do"; and in schools, it is primarily the "Do-Look-Learn" approach. Although it is easy to quibble with oversimplifications of this type, there is more than a kernel of truth here. Few of us who have studied schools or who have worked with them would dispute that it is "doing" that is of critical importance at the school level. The context of the school constantly drives teachers in this direction. "Classroom press" is the label Huberman (1983) uses to describe the classroom environment, emphasizing characteristics such as immediacy and concreteness, multidimensionality and simultaneity, unpredictability, and personal involvement. Schools are arenas of action, not reflection.

What are the implications of this type of school reality contrasted with higher education and R&D, particularly in terms of implementing findings of alternative inquiry paradigms? Obviously there are many, especially with respect to effective strategies for increasing the likelihood that knowledge produced through inquiry will be reflected upon and ultimately be used by people in schools. First, however, we must ask ourselves if we can assume that, within their reality, school people have a shared paradigm—or that they would recognize or own any of the alternative paradigms described here. Can we assume that Lincoln's "intrapsychic need for coherence, order, and logic" is applicable in the same manner for those who do not see themselves as sharing in a particular paradigmatic view?

We can agree that paradigms will exert unconscious influence over choices, but, if we are correct in our suspicion that it is the few rather than the many who actually share in a coherent, internally consistent, articulated paradigm, what are the implications for deciphering these influences? And, if practitioners are to be part of the inquiry process, as Green and Chandler suggest, what problems does this presumed lack of understanding regarding paradigms create?

This is not to argue that we do not all act on particular paradigm-based assumptions, beliefs, and theories, though we are likely not to be conscious of many of them. But it seems unrealistic to expect internal consistency to prevail when the potentially dominant paradigm is unrecognized let alone unarticulated. Similarly, it is equally unrealistic to expect individuals to understand how these often unconscious paradigm-driven assumptions can skew the interpretation and application of findings from alternative inquiry processes, often without recognizing that this is even occurring.

There appears to be some agreement among all the keynote speakers that, regardless of the objectivity or subjectivity of knowledge (or whether or not one would "own" a particular paradigm), people are not passive recipients of information. Similarly, there is no denial of the social construction of at least perception and beliefs, if perhaps there is disagreement about its impact on knowledge. Without becoming sidetracked on either a discussion of what it means to know something or whether knowledge is socially constructed—both of which are important to the discussion but neither of which we can do justice to in such a brief response chapter—it seems likely that most of us could agree that people are at least as likely to act on what they believe, feel, and think as they are to act on what they "know."

From a pragmatic perspective on implementation, this is a critical point because our concern is with causing some action to occur. Only secondarily are we concerned with knowing, at least at the outset. If this is the case, then many of the epistemological distinctions we are discussing take on secondary importance and we may be able to shift the discussion to more common ground.

That common ground has to do with "knowledge" use—*knowledge* being much more loosely defined than at least Denis Phillips (this volume) is likely to find acceptable. From a pragmatic perspective, I suspect that a discussion of implementing the outputs or findings from alternative inquiry paradigms is not unlike a discussion of general knowledge use and dissemination. Clearly the complexity of the discussion is raised substantially. We can no longer simply discuss "knowledge" but must instead discuss knowledge within the context of a particular paradigm as well as that same knowledge within the context of alternative paradigms. If we believe that one's paradigm serves as a lens that distorts (often unconsciously) understanding, manipulation, and application of information, then it will be necessary to discover techniques or strategies that allow "translation" of findings from one paradigm to another without mutating meaning beyond recognition. And, of course, one person's knowledge use constitutes another's knowledge creation so the hall of mirrors effect can be quiet disorienting.

Nevertheless, regardless of the added complexities, it is important not to ignore the obvious. To begin with, what do we know about knowledge use in schools? Huberman (1983) provides a number of insights into the dominant realities of practicing educators:

- Operational and practical uses of knowledge ("how") are of more interest than conceptual and explanatory uses ("why").
- The validity of new information is assessed by its "fit" with personal experience; also important are peer confirmation, message plausibility, and source credibility.
- Personal acquaintances and written materials—what is easily accessible—are the primary sources of knowledge.
- The exchange of "recipe knowledge" is much more common than reading, taking courses, participating in in-service activities, and seeking information and practices, although all occur.

Although there are many barriers to the use of new knowledge in schools, there is increasing understanding of strategies to overcome these problems. In their study of general assistance and dissemination strategies, Louis and her associates identify two critical factors in facilitating or blocking knowledge use: (a) incentives and (b) assessing/social processing (Louis, Kell, Dentler, Corwin, & Herriott, 1984). Incentives can be personal (e.g., improving professional skills, achieving great efficiency, gaining support for ideas/plans) and/or organizational (e.g., mandates, collegial pressures). According to Louis, Kell, Dentler, Corwin, and Herriott (1984, p. 130):

Current research has tended to neglect or trivialize the range of relevant incentives that people bring to knowledge use settings. Often people are motivated only by the "ownership" incentive. . . . Individuals are actively engaged in meeting their own needs as they assess and use information, and . . . personal incentives are generally more powerful than the organizational pressures that are brought to bear.

The second factor identified by Louis and colleagues—assessing and social processing—is equally, if not more, important for our conversation. People respond to the information they receive by assessing and processing it with their colleagues. According to Louis, Kell, Dentler, Corwin, and Herriott (1984, p. 119):

Because both *assessment* and *social processing* involve further analysis of the information, in effect the knowledge that emerges after they occur is different than that which existed before. Thus, the decision-making activities transform the information from something that was not part of the individual and organization to something that is personalized and customized for potential use.

This second aspect of knowledge use—what one of our colleagues refers to as "meaning making"—seems critical to our discussion of implementation. It is at this meaning-making stage that implementors can take into account differing paradigms and can begin the process of bridging or translating between/among inquiry processes to create shared meaning, which in turn (we would hope) will lead to changed behavior. But how does this process occur? Who is involved and in what roles? How might sensitivity to differing paradigms be embedded in this process?

There is much research on who can play what roles in providing assistance to facilitate the use of new knowledge in schools (see, for example, Crandall & associates, 1983; Emrick, Peterson, & Agarwala-Rogers, 1977; Havelock, 1973; Loucks-Horsley & Hergert, 1985; Louis & Rosenblum, 1981). Louis, Kell, Dentler, Corwin and Herriott (1984, p. 164) suggest that disseminators should ask themselves three questions about providing services and assistance:

a. Can opportunities for direct, preferably face-to-face, interaction between users and disseminators be built in?

b. Can those interactions be made into *multiple* occasions?

c. Can the interactive arrangements be arranged to endure across a period of a school year or more?

They similarly identify a list of key questions about the content of what is to be disseminated—questions those engaged in the inquiry process might find equally useful to ponder:

a. Has the knowledge been constructed with a view to its field-tested useability?

b. Has the social context of prospective users been incorporated into the knowledge?

c. Is the knowledge accessible to inexperienced users?

d. Does the knowledge have a strong inspirational, idealistic, or altruistic thrust in its message?

e. Is there a way built into the knowledge base for users to assess the knowledge on their own terms?

f. Does the knowledge initiate or encourage local adaptation? (Louis, Kell, Dentler, Corwin, & Herriott, 1984, pp. 163-164)

Obviously these questions do not indicate how to implement or translate findings across alternative paradigms. They do, however, remind us of factors that are important to increasing the likelihood that people in schools will use the knowledge that emerges from inquiry, regardless of the paradigm. To return to my position at the outset of this chapter, for us, implementation is successful only if it results in changes in behavior. This requires that people use the information that is emerging (i.e., assess and process it into some local/individual understanding and action), whether or not they have been a part of the formal inquiry process.

But as Louis and her associates point out, as information is incorporated into a new context, it is likely to be altered. Is this mutation of information desirable? If not, is it preventable? Can information be "translated" in a manner that allows it to have meaning for those using it while remaining consistent with the inquiry paradigm through which it was generated? These are, in part, questions of fidelity versus adaptation and are thus familiar to those involved in educational change and innovation. But the dispute takes on new meaning within the context of alternative paradigms.

Although we do not have answers to these questions, we suggest that this chapter and the Green and Chandler chapter provide a stepping-off place to examine this next set of issues, which focus on *translation* (e.g., Can findings that flow from one paradigm be translated to another with fidelity? Is this necessary or desirable?) and *meaning making* (e.g., What are the consequences of paradigmatic lenses distorting "knowledge"? Is fidelity an issue? Is "meaning" translatable across paradigms?). I suggest that we turn to these issues now.

[17]

Discussion on Implementation

CORRINE GLESNE

Univeristy of Vermont

Because Judith Green, the session presenter, is a sociolinguist, it wasn't surprising that much of the discussion in our sessions focused on words and their meaning. Eight particular words seemed to dominate. I have paraphrased some of the conversation around these and shaped a dialog to give you the flavor of the discussions.

Commentator: "Word one is *implementation*. We know very little."

Respondent: "We know a great deal."

C: "We know about change. The second word is *change*."

R: "Is change a goal of alternative paradigms? Do we inquire in order to change social phenomena?"

C: "Or do we inquire in order to understand?"

R: " . . . and then use that knowledge to improve."

C: "No, I'd say we use that knowledge to inform."

R: "Implementation may or may not contribute to change. And change happens whether or not we want it to."

C: "But we cannot ignore the change literature when talking about implementation. The third word is *role*. Researcher, practitioner, policymaker."

R: "Different words or different roles?"

C: "I can be all three, but it's difficult to be so simultaneously. My role determines what I want out of implementation."

R: "Most of us are more one role than another and we interact differently with implementation in each case."

C: "The case, or a fourth word, *context*. Each situation is a unique case. We need to uncover the uniqueness and understand implementation in that light."

R: "But then we are context bound and that makes for a problematic policy environment. Perhaps we know more than we think we know and can move faster toward implementing our knowledge."

C: "It's not just a matter of us moving faster but of others moving faster too. The fifth word is *audience*."

R: "Who is the audience? Participants? Our others? The 'they'?"

C: "We talk of teachers, administrators, journal editors, and colleagues."

R: "Don't forget the children in the schools. How do we hear the voices of the learners?"

C: "Implementation requires linkage with the audience."

R: "Implementation requires sensitivity to the audience as we discover, and as we present, our understanding."

C: "But how? The sixth word is *transformative*. We desire a transformative experience, not one that is top down."

R: "Move away from consumer and transmission models."

C: "In implementation, the audience must participate, must be a part of reconstruction."

R: "But what if, through democratic participation, we vote ourselves into ignorance? Should the audience drive implementation?"

C: "No, it takes a seventh word, *dialog*. Something we need to do more of, but how?"

R: "Through an eighth word, *language*. We learn to code-switch, to speak the languages of our different audiences, to use what Bruner calls the storied nature of our lives."

C: "But do we—you and I, the researcher, the practitioners, and policymakers—still speak the same language? Perhaps we need to continue constructing and deconstructing our own language of inquiry, learning to speak the same language among ourselves."

KNOWLEDGE ACCUMULATION

[18]

Three Views on the Nature and Role of Knowledge in Social Science

JENNIFER C. GREENE

This chapter examines the perspectives of postpositivism, interpretivism,[1] and critical theory on issues related to social scientific knowledge accumulation. The discussion is spirited by efforts both to honor the paradigmatic pluralism of this era and, given my own strong pragmatic orientation, to question what it all means for the practical import of our work. For each inquiry framework, in turn, honor is paid via an introductory sketch, both the form and the substance of which are intended to be illustrative; a brief review of the paradigmatic assumptions most germane to knowledge issues; and a focused discussion of the nature of knowledge and its links to the form and function of knowledge accumulation. Then, the challenge is offered via a critique of the implications of each paradigm's view of knowledge accumulation for the purpose and role of science in our world, with an emphasis on the interrelationships of theory, research, and practice.

As a baseline for this discussion, the perspectives of the conventional inquiry framework on these knowledge accumulation issues are offered first. Within our long-standing scientific tradition, knowledge has been equated with theory, where theory comprises a precise,

AUTHOR'S NOTE: My sincere thanks to Cathy Campbell, Charles McClintock, Bill Trochim, Deborah Trumbull, and particularly Egon Guba for their constructive comments on this chapter.

testable network of universal, lawlike relationships among clearly defined variables, a network that is determinate, explanatory, predictive, and verifiable. In conventional science, theories are developed, tested, and refined through empirical research. So, research is intentionally cumulative, and hallmarks of good research studies include clearly defined hypotheses derived from existing theory and results that take the form of generalizable theoretical propositions. The task of the scientist is thus to develop theory. Once developed, scientific theories can be used to address problems or advance life quality in the world of practice. In conventional science, that is, there is a "categorical distinction" between research and practice, between the development of scientific theory and applications of this theory to practical problems (Bernstein, 1976, p. 44).

In relationship to this conventional portrayal of knowledge accumulation, three alternative images frame the present discussion. As the paradigm that represents "old uncertainties unthroned, but not abolished" (Cook, 1985, p. 37), postpositivism also embraces a *social engineering* view of the role and purpose of science. Interpretivism, however, seeks not to adjust the conventional framework but to replace it. With its grounding in phenomenology, hermeneutics, and value pluralism, interpretivism's perspective on the role of social science in the world is likened to *storytelling*.

Critical theory rejects both postpositivism and interpretivism as stand-alone paradigms because of their silence on issues of politics, values, and ideology. This critical inquiry framework seeks to make such issues central to science, thereby intertwining the purpose of science with that of *political engagement and action*.

This chapter then concludes by identifying key issues that cut across these diverse images in the spirit of what Gareth Morgan calls "reflective conversation" (Morgan, 1983b, p. 374). In this era of paradigmatic pluralism, Morgan urges such conversation as a way of facilitating more thoughtful research practice, and especially greater responsibility among social scientists, for "their role in making and remaking social science as we know it today" (Morgan, 1983b, p. 376).

Stances

As one additional set of introductory comments, I believe it is important to share my own predispositions regarding the three paradigms and the knowledge accumulation issues to be addressed. These comprise four main themes. First, regarding my own expertise or my qualifications for this discussion, I can claim modest mastery of the foundations and perspectives of both postpositivism and interpretivism but consider myself more of a novice with respect to critical theory. My discussion of this latter inquiry framework should thus be viewed as more tentative. Second, my paradigmatic loyalties continue to be troublesomely divided. I have substantially rejected the conventional paradigm that initially shaped my identity as a social scientist but, as yet, am unwilling to swear allegiance to a single alternative. I have opinions about various aspects of different paradigms, but, in the main, I remain a learner, intensely curious and eager to continue learning about the multiple inquiry frameworks that abound in this pluralistic era (Lincoln, 1989). Third, I count myself among those "who believe that science is a remarkably different validity-producing social system [say, than the arts or religion] and at the same time are puzzled as to how this can be so" (Campbell, 1988, p. 498). With the nearly universal recognition that values, ideology, and beliefs permeate the very fabric of social science, what then sets the logic and validity of science apart from any other human endeavor? Finally, and perhaps most important, I believe that all of this self-conscious and often rarified discourse about the assumptional bases and coherence of our work really does matter. This is reflected primarily in this chapter's explicit emphasis on the practical significance of social science. Miles and Huberman (1984) have argued that epistemological purity does not get research done. In counterpoint, I would contend that epistemological integrity does get meaningful research done right. The important "evaluation criteria that can be brought to bear on the nature of knowledge . . . relate [primarily] to the way knowledge serves to guide and shape ourselves as human beings—to the consequences of knowledge, in the sense of what knowledge does to and for humans" (Morgan, 1983b, p. 373).

Postpositivism: Social Science as Social Engineering

Sketch

Thomas Cook's *Postpositivist Critical Multiplism* (1985) is a leading example of postpositivist thought. This approach to inquiry aims to "approximate the ultimately unknowable truth through the use of processes that critically triangulate from a variety of perspectives on what is worth knowing and what is known" (Cook, 1985, p. 57). The multiplism argument is rooted in the classic methodological ideas of multiple operationalism (Campbell & Fiske, 1959) and between-method triangulation (Denzin, 1978; Webb, Campbell, Schwartz, & Sechrest, 1966). But, in direct response to the philosophical attacks on conventional science, Cook proposes such additional forms of *methodological* multiplism as multiple analyses of the same data set. He also extends the triangulation argument to *theory-related* forms of multiplism, including, for example, the testing of multiple explanatory models for a given set of data (rather than assessing the goodness of fit of a single model). Further, to redress the disappointing failure of social science to contribute meaningfully to the reforms of the Great Society era, Cook advances forms of multiplism that acknowledge the *politics and value pluralism* of such policy contexts, for example, the inclusion of multiple and diverse constituencies in formulating the research agenda.

The Nature of Postpositivist Knowledge and Key Underlying Assumptions

Cook's proposal for critical multiplism, in concert with the remarks on postpositivist "myths and realities" by Denis Phillips (this volume) in the present forum, provide a view of the nature of knowledge in postpositivist thought.

Knowledge remains theory in postpositivism, where theory is construed as a "model" (Cook, 1985) or a "huge fishnet" (Phillips, this volume) of complex, mutually interacting casual relationships among specified constructs or variables. That is, postpositivists believe that human phenomena can best be explained in terms of causal relationships. But this causality is assumed to be complex, multiplistic, and interactive. "Human and social relationships are more like pretzels than single-headed arrows from A to B . . . more like convoluted multivariate statistical interactions than simple main effects" (Cook, 1985, p. 25). Moreover, good theories accurately explain and predict human phenomena but may or may not actually correspond to truth. For, given the realist ontological stance of postpositivism—the belief that there is a natural world out there and that our task as scientists is to know and understand it, in order to explain and predict it—truth remains a "regulative ideal" (Phillips, 1987b, in press). However, because "no longer can it be claimed there are any *absolutely authoritative foundations* upon which scientific knowledge is based" (Phillips, this volume; see also Bernstein, 1983), truth is acknowledged as "ultimately unknowable" (Cook, 1985). Hence, theory in postpositivism is more like *small theory* and knowledge claims are concomitantly more modest. "Any return to grand theory in human sciences . . . is a selective and wishful interpretation of social science research" (Overman, 1988, p. xvi).

In fact, postpositivist knowledge claims or theoretical propositions are viewed, from Dewey, as "warranted assertibility" (Phillips, this volume) or as established regularities or probabilities about human phenomena rather than as universal laws that govern human behavior. Knowledge claims gain warrant when they are supported by carefully marshaled, objective evidence and when their argument is credible, coherent, and consensual, in other words, when they have survived a *critical tradition* of evaluative challenges and unsuccessful refutations (Cook, 1983, 1985; Phillips, in press). This notion of a critical tradition, derived from Popper, constitutes the essence of Cook's multiplism proposal; he advocates multiplism precisely to invite open criticism from diverse and pluralistic perspectives. "So long as ultimate truth is not accessible, the process of assigning validity is social and partly dependent upon a consensus achieved in debate" (Cook, 1983, p. 89).

Survival of the critical tradition is similarly integral to the post-positivist conception of objectivity. For all alternative inquiry frameworks, acceptance of Hanson's insight that no observations are theory or value neutral (Phillips, 1987b, in press) forces either a reformulation or a rejection of the conventional view of objectivity as freedom from bias. Postpositivists have opted for reformulation, arguing for a view of objectivity as "critical intersubjective verifiability across heterogeneous perspectives" (Cook, 1983, pp. 83-84; see also Campbell, 1984). Knowledge claims so verified are more objective and thus more warranted or more likely to be true. This reconstrual of objectivity also shifts its locus from the individual scientist and the context of discovery to the "community of inquirers" and the context of justification (Phillips, in press). "The objectivity of science is not a matter of the individual scientists but rather the social result of their mutual criticism" (Popper, quoted in Phillips, in press).

Knowledge Accumulation in Postpositivism

With a view of knowledge as small but convoluted, pretzel-like theory and a belief in truth as a regulative ideal, postpositivism maintains as the goal of empirical research the development of generalizable theoretical propositions, yet views such generalizations as attainable only tentatively and probabilistically. "Most scientific results have the character of hypotheses, i.e., sentences for which the evidence is inconclusive . . . [and which are] liable to be superseded in the course of scientific progress" (Popper, quoted in Campbell, 1984, p. 4). Further, with a commitment to an open critical tradition and a concomitantly muted confidence in methodology, postpositivism's empirical quest for knowledge emphasizes replicability across heterogeneous populations, settings, times, perspectives (see, for example, Cronbach, 1982) and deductive, critical refutation. Scientific generalizations gain warrant only through such replication and criticism. Thus knowledge in postpositivism is accumulated or small theory developed not via the single definitive study but from programs or traditions of empirical research, and past research serves less as the foundation and more as the catalyst for future inquiry.

As Howe (1985) and Phillips (this volume) describe this relationship between research and knowledge growth in postpositivism, empirical evidence can either provisionally confirm a theoretical hypothesis or prove inconsistent with it. If the latter, and the evidence is accepted as credible and thus falsifying, then postpositivists can use this evidence in a variety of ways. No one specific change, i.e., rejection of the given hypothesis, is necessitated (Phillips, this volume). This is because the empirical test does not apply to this hypothesis alone but to the entire theory within which it is embedded. So, different scientists may decide to modify different portions of the relevant theory or even to make no theoretical modifications, awaiting further evidence. That is, decisions about how to modify theories and thus contribute to knowledge growth require professional judgment; they cannot be made mechanically (Phillips, this volume). Nonetheless, while acknowledging the role of professional judgment in scientific growth, postpositivists continue to question how such growth can be rationally justified. And on this, Phillips asserts, "there has been much debate, but little consensus" (Phillips, this volume).

So Why Do Social Science?
The Postpositivist Response

> The ideology of the experimenting society is a *method* ideology, not a content ideology. That is, it proposes ways of testing and revising theories of optimal political-economic-social organization rather than proposing a specific political and economic system. (Campbell, 1984, p. 16.)

> [The social scientist's job] is to interpret the world, not to change it; he [or she] interprets it by offering and testing theoretical explanations. . . . Therefore, he [or she] endorses a categorical distinction between theory and practice or action. (Bernstein, 1976, p. 44)

These quotes well illustrate the *intended* political and value neutrality of postpositivism and its continued separation from the world of practice. The line demarcating social science from practice is more permeable in postpositivism than in conventional science. For example, Cook argues that social science must interface with the pluralistic politics and values of applied contexts, especially policy contexts, and that social scientists must not just "build the restricted set of assumptions of the powerful into their research" (Cook, 1985, p. 37). Also arguing largely within the context of applied social policy, Campbell (1984, p. 4) quotes Popper as saying, "Practice is not the enemy of theoretical knowledge, but the most valuable incentive to it."

Nonetheless, the postpositivist social scientist's main job is to participate in the critical community of inquirers whose collective task it is to develop warranted scientific knowledge. The individual scientist's participation is marked by his or her own values, theoretical predispositions, and beliefs, thereby generating a critical but not a normative warrant for the community's collective product of theory. This theory then is to be used to enhance or extend the quality of human endeavors in the world of practice. "How people use the theory to guide practice is not a question of science but of politics" (Popkewitz, 1984, p. 39). So, practical action is a potentiality of the theory because the theory contains valued instrumental knowledge about manipulanda (Cook, 1983), but theory and action remain separate. And so, belying its claims for neutrality and consistent with the character of social engineering, postpositivism clearly rests on a value foundation of utilitarianism, efficiency, and instrumentality.

Interpretivism: Social Science as Storytelling[2]

Sketch and Key Interpretivist Assumptions

The constructivist paradigm developed and continuingly nurtured by Yvonna Lincoln and Egon Guba (Lincoln, this volume; see also Guba & Lincoln, 1981, 1987, 1988a: Lincoln, 1988, 1989; Lincoln & Guba, 1985, 1986a) constitutes a major example of interpretivist thought and a significant influence within contemporary paradigm debates. The following is a brief sketch of this paradigm, drawn largely from Lincoln's chapter in this volume, in a form that approximates its own voice.

The impersonality of the small conference room—its institutional-beige walls absent any adornment and its hard, uncomfortable black chairs arranged in neat precise rows like soldiers on a parade ground—only heightened the drama unfolding with the current speaker at the front of the room. She spoke of a constructivist paradigm for social inquiry, a paradigm erected from the rubble that ensued when the tower of conventional science, besieged by the batterings of the new philosophy of science, finally toppled. Constructivism, she argued, is based on an entirely different, synergistic set of assumptions about the world and the manner in which we can know it.

One such assumption is that "reality is a social, and, therefore, multiple, construction" (Lincoln, this volume). As social, this reality derives from human interactions aimed at meaning making, comprises intersubjective meanings that "exist only by social agreement or consensus among participants in a [given] context" (Eisenhart, 1988, p. 103), and thus is multiplistic as well as ever changing. Moreover, "the ways in which [humans] interpret their own actions and those of others are not externally related to, but constitutive of, those actions" and of human beliefs, practices, and institutions more generally (Bernstein, 1976, p. 156). Other constructivist assumptions are that "knower and known are interactive, inseparable" and that "inquiry is value-bound" (Lincoln & Guba, 1985, p. 37). These represent, the speaker noted, not just acceptance of Hanson's insight but actual celebration of it "as an opportunity to be exploited" (Lincoln & Guba, 1985, p. 101) as in maximizing the power of the dialectical interaction between a cooperating respondent and a human inquiry instrument to generate meaningful understanding.

Beyond these bold strokes of scientific philosophy, the other contribution to this drama was the speaker's integration of the personal with the scientific in her presentation. She spoke of her immersion in constructivism as an "enlightening, curious, idiographic, and piquant voyage" (Lincoln, this volume). She shared her struggles to respond to critics along the way and to make whole and coherent *her* vision of social inquiry. As we share many value stances, my vision of constructivism would be similar. But I can't help but imagine that there are constructivists with different personal values, and then I wonder, what do their visions of constructivism look like?

The Nature of Interpretivist Knowledge

From Lincoln and others, interpretivist knowledge comprises the reconstruction of intersubjective meanings, the interpretive understanding of the meanings humans construct in a given context and how these meanings interrelate to form a whole. Any given interpretive reconstruction is idiographic, time- and place-bound; multiple reconstructions are pluralistic, divergent, even conflictual. Hence, interpretivist knowledge resembles more context-specific working hypotheses than generalizable propositions warranting certainty or even probability. But what is the character, the form and substance, of these working hypotheses and thus of interpretivist knowledge?

- Interpretivist knowledge is grounded knowledge (Glaser & Strauss, 1967), not developed from armchair speculations or elegant deductive reasoning but both discovered and justified from the field-based, inductive *methodology* (Guba & Lincoln, 1988a) of interpretivist inquiry.
- Interpretivist knowledge represents *emic* knowledge or inside understanding of the perspectives and meanings of those in the setting being studied, and it encompasses both propositional and tacit information (Stake, 1983; though see Phillips, 1987b, pp. 92-94, for a critique of this claim). That is, the understanding communicated in interpretivist knowledge comes not only from its words but also from the broadly shared contexts of natural experience within which it is embedded.
- Interpretivist knowledge constitutes not nomothetic models but holistic "pattern theories or webs of mutual and plausible influence" (Lincoln, this volume), webs that reflect a hermeneutic intertwinement of part and whole and a view of knowledge that is more "circular" or "amoebalike" than hierarchic and pyramidlike (Lincoln, this volume).
- Interpretivist understanding also aims for internal consistency and coherence. "Correspondence theories identify truth with a relationship *between* language and reality; coherence theories identify truth with internal consistency among claims *within* a language" (Howe, 1988, p. 15).
- And interpretivist knowledge is value-bound and hence "conflictual," "problematic and contested . . . locally and politically situated" (Lincoln, this volume). Moreover, "from this [interpretivist] perspective, social inquiry is meaningful only because it does involve values" (J. Smith, 1983, p. 47).

Knowledge Accumulation in Interpretivism

As is evident by this portrayal of interpretivist knowledge, inter-pretivism denies the possibility of universal social laws and empirical generalizations.[3] If all knowledge is socially constructed, value bound, and indeterminate, "only time- and context-bound working hypotheses (idiographic statements) are possible" (Lincoln & Guba, 1985, p. 37). So, interpretivist research generates working hypotheses that are connected not to a priori theory but to a context-specific, often emergent inquiry problem, which may or may not be informed by existing knowledge.

> The evidence generated by interpretive research is much more likely to be of an evocative rather than a comprehensive kind, to be sustained, rejected, or refined through future studies. The conclusions of one study merely provide a starting point in a continuing cycle of inquiry, which may [or may not] over time serve to generate persuasive patterns of data from which further conclusions can be drawn. (Morgan, 1983c, p. 398)

Yet, if all knowledge is context-specific working hypotheses and if research studies may or may not be connected to one another, how is knowledge accumulated within this inquiry framework? What is the meaning of interpretivist scientific progress? Two forms of response to these questions will be offered.

First, within interpretivist circles, the challenge of knowledge accu-mulation has been primarily addressed by the general concept of *transferability*. This concept shifts the inquirer's responsibility from one of demonstrating generalizability to one of providing sufficient description of the particular context studied so that others may ade-quately judge the applicability or fit of the inquiry findings to their own context. The locus of judgment about transferability thus also shifts from the inquirer to potential users. (See Cronbach, 1982, for similar themes presented for evaluative inquiry.)

Robert Stake's (1983) *naturalistic generalization* is one version of this transferability concept. Stake argues that "naturalistic generalizations develop within a person as a product of experience. They derive from tacit knowledge of how things are . . . [and] seldom take the form of predictions but lead regularly to expectation" (Stake, 1983, p. 282). Further, the interpretivist case study can provide a basis for such generalizations because it vicariously communicates natural experience as well as tacit knowledge. The importance of communicating "vicarious, 'déjà vu' experience" is also emphasized in Lincoln's formulation of criteria for constructivist case studies (Lincoln, 1988, this volume). And Lincoln and Guba offer transferability (to replace generalizability) as one of their four trustworthiness criteria for the constructivist inquiry process (Lincoln, this volume; Lincoln & Guba, 1985, 1986a). Regarding the latter, Lincoln and Guba contend that the inquirer must provide, at minimum, a thick description of the inquiry context and of the transactions or processes observed in that context that are relevant to the inquiry problem (Lincoln & Guba, 1985, p. 362), though they also acknowledge that "it is by no means clear how 'thick' a thick description needs to be" (Lincoln & Guba, 1986a, p. 77). Then, "the final judgment [about transferability] . . . is vested in the person seeking to make the transfer" (Lincoln & Guba, 1985, p. 217). Such persons may be interested readers, other researchers, or practitioners, lending multiple meanings to the transferability concept. In short, interpretivist inquirers must provide for the possibility of transferability, but its actualization—in the form of scientific knowledge accumulation or enhanced practice—depends on the interests of potential users.

Second, Lincoln's comments in the present forum openly invite further work on these issues of knowledge accumulation within constructivism. Arguing that we do not yet have a language for talking about forms of knowledge that are not hierarchic or taxonomic, neither do we have a language for conceptualizing connections between nonhierarchic knowledge forms. Maybe, she argues,

> we ought to be talking not about "building blocks of science" but about extended sophistication, or the artistic and expressive process of creatively conjoining elements in ways that are fresh and new. We ought to think of bridging, . . . or of synthesizing, . . . or of some other linkage processes. . . . we have no models for scientific knowledge that account for nonhierarchic learning, and we may have to borrow from the poet, the artist, the madman, the mystic. (Lincoln, this volume)

This importance of this challenge is underscored by the problematic character of the relationship of interpretivist knowledge to the world of practice, as discussed next.

So Why Do Social Science?
The Interpretivist Response

As grounded knowledge, interpretivist knowledge is embedded within the world of practice. Being value laden, interpretivist knowledge is not neutral or even critically neutral but *interested* knowledge, embued with the normative pluralism of the world of practice. Being value-laden, interpretivist knowledge is also permeated by the values and interests of the inquirer. Constructivism does aim to monitor and minimize the intrusion of inquirer biases into the inquiry process. When such reflexivity is successful, the inquiry findings represent primarily the meanings and values of respondents, and the inquirer's role becomes one of translator or intermediary among differing communities (Bredo & Feinberg, 1982b, pp. 430-431). Yet, any efforts to mute inquirer interests can be only partially successful at best. As Lincoln observed, the "research process itself [is] a political endeavor" (Lincoln, this volume).

Lincoln's interests as an inquirer are oriented around those of inquiry stakeholders and include fairness, action, and empowerment. She is seeking "a mainstream rethinking of the role the social sciences play in everyday, ordinary life" (Lincoln, this volume), a role that includes stakeholders as collaborators in inquiry, that fairly presents the constructions and values of all stakeholders in a setting, and that enhances the ability of stakeholders "to take action, to engage the political arena on behalf of oneself or one's referent stakeholder or participant group" (Lincoln, this volume). I believe these interests reflect Lincoln's vital immersions in the domains of social policy and program evaluation. And, as noted earlier, I share some of this experience and many of these values. But I believe they are our values as inquirers and not inherently those of the interpretivist inquiry paradigm.

Rather, the interpretivist paradigm must be characterized as value relative. Interpretivist knowledge inevitably reflects the values of the inquirer, even as it seeks to reconstruct others' sense of meaning and supporting beliefs. Further, as argued previously, uses of this knowledge depend on the interests of potential users, whether other researchers, policymakers, practitioners, or social program beneficiaries. So, even though interpretivist knowledge is embedded within the normative, pluralistic world of practice, interpretivist inquiry "is not directly [or necessarily] concerned with judging, evaluating, or condemning existing forms of social and political reality, or with changing the world" but with describing and understanding its constitutive meaning (Bernstein, 1976, p. 169). And so, given its value relativity, common goals of interpretivist inquiry can only be to enrich human discourse, "to bring us in touch with the lives of strangers . . . to converse with them" (Geertz, quoted in Rabinow, 1983, p. 66), "to enlarge the conversation" (J. Smith, 1984, p. 390) with our own understandings and our own stories. That is all?

Critical Science: Social Science as Political Engagement

Sketch

The sketch for the third inquiry framework, critical social science, is presented as a conversation, illustrating the communication and dialog essential to critical science. The setting is a community housing agency that seeks adequate housing for homeless and other low-income individuals in the community. The participants are Elena, an agency staff member for the past five years since her graduation from college, and Bill, a middle-aged, unemployed, temporarily homeless steel worker who is one of the agency's more active and outspoken clients.

Elena: Hi Bill. You wanted to talk with me as soon as possible. What's up?

Bill: Hi Elena. How's the bum-and-crazy business these days? Just kidding. Actually, I wanted to know if you heard Marcia Wilcox's talk last night at the YWCA about her research on housing in this town.

Elena: No, I didn't go. I'm really sick of researchers and their so-called facts and figures.

Bill: Well, Marcia was different. She started with history, saying that since the Depression days in this country, federal policy on low-income housing has never been more than an empty promise, or at most a half-hearted one. Oh sure, there have been some good guys—and gals—and some good intentions in the government all along. But, these intentions never really had much of chance, because they were opposed by the development interests of business and industry.

Elena: We all know that, that's nothing new. And, besides, these intentions
         you mentioned—they're not empty or half-hearted at all. They
         represent the fundamental ideals and values in this county.
Bill: Yes, I know, and Marcia agreed, too. She talked about these values
         as underlying the intent of federal housing policy over the years.
         But, as I was saying, this intent has always been opposed by the
         development interests. *And*, the way our government is set up
         automatically favors these interests over our ideals. She said some-
         thing like, the political structure inherently contradicts the values
         of social policy intent.
              Then, Marcia got local—and here is where you should be inter-
         ested. She said that the same thing happens at the local level, and
         that in this town, agencies like yours are part of the problem.
Elena: Part of the problem! I don't understand! Our whole reason for
         being is affordable housing for low-income people. We also have a
         good working relationship with the Downtown Business Associa-
         tion. And I've always thought that was good political strategy, you
         know, like the lamb lying down with the lion.
Bill: Yeah, but by lying down with them, you're doing a whole lot more
         than just resting. As Marcia said, you're buying into what they
         represent. And you're therefore reinforcing a local political situa-
         tion that, just like national politics, favors growth and development
         even without trying to do so. These priorities are built into the
         whole structure of the political system. So, what's really needed are
         some challenges to this structure. Without them, low-income hous-
         ing will always remain but a quadrennial campaign promise.
Elena: Like what kinds of challenges?
Bill: Marcia gave us some good leads on this. I've made some phone
         calls and a group of us are meeting tonight to talk more about her
         ideas. Want to join us?

On Critical Social Science

This sketch is intended to illustrate three key knowledge-related
attributes of critical social science: its embeddedness in history and
ideology; its own ideology, as revealed in the meaning of *critical*; and
its dialectical synthesis of historical dualism. (Critiques of these and
other tenets of critical social science are offered by Bredo & Feinberg,
1982a, 1982b; Fay, 1987.)
   According to Popkewitz (this volume) the rules, standards, and
logic of science do not have constant meanings, but embody different
concepts that are historically constructed and tied to social agendas

(see also Popkewitz, 1984). So, varying views of science, as represented by alternative inquiry frameworks, reflect different intellectual traditions that both arise from and embody different interplays of history and ideology. The assumptions, value dispositions, and methodologies of each tradition coherently interrelate to generate its definition of what counts as legitimate scientific knowledge.

The values explicitly promoted by critical social science are well articulated by its concept of critical,[4] and Popkewitz (this volume) offers two senses of what is critical about critical social science: (a) an analytic posture by which the logical consistency of arguments, procedures, and language receive continual cross-examination and scrutiny (not unlike the critical tradition of postpositivism), and (b) a lens for this posture that "give[s] focus to skepticism toward social institutions and . . . considers the conditions of social regulation, unequal distribution, and power" (Popkewitz, this volume). A critical social scientist would ask, for example, whether observed patterns of relationship "reveal invariant regularities of social action" or "express ideologically frozen relations of dependence" (Bernstein, 1976, pp. 230-231). Critical science also embodies an action-oriented commitment to the common welfare. It "has a [fundamental] practical interest in the fate and quality of social and political life . . . in radically 'improving human existence'" (Bernstein, 1976, pp. 174, 180).

Finally, Popkewitz (this volume) describes critical social science as a tradition that exposes the ideological bases and thus the poverty of such dualisms as objectivity and subjectivity, rigor and relevance, discovery and verification, and even ontology and epistemology. For example, "[objectivity and] relativity [are] issues only within the context of foundationalist epistemologies which search for a privileged standpoint as the guarantee of certainty" (Lather, 1988c, p. 10). In short, "phenomenology negates positivism, and philosophies of praxis [or practical action] are concerned with negating the dualism thus created" (Morgan, 1983b, p. 372; see also Bernstein, 1983).

The Nature of Critical Knowledge

Following directly from these attributes, knowledge in critical social science is, substantively, nonfoundational knowledge about the historical, structural, and value bases of social phenomena as well as about contradictions and distortions therein. Knowledge in critical science is also interested knowledge or knowledge that reflects the values and priorities of a particular intellectual-cultural-social tradition. In the critical theory of the contemporary Frankfurt school, advanced most notably by Jürgen Habermas (1971), legitimate interests include the technical-instrumental and practical-communicative knowledge claims of postpositivism and interpretivism, respectively. But, in part because neither of these informs us how to tell good from bad, their inquiry paradigms are supplemented and superseded in critical theory by one that takes a third emancipatory, action-constitutive interest as fundamental (Bredo & Feinberg, 1982a, p. 275). "An empirical statement [or critical knowledge claim] must be judged by its intentions for the good and true life" (Fischer, 1985, p. 251, from Aristotle via Habermas).

So, critical knowledge is also practical, action-oriented knowledge that enlightens and thereby catalyzes political and social change. Critical knowledge enlightens an audience by revealing the structural conditions of their existence, specifically, how these conditions came about and what distortions or injustices they currently represent. Such enlightenment carries within it an enabling, motivating force to stimulate action, a catalyst for self-reflection toward greater autonomy and responsibility and for strategic political action toward emancipation (Bernstein, 1976). Critical knowledge does not prescribe such action, for that would be action in its merely technical sense. Rather, critical knowledge represents "a genuine unity of theory and revolutionary praxis where the theoretical understanding of the contradictions inherent in existing society, when appropriated by those who are exploited, becomes constitutive of their very activity to transform society" (Bernstein, 1976, p. 182).

Knowledge Accumulation in Critical Social Science

So, how does knowledge—as an interested, emancipatory account of the history and values underlying social phenomena—accumulate in critical social science? As I understand this inquiry framework, the short answer is that it doesn't. Nor is it intended to. As Popkewitz (this volume) argues, the belief that scientific knowledge is a progressive development in which evidence continually clarifies and modifies what is known is erroneous. The logic of science is historically formed and changes in a manner that is not necessarily cumulative. From a critical perspective, knowledge accumulation in its building-block sense reifies "the social and historical conditions in which knowledge is produced and transformed" (Popkewitz, this volume) rather than respects the ideological and dynamic character of such conditions. With such respect, what counts as knowledge, including critical knowledge, changes with the times. Moreover, knowledge itself, as practical and action oriented, changes the social-political conditions in which it is produced. So, to endeavor to build on prior work is to estrange it from its own social-historical context, to deny, in turn, its impacts on that context and thereby to strip it of meaning.

Popkewitz (this volume) does say that "we need to understand what others have said and done before us" and that this involves a complex process of interpretation and analysis. Just what this means, however, is not entirely clear.

So Why Do Social Science?
The Critical Science Response

The practical import of critical social science, its role and function in the world of practice, *is* entirely clear and, moreover, is vitally integral to this inquiry framework. Critical social science denies the distinction between *is* and *ought*, between science as theory and research, and practice as normative, ideologically based action. Critical science seeks to reclaim the critical function of theory (Bernstein, 1976); to reassert the scientist's role as an interested observer who speaks with "a critical voice of social consciousness" (Popkewitz, this volume); to have a "practical political impact" (Fay, 1987, p. 2); "to change the world, not to describe it" (Popkewitz, 1984, p. 45).

Critical social science strives to meet these aims via the action-constitutive nature of its knowledge, its "unity of theory and revolutionary praxis" (Bernstein, 1976, p. 182).

> Critical social science is an attempt to understand in a rationally responsible manner the oppressive features of a society such that this understanding stimulates its audience to transform their society and thereby liberate themselves. (Fay, 1987, p. 4)

Causing some disquiet here is my difficulty in giving concrete form to knowledge that inherently but nonprescriptively catalyzes political action. Just what does such knowledge look like?

Concluding Comments

This discussion about the nature and role of social scientific knowledge in postpositivism, interpretivism, and critical science has been with intention minimally comparative and largely descriptive. I endeavored primarily to present the arguments of each inquiry framework with some measure of internal integrity rather than in reference to selected concerns or criteria. I hoped thereby to invite broad participation in the identification of important issues for further conversation. Some people may be most interested, for example, in issues related to causality, others in questions about subjectivity. My own nominations of agenda items for further conversation are reflected in the critiques made of each paradigm's stance on the role and purpose of social science in society. In concluding this discussion, I would like to return to these issues. Their presentation here highlights both the language and the concepts that differentiate the three inquiry frameworks and some of their common challenges.

(1) Given the acknowledged, though varied, complexity of and the contextual and/or historical boundaries on social knowledge, can it serve other than local or micro-level interests? Can and should social scientists aspire to serve the common good, or do we need a social scientist in every community?

(2) Given that all social knowledge is value bound, value laden, or value based, is all social science fundamentally about human values? Can and should social scientists seek to "recapture moral discourse" (Schwandt, 1989b) as our most significant societal role?

(3) As social engineers, as storytellers, or as catalyzers of political action, what moral and ethical responsibilities do social scientists have for the consequences of our work?

(4) Even as social scientists from quite different perspectives share a commitment to the improvement of social life through our work, we diverge in how this commitment is actualized in the world of practice. Is relativism justifiable in this context? Whose interests should be served by social science?

And now, please, let us converse.

Notes

1. Throughout this chapter, the more generic term *interpretivism* is used to include the constructivist inquiry framework set forth by Lincoln (this volume) and the terms *paradigm* and *inquiry framework* are used interchangeably.

2. This discussion will focus on the constructivist view of interpretivism, including similar and related views, but excluding dissimilar qualitative traditions (see Atkinson, Delamont, & Hammersley, 1988; Jacob, 1987, 1988; M. Smith, 1987).

3. Here, there is a sharp break between interpretivism (especially as constructivism) and some other qualitative traditions. Ethnography, for example, does address general theories of culture and does acknowledge the possibility of generalizable knowledge (see the references listed in note 2).

4. Bredo and Feinberg (1982b) criticize other inquiry frameworks for not fully acknowledging or justifying their value positions. Critical theory, they say, at least attempts to do so, notably, Habermas's efforts to define the "universal pragmatics" of a theory of communicative competence (Bredo & Feinberg, 1982b, p. 436).

[19]

Emergent Paradigms
How New? How Necessary?

MARGARET D. LeCOMPTE

I begin this response by suggesting that conflict and incompatibility among paradigms is more at issue in education than it is in the social sciences generally. Of concern is not so much research in the social sciences but research in education, and how debates in science and philosophy do *not* trickle down into educational practice (Popkewitz, this volume). My purpose will be to broaden the discourse somewhat by asking, What are the social sciences? I then shall look at the definitions given for each of the paradigms under consideration—the postpositivistic, constructive, and critical theoretical. Finally, I will talk about what knowledge really is, and the kinds of knowledge that might be additionally sought, given the definitional constraints posited by the keynote addresses for the conference on which this book is based.

The enthusiasm of formerly positivistic researchers for alternative methods for investigating human problems seems to derive from the domination of American pedagogical studies by psychology and especially behavioral psychology, with its attendant commitment to testing, measurement, and experimental research. This has been coupled with a very American fascination with efficiency and causality; these have made educational research and practice vulnerable to the worst excesses and rigidities of logical positivism.

AUTHOR'S NOTE: I am indebted to Kenneth Howe for his insightful assistance with interpretation of philosophical debates and assertions, and to A. Gary Dworkin for background in sociological theory.

Paradigms and Intellectual Ethnocentrism

Firestone (this volume) defines *paradigms* or *disciplines* as cultures that constrain the behavior and beliefs of their members. Further, never having been exposed to alternative ways of doing things leads one naturally to assume that the way one has been taught is the only way to think and operate. A corollary to cultural isolation is lack of awareness of the existence and legitimacy of other cultures—which can lead to ethnocentrism (Atkinson, Delamont, & Hammersley, 1988). The converse is what Warshay (1962) calls possessing a breadth of perspective.

How New, and How Emergent, Are the "New" Paradigms?

The enthusiasm for new paradigms may simply be the excitement one feels when immersed in a foreign and unfamiliar culture—before culture shock sets in. Further, the new paradigms described in this conference really are not new. Postpositivism (Phillips, this volume) resembles pragmatism, especially in its approach to methods and processes of verification. Constructivism, with its emphasis on multiple constructed realities and *emic*, or subject, meaning, is a combination of symbolic interactionism, ethnomethodology, and other phenomenological approaches to inquiry. Critical theory originated in Europe after World War I. In fact, the issue of how problematic conventional science inquiry becomes when empirical realities change has been of concern for a long time in other social science disciplines (Eckberg & Hill, 1979; Friedrichs, 1970; Gouldner, 1970). What *is* new is the use of these perspectives by pedagogues and educational researchers.

Some of the contemporary paradigmatic soul-searching in education may have resulted because educators bought wholeheartedly into a model more appropriate for laboratories or hard sciences— behaviorism and statistical methods adapted from genetics and agricultural economics. It did not fit what they were studying but they nonetheless clung to it like a religion in order to emulate *hard* scientists. Consequently, the use of qualitative methods felt like a breath of fresh air compared with the rigidities of quantification. What I suggest is that the fresh air had existed all the time—in other social science disciplines.

Hence, we may not really need new paradigms; we may only need to use more fully and imaginatively those we already have. We especially should not substitute for science the techniques of literary criticism or *storytelling*—a metaphor for authentic products of inter- pretive research often ascribed to Geertz (1973, 1988) in what I believe to be a misreading. An example can be drawn from the clinical work of the neurologist Oliver Sacks (1986), who used the often poetic insights and frequently mad alternative realities of his brain-damaged clients to inform and enhance his scholarly research. While he called for a new form of science and treatment of the mind that blended research findings with the "realities of madmen and poets" (see Lincoln, this volume), Sacks never ceased being a scientist.

What Are the Social Sciences?

Weber (cited in Berger, 1977, p. 162) used the terms *social science, cultural science,* and *history* synonymously—as, to some extent, does Popkewitz (this volume). In so doing, he emphasized the human, contextual, social, and, hence, interactional nature of what the social sciences investigate. Today, the social sciences usually include sociol- ogy, psychology, economics, political science, and anthropology. Each asks its own peculiar questions and has its own mode of inquiry and ways of looking at the world. But history now is grouped with the humanities—literature, poetry, languages—and most university ad- ministrations do not consider it to be a social science. Even the credentials of anthropology sometimes are questioned; it may be considered a humanity or lumped with geography. Yet, cultural stud- ies and history *are* the foundations of the social sciences. They are critical to our understanding of educational processes—as are all of the social sciences.

Paradigmatic monotheism derives from intellectual isolation from other scientific traditions. Such isolation is dangerous, because it leads to "intolerance. . . fruitless polemic, [and] hypercriticism. [It also] leads to the belief that new thoughts are revolutionary and [to] neglect of relevant scholarship received to be outside the paradigm simply because it 'belongs to another tradition' " (Atkinson, Delamont, & Hammersley, 1988, p. 233). Instruction in American colleges of edu- cation has been typified by this kind of isolation. Textbooks in research design, which really are texts in experimental design, typically devote only a chapter or two to all other models. Until recently, the majority of colleges of education had no courses in field or qualitative methods; in most, they are still electives. Few colleges of education teach historiography; none teaches it regularly.

Although I by no means wish to denigrate the great contributions psychology has made to our understanding of human life and cognition, the focus of psychology is the isolated individual, decontextualized, and laboratory bound. It provides neither a complete nor in ideal model for studying *social, cultural,* and *historical* men and women. The "headlock that educational psychology has had on educational research" (Spindler & Spindler, 1989) has created the so-called conventional science model, which, indeed, is too narrow. It has led to the sort of intractable problems of explanation that have long frustrated educational evaluators struggling with its application to events in the real world (see Eash, 1985; Guba & Lincoln, 1981; LeCompte, 1972; Stake, 1985). It also has imposed significant limits upon the question: What constitutes legitimate knowledge and modes of knowledge accumulation?

The so-called conventional science paradigm generates and legitimates only a particular kind of knowledge—that which can be quantified and measured. However, other paradigms, appropriate to other social science disciplines, inform our investigations in education. And cross-disciplinary approaches not only will help us avoid the danger of creating new, equally rigid and restrictive canons for critical, post-positivistic, and constructive investigation but will prevent us from celebrating the death of an old orthodoxy by creating a new one just as doctrinaire.

What Is the Nature of Knowledge?

My next concern is with the definition of the nature of knowledge. Three assumptions about *emergent* paradigms were implicit in the conference keynote addresses. First, the paradigms are philosophically and operationally incompatible. Second, they are based upon different definitions of reality and, hence, generate substantively different kinds of knowledge. Third, they lead to different versions of the truth. To address these assumptions, I feel that we must define the term *knowledge* more carefully and in terms of a broader definition of the social sciences than that embraced by the conference conveners.

By definition, the various social science disciplines concern themselves with different aspects of human social and cultural life. Economics addresses issues of exchange, distribution of resources, and production. Political science looks at the arrangement of power and control. Sociology and anthropology examine the structure and dynamics of human organization as well as their genesis. Psychology examines the workings of the individual human psyche. Clearly, staying within the confines of one discipline restricts the scope of questions that can be asked, the methods to be used for investigation, and the explanations that inquiry generates. The result is a serious problem for accumulation of knowledge: without a cross-disciplinary perspective, the types of knowledge that can be generated are limited (Cahnman, 1965).

A second problem is that confusion exists over distinctions among *information, knowledge,* and *truth.* The question at issue is this: How can we verify the truth of research results we have generated? My response: Although we can generate and accumulate knowledge in any scientific tradition, we will have a very hard time generating and accumulating truth.

Because it must at least be capable of falsification, scientific knowledge refers to information and facts about reality, whether viewed as context specific or not. Truth, however, has three connotations: (a) warrantability, practical value, or utility; (b) a universal and permanent definition of reality; and (c) correctness or rectitude in behavior. The first two clearly involve debate between realists and idealists, which plays itself out both in philosophical ponderings and in scientific investigation and upon which I hold both a pragmatic and agnostic position. The third addresses what I feel are cultural issues governing proper forms of interaction among people. Failure to make these distinctions creates a confusing logic that begins with science and ends with religion: "Having now defined what real or true knowledge is, and having delineated how one goes about acquiring it, it is clear (here making the shift from description, or science, to prescription, or religion) that there is only one right or true way of carrying out investigation!"

Both knowledge and truth deal with understanding, but of different kinds. Knowledge and information fall into the realm of science, while truth is an issue for philosophy and religion. Knowledge and information address what Weber (1968, cited in Heap, 1977, p. 177) called "direct observational understanding," or the sense or identity of acts or phenomena. Observational understanding allows us to see actions as what they are and is required to locate and perceive patterns of like actions. They also can address explanatory understanding (Weber, 1968, p. 8), or that which tells us the motive or purpose for an act. Explanatory understanding is, however, valid only within a given social or cultural context. When what is valid for a given context is seen as appropriate for, or mistaken for *truth* in, all contexts (as has been the case in American educational research for many decades), the mischief starts.

Knowledge then is a representation, or picture, of empirical reality in the human mind; it is, in fact, an abstraction, because the limitations of the mind dictate that humans choose to attend to those phenomena that are value relevant or culturally significant for them (Berger, 1977). While principles of abstraction, or value relevance, differ, of course, from group to group, the use of the principle of value relevance tells us what is important to look for. It permits us to look for two kinds of information: (a) the ideas that motivate people and (b) the activities that they carry out because of what motivated them—or, as Popkewitz (this volume) calls them, the objective and the subjective. This perspective facilitates the accumulation of information and knowledge. It also permits an examination of truth—at least truth as defined by those who are being studied. It answers the somewhat unanswerable question, "What is Real?" in terms of the pragmatists' notion of warranted assertability. However, it does not resolve the problem of relativity, upon which Lincoln (this volume) holds an uncompromising position. Complete relativism, I think, is dangerous. It leads to complete reductionism; it means that people cannot even talk to one another and that interaction and meaning become random (Long, 1958). I am uncomfortable with that position on political and cultural as well as scientific grounds.

What Knowledge Can be Accumulated in Each of the Postconventional Science Models?

Greene (this volume) uses three metaphors to describe the emergent paradigms. Postpositivists are social engineers, constructivists are storytellers, and critical theorists are social activists. For postpositivists, reality is what works, what can be warranted or verified; knowledge is *small theory*; and truth is a regulative ideal. Knowledge accumulation then consists of building ever more complex and complete, if probabilistic, explanations of phenomena at the small theory level, facilitating an understanding of specific group mechanics across and within specific, not universal, groups.

For constructivists, reality is a social and multiple construction; knowledge is derived from understanding and consists of a consensus within a given context of individual perceptions, constructions of meaning, and the values that underlie them. It is acquired in the investigation of almost dyadic interaction where the knower and the known are inseparable—or "interactive monism" (Lincoln, this volume). Because individual interpretations are ideographically bounded by time, place, and persons, and multiple reconstructions are pluralistic, divergent, and conflictual, knowledge accumulators become folklorists, devoted to the collection of stories. Truth is completely relative to the context.

Critical theory and constructivism have a great deal in common. Both view reality as context specific and believe that human activity is generated by the motivations and interests—or ideologies—underlying them. However, critical theorists place their analysis squarely on a macro-historical plane, while constructivists appear to be more concerned with microlevel patterns of interaction. For critical theorists, reality is ideological and dependent upon the interests, values, and priorities of the particular intellectual-cultural-social tradition of those who develop it; it becomes "real" to people insofar as the social permeates the consciousness of individuals. Knowledge then consists of histories that are located in society and implicated in shaping the productive, administrative, and structural dynamics of the given society (Popkewitz, this volume). For critical theorists, knowledge is purposive and linked to practice and the promotion of change. It cannot, therefore, be accumulated, because to do so would make it "real" when, in fact, it is context dependent. The implication might seem to be that there is no truth, for it too would have to be dependent upon its historical context.

However, time *does* stop for critical theorists, because the goal of knowledge or practice is what is "good," "right," "responsible," and "empowering for individuals." These concepts are themselves historically bound; they are deeply rooted in western European philosophical traditions dating from the seventeenth and eighteenth centuries. Truth then, for the critical theorist, is whatever leads to the achievement of these conditions.

What Knowledge Can We Accumulate?

The term *accumulate* is an interesting one, with a descriptive valence all its own. It reminds me of cotton pickers dragging behind them their tow sacks, which grow increasingly heavier as the day progresses. It implies a horizontal, rather than hierarchic, accretion. In scientific terms, this means that, while we may be able to add to our knowledge base descriptive information about how our world works, we may not be able to generate causal laws that will hold true regardless of the context. We may be able to accumulate (a) information about the ideas that motivate people and groups of people and (b) information about the activities they carried out because of what motivated them (Weber, 1968). In this chapter, I will address this form of knowledge accumulation in each of the three *emergent* paradigms, accepting for the moment their own terms and definitions of knowledge, and without exciting philosophical debates about truth. I will not discuss postpositivism at length, because, as *neopragmatism*, it is a familiar perspective. Knowledge accumulation simply involves constructing better, if less grand and presumptuous, explanations of phenomena. I will devote my comments to Greene's (this volume) discussion of critical theory and constructivism, beginning with the most troublesome for me—the constructivist paradigm.

Knowledge and the Constructivist Paradigm

Greene (this volume) states that the constructivist paradigm defines knowledge as what people "know" or how they define their situations; as I understand her formulation, the task of the knowledge accumulator in the constructivist paradigm is that of the folklorist or collector of stories. This strikes me as insufficient. It is an overreaction, an attempt to be artful in response to the aridness characteristic of conventional scientific writing. All of a sudden, social scientists have discovered passion, art, portraiture, and the multiple jabberings of a peopled reality. They have jumped from the methods of somewhat reified science to literature. But neither artful portrayal nor thick description necessarily creates knowledge, though they could produce an initial data base. The real issue is this: Of what should the data base consist? Here the lack of sociology in Lincoln's (this volume) description of constructivism is most apparent.

Lincoln's constructivist model could be subject to the same critique leveled at some interpretive, interactionist, and phenomenological approaches to understanding human behavior: it is decontextualized, hanging in air. It posits the existence of a cobweb of multiple negotiated realities but never delineates the interests they reflect, the rules that govern the negotiation of reality, or their historical antecedents. Yet these are the warp and weft of social life—and constitute the realm of culture and society. While human life may be individually *interpreted*, it also is *socially* defined (Ritzer, 1980). It is governed by ideas that people develop concerning desirable or obligatory ways in which their coexistence should be structured. The ideas, norms, or values are not automatic or natural, but, while out*side* of people, they still are " 'artificial' and man-made; they are called norms and values because adherence to them is not merely contemplative, but involves the recognition that the actor who holds them somehow has the duty or task to attempt their practical implementation" (Berger, 1977, p. 168).

General cultural values are ideas that groups of people have developed concerning the regulation of their activity. Thus the concepts of actor, act, role, norm, value, expectation, obligation, and institution are sociological concepts that constitute the building blocks of human social life—the carpet that underlies the design (see Sacks, 1986, p. 176). They also are embedded in the history of the group, not simply created *de novo* in every social interaction. If this historical dimension is not kept clearly in mind, studies of human social life seem to suffer from a kind of collective Korsakov's amnesia, wherein the items and events in the present must constantly be re-created each instant because no past exists to guide, constrain, and connect them to an identity.

The constructivist paradigm concentrates on delineating interaction and meaning *at the moment*; it leaves one with a curious sense of ephemeralness and impermanence. Missing is the *social definition*, or knowledge of the social rules, the framework, that lies *outside* immediate action. Both—the immediate and particular as well as the constant and universal (for the group)—are needed for an authentic portrayal of human social life. Thus there are prior conditions, rules, and sets of circumstances that restrain and guide the identities and expectations that people have; these in turn structure their negotiations as well as their definition of their own situations. Consideration of the writings of sociologists like Peter Blau (1964, 1977), George Homans (1950, 1974), George Herbert Mead (1934/1967), Alfred

Schutz (1932/1967), and others would be helpful. These works set out a framework for the constraints that shape interaction, both at the individual and the group levels, both for researchers and those they study.

Knowledge Accumulation and Critical Theory

I disagree with Greene's (this volume) statement that critical inquiry does not and is not intended to accumulate knowledge. My reading of critical theory is that, although knowledge does not, it is true, accumulate in the sense that it moves hierarchically toward ever more refined and accurate versions of the truth, it can accrue horizontally in time. In other words, the tow sack can be filled, and its contents can inform our actions. I believe that what the critical theorists are saying is that knowledge about people's ideas and their actions can be collected and accumulated; however, it is a knowledge base suffused with a specific analytic posture that moves away from a preoccupation with method, roles, and technique and toward an understanding of issues of value—the tacit and interest-based assumptions that structure contemporary life. In this way, our critical senses, once dulled by overriding concern with procedures, can be awakened to a context-bound form of knowledge and investigatory methods that explicitly are *not* value free or hierarchic.

Rather, they will emphasize accumulating historically based, context-bound description, confronting the values and interests inherent in both the method and the results of the research. In this way, the data basis for continuing, historically informed dialog and analysis can be established.

[20]

Discussion on Knowledge Accumulation

JUDITH PREISSLE GOETZ

University of Georgia

As the section of formal presentations on knowledge accumulation concluded yesterday, an individual in the audience objected to how the day had been laid out to that point. She found it to be inconsistent for researchers focusing on interaction and meaning to frame the major part of the conference as traditional lectures. As a consequence the group reorganized the room into a circle of chairs, and this is how we organized our space for the discussion. Both days the discussion proceeded with about 25 people present. It was noteworthy that everyone remained for the discussion period, and the first day we actually ran over our time by five or ten minutes. A number of recurrent themes, issues, and questions emerged.

First, power over and control of knowledge was a key issue. People were concerned that those for whom much educational knowledge is supposedly generated—that is, the school people—were absent from this conference. Other people voiced a concern about the larger proportion of men to women on the program and the near absence of all but White faces. These factors raised questions about just how seriously critical theory is taken at this conference. That discussion led to critiquing critical theory itself as discussants noted its very Western bias toward the empowerment of individuals as opposed to the empowerment of groups.

Participants returned repeatedly to the notion of *paradigm*, how effective paradigm is as a construct describing activity in the human sciences and how the various so-called paradigms are similar to as well as different from each other. In this discussion a value emphasized was the way the construct of paradigm at least allows us to reflect and introspect on what we are doing.

Related to this issue were efforts by participants to place all the presentations within the history and development of the human sciences during the past 3,000 years. Several individuals expressed concern that speakers were reinventing the wheel long debated by philosophers and methodologists.

Participants also worried about the issue of reality. To quote a participant, "Is [it] the assumption that you understand each other's realities?" Another quote: "It must be shared, constructed, and objectified through the history that we share." A third quote: "What I know about you is always in jeopardy and always incomplete."

Another theme was that of responsibility. This, of course, is related to issues of power and control. What are the responsibilities of the knower and the known? How does some knowledge get legitimated while other knowledge is denigrated? Why is practical knowledge denigrated while theoretical knowledge is legitimated? Why is men's knowledge legitimated and women's knowledge denigrated? What is the relationship between knowledge and action?

Participants speculated about the relationship of science to other forms of inquiry and to such other areas of human endeavor as art and literature. "Behind fine writing is technique and discipline," commented one participant. The statement led to questions and comments about how quality is assessed across the areas of human activity.

Much of the discussion focused around how paradigms are assumed to operate. If paradigms are unconscious *worldviews,* then surely researchers cannot choose among them. How deterministic are they then? Have investigators no choices? And if researchers can learn their paradigms and make choices, are they bound to single traditions? Must researchers succumb to the tyranny of method? An astute participant responded that, after all, human growth may be fostered best by stepping outside our customary worldviews and looking freshly at the world.

METHODOLOGY

[21]

Paths to Inquiry in the Social Disciplines
Scientific, Constructivist, and Critical Theory Methodologies

THOMAS R. SCHWANDT

In one of the earliest attacks on Cartesianism, Charles Sanders Peirce (Buchler, 1940, p. 54) advised that we "not block the way of inquiry." He labeled any philosophy that barricaded the road of advance toward truth as "the one unpardonable offense in reasoning" and a "venomous error." Further, he observed that this sort of error assumes four familiar shapes: absolute assertion; the claim that certain things can never be known; the claim that certain elements of science are basic, ultimate, independent of all else and utterly inexplicable; and the claim that a particular law or truth has found its last and perfect formulation.

Although we may quarrel with Peirce's pragmatic formulation of what constitutes an advance toward truth, his advice about unblocking the path to inquiry is sound. And I have taken it to characterize both the overall intent and the tenor of this symposium as well as my general goal in discussing the nature of methodologies, or paths to inquiry if you will, appropriate to the three paradigmatic persuasions introduced in the conference's keynote addresses. As we examine what we are about when we inquire using these different methodologies, we would do well to remember that the path to understanding will surely be blocked if we forget even the most carefully stated postulate is but a proposition as easy to doubt as to believe; that the history of inquiry in every discipline teaches us that what we once thought imperceptible or perceived only dimly has often been shown to be knowable; and, that likewise, the history of science, as well as current investigations in moral philosophy, reveal that all attempts to establish an indisputable foundation for our knowledge have met with failure and that our knowledge of both the external world and the ways and means of human interaction is always evolving.

In this chapter I shall explore the topic of methodology in a four-part treatment, focusing first on what we mean by the term *methodology*; second, on the nature of methodology in each paradigmatic persuasion; third, on the regulative ideals that shape and direct each methodology; and, fourth, on the issue of methodological compatibility.

Postpositivistic Methodology

If by virtue of nothing else than an accident of birth, all of us are participants in a postpositivistic culture of inquiry. By that I mean we are thinking about and conducting our inquiries in a zeitgeist that is characterized by a general rejection of the logical positivist or logical empiricist program of inquiry. For at least the past 25 years, discussions of methodology in both the natural and the social sciences have been dominated by criticisms of that program and by formulations of alternative views of the nature of scientific inquiry. To be aware of current conceptions of inquiry in both the social and the physical disciplines is to understand that there is no indisputable foundation for knowledge, to recognize that knowledge is in principle uncertain and contingent, and to have made some kind of, at the very least moderate, "interpretive turn" to borrow a phrase from Clifford Geertz. It is in this zeitgeist that we must first examine what it means to talk about methodology. Hence, what follows is an attempt to describe the concept through a series of propositions. My intent is to sensitize the reader to the meaning of the term more so than to offer a definitive view.

First, as the examination of any methods text in the social disciplines will show, we have tended to derive our understanding of methodology from the conception of *scientific* method—the principles and procedures that govern investigations of the physical world—

and not from the humanistic disciplines. In part, this is testimony to the pervasive secular and professional belief in the naturalistic interpretation of the social sciences. In the current zeitgeist, this belief is being challenged. For example, in an essay exploring the rise of the interpretive turn in the social sciences, Clifford Geertz (1980, p. 166) claims that social thought is being refigured, that, in the social disciplines, "something is happening to the way we think about the way we think." This refiguration is taking the form of a revised style of discourse in which many social scientists are turning away from a "law and instances ideal of explanation toward a cases and interpretations one, looking less for the sort of thing that connects planets and pendulums and more for the sort that connects chrysanthemums and swords" (p. 165) In this refiguration, the methodology of the natural sciences is being discarded as a guide, and it is being replaced with explanatory schemes and methods drawn from literature, law, theater, and the like.

Second, and in a related way, we tend to regard scientific methodology as the paradigm case of methodology (or the paradigm case of forming justified beliefs) and the one sure tradition-independent way of rational argumentation. In other words, we tend to equate being rational or reasonable with using this particular way of knowing. This view is evident, for example, in D. C. Phillips's (this volume) claim:

> Scientific reason is not marked off from other forms of human intellectual endeavor as a sort of model of perfection that these lesser activities must always strive (unsuccessfully) to mimic. Rather, science embodies exactly the same types of fallible reasoning as is found elsewhere—it is just that scientists do, a little more self-consciously and in a more controlled way, what all effective thinkers do.

Here, Phillips expresses the view that scientific reasoning is epistemologically similar to all forms of human reasoning and that all "effective" (read, "reasonable" or "rational") thinkers employ a method of inquiry similar to that of scientific method. What Phillips implies here is that, at least in principle, all disagreements about claims to know can be rationally settled and that we can know in advance the kind of evidence, or at least the kind of procedure, needed to resolve these disagreements in a rational way—in a phrase, that procedure is scientific method.

This claim has been severely attacked in recent years. Richard Rorty (1979, p. 316), for example, argues that embedded in our conception of scientific method is a fundamental belief that all contributions to a given discourse can

> be brought under a set of rules which will tell us how rational agreement can be reached on what would settle the issue on every point where statements seem to conflict. These rules tell us how to construct an ideal situation, in which all residual disagreements will be seen to be "non-cognitive" or merely verbal, or else merely temporary—capable of being resolved by doing something further.

Under the influence of this biased view, we tend to regard scientific method as *the* way of conducting rational inquiry. In his keynote address, Popkewitz (this volume) echoes Habermas's (1971, p. 4) claim that we have collapsed epistemology into scientific method:

> The philosophy of science that has emerged since the mid-nineteenth century as the heir to the theory of knowledge is methodology pursued with a scientistic self-understanding of the sciences. "Scientism" means science's belief in itself: that is, the conviction that we can no longer understand science as one form of possible knowledge, but rather must identify knowledge with science.

Third, within the current zeitgeist, we recognize that methodology is historically situated and that it evolves. Our understanding of what constitutes scientific methodology—or, for that matter, the methodology of legal interpretation, literary criticism, medicine, and so forth—changes over time. This is readily apparent, for example, if we examine the various formulations of scientific methodology found in the writings of Descartes, Bacon, Herschel, Whewell, and Mill (Blake, Ducasse, & Madden, 1960). The Aristotelian notion of scientific methodology as grounded in plausible opinion or persuasive speculation was supplanted in the seventeenth century by Renaissance notions of methodology as a combination of mathematical and experimental procedure bestowing upon results thereby attained a final and assured certainty. This Cartesian notion has given way in the past few decades to acceptance of a hermeneutical element in scientific methodology (Bernstein, 1983; Brown, 1977; Toulmin, 1983).

To claim that methodology evolves is to recognize that salient terms (e.g., *induction, observation, theory, hypothesis, empiricism*) that we often take for granted in our discussions of methodology have changed in meaning; that there is no such thing as *the* scientific method forever fixed and unchanging; that methodology does not develop *ex nihilo;* that there are no absolute standards against which methodologies can be evaluated (just as we have come to recognize that there are no absolute foundations for knowledge). Our inquiry methodologies and our standards for judging the implementation of those methodologies develop together and are continually revised by a process of mutual adjustment.

Fourth, to study a methodology is not simply to examine the exercise of method, it is to study a way of knowing; in other words, methodology and epistemology are linked. Ways of knowing are guided by assumptions concerning what we are about when we inquire and by assumptions concerning the nature of the phenomenon into which we inquire. Phillips (following Popper and others), for example, calls the former "regulative ideals" and they include notions such as objectivity and truth. The latter are illustrated by Gouldner's (1970) notion of "domain assumptions"—beliefs or predispositions about the nature of people, the nature of society, the relationship between people and society, and so forth that shape investigations. Examining how these two sets of assumptions (which themselves evolve) shape our understanding of inquiry and guide the development and evaluation of methods is what makes the study of methodology more than an examination of the "how-to" of inquiry. To study a methodology is to explore a logic of justification or a meta-framework for understanding the exercise of method, that is, for examining the principles and procedures by which we formulate inquiry problems, develop answers to those problems, and evaluate the correctness and profundity of those answers.

Finally, we undertake a study of method not because it is likely to improve actual practice but because it will cast some light on our understanding of that practice. Newton-Smith's (1981, p. 209) advice on this matter as it pertains to scientific methodology is equally applicable to the study of any methodology:

> The study of scientific methodology will not produce a methodologist's stone capable of turning the dross of the laboratory into the gold of theoretical truth. This pessimism about the fruits of methodological

studies should not deter us from proceeding. Even if it will not make us better scientists, it will give us a better understanding of the scientific enterprise.

It is against this background of general features of methodology that the discussion of the three paths to inquiry in the social sciences is cast. What follows is not a review and critique of individual methods. I would not know where to begin to sample fairly the many methods controversies embedded in each path to inquiry. Instead, I have chosen to examine each path by first commenting briefly on its origins, then offering a characterization of its methodology. Because all three of the methodologies to be discussed are postpositivistic in the sense described above, I prefer to call the first *scientific methodology* because it reflects the mainstream view of what it means to investigate a phenomenon scientifically. The other two approaches are referred to as *constructivism* and *critical science*, respectively.

Scientific Methodologies

These methodologies issue from the naturalistic interpretation of the social sciences—the view that the aim of the social sciences is the same as that of the natural sciences and that the social sciences, as Phillips (1987b, p. 204) observes, "have no features that offer insuperable obstacles to the adoption of the methods of the natural sciences." The failure of the social sciences thus far to achieve the kind of powerful explanations characteristic of the physical sciences is attributed to the immaturity of the former and not to any logical incompatibility of subject matter and methods. Echoing both Popper (1961) and Nagel (1961), Phillips (1987a, p. 395) tells us that "epistemologically, the two sciences are rather similar—the relationship between the evidence that is appealed to, and the knowledge claims that are made, is the same."

The scientific path encompasses three types of inquiry strategies that can be roughly characterized as experimental and quasi-experimental strategies, ex post facto or causal-comparative strategies, and descriptive strategies (e.g., correlational studies, survey research). Each of these strategies has its own methodological logic (Soltis, 1984), but what concerns us here is a more generalized conception of scientific method.

At the risk of gross oversimplification, it can be said that scientific methodology is principally concerned with procedures for the development and testing of causal hypotheses, although well-conceived and executed descriptive studies are important and valuable. Observation, measurement, experiment, and theory building are the cornerstones of the methodology, with statistics playing a major role in the formulation and testing of some types of hypotheses. If one were to characterize the nature of scientific methodology in a word, it would be *experimental*, for what is most important in the scientific undertaking is some framework that permits a good test of a hypothesis, conjecture, or hunch, if you will. Experiments, in their many forms (e.g., true experiments, time-series analyses, or causal-comparative studies), provide this framework by allowing for controlled comparisons in testing the hypothesis of interest. To be sure, varying degrees of control are afforded by different types of experiments.

A salient feature of scientific methodologies is their insistence on separating normative and empirical theory. These are methodologies for investigating what is, not what ought to be. Empirical theory in the social disciplines may yet be in its infancy and disagreements may arise over whether explanations are best afforded through hypothetico-deductive structures of reasoning or functional analyses, yet such theory is a goal at which social scientific approaches aim. Scientific methodologies deal with social facts; the stuff of normative theory—social and political goals, aims, morals, and values—is not their concern.

Constructivist Methodologies

Two recent reviews by Jacob (1987) and Atkinson, Delamont, and Hammersley (1988) highlight the fact that this family of constructivist methodologies is far less uniform in aims and strategies than the methodologies constituting the empirical-analytic or scientific approach to inquiry. Nonetheless, these paths to inquiry share a general rejection of the naturalistic interpretation of the social sciences and seek to inquire into, portray, and interpret the realm of intersubjective meanings as constituted in culture, language, symbols, and so forth. Within this family of approaches, at least three strands are evident—the ethnographic, the ontological, and the moral-political. The first of these is my primary concern in this chapter, although I shall try to at least outline the features of the other two.

Ethnographic Strand

The ethnographic strand includes inquiries variously referred to as fieldwork or field research, ethnography, case study research, anthropological research, and naturalistic inquiry. Within this strand in the field of education, the work of Harry Wolcott (1973), Phillip Jackson (1968), Louis Smith and William Geoffrey (1968), and Alan Peshkin (1986) is representative as are the discussions of research strategies and methods by Bob Stake (1978), Judith Goetz and Margaret Le-Compte (1984), Yvonna Lincoln and Egon Guba (1985), and Robert Bogdan and Sari Biklen (1982). Outside of education, Clifford Geertz's (1973, 1983) collected essays and Robert Emerson's (1983) reader illustrate many of the methodological issues confronting this strand.

The ethnographic methodologies have two characteristics in common. First, the methodologists of the ethnographic strand share in the goal of documenting the unique subject matter, methods, and aims of the social or human sciences and defending its methodologies as objective (i.e., confirmable, warranted). In so doing, these methodologies reflect the hermeneutic interpretation of the social or human sciences first set out by Dilthey as explained in the following passage from Bernstein (1983, pp. 112-113):

> Nineteenth-century hermeneutics developed as a reaction against the intellectual imperialism of the growth of positivism, inductivism, and the type of scientism that claimed that it is the natural sciences alone that provide the model and the standards for what is to count as genuine knowledge. The character of hermeneutics was shaped by the assault on the integrity and autonomy of the human sciences. The primary task was seen, especially by Dilthey, as that of determining what is distinctive about humanistic and historical knowledge and of revealing its characteristic subject matter, aims, and methods in a manner that would meet and challenge the belief that only the natural sciences can provide us with "objective knowledge."

Second, the ethnographic methodologies largely (although not exclusively) view themselves as sciences. In the Anglo-American tradition, we typically divide intellectual endeavors into the natural sciences, the social sciences, and the humanities. The ethnographic strand, while rejecting a collapse of the social sciences into a natural science of individuals and their social relations, nonetheless, defines itself as a science, and in so doing demonstrates greater affinity with natural science than with the humanities. In characterizing this approach, Geertz (1973), for example, refers to it as an interpretive science in search of meaning in contrast to an experimental science in search of law.

When we speak of constructivist methodology, we tend to have in mind the ethnographic strand, for it is the easiest to cast in a dialogue with scientific methodologies. As will be seen shortly, the other two strands are less amenable to our social scientific sense of method.

Although there are important differences among methodologists within the strand, Guba and Lincoln (1988a) and Sherman and Webb (1988) provide us with an overview of the salient features of this kind of inquiry: First, these methodologies are directly concerned with understanding as nearly as possible some aspect of human experience as it is lived or felt or undergone by the participants in that experience. Second, to achieve that aim of capturing the qualities of an experience, the methodologies encompass procedures for bounding an inquiry within a particular context, for it is only within some context that the experience has meaning. Third, these contexts must be naturally occurring as opposed to contrived or fabricated (hence, the label *naturalistic* inquiry). Fourth, the inquirer follows procedures for considering the context and experience as a complex temporal, sociocultural, and geographic whole. Fifth, the inquiry is conducted using the investigator-as-instrument who employs ordinary fieldwork methods (Wolcott, 1988). Sixth, the inquirer disavows a hypothetico-deductive paradigm in favor of forms of inductive analysis (Charmaz, 1983; Katz, 1983; Strauss, 1987) and, as a result of that analysis, produces not a technical report but a type of narrative, text, or case report.

Ontological Strand

I have labeled a second strand of interpretive methodologies *ontological* because it appears to take its cue from Gadamer's notion that interpretation or understanding is not a methodological problem but an ontological one. In the ethnographic strand, hermeneutics is a method of achieving interpretive explanation, of engaging in what Geertz described as an elaborate venture in thick description. In the ontological strand, hermeneutics is not a method or, to borrow a phrase from Bernstein (1983), not "an intellectual stepsister to the methods of the social sciences." Rather, following Heidegger (1962) and Gadamer (1975), the ontological strand views hermeneutics as a way of being-in-the-world. As Ricoeur (1981, p. 67) explains, Gadamer questions "the primacy of judgment in man's [sic] behaviour towards the world,

> and the only philosophy which sets up judgment as a tribunal is one that makes objectivity, as modelled on the sciences, the measure of knowledge. Judgment [is a] dominant category only in the type of philosophy, stemming from Descartes, which makes methodical consciousness the key of our relation to being and to beings.

This sentiment is clearly explicit in the work of Elliot Eisner and his colleagues who engage in educational criticism. William Pinar (1988) argues for a difference between "Eisnerian" forms of qualitative inquiry and ethnographic research, and it is Eisner's concern with the primacy of experience—his view that knowledge occurs in the experience of situation—that makes this work exemplary of the ontological strand. Eisner (1988, p. 16) claims that, ultimately, all forms of representation (e.g., science, art)

> must give way to the primacy of experience. In the end, it is the qualities we experience that provide the content through which meaning is secured. Meaning is not located in propositional language or forms of art independent of a competent and creative reader who is able to secure from them a particular quality of life.

A second feature of the ontological strand that distinguishes it from the ethnographic strand, is that the former appears to find greater affinity with the humanities than with the social sciences. This too reflects the German tradition of viewing the social disciplines as forms of moral sciences (*Geisteswissenschaften*) sharing characteristics with the humanistic disciplines (Bernstein, 1983).

Moral-Political Strand

There may well be a third strand of constructivist methodology—a moral-political one—although it might be argued that this third strand had greater affiliations with critical theory than with constructivism. I think that this strand at least bridges the two paths to inquiry. What I have in mind here is the work of Robert Bellah (Bellah, Madsen, Sullivan, Swidler, & Tipton 1985), William Sullivan (1986), Norman Birnbaum (1988), Alasdair MacIntyre (1984), and others. Their work draws on the tradition of the social construction of reality (like the ethnographic strand) but it takes on an avowedly moral and political character. These individuals seek to restore the idea of social science as public philosophy, to reunite social sciences with moral analysis.

Critical Science Methodologies

Critical science in its many forms (critical theory, critical social science, new paradigm research, praxis-oriented research, critical inquiry, emancipatory social theory, emancipatory research, feminist research) seeks to recover the function of critical reflection in the social disciplines and in the practice of social inquiry. If constructivism can be characterized by its concern with a hermeneutic consciousness—capturing the lived experiences of participants—then critical theory can be characterized by its critical consciousness—systematically investigating the manner in which that lived experience may be distorted by false consciousness and ideology (where ideology can be defined after Ricouer, 1981, p. 80), as "an allegedly disinterested knowledge which serves to conceal an interest under the guise of a rationalisation"). If the constructivist methodologies are preoccupied with the restoration of the meaning of human experience, then critical science methodologies are preoccupied with reduction of illusions in human experience.

Critical science is grounded in a critique of the dominant ideology of the present day, namely, the ideology of science and technology (Fay, 1987; Giroux, 1983; Habermas, 1971). The most prominent feature of this ideology is the production and sustenance of a technical or instrumental rationality that systematically distorts the communicative capacity of human beings. Under the influence of this ideology, all aspects of human affairs (e.g., the process of inquiry, knowledge, or human relations) have undergone a process of reification such that we no longer recognize the distortions of communicative action and language. From a methodological, or perhaps more accurately an epistemological, point of view, recognition and understanding of this state of affairs—that is, the development of a critical theory of society—can be achieved through a critique of ideology (as practiced by Marx) or the method of psychoanalysis (modeled, in part, on Freud).

The critical theorist and the people he or she studies engage in a process of dialogue or depth hermeneutics through which, as Bernstein (1976, p. 199) explains, "the participants achieve self-knowledge and self-reflection which are therapeutic and effect a cognitive, affective, and practical transformation involving a movement toward autonomy and responsibility." It is in this way that critical theory is said to link both theory and practice.

Critical science incorporates the practices and aims of both scientific (empirical-analytic) and constructivist (historical-hermeneutic) methodologies, and juxtaposes empirical and interpretive accounts to facilitate the dialectical and critical aims of its own methodology (Comstock, 1982). As Habermas (1971) explains, the role of the theorist as critic is ruled out by methodological prohibition in standard conceptions of scientific methodology. Critical science seeks to recapture that role of the theorist as well as that role for social and political theory in general.

Regulative Ideals in Methodologies

As noted at the outset of this chapter, the various research strategies and methods that constitute the three methodologies in question are directed or guided by specific regulative ideals or goals. In this section, I shall attempt to draw attention to several salient regulative ideals operative in each methodology and, in so doing, demonstrate similarities and differences.

Shared Concern with Objectivity

All three methodologies embrace the regulative ideal of objectivity in inquiry. Owing in part to the positivists' program of seeking ultimate foundations for knowledge, this ideal has often been misinterpreted as *objectivism*, defined by Bernstein (1983, p. 8) as "the basic conviction that there is or must be some permanent, ahistorical matrix or framework to which we can ultimately appeal in determining the nature of rationality, knowledge, truth, reality, goodness, or rightness." We now recognize that the logical empiricists' program to locate this indisputable foundation is bankrupt. But the ideal of *objectivity* survives if by that term we mean, in Bernstein's (1976, p. 111) words, some set of "intersubjective standards of rationality or norms of inquiry by which we attempt to distinguish personal bias, superstition, or false beliefs from objective claims." Without such norms, knowledge remains private and incorrigible and, hence, incapable of criticism.

The confusion over the meaning of objectivity as a regulative ideal has arisen from confounding it with the notion of *objectivism* and from juxtaposing the latter with *relativism*. Recognizing that objectivism is a bankrupt notion in no way entails rejecting the bid to be objective, neither does it follow that we must slide down the slippery slope of relativism. As the philosopher James Giarelli (1988, p. 24) explains:

> What the refutation of objectivism does is to radically revise . . . the problem of thought and inquiry. Instead of a concentration on the mechanics (e.g., deduction, decision by formal rule, appeal to abstractions and universals) of an ahistorical closed system, the pragmatic tradition locates the problem of thought and inquiry in the development of the complex rationality of judgment and argumentation necessary for intelligent conduct. While judgments may not have [objectivist] justification and our arguments may be indeterminate and contestable, we still are making judgments and arguing for choices, and thus we are not relativists in any practical sense of the term.

Thus, within each methodology, we find discussion of norms for proceeding with a particular form of inquiry in a rational manner, for justifying claims according to some set of good-making criteria for those claims. That there are different paths by which the goal of objectivity is to be realized within different communities of inquirers is not surprising in view of our having abandoned the regulative ideal of objectivism. Lather (1986a), for example, writes of what is required to justify a claim in critical science; Lincoln and Guba (1985) and Goetz and LeCompte (1984) disagree over what is required to evaluate a claim in constructivist approaches, and Campbell (1986) and colleagues (Shadish, Cook, & Houts, 1986) continually refine their views of norms for judging the correctness of a causal claim in scientific approaches. From the fact that there are no *absolute* or a priori foundations for evaluating claims and arguments it does not follow that there are *no* such ways of reaching agreement within different epistemic communities that follow different paths to inquiry.

Having emphasized this shared focus on the regulative ideal of objectivity, I should like to point to some fundamental differences in the three paths in light of other regulative notions.

Scientific Methodologies

Three additional regulative ideals are most salient in these methodologies: primacy of method, truth, and progress. Peirce and Dewey were among the first to introduce the ideal of primacy of method. Peirce's defense of the scientific method did not consist in claiming that scientific *beliefs* are somehow more stable than other types of beliefs but in claiming that the *method* of science is itself firmer or more dependable than any other method of knowing (Scheffler, 1974). It is in this sense that knowledge produced via the scientific method is rationally justified, and, by implication, knowledge generated by any other means is not. This regulative ideal of the primacy of method has informed the development of scientific methodology: It is readily evident in classic discussions of this methodology as found, for example, in Max Black (1952) and Ernest Nagel (1961); it underlies Popper's (1968b) explication of the logic of scientific discovery and is apparent in Phillips's (1987b) recent writings on what constitutes adequate warrants for scientific claims.

Although I have no intention of opening the Pandora's box that contains the intertwined serpents of truth and realism, it is reasonable to say that science aims at learning truths about the empirical world. Scientific methodology is grounded in the view that there is a property called truth and that there is such a relation as reference by which the phrase "is true" has meaning. Debates within the scientific community are not centered on whether truth ought to be a regulative ideal but on how to define the property called truth and how to determine what is entailed in the relation of reference. For example, Putnam's (1987) explication of internal realism and conceptual relativity, Hesse's (1980) theory of truth for some theoretical sentences, and Campbell's (Shimony, 1981, p. 102) position of accepting "the correspondence meaning of truth and goal of science, and acknowledging coherence as the major but still fallible symptom of truth" are all testimony to the power of this regulative ideal in scientific methodology.

Closely related to the regulative ideal of truth is another characterized here as *progress*. This is the assumption that the successful application of scientific method yields some form of accumulation, progress, or convergence of scientific theory toward the truth. Hesse (1980, p. xi) highlights this regulative ideal when she explains that "natural science is instrumentally progressive . . . in the sense that we now have vastly increasing pragmatic possibilities of predicting and controlling empirical events by means of experimentation and theory construction." In the framework of the naturalistic interpretation, this ideal governs the methodology of the social sciences as well. As Bernstein (1976, p. 52) explains, we believe that scientific knowledge of social and political affairs must bring progress toward ideals and social goals accepted by reasonable human beings.

The ideal of progress entails a belief in the rationality of scientific methodology in particular and in the entire enterprise of science in general. In light of challenges to the received view of scientific methodology (i.e., dissolution of the belief in an indubitable foundation for the evaluation of scientific claims, evidence of historical and sociological elements governing theory development and choice, and the like) postpositivistic scientific methodology has been concerned with redefining the rationality of science. Newton-Smith's (1981, pp. 183-184) notion of "temperate rationalism" founded in his thesis of verisimilitude is exemplary here.

Constructivist Methodologies

Unlike scientific methodologies, constructivist methodologies are guided by the ideal of fidelity to subject matter (versus primacy of method). That is, they claim no special status for a particular way of investigation, and rather than impose a general set of methodological principles on all forms of experience, the constructivist will adapt both design and method of investigation to the nature of the phenomena at hand (Diesing, 1971). This ideal entails numerous practices involving emergent design and the adoption of a fieldworker role. It is also manifest in the notion that fieldworker-respondent relations unfold within a covenantal as opposed to a contractual ethical framework (May, 1980).

Fidelity to subject matter is related to a second regulative ideal that I shall call *complementarity*, which literally means that the inquirer complements the inquiry, that is, makes it complete or whole. To understand what is distinctly human in shared experience, the knower must participate in the known. Constructivist methodology sees this participation, this interaction if you will, as necessary to the acts of discovery and interpretation. Again, there are disagreements on how best to manage this participation to avoid the charge that the product of inquiry is a private and inaccessible reconstruction of others' lived experience, but, without such participation, without complementarity, there can be no truly constructivist or interpretive inquiry.

Given the constructivists' view that there is an inevitable dependency of inquiry findings or outcomes on the methods used to produce those findings and that inquiry is contextually and sociotemporally bound, it follows that there is no clearly conceived regulative ideal of truth. At best, for the constructivist, the property of truth and the reference "is true" refers to the degree of correspondence between the inquirer's account of participants' lived experience and the participants' own views on the matter. Accordingly, constructivists such as Lincoln and Guba (1985), Douglas (1976), Bloor (1983), and Schatzman and Strauss (1973), for example, propose verifying findings through some procedure of member validation or member checking. Yet this procedure does not yield incorrigible results, for, as Geertz (1983) points out, the ethnographer cannot capture participants' constructions of their reality *in themselves*; the inquirer's account is always mediated, such that there can be no ultimate verification. Emerson (1983, p. 107) makes this point clearly: "Exposing findings to the scrutiny and response of those studied does not produce absolute 'truth' against which to measure and evaluate those findings, but only another statement whose meaning must be inferred or determined by the fieldworker." Put somewhat differently, for the constructivist, there is no escaping the hermeneutic circle.

Finally, the regulative ideal of progress that informs scientific methodologies is absent in constructivist accounts. It is impossible to speak of progressively true descriptions of the sociobehavioral world when those descriptions are but a series of different interpretations. Of course, this does not mean that real learning cannot take place from examining those interpretations or that intellectual and political choices are not made between competing interpretations or explanations. As Geertz (1980, p. 178) explains, we may still believe that "social events do have causes and social institutions effects; but it just may be that the road to discovering what we assert in asserting this lies less through postulating forces and measuring them than through noting expressions and inspecting them."

Critical Science Methodologies

The overriding regulative ideal in critical science is the achievement of true as opposed to false consciousness and the kind of empowerment and emancipation that this entails. However, this ideal does not presuppose a conception of absolute truth, as Bernstein (1976, p. 109) explains, "we can show the falsity of an ideology without claiming that we have achieved a final, absolute, 'true' understanding of social and political reality."

This ideal of achieving true consciousness characterizes the project of feminist research (Benhabib & Cornell, 1987; Bowles & Klein, 1983; Griffiths & Whitford, 1988) as well as the work of the radical curriculum theorists Michael Apple (1979) and Henry Giroux (1983). The besetting sin of critical science is its failure to move beyond this critique of ideology to socially transformative action (i.e., empowerment and emancipation), or, as Giroux (1988, pp. 192-193) has noted, to "move beyond the language of critique and domination" to develop a "language of possibility."

It is in light of this ideal that critical science can also be said to embrace the regulative ideal of progress. However, as Brian Fay (1987) argues, critical theory, contrary to standard conceptions of scientific theory, is not concerned with an instrumental use of knowledge but with self-knowledge that liberates individuals from the oppressiveness of their social arrangements. This he terms the "educative conception" of social theory in which theory

> is seen as a means by which people can achieve a much clearer picture of who they are, and of what the real meaning of their social practices is, as a first step in becoming different sorts of people with different sorts of social arrangements. (Fay, 1987, p. 89)

Thus, although the particular use of theory differs in critical science and scientific methodologies, both share the (rationalist) assumption that theory possesses the power to affect progress in or transform human life.

Finally, critical science is guided by the regulative ideal of truth; however, its definition of truth is also significantly different from that embraced by the scientific methodologies. Habermas (1971) provides the key to understanding this ideal, although his notion is very complex and I can do no more than outline my elementary understanding of his view here. The regulative ideal takes the shape of a consensus theory of truth in which to claim that one is acting rationally entails the making of claims about the truth, legitimacy, and justification of the specific statement made and of the maker (speaker) of the statement. Truth is embedded in communication or discourse, and to say something aiming at truth is to invoke (or at least recognize) the authority of a particular community of inquirers that is competent to evaluate the particular claim made. A statement aiming at the truth can neither be made nor evaluated if something like the ideal speech (communication) situation does not obtain. The philosopher Anne Sellar (1988, p. 177) captures this idea in her observation that "if our communities are to be epistemologically effective, then they cannot be politically coercive." The regulative ideal of truth in critical science entails striving for this ideal situation.

Conclusion

Thus far in this discussion of methodology, I have examined its general nature, sketched some of its characteristics in scientific, constructivist, and critical science paths to inquiry, and briefly examined regulative ideals that give shape to different methodologies. It should be apparent that each methodology represents a fairly distinct and different path to inquiry in the social disciplines. To conclude this discussion, I shall briefly comment on the notion of undoing the myth of methodology and on the issue of methodological compatibility.

Putnam (1987, p. 86) is among the many who argue that the time has come to reject the project of Epistemology with a capital "e"—"the project of a Universal Method for telling who has 'reason on his [or her] side' no matter what the dispute." To many of us it comes as little surprise that the search for the holy grail of Method (with a capital "m") is over. We have found it, and it is a beaker of our own making. Regardless of whether we believe that scientific, constructivist, and critical theory modes of investigation in the social disciplines are different types of inquiry or hold that they are different moments in theorizing about social and political life (Bernstein, 1976), what is most important is that we recognize that these are human practices reflecting lived conduct rooted in our attempts to make sense of complex social and moral reality. Under such a pragmatic perspective, we recognize with Giarelli (1988, p. 26) that neither epistemology nor methodology is "about the nature of truth, but rather involves the study of the social practices by which communities develop a basis for warranted belief and action."

Finally, in a recent article, Kenneth Howe (1988) argues that we must resist the "tyranny of methodological dogma" and close down the quantitative versus qualitative debate. I agree with Howe that we must resist the elevation of any path to inquiry to the status of an orthodoxy and that adopting a pragmatic stance toward the nature of thought and inquiry makes many distinctions between the paths (e.g., descriptive versus evaluative or hard versus soft) once thought categorical to be of relatively little use in developing an account of inquiry in the social disciplines. However, from this it does not follow that distinctions like quantitative-qualitative or scientific-constructivist-critical science are meaningless. Each of these is a different practice shaped by different aims, standards, values, and social and political realities, and, as Howe himself admits each is situated within a complex web of background knowledge. In other words, these paths to inquiry are rooted not simply in matters of epistemology but in relations of power, influence, and control in communities of inquirers (Eisner, 1988). To dismiss them as so many methodological dogmas is to reduce social inquiry to matters of technique separating the means of inquiry from the issues of purpose, value, and assumption that shape the very act of inquiry itself (Schwandt, 1989a). To view inquiry as a kind of technical project characterized only by types of logics or methods in use is to empty inquiry of its significance as a kind of practically and historically situated undertaking.

[22]

Ruminations on Methodology
Of Truth and Significance

GAIL McCUTCHEON

This chapter contains reflections on methodology related to Schwandt's chapter but not tied solely to it. This set of ruminations begins where Schwandt begins with C. S. Peirce on truth. Then it turns to alternative paradigms. I close by discussing interrelated matters associated with significance, truth, and associated methodological matters. This chapter also relates to J. Smith's (this volume) chapter about criteria because I concur with him that "one has not seriously thought about the nature of social and educational inquiry until one has confronted the criteria issue." Neither can we disentangle methodology from the issue of criteria when considering alternative paradigms.

Doing qualitative research and commenting on a chapter are somewhat akin to seeing shapes in clouds or patterns in an oriental rug. Although I'm sure you see different shapes and patterns, I'll trace ones I see as important and germane to research methodologies using alternative paradigms.

As researchers, we should not be complacent but I believe we are doing a good job of thinking about and employing varied new paradigms of research. Alternative paradigm research has found acceptance at conferences and in research journals. Those of us using different paradigms publish books, secure and keep jobs. In my own college, many colleagues desire to understand alternative paradigms of research and almost routinely require advisees to take methods courses likely to be used in at least two paradigms rather than settling just for one; they accept students doing dissertations resting on new alternative paradigms and ask interesting questions in the defenses about the research. Students' and colleagues' scholarship based on different paradigms is recognized and rewarded. Research retreats about alternative paradigms are sold out. Courses in qualitative research overflow with students. Many healthy debates about what constitutes scholarly inquiry and how it should be done have ensued in different settings from search committees, to the college senate, to student advisory committees, to research retreats.

But somehow I feel we're falling short of the mark in research using different paradigms not only in Columbus; so let's not puff up our chests and gloat too much, for I also have a sense of unease that, while we are doing acceptably well with data collection and analysis, we are not pushing ourselves sufficiently beyond a technical sorting of data into categories (analysis) much as an accountant works. We have clear descriptions of how to collect and analyze data. For example, Miles and Huberman (1984, p. 15) define these purposes for qualitative data analysis in order to determine valid analyses and be scientific when they say:

> How can we draw valid meaning from qualitative data? What methods of analysis can we employ that are practical, communicable, and non-self-deluding—in short, *scientific* in the best sense of the word?

Peirce on Truth

Schwandt starts us off on a productive track with Peirce's theory of truth. Rather than being a correspondence theory of truth, Peirce's theory focuses on properties associated with the operation of an object (such as litmus paper) on the world. He is a pragmatist.

Here, Peirce (1878) discusses how we arrive at belief and its relationship to rules for action, which he calls "habits":

> We have seen that it [belief] has three properties: First, it is something that we are aware of; second, it appeases the irritation of doubt; and, third, it involves the establishment in our nature of a rule of action, or, say for short, a *habit*. As it appeases the irritation of doubt, which is the motive for thinking, thought relaxes, and comes to rest for a moment when belief is reached. But, since belief is a rule for action, the application of which involves further doubt and further thought, at the same time that it is a stopping-place, it is also a new starting place for thought. That is why I have permitted myself to call it a thought at rest, although it is

essentially an action. The *final* upshot of thinking is the exercise of volition, and of this thought no longer forms a part; but belief is only a stadium of mental action, an effect upon our nature due to thought, which will influence future thinking.

The essence of belief is the establishment of a habit, and different beliefs are distinguished by the different modes of action to which they give rise.... To develop ... meaning, we have ... simply to determine what habits it produces, for what a thing means is simply what habits it produces, for what a thing means is simply what habits it involves. (Peirce, 1878, p. 39, emphasis in original)

One positive aspect of Peirce's line of thinking rests on the relationship between action and thinking. Further, his conception of how one belief affects others relates to research using alternative paradigms in that it is developmental and cyclical; what I learn in one study can be carried onward to the next, so it has continuity.

The meaning of a window then, for Peirce, is that it is transparent, so the way it acts upon the world is to let us see through it; a heartily swung baseball bat would operate on it to shatter it; it separates outdoor and indoor weather (Pratte, personal communication, 1988). Hence, the "truth" of our research for Peirce is how it operates on the world in at least two ways. One constitutes how a phenomenon we study operates on the world. Another is how the research itself operates on the world. This point is elaborated upon further at the end of this response as I discuss significance.

Peirce's theory of belief, truth, and meaning rests on empiricism and is probably more objective than some of us might prefer. It also implies elements of causality and instrumentalism we might question. Others might find it helpful because truth is somewhat slippery, belief and action are interrelated, and the work is acknowledged as developmental and cyclical. It relates well to practical thinking and action in education because it rests on the idea of how something operates on the world.

Some Observations on Alternative Paradigms

Epistemologies many of us follow are based on ethnography, other forms of interpretivism, and critical theory. A common attempt for many is an attempt to uncover different structures. Many ethnogra-

phers, for example, strive to unearth various social structures underlying the lived-in world in order to produce understanding. Critical
theorists aim at illuminating various taken-for-granted structures and
practices that produce and support hegemony so we can ultimately
liberate ourselves from them in striving for equity. Each perspective
yields interesting insights into education, and I'm not totally convinced that anything is wrong with trying to disclose and understand
such structures. On the other hand, many poststructuralists eschew
structure, and yet I find that their perspectives illuminate matters as
well.

Other qualitative researchers such as some interpretivists and educational connoisseurs and critics seek to understand the nature of a
phenomenon; rather than looking for a structure, these researchers
seek to capture the essence of a matter.

One danger for all of us is to fall prey to issues of validity and
objectivity characterizing a positivistic correspondence theory of truth.
An examination of the indexes of major books about qualitative
research methods illustrates the problem; we can find validity and
objectivity listed along with techniques such as member checks, audit
trails, and referential adequacy (which I take to mean the presence of
sufficient evidence to warrant an interpretation or analysis). The
danger is that, if we only concentrate on whether our work is "true"
in a sense of corresponding to reality, we sell ourselves short and
should also worry about significance, to which we now turn.

Significance

Significance has two interrelated meanings associated with qualitative research. One concerns *meanings* of observations (see McCutcheon,
1981). In this case, Jacques Maquet (1964, p. 49) reminds us that

> social phenomena, even when reduced to their simplest components,
> differ from physical phenomena in that the former have one of several
> meanings as integral parts. . . . Two completely different social phenom-
> ena, an act of magic and an act of ritual, may have, as it were, the same
> behavioral manifestations. Without its meaning, an observable behavior
> is not a fact for the anthropologist. And the meaning of such behavior is
> rarely obvious; it requires interpretation—often much interpretation.
> The observer's general knowledge, his intellectual skill, and his imagi-
> nation are important assets in that interpretation [sic].

In schools I often observe mysterious events and must interpret them. Sometimes this is quite simple, and, on other occasions, it requires a great deal of interpretation to understand what in the world is happening because the meanings are slippery and multidimensional.

Mysteries in classrooms appear with some frequency, and we have to interpret them to understand their significance (meaning). Some interpretations are low-inference ones, and interpretations are possible simply through further interview about them. This is not always the case, for many such mysteries have to be made sense of by considering them deeply rather than merely asking someone for more facts.

As this form of significance implies, we have to wonder about what our observations signify—mean—for our work to have potency.

Interpretation calls for us to take a deep breath and turn inside while considering our data and the experiences of collecting them to imagine, reflect, and ultimately understand what we experienced in our research. It is probably only partly a rational process and also partly an intuitive one. Maybe this is one reason why it escapes our attention in considering methodology: Intuition, after all, isn't scientific! Yet, it seems most creative geniuses have relied on it. I think it was Thomas Edison who said that his work was 1% inspiration (is this intuition?) and 99% perspiration (is this data collection and analysis?). Peirce (1896, pp. 196-197) relates to this when he says:

> When a man desires ardently to know the truth, his first effort will be to imagine what the truth can be. He cannot prosecute his pursuit long without finding that imagination unbridled is sure to carry him off the track. Yet nevertheless, it remains true that there is, after all, nothing but imagination that can ever supply him an inkling of the truth. He can stare stupidly at phenomena; but in the absence of imagination they will not connect themselves together in any rational way [sic].

Analysis and interpretation are interconnected in that, after (and while) we collect and analyze data, we have to interpret their significance.

A second meaning of significance appropriate to our work is importance. It is in this area where we particularly fall short and to which I think we must attend when considering methodology. Peirce's theory of belief and truth would imply that we should consider the practical significance—illuminative significance—of our work: its implications for operating on the world by contributing to and perhaps changing actions and thinking in education. I call this "illuminative significance" because it can shed light on our endeavors. Thinking and acting should be construed not as separate here but as dialogically interrelated. This is the case because, even as we act on the world—through speech or otherwise—we think and sometimes modify our actions. Similarly, as we think, we envision actions as we mentally rehearse them and alter our thinking for we "see" that such actions would simply not be appropriate or might not be effective. As we teach, research, advise, write, and administer, this dialog between thinking and action goes on virtually constantly and is probably the main reason for saying we take our work home with us, unlike what we imagine of the grocery baggers and TV repairers of the world.

One way we can think of illuminative significance is to consider the impact of our research in implanting concepts, ways of viewing the world, and language into educators' thinking, literature, and actions: the extent to which our research shapes our field's consciousness in its interpretations and the sort of questions raised, that is, its mark on education. It is important here to note that this influence is probably unlikely to be neatly and tidily one to one. Merely because we find out "A" in setting "1" does not necessarily mean it will play itself out as "A" in setting "27."

Nonetheless, our interpretation "A" may transfer in significant ways to other settings, even though they are observably different. Such interpretations then move into our thinking and help us frame our questions in our research. Weiss (1980) refers to this sort of conceptual movement as "knowledge creep." Linked to an earlier point, knowledge creep about significant matters affects both our thinking and our actions in education because the two have a dialogic relationship. This further relates to Peirce's theory of belief and truth in that significant findings creep into our ways of thinking, the questions we raise, and ultimately how we and the findings operate on the world. The activities of analysis and interpretation differ in important ways.

Implications for Methodology

Assuring that we have told the "truth" of our research, in terms of how a matter operates on the world, is important, but how might we go about achieving significance in our work? Here, I'll be autobiographical to demonstrate some examples of courses of action to address this problem. Studying how 12 elementary school teachers planned their lessons (McCutcheon, 1980) led me to collect more than a filing-cabinet drawer full of data from observations, interviews, and teachers' lesson plans. I began telling the story of the study to the 12 teachers involved, to my graduate assistants, and virtually to anyone who seemed to listen. A breakthrough came when I told the story to Chris Clark, who admonished me to listen more closely to my own story so I could understand its meaning: that the important facet of teachers' planning is its *mental* activity, not what is written on paper.

Similarly, a study of homework practices in a local school system yielded reams of data from administrators, parents, teachers, and students. Not until I presented this at AERA did I understand some of my own data. In this case, Robert Tabachnick was my discussant, and he raised one simple point that amazed me. He said he was surprised that I hadn't suggested that elementary school teachers might consider assigning homework where an adult was also to be involved (because those children had enthusiastically implied that one aspect of homework they enjoyed was the attention they got for it). I was amazed merely because it was so obvious, as had been my point with Chris Clark, yet both obvious points had eluded me as had one point about the unintended support of sexism in one teacher's practices in physical education class in an earlier study (McCutcheon, 1979) until I told it to a group of undergraduate education students who raised the issue.

What do I draw from this partial autobiography of research? It seems clear to me that we need to be patient with ourselves, and realize that significant interpretations may be a long time in coming, and to give ourselves advice to tell the story of our research many times to other people but also to listen carefully to ourselves as we tell that story to hear our own focus and concern. We need to turn inward to try to involve our imagination and intuition. A supportive outsider may be capable of understanding its significance. Perhaps we get so close to our data as we live in a setting and involve ourselves in our research that it virtually blinds us to its significance. It's almost a wrenching experience to leave the site and to turn inward to our intuition and imagination, for we lived in that setting so fully and for so many hours. An outside consultant role of listening to the story actively and hearing its main messages for us may be very helpful. This role extends beyond that of being a peer debriefer by helping to focus on what constitutes the essence of the research. It further extends the work beyond reliability and objectivity to the criterion of significance.

Another factor relating to significance may be our closeness to our subjects—both the foci of our work and the people inhabiting our settings. Too much distance from them probably renders our position too external to reach a sufficiently full understanding of it to be able to render it richly and to understand it.

Obviously, reading relevant literature may also help us to develop conceptually significant interpretations, but this endeavor could also be problematic because we might maintain status quo findings and continue to ask previously asked questions rather than pushing into new realms.

Summary and Conclusions

Adopting Peirce's theory of belief and truth might help us ponder significance rather than dwelling exclusively on validity, reliability, and objectivity, which are criteria from the positivist paradigm. Although I suppose they are necessary, they are clearly insufficient if we hope to reach our potential as educational researchers. I further have argued for ways to strive for significance in our work as we consider its meanings and its importance in influencing thought and actions in education through "knowledge creep." *Significant* educational research can be used by others to ponder their own research and actions because it illuminates their work.

Although analysis of data (à la Miles and Huberman 1984, for instance) is necessary during and following fieldwork, qualitative researchers are not merely technical accountants filing the data into this category or that. We are also meaning developers. Although the data can "speak" to us as analyses emerge out of the data, it is through our active, mental work that we develop interpretations, and this is the more significant part of treating our work where we knit together seemingly disparate data and convey their meanings. In some respects, this is the most frustrating aspect of doing research. I, at least frequently, have the uneasy, gnawing feeling that the meaning is escaping me, although I know there's more to it than what I've said so far. Having been in a setting for six to eight weeks and tried to understand it, is it all for naught because I don't understand the significance of its stories? I am reminded here of Agatha Christie's Jane Marple (Jones, 1987), televised by PBS in the United States on *Mystery*, who occasionally worries, "Something's going on here. But I fear I'm missing it. The bits and pieces just won't come together for me." She seems more patient that I, sipping her tea until the facts converge for her. Actually, she probably sleuthily thinks about human nature and motivation, past solutions, and the particulars of this crime to reach a solution. She's probably only outwardly calm as she sips her tea, for facts don't simply converge. We actively fit data together; it's an *active mental* process because we have to arrange data in a conceptual scheme rather than arraying them in some separated fashion, for research is more than merely a quest for facts.

Our work also demands time and patience (and perhaps several cups of tea). But then Jane Marple is on television and resides in a fictional world, not in educational research. Stories told in movies and television always work out, don't they? I believe our research stories will also work out if we give ourselves adequate time and turn our attention to developing *significant* interpretations.

[23]

Discussion on Methodology

MARION LUNDY DOBBERT

University of Minnesota

Both methodology discussion sessions focused on general issues of paradigmatic accommodation. In one session, *methodology* was defined as a study of methods, a study in which we lay bare our choices of method and define the way these choices fit our research problem. Methodology was discussed at this level in both sessions rather than at the level of selection or development of research techniques. The discussions were not linear or sequential but developed as sets of parallel, intertwined themes that ran throughout the hour-plus dialogs.

A number of definitional issues requiring clarity were raised and discussed in both sessions. These discussions clarified concepts not by achieving definitive solutions but by adding layers of information and interpretation. For example, we mulled over the definition of the term *paradigm*, which, from the classic Kuhnian perspective, someone pointed out, is misused in social science. As might be expected, we also tried to specify the differences between the three paradigms under consideration at the conference. One participant asked for a clarification of the positions of the three paradigms within anthropology and sociology. Another participant responded by noting that both disciplines have subfields or cohorts of researchers that adopt each of the paradigms. Tom Schwandt's paper, which opened both sessions, stimulated debates on the roles of criticality and change in the critical traditions; the paper identified three differing strands within the critical research tradition. Other discussion embodied our collective reflection on major conference issues such as the philosophical and practical consequences of the arbitrariness of the axioms underlying all paradigms, the importance of surprise in all research, and the current trend toward multimethods research, including multiparadigmatic methods. The report merely notes the presence of these discussions and focuses on major issues that developed that either were not discussed in the keynote addresses or that were developed beyond the points that the keynoters were able to reach during their assigned time periods. Four major issues surfaced, as follows.

Arrogance in Research

Four varieties of arrogance were identified. The first was the arrogance of positivist research wherein the researcher makes all the decisions about the conditions of the research and decides upon the nature of the intervention for the clients. A second form of arrogance is to be found in researchers who refuse to discuss their procedures and paradigms but just want to "get on with it," that is, the self-satisfied. The arrogance of deciding that other people need empowering and are not already powerful was the third form identified. In the discussion of this form of arrogance, the example was offered that teachers are, in fact, very powerful. Fourthly, there is the arrogance of not asking where *we* need critical perspectives to liberate our own thinking, of not asking those we study to help us become liberated.

Paradigms and Practitioners

A second major theme to surface was the question of the relationship of this conference and its issues to practitioners. A number of discussants opined that this conference is not likely to be of much use to those working on practical issues in their daily lives within the educational context. Although we have the leisure to sit here and discuss the paradigms, even we are having difficulty interpreting them. Who, it was asked, will interpret for practitioners? Other discussants strongly rejected questions and comments in this vein, saying that practitioners are fully capable of thinking for themselves and have the ability to interpret paradigmatic issues.

Another approach to issues of practicality centered on information needs: Why do we not ask what research is *needed* in the field before we select an issue to study? Why is it, as a case in point, that innovations such as pre-first grades occur without previous research underpinnings? There is a great need for research with respect to educational innovation, and yet most innovations seem to be undertaken in response to needs of the educational system without previous research support.

In both sessions, participants commented that researchers and educators in the field live in different worlds. In one session the assertion that, despite our changes in research strategies (based on the critical and constructivist paradigms), researchers and practitioners are not getting closer together went unchallenged. In the other session it was noted, contrarily and, again without challenge, that the relationship between researchers and practitioners has changed a great deal, that we now have *negotiated we's* and *countertexts* among our report forms, although these are still difficult to get published in journals.

Finally, one of the central issues of the conference, the definition of truth, surfaced in this context. A participant asked whether we might not define truth not in terms of correspondence theory, or some other historical, philosophic theory, but in terms of its significance to the people studied. Taken as a whole, the practitioner theme in the discussions suggests that the methodology section may have identified a fourth research paradigm that was not on the conference agenda, a practical/practitioner paradigm.

Writing Multiparadigmatic Science

A major strand of discussion in one of the sessions was the question of how we might write multiparadigmatic science. The participants agreed that homogenization of paradigms should not and could not occur and then asked how we ought to write up our research if we assumed paradigm separateness.

Five rather practical solutions or parts of solutions surfaced: First, we might use several different type fonts in a report to represent the perspectives of the differing paradigms. The result would be like a formal news show discussion, where each participant systematically is given the opportunity to comment on each issue. Second, a report might present a number on clear, compelling stories, one from the perspective of each research paradigm used. Third, we might treat a study like a document in need of translation and assign a serious responsibility for both translation and careful listening. With respect to alternative paradigms, this approach would entail a bilingual or trilingual model wherein we recognize that translation and comprehension won't be perfect but we agree to try. Fourth, we might attempt to use a sharing model instead of a debate and competition model. In this model, successive contributions from alternative paradigms would attempt to be additive and to contribute to the building of a whole rather than negative as is so frequently the case with interparadigmatic critique. A fifth suggestion was that we attempt to ground interparadigmatic discussions in the data of real studies. (The term *data* was used here, as I understood it, to cover the meanings employed in all three paradigms.)

Social Uses of Paradigms Within the Scientific Community

Participants pointed out that the paradigms we use stem from *warrants* and *charters*, often embodied in foundational documents that contain different rules for appealing to each paradigm's basic tenets. These warrants are historically situated. The basic warrants may be used in two ways. Individuals may read the foundational documents and subscribe to them, adopting their values. Such a choice will then serve as the foundation for an individual's work and belief system about research standards. Alternatively, an individual can read the warrant documents and use them as standards for judgment, using them *as if* he or she subscribed to them. We use this sort of application of warrants when we judge articles for a journal by temporarily adopting their criteria as formal standards by which to judge an article's internal validity. But, a participant pointed out, not everyone is willing to make this type of formal use of warrants and their derivative criteria. Many journals, for instance, control papers accepted by refusing to adopt other warrants, even temporarily. Empiricist researchers seem less inclined to the temporary adoption of alternative warrants than researchers from the other two paradigms.

These considerations raised a number of questions: When and where are members of a research community willing to adopt the warrants of other communities for temporary judgment? When will researchers use form criteria rather than belief criteria? Why do the frequencies and distributions of such choices vary by research community and over time?

TRAINING

[24]

So-Called Training in the
So-Called Alternative Paradigm

SHULAMIT REINHARZ

Some Context and Connection

I am a sociologist working in the United States in the last quarter of the twentieth century. In my discipline—sociology—as in all others, differences of opinion exist as to what constitutes good work (Reinharz, in press). The two major points of view in sociology at this time—the last quarter of the twentieth century—and in this place—the United States—are that (a) research should be done in such a way that the outcome rests on statistical reasoning or (b) research should be done in a way that relies on the interpretation of descriptions of behavior and reports of speech. Put briefly, these two alternatives are labeled positivist and antipositivist, or quantitative and qualitative.

Because I mentioned time and place in my opening statement, I want to make a comment about each, dealing first with the issue of *time* or historical period. In my view, the tension concerning method is currently high, although not the highest it has ever been. In fact, the tension between the two perspectives has ebbed and waned in sociology. Sometimes the tension concerning method in the discipline has paled in comparison with other differences of opinion, for example, should we or should we not take a stand as a group for or against a particular national policy?

In his opening address, D. C. Phillips (this volume) seems to disagree with my assessment. According to Phillips, we find ourselves in a special historic moment. He claims that positivism, the "dominant older view," was "in its death throes" in 1956, subsequently enabling us to enter the period of "postpositivism." Perhaps this is so in some fields, but in sociology the transition has not been so clear-cut. I find that we are still in conflict and that neither side has experienced "death throes."

This view seems to be shared by Popkewitz (this volume). Casting a glance on American social science from his temporary perch in Sweden last year, he concluded his chapter with the idea that "positivism dominates American culture and science" but that we can also characterize positivism and antipositivism as "competing traditions." Thus there not only are possibly competing traditions but conflict about whether or not one party to the competition is dead!

And now, as to *space*. For the sake of illustration, I want to contrast the United States with Israel. During my recent sabbatical in Israel (1987-1988), I had a chance to view briefly the sociology departments in that country's major universities. There I found the tension between the two perspectives to be minimal (Reinharz, 1989). The reasons for this state of affairs are the following:

> First, all the departments are combined sociology and anthropology departments; second, the most prestigious members of the most prestigious departments do qualitative research; third, Israel is connected both to American and to European sociology, where American is understood as mathematically oriented and European as theoretically oriented; and finally, when departments are small, as these departments tended to be individuals tend to engage in both kinds of work.

Reviewing the history of sociology in Israel, Erik Cohen (1988, p. 88), dean of social sciences at Hebrew University, wrote that

> at an earlier stage there was a tendency in the small nucleus of early sociologists to fuse qualitative and quantitative methods of study, [but that] a gradual separation between sociologists with a qualitative and those with a quantitative orientation took place as the number of academic sociologists in Israel expanded.

The situation in the United States in this period is less harmonious than in Israel. Here I find that methodological differences are sharply drawn. The tension between the two methodological perspectives is manifest in two classic ways—silence and dualistic metaphors. The metaphors and silence, in turn, *contribute* to the sharp divisions. I will now discuss these ideas, turning first to silence.

Silence

Why do I say *silence*? The answer for me is lodged in the following illustration. I think it is fair to say that *all* American sociologists recognize that both perspectives exist. Thus textbooks on research methods in sociology consistently cover *both* approaches, yet, at the same time, the two perspectives are generally not given equal *space* in the research textbook. For example, a popular methods textbook by Earl Babbie (1983) contains five parts, one of which is "Modes of Observation." In this section he devotes one chapter each to experiments, survey research, field research, unobtrusive research, and evaluation research, thus acknowledging the existence of various forms of research. However, in the six chapters of the next part—Analysis of Data—nearly all the material relates to mathematics (the chapter titles are "Quantifying data," "Elementary Analyses," "Indexes, Scales and Typologies," "The Elaboration Model," "Social Statistics," and "An Overview of Advanced Analysis"). The hidden message is that what is meant by *data* is numbers. The other data are silenced. The previous section's acknowledgment that description and transcription are data disappears in this section.

This common feature of many textbooks suggests that, when qualitative methods are included, it is more the product of lip service than of conviction. We know from sociological studies that, when the members of one group are silenced, they generally survive in a separate culture. Thus, whereas one can receive good instruction in quantitative methods from such texts, one has to turn to specialized texts to get guidance for qualitative research methods. However, because of the great variability in qualitative methods, resulting from the fact that researchers must become part of idiosyncratic individuals' social worlds or part of highly variable social settings, it is difficult for *any* text on qualitative methods to provide instruction useful for *all* projects. For this reason, a helpful source for learning these methods is the appendixes or methods chapters of books reporting a study similar in some way to the qualitative study a person plans to undertake (Reinharz, 1984a). This type of learning represents a form of apprenticeship.

Dualistic Metaphors for Method

Beyond the phenomenon of silencing, manifest in the amount of space devoted to each of the perspectives, we can also examine the language used to describe the two perspectives (Blakemore, 1988). When we do this, it is easy to see that there is an antagonistic relation, expressed in military and social movement metaphors. Metaphors are important conveyors of value in sociological and other academic work (Reinharz, 1987). For example, eminent sociological theorist, Randall Collins (1984, p. 330), wrote:

> Sociology is split into two antagonistic or mutually oblivious wings: quantitative and nonquantitative. . . . In recent years, the antipositivist side has become much more prominent within sociology, as well as more militant. . . . However, positivist sociology has certainly not retreated. . . . Recent statistical sociology makes no concessions of intelligibility toward outsiders and shows almost no interest in linking up with larger theoretical concerns. On the other side, anti-positivists, once a somewhat embarrassed minority, militantly advocate their own programs of inter-pretive, historical, Marxist, structuralist, or ethnomethodological sociology and condemn their positivist opponents in absentia.

To diminish this estrangement, some brave souls of the positivist camp have invited representatives of the other side to display their goods, that is, to teach them what qualitative methodology is all about. As a person who is frequently called upon to play this consultative role, I find it remarkable how frequently quantitative types realize they could actually like qualitative types if they only got to know them better. After the brief encounter, however, each group probably returns to its typical practices and former prejudices, enlightened merely by a little more understanding or tolerance.

Rosabeth Kanter (1980) has done interesting studies of dualism based on her notion of tokens. Using her terms, people who do qualitative research are tokens in the larger research world. One characteristic of tokens is that they always have to explain themselves and teach others who may be hostile (Kanter, 1980). Another characteristic of tokens is that they do not generally ask those who are not tokens to explain themselves.

To use a race or ethnic relations metaphor, we could say that our research methods textbooks provide pseudointegration of the methodological groups and that proponents of the two methods spend most of their time in segregated areas. Advocates of each position usually do not understand one another, nor do they usually work together on a joint project. In some cases, the distance between the two perspectives reflects actual antagonism; in other cases, the distance reflects a liberal "live and let live" attitude.

An outcome of dualism in race and methods can be observed in efforts at integration or intermarriage. Thus, in the case of research perspectives in sociology, a few integrationists on both sides argue that the research is at its best when it combines the virtues of both strategies (Eckert, 1987; Jick, 1983; Pillemer, 1987). Instead of using the term *intermarriage*, of course, the term *triangulation* is preferred.

To return to the military metaphor, I would say that lip service, tolerance, consultation, and triangulation are minor cease-fires. The more general pattern is two groups of sociologists each going about its own work, mildly aware of and irritated by the presence or existence of the other, referring to each other with wit, sarcasm, and methodological ridicule. Each has its own "founding fathers and mothers" and proud historical moments (Becker, 1970). Each has its own epistemology. Each forms its own professional organizations, publishes in its own journals and books, and awards its own prizes. Together they are part of a few larger umbrella organizations, but, when the large disciplinary groups meet, members of the two camps quickly move to their own corners of the conference site.

The problem with the picture I have painted is that it is too balanced. It does not take into account the relative difference in power, resources, and prestige between the two perspectives, so I will try to use power-laden dualistic metaphors now. The quantitative approach is the taken-for-granted one, the one with the human, capital, and ideological power; the qualitative approach is the *alternative paradigm* or, as Simone de Beauvoir (1952) has put it, "the Other." The quantitative is the Establishment and the qualitative is the social movement protesting the Establishment. The quantitative is the regular army and the qualitative the resistance. The qualitative approach is the outsider trying to get in by showing that the Emperor has no clothes. The quantitative approach is the Emperor sitting on the throne not examining whether or not he is nude. The qualitative one is the person writing about the problems with quantitative research; the quantitative one considers how much lip service to pay to the qualitative one. To use the military metaphor, quantifiers think qualitative research is good for exploratory investigation, the testing of the mine field. Then the big guns with the large data sets can come in.

Using the metaphor of body and gender (Keller, 1985), the quantitative is male; the qualitative is female. In general, quantitative research defines itself as hard, firm, real, concrete, solid, and strong; it defines qualitative research as soft, mushy, fuzzy, and weak. Qualitative research, on the other hand, defines itself as thick, deep, and grounded and defines positivist research as dry, thin, meaningless, and unintelligible. Qualitative researchers *immerse* themselves in their data; quantitative researchers *control* the variables. Therefore, the danger for qualitative researchers is drowning in data; and the danger for quantitative research is having dirty data. Like geologists and problem-solvers, positivists come up with *findings* and *results*; like classicists, antipositivists read texts and develop themes.

Let me put some life into these grim metaphors by quoting from a letter I received from a male doctoral candidate in a large, midwestern University, the day I started writing this. (Ironically, in a chapter I wrote in 1980, I used the same technique of drawing on letters received that day; Reinharz, 1981). Sadly, the theme of the letter quoted below is the same as in that quoted nine years ago.

Dear Shula, I am sending you my bound copy of the qualitative reader I put together some years ago. . . . For political reasons at the time, I did not claim status on the title page as the organizer and "compiler" but that was in fact my role. In this department, qualitative methods have always been under fire from the "quantifrenics." As I was so closely identified with one faculty member who openly favored use of qualitative methods when appropriate, it was wise, for the purposes of encouraging wider participation, to present a more corporate appearing sponsorship of the graduate students' "study group." As no graduate course offerings in qualitative were permitted by the powers that be [one woman was allowed to teach only a sophomore undergrad course, and then they scuttled that too—a long story], the semi-organized study group format was my response as a graduate student who longed for some intelligent methodological discussion on a regular basis. To broaden participation, I was able to get one of the older faculty members, now retired, to act as a conduit for students who wanted to register for independent study credit.

The debate between qualitative and quantitative research almost always takes place on the linguistic turf of positivist research. From the perspective of the dominant paradigm, qualitative research is good to the extent that it satisfies the standards set up by the quantitative standard. Because qualitative research has less ideological and institutional power, it usually does not devise the terms by which the two sides are labeled. An exception is Barney Glaser and Anselm Strauss's *Discovery of Grounded Theory* (1967). In my view, one of the reasons their book has been so widely adopted is that it proposed new language that emerges from the qualitative perspective. These terms were then used to describe both sides. It labeled conventional research as drawing on the logic of verification and grounded theory research as drawing on the logic of discovery.

Because the positivist paradigm typically defines the terms, it is able to assert quantification as hard, objective, concrete, difficult, and definitive and to describe descriptive research as soft, subjective, exploratory, and easy. Much of the discussion then *begins* with qualitative research defending itself against having these labels applied or against having these labels defined pejoratively. Such a beginning typically leads the qualitative researcher into modifying the nature of qualitative research in order to meet the criticisms of positivists.

Issues of dominance, apparent in the qualitative/quantitative tension, reflect issues of dominance and powerlessness in our society. The power of quantitative research in social science derives not from its explanatory power but is a halo effect of the status of the physical sciences, in contrast, for example, to the status of the arts. In our society, White males are trained for and associated with the world of the mind and the physical sciences; Black men with the world of the body, music, and soul; and women of both races with reproducing, serving and caring. Those who conduct quantitative research obtain resources and prestige. This prestige is not universally obtainable. To the extent that some children are poorly trained in mathematics in our public schools, the ability to conduct such research becomes the prerogative of a certain class, gender, and race. These same people are socialized to control—from the pulpit, from the lectern, from Capitol Hill, in the doctor's office, in the experimental laboratory, and in the collection of data. People not socialized to control others are well suited for qualitative research. As Harriet Martineau (1838/1988, pp. 20-21) put it, more than 150 years ago:

> Every observer and recorder is fulfilling a function; and no one observer or recorder ought to feel discouragement, as long as he desires to be useful rather than shining; to be the servant rather than the lord of science, and a friend to the home-stayers rather than their dictator.

Why the So-Called Alternative Paradigm

Today in this social setting that we have created, the antipositivists have hegemony for once. Thus we probably feel particularly free to formulate and use our own language. In preparation for our conference, therefore, I attempted to write a paper using words for what we do that are *not* derivative of the quantitative perspective. For this reason, I have avoided or infrequently used terms such as *nondominant, antipositivist,* or *alternative,* all of which are positivist centered. These words privilege positivism. I even find *qualitative* troubling because it implies the conventional contrast. To highlight this point, I have used the phrase *so-called alternative paradigm* in the title of this talk. The term *so-called* represents my psycholinguistic attempt to break away from being defined by others.

Feminists use the word *naming* to refer to this process of self-labeling. *Naming* frequently requires the invention of neologisms. Neologisms are liberating, refreshing, playful avenues for rethinking and getting out of old boxes and fetishes. It leaves outsiders uncomprehending. From the perspective of a radical feminist critic such as Mary Daly (1978, pp. 23-24), unless you start out this way, your journey leads nowhere. She writes:

> Elsewhere I have advocated committing the crime of Methodicide, since the Methodolatry of patriarchal disciplines kills creative thought. . . . Gynocentric writing means risking. Since the language and style of patriarchal writing simply cannot contain or carry the energy of women's exorcism and ecstasy [I must therefore] invent, dis-cover, re-member. At times I make up words (such as gynaesthesia for women's synaesthesia). Often I unmask deceptive words by dividing them and employing alternative meanings for prefixes (for example, re-cover actu-

ally says "cover again"). I also unmask their hidden reversals, often by
using less known or "obsolete" meanings (for example, glamour as used
to name a witch's power). Sometimes I simply invite the reader to listen
to words in a different way (for example, de-light).

By disposing of articles, Black feminist writer Bell Hooks (1984)
complements Mary Daly's reviving of nouns. For example, Hooks
writes of "feminist movement" not "the feminist movement." She
shows how different the phrase "I am a feminist" is from "I advocate
feminism." Bell Hooks and Mary Daly have helped me see once again
how the dominant paradigm defines the so-called alternative paradigm and how a true alternative would have to spring from autono-
mous roots. Assuming I have explained why I use the term *so-called*
alternative paradigm, now I would like to explain why I use the term
so-called training.

Why So-Called Training

Training for so-called alternative work raises questions that differ
from training for dominant work. For example, the fact that statistical
research usually requires large samples means that large sets of people
will have to be organized to conduct the research. This prerequisite
abets the formation of hierarchic research teams, which affect the
psychology of all its members, the kind of projects that will be undertaken, and the kind of effect on interpretation of data that people of
different statuses can have.

The conduct of large-scale quantitative research, furthermore, requires capital. This capital is generally available from two sources—
the federal government and research foundations. These institutions
must be expected to protect their vested interests. One need only look
at the U.S. president's manipulation of Dr. Sullivan, the head of the
Department of Health and Human Services, to understand the extent
to which this organization must serve vested political interests. Most
government research funds come via this agency. Two major activities
of universities are the obtaining of funds from the government and
competing against other universities. Universities that successfully
obtain funds are able to attract researchers who will attract attention
through their publication and thus attract students. The pursuit of

money to do the research has become an end in itself. Research that is expensive is more prestigious than research that is cheap or free.

Qualitative research—the so-called alternative paradigm—is frequently conducted without hierarchically organized research teams and without the flow of much funding. As Virginia Woolf (1979) wrote, women have become writers because paper is inexpensive. The skills that so-called alternative research requires include the ability to form relationships of trust with people, the ability to listen carefully, and good verbal and writing skills. These are the skills of women and others without power, as a result of the way they are socialized in our society.

Because these skills are not highly valued in our society, the people who possess them are not highly valued. For this reason, many schools do not offer any training in qualitative methods, while other schools offer very limited training. These same schools are unlikely to grant tenure to someone whose work and teaching is primarily *so-called alternative*. Thus to train students in these methods is possibly to train them for unemployment or difficulty in landing a conventional position, and definitely to train them to have to explain themselves to others.

In these schools, senior scholars may offer training in these methods because their job security allows them to do whatever they want. However, their own lack of training may lead some people to try their hand at qualitative research without training, with the expectable poor quality results and self-fulfilling prophecy in the eyes of the quantifiers. I see this problem of poor quality frequently in qualitative papers I review for journals.

This semester I am once again teaching the graduate research methods seminar at Brandeis University. Before the course began, I received many phone calls from students at other universities in the Boston area asking if they could enroll because an analogous course was *not* offered in their universities. Because I was on sabbatical last year, there was also a larger than usual group of students in my own department who wanted to take the course, as was true in another division of the university that typically sends its students to the course for so-called training. Because pre-enrollment began to be too large for me to have a course with any value, I limited enrollment only to students in my department and suggested to other students that they suggest to their departments that faculty be hired in this field.

It will, therefore, come as no surprise that, because I teach at the American university whose sociology department is most connected with the so-called alternative paradigm, I am frequently called upon to consult by people who want to do this kind of research but who can find no one in their own department who can really guide them. On one level, this is flattering. It is good to know that one's abilities are respected and that there is a market for what one has to offer. But, on another level, frankly, it is demoralizing. It indicates to me that there are too few people to call upon, and that universities are not adequately hiring people with these skills.

Why are there so few teachers of *so-called alternative* methods? The answer is quite simple. Positivists still have that power over most academic departments, and although they may respect proponents of alternative paradigms, they will not necessarily hire them, especially when resources are scarce. If so-called alternative paradigm researchers are not being hired, then they are not available as trainers. Thus the first question concerning training is *who is going to do it*? Where is the human, material base? We should study which graduate programs offer training in the so-called alternative paradigm and which do not. Johns Hopkins University Sociology Department, for example, has four methods requirements and does not teach qualitative methods at all.

Second, if the people actually teaching alternative paradigm research were not hired or trained to do it, then who *are* they? The answer may be that they are people who discovered it for themselves when they became disenchanted with whatever else they were doing. Yvonna Lincoln (this volume) hints at this in her keynote paper: "I did my usual number when someone asks me a question to which I haven't a clue: I made it up as I went along." This idea was also discussed by feminist physicist and philosopher, Evelyn Fox Keller, in a talk at Brandeis University in the fall of 1988 in which she attempted to explain why Brandeis University had produced so many eminent feminist scholars. Her answer was that students at that university were taught what was wrong with the conventional paradigm but were not taught an alternative. Thus they had to make something up. Those conditions practically compel people to be bold and creative. I try to keep this lesson in mind when I so-call *train* people in alternative paradigms, that is, I try to create the conditions in which they will invent an alternative.

Creating A Research Support Group

I am arguing that we must first deal with the problem of whether the methods associated with the so-called alternative paradigm will be taught at all. Then, once someone has been hired or inspired to teach such a course, the question is this: What language will she or he speak? The language of validity, reliability, data, human subjects review, and sampling, for example, comes from the nonalternative world. What is the preferred language in alternative paradigm research? How can training in qualitative research label itself?

Thus to train someone in the paradigm in which we are interested is first of all to decide how to name what it is one is training people to do. Those who train people to be qualitative researchers are mentors of tokens. How we label our work, and what words we need to invent to describe it, would be my first steps on the journey. Another way to say this is that we begin with the understanding that the quantitative perspective is the one that most students believe to be the *normal* paradigm. It is the one students are exposed to in courses simply labeled *research methods*. Courses in the so-called alternative paradigm have specific names such as *field methods* or *qualitative methodology*, in other words, a variant of the normal, a deviation. We have to question this way of naming ourselves.

In the conventional paradigm, *to train* implies an explicit set of skills that can be transmitted. If we start from the position of being "Other" or different, we may find that we have to create a new culture in which the process of our so-called training is the product itself. The process is the product in many social settings, one of which is a research support group (Reinharz, 1984b). I think we can develop a model for training that draws on what we know about such groups.

Parts of the process include considering the space itself: What is the size of the room and the shape of the table? Can everyone see and hear each other comfortably? What is the meaning of the time we meet? How do we learn each other's names? What brings us all here? Why is it that some of us are anxious and some exhilarated? Who can speak with us about the research problems they are currently experiencing? How should we spend our time? How can we include ourselves in our work? This may be the appropriate model for adult learners.

In my own efforts to model training on the basis of a *support group*, I find that we make decisions together as we proceed. We have had sessions where everyone brings in their favorite piece of research and explains how it earned this status in their eyes. We describe the physical properties of the space in which we do our work at home or are unable to do our work at home. We bring in our favorite office supply and explain how we use it. We read each other's work constantly. Some of us work on individual projects and others work with a partner. We discuss our feelings about writing. We assume that we are building an invisible college by contacting people by phone and networking. We all assume we are going to publish what we write no matter where we are in our level of education.

We assume work is not good until it is revised. We argue with each other because we don't all share the same viewpoint. I write memos after each session sharing some material for which there was insufficient discussion time. We make decisions together. We question everything we can think of questioning. The role of the leader is assumed by the faculty member, but the role of the teacher is assumed by everyone in the group and by the group as a whole. We help each other listen to the language of our interviews. We read each other's field notes. We help each other choose what we can or must study.

No two occasions in which I have offered this course cum support group have been alike, just as the process of supervising dissertation students is never exactly the same. The students are unique, and I am changing. But the pleasure of not being defined by a paradigm in which I do not do my work is great. It is almost as pleasurable as the enjoyment I feel when reading the products of the research projects that emerge from the class.

[25]

A Response to So-Called Training in the So-Called Alternative Paradigm
Reactions to the Dark Half

JERI R. NOWAKOWSKI

Let me start out by acknowledging that Dr. Reinharz's chapter is an important perspective; and it is well argued, well described, and thoughtful in its movement at the end toward a kind of action that redeems the preceding frustration. The perspective is recognizable because we have seen it and heard it before from colleagues—some of them involved in this conference. If iteration is testimony to shared reality, certainly the academic world she describes is one that reflects the reality of a number of scholar-teachers in the so-called alternative paradigm.

Nonetheless, I'll challenge Dr. Reinharz's comments, at least to suggest that her perspective is not inevitable, further arguing that it isn't a helpful legacy. My remarks will focus on three topics: training, practice, and the metaphors and language of inquiry.

Dr. Reinharz's chapter has six parts. It begins with "context and connection," establishing the personal and social context of her remarks. This is followed by the section on "silence," and then by lengthiest section, which focuses on "dualistic metaphors." In this section, she uses metaphors of gender, marriage, race, and the military to underscore the "grim" dominance of the positivistic perspective in higher education research settings. In subsequent sections on the "so-called alternative paradigm" and "so-called training," she coins terms that are purposefully nonderivative of the quantitative perspective. She distinguishes training in the so-called alternative paradigm in several ways. She maintains that statistical research usually takes large hierarchic teams, is expensive, and, bottomline, is presently the funding choice of a number of federal agencies. On the other hand, skills prerequisite to qualitative inquiry are not highly valued. This, she maintains, affects the pool of potential instructors and students, the number of course offerings, and ultimately the tenure possibilities for professors of the alternative paradigm. Finally, in the last section of the chapter concerning the "research support group," Reinharz describes a model for training that calls upon what we know about support groups. This process of training, the one she uses, becomes an important product in its own right.

Training

Dr. Reinharz's chapter ends with a wonderful description of training, the kind she does in her classes. It describes students who are required to be metacognitive or think about how they think and learn, to work collaboratively and support each other, to question assumptions, to engage in inquiry activities that are authentic and useful, to set high expectations, to see their professor as a facilitator and guide. That's where my reactions to the so-called training chapter begin.

Shulamit Reinharz's training course, as she describes it, is good because it reflects the best of what we know about effective teaching and learning, not because it is about the alternative paradigm. And, as Shulamit may suspect, her strategies would be suited as well for training in the so-called dominant paradigm. In fact, one needs only to turn to some of the work being done in math and science education to see how effectively, say, algebra can be taught using these same methods (Schoenfeld, 1985).

Let me explain why I think this is an important point. Training in higher education in general does not enjoy a very positive reputation. Even in colleges of education where methods of teaching are part and parcel of the curriculum, there is a disheartening disparity between what research indicates is successful instruction and what goes on. So, it is important to underscore the innovativeness and effectiveness of the training strategy Dr. Reinharz uses. Then it's important to connect it with the growing body of research on teaching and learning that both articulates and advocates the kinds of strategies she is using. And, finally, it is well to point out that, although one could argue that qualitative inquiry may more readily lend itself to these strategies, statistics courses would be fair territory for their application as well.

This leads me to suggest that the training challenges described by Dr. Reinharz might well be set in a broader context. She sets the stage for this when she suggests that the instructional process she uses is part of the product—part of the curriculum itself. This is perhaps one of the most important points in her chapter. Although previous sections characterize the paradigm debates about how and when it is we come to "know," this last section describes her assumptions about training and how students come to learn. She senses there is symmetry between the two in her course.

Let us separate out for a moment the learning process. The vision of the learning process in institutions (or courses) determines the nature of curriculum, instruction, assessment, and even their organizational structure. The prevailing industrial metaphor, for example, suggests that learning is an additive process whereby students cumulate information and basic skills provided to them by instructors until they are finished with their degrees.

Research emerging from cognitive psychology, philosophy, and multicultural education provides a richer definition of learning and thinking. This definition maintains that learning fundamentally involves making sense of information at hand and that this happens best under certain conditions. (1) It happens when learners actively participate in the learning process and internalize criteria for making decisions and judgments. (2) Students are empowered because they have a repertoire of strategies for thinking and for thinking about their own learning. (3) Learning and thinking are enhanced because students are allowed to apply what they have learned in authentic tasks while working with others. (4) Learning is empowering because teachers build on the strength of what students already know—their prior knowledge. (5) Learning is enhanced because instruction accommodates cultural and gender differences. That is, students from different cultures and backgrounds may learn in different ways and may come to the learning setting with different sets of prior knowledge. These students can learn and can learn from each other (Jones & Fennimore, 1990).

Paralleling these changes in the vision of learning is a reconceptualization and renewal of the ways we think about expert teaching and professional development. Now researchers argue that expert teachers have the same characteristics as expert learners. They have a rich knowledge base not only of their content area but also of learning, teaching, and classroom strategies (Berliner, 1984; Duffy, Roehler, & Rackliffe, 1986; Leinhardt, 1986). They have powerful repertoires of cognitive and metacognitive learning strategies to help them process information, control their own learning, and design learning experiences for others (Borko & Shavelson, in press; Clark & Peterson, 1986; Shavelson, 1983; Shulman, 1987). And teacher educators are underscoring the need for teachers to work collaboratively and to plan activities for their own professional development (Schoen, 1987).

Again, I'd pause to remind you of the description of Dr. Reinharz's instructional strategy, her sense of context and prior knowledge, her emphasis on collaboration, and her descriptions of her own ongoing efforts to revitalize herself through, for example, continued study and ongoing dialog with students. Not all instruction in the alternative paradigm looks like this. In fact, some courses are structured so that students listen, basic information is provided by the teacher, work is solitary, exchange is modest, students who come to the course questioning the credibility and usefulness of this inquiry perspective are isolated, and a modest amount of time, if any, is spent engaged in an authentic qualitative inquiry activity.

I'd probably agree with those who argue that the latter description is more apt to describe course work in the "other" paradigm, though at this point I wouldn't agree that it is inevitable even in conventional statistics and research courses. I'm not sure that Dr. Reinharz is arguing so either. Hubert Dyasi makes scientific inquiry come alive for children and teachers in his New York City College Workshop Center using the learning strategies described above. Even the study of something so mundane as chewing gum becomes a starting point for inquiry that moves through chemistry, geography, sociology, and history—touring Belize and stopping at Wrigley's doorstep (Dyasi, 1989).

There are several important points to be drawn here. First, training or instruction has a considerable research base of its own. There also is renewed interest in and research on learning. Together these research bases tell us that training that respects learner background and prior knowledge and moves the learner toward becoming a more deliberate, empathic, knowledgeable and self-conscious thinker is of value. Such a vision of learning can be embedded in any content area and, in some K-12 contexts, already is. We would do well to reassess the fit between message and medium in our inquiry courses.

Second, the inquiry process, which is the backbone of individual learning, must be part of what and how we teach. When we teach inquiry, we must be aware of our assumptions about how students will learn—what inquiry process they will engage in to acquire information about a paradigm. They too should be self-conscious about how they are learning. In a sense, training in the so-called or other paradigm allows Pirandelloish plays-within-plays where students can juxtapose the inquiry procedures they use to learn with the inquiry process they are studying as a way to know about the world.

Third, current research on learning makes a point of the importance of assessing and recognizing what students bring to a learning setting. That is the base upon which they will build. Deny that base, and they begin without bedrock. Use that base, and they will begin in important ways ahead of the syllabus.

There are several important implications. The first is to realize that students come to us with a repertoire of learning strategies—strong and weak. The second is that they come to us with considerable, if not self-conscious, background in inquiry. This means that the one or two inquiry courses they take within their own department or degree programs will never constitute what they know about inquiry—scientific or personal. Third, it is important to build on what bedrock comes with a student and not begin by dispelling all they think they know.

Let me provide a personal example. I had a master's degree in English when I applied for admission into an educational leadership and policy studies program. I still remember watching my adviser shake his head through 55 hours of coursework in English. Perfunctorally checking off Melville, T. S. Eliot, History of the English Language, and Spanish and French literature courses, he commiserated with me. None of these can be used, he explained, in your new program. And they weren't.

It was up to me, years later, to forge the relationship between my two degrees. In fact, research methods and critical analysis skills learned in literature moved gracefully to evaluation research. There was a similarity in looking for evidence in descriptions of educational programs and looking for evidence in stories about whales and medieval travelers. Hermeneutics, textual analysis, precisely communicating evidence, organizing, interpreting, and representing conclusions were grounded upon language and critical analysis skills in both fields. This was not a bridge made for me by my teachers.

Those I know who trained in evaluation about the same time as I had one or two courses, if any, in qualitative inquiry. Those ten years our senior, from whom we often learned, had no such courses. Colleagues with whom I share many common practices and values in education received their training in religion, anthropology, educational psychology, psychology, sociology, and, yes, literature. Most of us who now feel comfortable in the so-called alternative paradigm didn't receive our training in it but accrued skills through experience layered on top of earlier degree programs.

We cannot afford to forget, we who teach evaluation paradigms in the social sciences, that we have across the campus a number of partners. We aren't alone in the effort to train students to have solid inquiry skills—to hone their skills in description, to interpret carefully what they see and read, to sort through and make sense. These skills are taught at multiple points in a student's career, under different course titles, and within different colleges.

Practice

Epistemological debates aside, more and more evaluators find qualitative and quantitative skills important in their armory of tools. Dr. Reinharz focuses on graduate or preservice training in the so-called alternative paradigm. My own perspective is that practicing evaluators, on the job and through continuing education, are attempting to pick up qualitative and quantitative skills they did not get in their undergraduate or graduate programs. Program auditors at GAO and in state agencies are seeking to expand evaluation research methodologies and quite commonly use qualitative methods.

There are about 800 members in the qualitative topical interest group in the American Evaluation Association. Presessions on ethnographic software are filled. Most practicing evaluators attending the conference, including program auditors, acknowledge they are using qualitative and quantitative methods.

When evaluators must be hired, and evaluation costed out, evaluators with qualitative skills are harder for our laboratory to contract. There are fewer of them, and the best are in demand. The expense, in my experience, of doing qualitative evaluation is greater than that of doing quantitative—at least on the local and state scales. Although national qualitative studies are more rare, I suspect they too are labor-intensive and expensive.

The brand of evaluation I practice, client driven and pragmatic, is not unlike that of many educational evaluators. Perhaps it straddles dualistic concepts, perhaps it has outgrown the old words that have been used to describe it, perhaps it needs, as Dr. Reinharz suggests, neologisms. It seeks to provide helpful information in the time allotted for the purposes described; it rarely promises truth, enduring or otherwise. It is, above all, a social service.

Metaphors and Language of Inquiry

The common, if not shared, language of inquiry is that of the "other." The greater space in research texts is devoted to math-based and positivistic language and methodologies. I agree with Dr. Reinharz. Also, the oldest and most conventional journals still hold pretty tenaciously to a provincial notion of research tidily separated into headings akin to those in a dissertation. Nowhere is the issue of dominance and methodological chauvinism so great as it is in the institution she describes. And to the degree that most of us who practice evaluation, and who advocate qualitative research, define our worlds by our university faculty, department, or even college, it can be a lonely vista. Simply put, the community we work in must be conceived of more broadly than that. A broadly based, albeit distant network of colleagues has many benefits—not the least of which is a richness and density of expertise that could never come from a single institution. New ways of linking, such as computer conferencing and teleconferencing, could do a great deal to sustain the dialog within this real and growing community.

Dr. Reinharz devotes a fairly substantial portion of her chapter to the language and metaphors used to characterize the alternative paradigm. I reject them all as worthy explanations of either what is or what should be. To accommodate the metaphor, for example, of gender, one has to accept the stereotype of the metaphor (i.e., female equates with soft and weak, and male with hard and strong) as well as the stereotypes of the paradigms. Ditto for metaphors of intermarriage, segregation, and battle. Both sets of stereotypes, wedded in each metaphor, poorly depict my own perspective of the status or complexity of the paradigm debate.

For me, the more damning metaphor distinguishing positivism and antipositivism or qualitative and quantitative is that of craftsman versus scientist. It's the notion that the tools used by the qualitative inquirer are comparatively primitive and crude, that somehow they are craftsmen doing lifetime apprenticeships. If good at their trade, they will become full-fledged carpenters. If statisticians get good at their trade, on the other hand, they become neurosurgeons. (Every time I think of comparing a chi-square table to an interview, this perception makes me smile.)

This brings me to my final point. Qualitative inquiry brings some critical precision tools to an important aspect of an inquiry process. One of the most important contributions offered up by qualitative inquirers for quantitative researchers is the distinction between study and report of study. As is clear in a number of research journals, quantitative researchers have not always seen or revealed the difference between their studies and reports of their studies. This oversight has led to a precision in language that belies the judgment and interpretation in the report and results in an exaggerated sense of objectivity and underestimation of the effects of rhetoric.

Criticism and objective study in the qualitative paradigm involves studying the interplay in written language between what is precise and verifiable and what is interpretative and judgmental. Qualitative researchers work hard to control this interplay in everything they write. Their study is composed of language as is their study report. They must step carefully from stone to stone allowing the reader to follow their thinking and methods and underscoring what is verifiable and what is interpretive. According to literary theorist John Ellis (1974), sound interpretations drawn of written text are like sound scientific hypotheses in that, the better they are, the more sense they make of evidence (in this case textual evidence) than rival explanations. Work by Miles and Huberman (1984), Guba and Lincoln (1981), and Schwandt and Halpern (1988) have helped provide more precise procedures and language for disentangling reports from their underlying studies. That is, the information accumulated by the researcher is distinguishable from the interpretation and resolution brought by the researcher. The shared territory of reporting may be fertile ground for mutual dialog and study among those in both paradigms.

Conclusion

Language used to depict or defend the qualitative paradigm should be selected carefully. What we say becomes reality. If we say in our training that the "ability to form relationships of trust with people, the ability to listen carefully, and good verbal and writing skills are the skills of women and others without power" it may become true. And this is a "blackness, ten times black" (Melville, 1959). It is not a language I want to pass on to students; it is not a reality I accept; it is not the legacy I choose for my nine-month-old son, who, as I write, is beguiling me from outside my glass-paned study door to offer up a hug. I wish these skills for him.

It is said that the dark side of Hawthorne came from his family's involvement in the Salem witch trials. He was a master at tales that traced such sin across generations. Ultimately in his stories, even though the crime was real, the blackness had to be abandoned or caught short before it was passed on to another generation. In other parts of our world, such as Israel, Dr. Reinharz tells us there is more methodological freedom. For students who take her classes, read her books, and walk the pathway she has broken, Dr. Reinharz creates a different worldview. I suspect the legacy she passes on through her training is quite different than the one she inherited.

[26]

Discussion on Training

JUDY BARFORD

School District #1, Charleston, Illinois

Inspired by Shulamit Reinharz's chapter, "So-Called Training in the So-Called Alternative Paradigm," and Jeri Nowakowski's response to it (this volume) participants in the discussion of the training issue immediately employed the spirit of the new paradigm. Chairs were moved to a circle arrangement. The group of fewer than 20 was small enough to permit personal introductions. Individuals represented a wide variety of professional affiliations (from publishers to early childhood people, from musicians to business managers). Many nationalities were represented including Brazilian, Canadian, Austrian, Australian, and Israeli researchers. All seemed eager for *interaction* after the three keynote addresses, the presentation of our own issue paper, and its formal response.

The discussion explored the questions: "How do you train people for inquiry?" "What is the ideal model?" Confronting students with *worldview* options and inviting a personal grappling with philosophies of science were suggested strategies. Making students aware that they do have paradigmatic choices was seen as crucial in an effective introduction to the study of inquiry. Students might choose tracks according to their own personal style or philosophical orientation or according to their preference for social interaction over number crunching. The student needs to appreciate her own intellectual bent. Though this kind of structure could reinforce dichotomies, it would have the advantage of encouraging students to consider the important assumptions that underlie various ways of collecting and analyzing data.

The general scarcity of persons to teach naturalistic inquiry was lamented as was the current expedient of recruiting (drafting!) those with little experience in alternative paradigm research to teach it. The current scarcity of qualified personnel results in vast differences in the quality and acceptability of alternative paradigm research from one faculty to another.

Participants discussed models of training that would fit specific characteristics of the alternative research paradigm. To be consistent, an alternative training model is needed for learning about the alternative inquiry paradigm. This training model would have its own language and its own culture.

Three suggestions for alternative training models emerged from the discussion. An *apprentice model* requires that the research work of students be carefully monitored by the professor. A class size allowing for optimal interaction is about 12 students. The students are apprenticed to the research task in three courses: In the first course, research literature is surveyed and reviewed. Published exemplars of research serve as models. Our discussion stressed the need to publish methodological sections in research reports. Including descriptions of the researchers in reports was also advocated. Personal descriptions would allow these individuals to become helpful models for trainees. Students also would contribute their favorite pieces of research. Just as free association can have therapeutic value, ideas of what students love can guide them. Research from many fields—psychology, anthropology, education, health, and sociology—can be compared and cross-referenced. The second course would center on data collection, and the third would emphasize data analysis. Students would seek help from each other throughout the sequence. Peer interaction would be highly encouraged. Although Shulamit's chapter suggests that these three courses could suffice, other participants thought as many as fourteen courses, six or seven in each paradigm, would be necessary to master the best of what we know. The two additional training models discussed were a *process model* based on the concept of the support group, which was cogently presented in Shulamit's chapter, and a *student-based model* in which students develop their own course work. The latter was elaborated by a participant.

Several other suggestions were offered regarding training. Because of the great problem of confidentiality in qualitative research, a plea was made for archives of research to be used for training. People who are doing qualitative research can be brought to class, thus stressing the significance of storytelling in qualitative reporting. The question of differentiating the training of practitioners who will be users only from those who will be producers of the research was raised but the idea of two tracks was opposed in the group. Because the polished researcher is one with significant experience, the group generally agreed that training programs must content themselves with the more limited goals of providing information and motivating students to actually conduct qualitative research.

The possibility of self-learning was suggested as an alternative to course work. If one needs multivariate statistics, for example, can't one learn enough from a book to meet one's needs? Several participants had, out of necessity, taught themselves qualitative methods. When training takes place as course work, the dissolution of distance and hierarchy between trainer and trainee must occur, and the freedom to disagree without stress or fear must be established.

Participants also recommended that training include the possibility of doing independent interpretations of data and being exposed to the difficulties of different kinds of data, such as speech data. The notion of social responsibility in research was stressed as a training topic. The costs of research should not be exorbitant. Training programs need to monitor questions of ethics and confidentiality carefully. Students need to be aware of the psychological impact of their work and to anticipate the cost to informants. Another possibility is *studying up*, studying persons with more power and prestige than the researchers themselves. The entire conference reinforced the importance of networking among those whose work involves training. (Several participants preferred the term *education*.)

Discussants expressed fears for the professional opportunities of those trained in alternative inquiry paradigms. Several told stories illustrating the continuing strength of logical positivism in practice. Alternative paradigm inquirers in training and those not yet tenured are often embattled individuals. Those tenured have more freedom to experiment and the opportunity to use their power to help others.

Questions remain. How shall we begin to meet the need for networking, the need for models from many fields, the need for application of the new paradigm in different cultures and different media? Participants regretted that the time allotted within the conference for the issues sessions limited the opportunity to share and discuss their own studies and their own teaching in sufficient detail. All agreed that the conference had generated considerable momentum and felt additional conferences might help sustain it.

VALUES

[27]

Reinscribing Otherwise
The Play of Values in
The Practices of the Human Sciences

PATTI A. LATHER

[Is it possible for social science] to be different, that is, to forget itself and to become something else . . . [or must it] remain as a partner in domination and hegemony? (Said, 1989, p. 225)

These are the days of disenchantment, of questions that cut to the bone about what it means to do empirical work in the human sciences. The erosion of the assumptions that support social inquiry is part of the relentless undermining of the Enlightenment code of values, which increasingly appears the key Western intellectual project of the late twentieth century. Those choosing to encourage rather than resist this movement are using it to stretch the boundaries that currently define what we do in the name of science. A behavioral science governed by adherence to methods and standards developed in the natural sciences is being displaced by what Harland (1987, p. 92) calls "a science for philosophers," which is emerging from those who work to rethink the theories and methodologies that undergird empirical aims and practices across the human sciences. Turning away from the enormous pretensions of positivism, their project is the development of a human science much more varied and reflexive about its limitations.

Science, as codified by conventional methods that marginalize value issues, is being reformulated in a way that foregrounds science as a value-constituted and constituting enterprise. Neutrality, objectivity, observable facts, transparent description, clean separation of the interpreter and the interpreted—all of these concepts basic to positivist ways of knowing are called into question. The exhaustion of positivism radically restructures the fact/value dichotomy. This chapter is both situated in that restructuring and written in the hopes of being anticipatory about the place of values in the development of a very different approach to inquiry in the human sciences.

I will proceed by first playing with the question: What is science? Here, I will argue that the objective, the apolitical, and the value neutral are cultural dominants that masquerade as natural, rational, and necessary but are less a fact of nature than of human production. They are, in spite of their denial, embedded in what Foucault (1980) terms "regimes of truth," the power/knowledge nexus that provides the constraints and possibilities of discourse. I will ground such arguments in an exploration of two key issues in what it means to reinscribe science, to do science otherwise: the issues of objectivity and relativism. Both are surveyed by probing the varied moves in feminist receptions of poststructuralism.[1] Finally, I will look at the place of values in each of the paradigms constructed by the conference on which this book is based: the postpositivist, the critical, and the constructivist. I will do this in a way that deconstructs the notion of paradigm itself.

What Is Science?

If we agree that there are no neutral observers . . . if we agree that we all take sides, the question is, then, How far do you go in taking sides? . . . the more we acknowledge our political positions, the freer we are to take a stand and become an advocate, the more we confront some very difficult ideas. (*Chronicle of Higher Education*, 1988, p. A8)

Legitimating itself in opposition to theology and aristocracy, science's claim to authority has been premised on its appeal to experience mediated by a purportedly value-neutral, logical-empirical method that promised the growth of rational control over our selves and our worlds. In this postpositivist era, it is easy to not see that what Comte termed *positivism* was part of the liberatory impetus of the Enlightenment project. This was recently underscored for me by learning that it was a British feminist, Harriet Martineau, who, in 1853, translated Comte's first lectures on the possibilities of a positive social science capable of leading the way to social betterment (Riley, 1988, p. 49).

But the intentions of science to liberate reason from the dictates of kings and priests were inscribed into practices of control and prediction. These practices were rooted in a binary logic of hermetic subjects and objects and a linear, teleological rationality; the innocence of both observable facts and transparent language was assumed. Quantum physics has problematized such concepts in the natural sciences and it, along with the human sciences, is still reeling from the aftershocks. Binary either/or positions are being replaced by a both/and logic that deconstructs the ground of both reductionist objectivism and transcendental dialectics (Derrida, 1978). Linearity and teleology are being supplanted by chaos models of nonlinearity (Gleick, 1987) and an emphasis on historical contingency (Foucault, 1980). Power is assumed to permeate all aspects of our efforts to know (Habermas, 1971), and language is theorized as constitutive rather than representational, a matrix of enabling and constraining boundaries rather than a mirror (Rorty, 1979; Tyler, 1987).

Within this context of the "postmodernism turn" (Hassan, 1987), the value-neutral claim at the heart of positivist authority is untenable. Foregrounded as an ideological ruse, the claim to value neutrality is held to delimit our concept of science and obscure and occlude its own particularity and interest. Truth, objectivity, and reason are reinscribed as what Foucault (1980) calls "effects of power," and the subject-object opposition implodes, collapses inward. Transhistorical assertions of value are seen as based not on an innocent reason or logic but on an alliance with power. Objectivity "creates its object to be objective about" (Harland, 1987, p. 104). Facts are not given but constructed by the questions we ask of events. All researchers construct their object of inquiry out of the materials their culture provides, and values play a central role in this linguistically, ideologically, and historically embedded project that we call science. By deconstructing assumptions of a knowing subject, a known object, and an unambiguous, complete knowledge outside of the unsaid and unsayable, science is, according to my present favorite definition, "a much contested cultural space, a site of the surfacing of what it has historically repressed" (Hutcheon, 1988, p. 72).

Contesting the suppression of values in the production and legitimation of knowledge has been led by the powerful and no longer ignorable conjunction of critical voices that has arisen in social theory over the last few decades. Linda Hutcheon (1988) calls these "the ex-centrics," the voices of the formerly silenced and/or marginalized, the voices of all women, men of color, the economically oppressed, postcolonials, lesbians and gays, all those who fail to fit the aggregation and generality at the heart of positivism's explanatory power. Laying the groundwork for the present focus on the politics inherent in any act of interpretation, they, in turn, have had their way prepared by the sociology of knowledge, broad intellectual traditions in social theory, and attention to the actual practices of science itself. Although the critique of scientism antedates Kuhn (1970), he was the first to show historically how infused with the social and the arbitrary were the allegedly neutral and empirical observations of science. Such work has propelled the surge away from positivism and toward an interpretive, value-searching conception of the human sciences that has been much augmented by the emergence of what Foucault (1980) terms "subjugated knowledges."

Both cause and effect of the loss of patriarchal/colonial authority, the formerly silenced have come to voice. What Nancy Hartsock (1987, p. 195) terms "the diverse and disorderly Others beginning to speak and beginning to chip away at the social and political power of the Theorizer" create a plurality of sites from which the world is spoken. Although by no means monolithic, either within or across categories of marginalization, the combined voices of the varied feminisms, postcolonialisms, and Marxisms have displaced an objective scientific reason with a consciously political and social reason. For example, feminist work in the area of methodology intensifies recent tendencies in philosophy of science (Harding, 1987, p. 184). In such discourse, issues of objectivity and relativism illustrate the recovery of the question of values within "knowledge projects called science" (Haraway, 1988).

Issues of Objectivity

While objectivity has been much critiqued and reshaped from a variety of directions within feminist discourse on science, the politics of knowing and being known have played center stage. Feminist philosophy of science has long argued that there is no innocent description and explanation, but what I find of most interest in feminist debates on objectivity is the unwillingness to give it up. This unwillingness seems rooted in what Harding (1986) identifies as the dilemma between the need for a postrepresentational science no longer dependent on the subject-object duality and transparent, inno- cent theories of language, and a "successor science" potent enough to unseat Enlightenment versions of science.

Harding's move is to argue that participatory values enhance objec- tivity. All knowledge springs from a perspective and should be legit- imated on that basis. "Objectivity" means being aware and honest about how one's own beliefs, values, and biases affect the research process: "It is politically value-laden research processes that are pro- ducing the more complete and less distorted social analysis" (Har- ding, 1987, p. 182).

Haraway (1988), however, argues against romanticizing and/or appropriating marginality as a "privileged standpoint." What the marginalized have going for them is not some *essential* goodness but their "preferred positioning" (Haraway, 1988, p. 584), positions from which they are a bit less likely to deny the workings of privilege, the shaping of hegemony, the interplay of dominance and subordination in all its many guises. Reclaiming objectivity as a necessary compo- nent in any science strong enough to unseat positivism, Haraway argues for "a feminist version of objectivity" where truth is more than rhetorical and science more than "contestable text and a power field" (p. 577). In a memorable passage, she argues,

> [There are] those of us who would still like to talk about reality with more confidence than we allow to the Christian Right when they discuss the Second Coming and their being raptured out of the final destruction of the world . . . the further I get in describing the radical social construc- tionist program and a particular version of postmodernism, coupled with the acid tools of critical discourse in the human sciences, the more nervous I get. (Haraway, 1988, p. 577)

Haraway's (1988, p. 580) urging of "a usable doctrine of objectivity" makes me nervous. How one paradoxically combines a successor science project coherent and "certain" enough to be potent in ideolog- ical struggles with "a postmodern insistence on irreducible difference and radical multiplicity of local knowledges" (p. 579) is a puzzlement. Longino (1988), for example, raises concerns that a denial of objective value necessarily commits one to the view that all judgments are "equal." In working through this puzzle of the grounds for non-foundational knowledge claims, the timeless issue of relativism becomes central.

Issues of Relativism

Relativism is reinscribed in contemporary cultural theory in ways that foreground Bernstein's (1983) question: Does the move away from foundationalist or absolutist epistemologies entail embracing "the spectre of relativism" as our inevitable companion?

Both "neoconservatives" and "progressives" reject the postmodern questioning of the "grand narratives of legitimation" (Lyotard, 1984) as a "French fad," which, by advocating the loss of foundational standards, propels us into irrationalism. While some lament the loss of "classical" standards and fear anarchy and cultural disintegration (e.g., Bloom, 1987), others see a slide into relativism that is dangerous for the dispossessed in its undercutting of the grounds for the social justice struggle and its feeding of nihilism and quietude (Dews, 1987; Hartsock, 1987; West, 1987). Feminist philosopher of science Sandra Harding (1987, p. 10) turns such fears of relativism upside down by arguing that we must "relativize relativism itself": "Historically, relativism appears as an intellectual possibility, and as a 'problem,' only for dominating groups at the point where the hegemony of their views is being challenged."

Caputo (1987, p. 262) asks, "How many of our questions arise from foundational compulsions, Cartesian anxieties?" To see relativism as a Cartesian obsession is to argue that it is an issue only within the context of foundationalist epistemologies that search for a privileged standpoint as the guarantee of certainty. Regardless of political positioning, the concept of relativism assumes a foundational structure, an Archimedean standpoint outside of flux and human interest. In Cherryholmes's (1988, p. 185) words: "If there is a foundation, there is something to be relative to; but if there is no foundation, there is no structure against which other positions can be 'objectively' judged."

If the focus is on the procedures that take us as objects and involve us in systems of categories and procedures of self-construction, relativism becomes a nonissue. If the focus is on how power relations shape knowledge production and legitimation, relativism is a concept from another discourse, a discourse of foundations that posits grounds for certainty outside of context. By positing some neutral, disinterested, stable point of reference, "relativism is the perfect mirror twin of totalization in the ideologies of objectivity; both deny the stakes in location, embodiment, and partial perspective; both make it impossible to see well" (Haraway, 1988, p. 584).

All thought is not equally arbitrary, Bakhtin (1984) argued over 50 years ago; positionality weighs heavily in what knowledge comes to count as legitimate in historically specific times and places. The world is spoken from many sites that are differentially positioned regarding access to power and resources. Relativism foregrounds the shifting sands of context but occludes the play of power in the shaping of changing structures and circumstances. As such, it is what Haraway (1988, p. 584) calls "a god trick . . . a way of being nowhere while claiming to be everywhere equally." In sum, fears of relativism and its seeming attendant nihilism or Nietzschean anger seem to me an implosion of Western, White male, class-privileged arrogance—if we cannot know everything, then we can know nothing.

Relativistic assumptions of a free play of meaning that denies power relations are of little use for those struggling to free themselves from normalizing boundaries and categories. Fraser and Nicholson (1988, p. 92) point out the practical political interests of feminism that have saved it from some of the hand-wringing of other leftists: "Women whose theorizing was to serve the struggle against sexism were not about to abandon powerful political tools merely as a result of intramural debates in professional philosophy." The point is that, although oppositional, critical work remains to be developed in the wake of postmodernism: "In periods when fields are without secure foundations, practice becomes the engine of innovation" (Marcus & Fischer, 1986, p. 166).

With practice as a privileged site for working out what it means to do emancipatory work within a postfoundational context, "The alternative to relativism is partial, locatable, critical knowledges" (Haraway, 1988, p. 584). Legitimacy is plural, local, and context specific: "Instead of hovering above, legitimacy descends to the level of practice and becomes immanent in it" (Fraser & Nicholson, 1988, p. 87). Interventions are situationally and participatorily defined. Cultural work becomes "a battle for the signified—a struggle to fix meaning temporarily on behalf of particular power relations and social interests" (Weedon, 1987, p. 98). Ellsworth (1987, p. 14), for example, asks, "How have we closed down the process of analysis and self reflection long enough to take a stand, and what or who have we had to put on hold or bracket in order to do that?"

As Fekete (1987, acknowledgments) notes, it is "strategically desirable to move people to think about the life beyond the horizons of the more nihilistic and paralyzing aspects of postmodernism." Fears of relativism are displaced by explicit interventions that collapse the boundaries between scholarship and politics. Absolute knowledge was never possible, anyway. Archimedean standpoints have always been shaped in the crucible of the power-knowledge nexus. We just thought otherwise, believing in gods and kings and, more recently, the "objectivity" of scientists.

All of this argues that something new is emerging, something embryonic, liminal, not yet in place. Derrida (1978, p. 293) calls it the "as yet unnameable which is beginning to proclaim itself." In terms of the human sciences, the shift is away from cognitive, rule-based, behaviorally focused empirical work and toward more reflexive, language-based, interpretive practices (Van Maanen, 1988, p. 76). While more emergent than codified and more experimental than standardized, such practices are much more cognizant of the inescapable incursion of politics, desires, and belief in what we do in the name of science.

The Postparadigmatic Diaspora: Recovering the Question of Values

> What is really happening, then, is itself a function of frames, which are a kind of fiction. (Hassan, 1987, p. 118)

Caputo's (1987, p. 262), term, "the post-paradigmatic diaspora," problematizes the concept of paradigmatic shifts so central to contemporary discourse in the human sciences. The central argument is that "paradigm" may be a useful transitional concept to help us move toward a more adequate human science but that "to still pose one paradigm against the other is to miss the essential character of the moment as an exhaustion with a paradigmatic style of discourse altogether" (Marcus & Fischer, 1986, p. x). Atkinson, Delamont, and Hammersley (1988) outline "the dangers of paradigms," "the dangers of Kuhnian rhetoric": the presentation of ideas as novel and distinctive that are better framed as historically rooted and relationally shaped by concepts that precede and parallel as well as interrupt them. They also note the "intolerance, fruitless polemic, and hypercriticism" that accompany paradigmatic allegiances.

"The play of ideas free of authoritative paradigms" (Marcus & Fischer, 1986, p. x) creates a moment in the human sciences that escapes, exceeds, and complicates Kuhnian structures. Although we need conceptual frames for purposes of understanding, paradigms can be dereified, de-Biblized, as my students term it, by foregrounding their presentation as but possible, even arbitrary framings of "the uneasy social sciences" (Fiske & Shweder, 1986). From this tentative position, what does each of the paradigms constructed by this conference have to say about the play of values in the practices of the human sciences?

Frame 1: The Discourse of Postpositivism

> Scientists firmly believe that as long as they are not *conscious* of any bias or political agenda, they are neutral and objective, when in fact they are only unconscious. (Namenwirth, 1986, p. 29)

The concept of Kuhnian paradigm shifts has permeated discourse across the disciplines for over two decades now. Kuhn's (1970) model of scientific change is rooted in the history of the natural sciences. In his view, the social sciences are a preparadigmatic hodgepodge of techniques largely borrowed from the natural sciences, too unformed to support productive normal sciences (Kuhn, 1970, p. 160). This aspect of Kuhn's thought has not been much noted, however, by those in the human sciences who have appropriated his language of successive paradigms, anomalies, revolutions, and competing modes of scientific activity. Within Kuhnian arguments, the central tension that causes a paradigm shift is internal to the discipline, technical breakdown brought on by the inability of the dominant paradigm to explain empirical anomalies (Gonzalvez, 1986).

Phillips (this volume) defines *postpositivism* as the more modest search for Deweyian "warranted assertability" as opposed to "truth." He distinguishes between *absolute* standards, as no longer philosophically tenable, and *no* standards, as the claim upon which "we have embarked on the rocky road to relativism." Method serves to provide some standards of logic, and evidence and objectivity serves as "a regulative ideal that underlies all inquiry," without which it makes no sense to do inquiry (Phillips, this volume). *Objectivity* is defined as that which withstands the test of critique by peers, "the social result of [scientists'] mutual criticism" (quoting Popper).

By assuming the descriptive adequacy of language as a mirror of the world, Phillips remains positioned in a representational logic. Seeking to capture the object of our investigations as it "really" is, independent of our representational apparatus, such logic denies the productivity of language in the construction of the objects of investigation. Additionally, by deemphasizing the political content of theories and methodologies, Phillips sidesteps how politics pervades science. As Cherryholmes (1988, p. 182) points out: "Policing some methodological rules to the exclusion of other sets of rules is a political as well as scientific activity." Searching for codifications and standards, "truth" is still procedural, methods still objectifying, values still to be controlled for and minimized in the effort toward precise, unbiased results.

In terms of the relationship between researcher and researched, what Dreyfus and Rabinow (1983, p. 180) term "the Great Interpreter who has privileged access to meaning" plays the role of adjudicator of what is "really" going on, while insisting that the "warranted assertabilities" uncovered lie outside the sphere of power. Willis (1980, p. 90) terms this claim of privileged externality, this assumedly politically neutral position, a "covert positivism" in its tendencies toward objectification, unitary analysis, and distanced relationships between subject and object.

Such criticism of what Van Maanen (1988, p. 54) calls the "interpretive omniscience" of the "high science stance" grows out of concern with the ways in which ideas about science serve particular political or economic interests. I turn now to the discourse of feminists and neo-Marxists, who raise the question, "In whose interest, by sex, race and class, has knowledge been generated?" (Gonzalvez, 1986, p. 16).

Frame 2: Discourse Toward a Critical Social Science

There is no social practice outside of ideology. (Hall, 1985, p. 103)

Efforts toward a critical social science raise questions about the political nature of social research, about what it means to do empirical inquiry in an unjust world. Based on Habermas's (1971) thesis in *Knowledge and Human Interests*, that claims to value-free knowledge obscure the human interests inherent in all knowledge, critical theorists are well represented by Popkewitz's (this volume) arguments that what counts as truth, adequacy, and procedure is tied to institutional history and social struggles. Scientific detachment and disinterest are historicized and contextualized and presented as political strategies that both served legitimating purposes and are undergoing radical challenges. "Values are in all layers of science," Popkewitz (this volume) writes; the focus on rules and procedures of science "dulls" us to the pervasiveness of values and creates a "methodological individualism" that is asocial, ahistorical, and mystifying in its promise of insulation from the incursion of values into our inquiry procedures.

Popkewitz's arguments mark how critical social science views methodology as inherently political, as inescapably tied to issues of power and legitimacy. Methods are assumed to be permeated with what Gouldner (1970, p. 51) terms "ideologically resonant assumptions about what the social world is, who the sociologist is, and what the nature of the relation between them is." Methods, then, are politically charged "as they define, control, evaluate, manipulate and report" (Gouldner, 1970, p. 50). Such a stance provides the grounds for an "openly ideological" approach to critical inquiry (Lather, 1986b) where the central issue is how to bring together scholarship and advocacy in order to generate new ways of knowing that interrupt power imbalances. The line between emancipatory inquiry and pedagogy blurs as critical researchers focus on developing interactive approaches to research. In addition, there is growing concern with the dangers of researchers with liberatory intentions imposing meanings on situations rather than constructing meaning through negotiation with research participants (Lather, 1986a, 1988b).

The linguistic, interpretive turn in social theory has rendered untenable Althusser's (1977) dream of a critical science outside of ideology. Although still a much debated term within Marxist discourse, *ideology* has been reconceptualized away from the concept of "false consciousness" and toward an understanding of ideology as the medium through which consciousness and meaningfulness operate in everyday life (Gramsci, 1971). As such, critical science is increasingly able to see that ideology can only be understood, not transcended (Hall, 1985). It has, however, found it more difficult to entertain the poststructuralist argument that no discourse is innocent of the Nietzschean will to power. Spivak (1987, p. 88), for example, cautions that "the desire to 'understand' and 'change' are as much symptomatic as they are revolutionary." In essence, poststructuralism argues that, whether the goal of one's work is prediction, understanding, or emancipation, all are ways of "disciplining the body, normalizing behavior, administering the life of populations" (Rajchman, 1985, p. 82). All are forms of knowledge and discourse that we have invented about ourselves; all define, categorize, and classify us. All elicit the Foucauldian question: How do practices to discover the truth about ourselves affect our lives?

Given such concerns, poststructuralism raises key issues in the movement toward a critical social science. What it means to do emancipatory work in a postfoundational context is a question receiving much attention in cultural theory these days.[2] The critical cultural practices of Marxism and feminism, critical practices that are sometimes complementary, sometimes contestatory, have intersected with the postenlightenment projects of Derrida (1978) and Foucault (1980) to aggravate the crisis of Enlightenment rationality of which they themselves are part. Unworkable constructs like "false consciousness" (Hall, 1985), the absence of what Haraway (1988, p. 586) calls "the fetishized perfect subject of oppositional history," including the essentialized Third World "woman" of much feminist discourse, inquiries into language and meaning and the consequent problematizing of the lust for totalities, universals, and certainties, the problems of vanguardism, of those who purport to speak for or on behalf of others—all illustrate how poststructural theory challenges Marxist and feminist explanatory systems.

Many Marxists and feminists fear the politics of postmodernity as undercutting the emancipatory project (Habermas, 1981). Others move to construct "a critical and adversarial postmodernism, a postmodernism of resistance" (Huyssen, 1987, p. xvi) to flesh out Deleuze's (1988, p. 30) announcement that "it is as if, finally, something new were emerging in the wake of Marx." Such an interventionary impulse propels oppositional intellectuals who, while recognizing the contingency and historicity of values, nevertheless, take a stand, act, assess, "self-consciously situating themselves at vulnerable conjunctional nodes of ongoing disciplinary discourses where each of them posits nothing less than new objects of knowledge, new praxis of . . . activity, new theoretical models that upset or at the very least radically alter the prevailing paradigmatic norms" (Said, 1986, p. 226).

In this poststructural space, the binaries that structure so much of emancipatory discourse implode from "us versus them" to a multi-centered discourse with differential access to power. The totalizing desire to establish foundations is displaced by a move toward a self-critique that traces our own collusion in the very cultural domi-nants we are opposing via the intersection of our liberatory intentions and the "will to power" that underscores interpretation. Foreground-ing the politics of knowing and being known, such a position notes how, too often in advocacy inquiry, research participants becomes objects—targets, Others to be acted upon—rather than agents who work to understand and change their own situations. From a post-structural perspective, the discourse of emancipation is as much a part of Foucault's "regimes of truth" as not.

Frame 3: Deconstructing Constructivism[3]

> Are we living in some great irruptive movement in which all will be changed? (Rajchman, 1985, p. 116)

Let me preface this section by remarking that, although it may appear that I have singled out for harsh criticism Lincoln's contribu-tion to our understanding of alternative paradigms for inquiry, I could as easily have deconstructed the words of Phillips, Popkewitz, or, best of all, myself. Believing firmly that, in a deconstructive practice that interrupts existent power arrangements, "our best examples must be ourselves" (Van Maanen, 1988, p. xv), early drafts of this chapter included a self-criticism of my own tendencies toward imposing order and structure rather than encouraging ambivalence, ambiguity, and multiplicity. Time and space decisions delayed this work,[4] and so I turned my deconstructive gaze upon Lincoln's words as constructiv-ism occupies pride of place in the lineup of paradigms that has been constructed by this conference: postpositivist, critical, and construc-tivist. That which goes last is assumed, often, to be the most complete or, at least, the latest, most-up-to-date articulation. That privileged positionality marks it as a site from which to begin to work through what it means to do empirical work in a postfoundational context that disallows claims to certainty, totality, Archimedean standpoints out-side of flux and human interest.

Lincoln chronicles her movement from an apolitical, ahistorical interpretivism to both a more "critical" position that recognizes how

politics permeates research and a somewhat "poststructuralist" position where she entertains Zeller's (1987) arguments on the illusions of
the fact/fiction duality. As such, I find the chapter illustrative of the
difficulties of fitting work into discrete "paradigms." One could probe
what Lincoln means by *constructivist*, an underexplicated term she
uses interchangeably with *naturalistic* and *ethnographic* and *phenomenological*. Her arguments for the necessity of both relativism and
paradigmatic allegiance, however, are what I find most problematic.
As my views on relativism have been dealt with in this chapter, I will
focus here on Lincoln's construction of discrete, coherent paradigmatic "views," which, coupled with a human "need" for order and
logic, "force," "demand," "dictate" that we "[choose] between one
view or the another."

I will deconstruct a paragraph of Lincoln's to illustrate how her
arguments work against themselves. (The paragraph begins: "The
thoroughly *universal* nature of any paradigm eventually forces the
choice between one view or the other.") There is much to be made of
the construction of Lincoln's arguments from a deconstructivist perspective. The deconstructive goal is to intervene in ongoing movements, to keep things in process, to disrupt, to keep the system in play,
to set up procedures to continuously demystify the realities we create,
to fight the tendency for our categories to congeal (Caputo, 1987,
p. 236). As an analytical place, deconstruction moves from the either/or
logic of ranked binaries to a both/and logic that probes the unsaid in
our saying.

With this brief overview of deconstruction in mind,[5] I will concentrate on Lincoln's primary rhetorical moves in the creation of the
binaries of universality/particularity, logic/irrationality, and coher-
ence/chaos. Each of these structuring dualities is presented as unified,
thereby hiding the multiple play of differences, "differences that
confound, disrupt, and render ambiguous the meaning of any fixed
bipolar opposition" (Scott, 1988, p. 48). I focus first on Lincoln's claims
regarding the universality and ubiquitousness of paradigms.

Universality. Claims to universality deny how our constructs are
social creations, rooted in historical and material specificity. The
concept of "paradigm" is such a construct, and it is part of a fundamental questioning of Western rationality. Lincoln makes some reference to this in her allusion to "a changing worldview in Western
society . . . that would change the face of research profoundly over the
years" but her movement in this paragraph is very much a totalizing

one: universal paradigms that permeate our lives and force choices. Totalizing moves unify with an eye to power and control as opposed to dispersing authority and "inciting multiplicity" to unseat univocal power bases. Probing the place of Lincoln's statement in the economy of power relations uncovers its homogenizing impulse versus a post-paradigmatic diaspora that views eclecticism as "a kind of anarchist or situationist strategy . . . an act of transgression" (Grossberg, 1988, p. 142).

For those engaged in experiments at the limits of their disciplines, the proper business of the methodologist is anarchistic, that of resisting the rigidity and pretension of rules, of interrupting received categories and procedures (McCloskey, 1983). From the use of interview data to construct a prose poem (Patai, 1988) to the "dada data" invoked by Clifford (1988, p. 149), new practices are emerging that reshape our sense of the possibilities for what we do in the name of the human sciences (Lather, 1989b). Lincoln's insistence on policing the boundaries of legitimate practice creates a form of disciplinary power that loses its interrogative capacities in the move toward positivity, toward an alternative canon characterized by totality, closure, and coherence rather than the ambivalence and open-endedness characteristic of nondominating, noncoercive knowledges that are located, partial, embodied (Haraway, 1988).

Rationality. Conceptions of reason and logic are not innocent. Standards of rationality have functioned historically to impose definitions of human nature from whence we deduce what we call common sense (Harding, 1982). It is in breaking out of common sense that we escape existing rationality, the exercise of power disguised as reason. To dissolve the rational/irrational binary is to break into some radical disjuncture with what is, some open space from which we can reinscribe otherwise by embracing that which has historically been labeled irrational, a different kind of reason that can only be unreasonable by the hegemonic standards of reason. "Common sense, the reasonable, that language of culture, conditions the *a priori.* . . . Reason cannot change the reasonable, for that is the role of history, of the irrational, and thus common sense—the reasonable—is the product of unreason, of the will, of passion, of ideology and power" (Tyler, 1987, pp. 168-169).

The universal and total appear so only through exclusion of that which does not fit their coherence. To think outside the structures of thought and consciousness that we have inherited, to avoid the "master's position" of formulating a totalizing discourse, seems to require more self-consciousness about the particularity and provisionality of our sense-making efforts, more awareness of the multiplicity and fluidity of the objects of our knowing. It seems to mean that we ground our action "not in terms of a stable opposition but in terms of an oscillation between several positions, in which the necessity of adopting a position in a given situation would include simultaneously calling it into question" (Rabine, 1988, p. 27). Such a way of being in the world requires a celebration of ambiguity and competing discourses, conditions that Lincoln fears invite psychological disaster.

Intrapsychic coherence. Grossberg (1988) traces the increased interest in postmodernism as being rooted in our affective sense that life can no longer be made sense of with our existent theoretical frameworks. We occupy shifting positions where the subject is constantly figured and refigured within a context of bombardment by conflicting messages, a "semiotic glut" (Collins, 1987, p. 25) spawned by the intensified sign production of consumer society. Self-identity "is constituted and reconstituted relationally, its boundaries repeatedly remapped and renegotiated" (Scott, 1987, p. 17). The subject is neither unified nor fixed. Identities are continually displaced/replaced. This focus on the fundamentally relational nature of identity results in the historically constituted and shifting self versus the static and essentialized self inherent in humanist conceptions of a unified self and an integrated consciousness. Rather than denying such a history of the present, deconstruction challenges fictions of unity and thereby helps us situate ourselves in the very different world that is already here.

One way of reading Lincoln's words is that the need for totality, rationality, and coherence inscribed in her words exemplify the dilemma of a successor science project referred to earlier as "epistemologically and politically powerful enough to unseat the Enlightenment version" (Harding, 1986, p. 150). The development of such a science is in tension with a postmodernism that struggles against claims of totality, certainty, and methodological orthodoxy. This dilemma requires a form of the "foxiness" and "versatility" recommended by Riley (1988) as a strategy that recognizes the "doubled moment" that characterizes knowledge claims in a postfoundational context. One-half of the movement is the refusal of hierarchic binaries as truth; the second half is to make this refusal in the name of differences that are more than multiple, differences that are situated, partial, embodied, that escape, exceed, complicate, and interrupt any fixed binary opposition.

Paradigms put order into an untidy universe, but to demand that all inquiry decisions be in line with the worldview embodied in a paradigm is problematic. Such a demand assumes a coherence and closure that is not existent in the emergent, open-ended processes of social inquiry in a time noteworthy for its disturbing of the formerly secure foundations of our knowledge. Lincoln's tendencies toward reification and totalization demonstrate the wisdom of Van Maanen's (1988, p. xiv) caution that "confident possession of some grail-like paradigm is at best a passing fancy or at worst a power play," but "the paradigm myth . . . dies more slowly than the post-paradigm reality."

Poststructuralism/postmodernism/deconstruction provides a transition to a readiness for a world evoked by Fekete (1987, p. x) as one where "the Good-God-Gold Standards," "the whole inherited inventory" of phantom foundations and absolutes has disintegrated. To move beyond the creation of counteridentifications entails figuring out how to position ourselves via recognition of our embeddedness in past practices and the continual shifts and realignments of the present. This is the grounds for movement into some radical reinscription of the fact/value dichotomy that marks the passage into a very different way of doing empirical work in the human sciences.

Conclusion

This chapter has interrogated the values underlying the cultural practices that we construct in the name of the human sciences. Contemporary history and philosophy of science, sociology of knowledge, and movement in science itself all have combined to impress upon us the interdependence of method, theory, and values (Mischler, 1984, p. 14). Postmodernism's delineation of the constructive and ideologically permeated dimensions of language serves as the latest in a long line of arguments that question the presentation of science as outside of politics and values, outside the shaping of the "reality" it attempts to capture. Preceded, paralleled, and interrupted by critical "ex-centric" discourses and global struggles for social justice, postmodern thought and practice open up new avenues for unmasking the politics of intellectual life.

What we are talking about here, in Lincoln's wonderful word play, "is not your father's" paradigm. It is an altogether different approach to the politics of knowing and being known. This approach, paradoxically, both calls into question "the dream of scientificity" (Barthes, quoted in Merquior, 1986, p. 148) and advocates for the creation of a "more hesitant and partial scholarship" capable of helping us "to tell a better story" (Grossberg, 1988, p. 17) in a world marked by the elusiveness with which it greets our efforts to know it.

Notes

1. For my purposes in this chapter, I use the terms *postmodern*, *poststructural*, and *deconstructive* interchangeably. For elaboration, see Lather (1989a, 1989b).

2. An example of this is the conference "The Politics of Postmodernity" (held in Quebec, May 28-30, 1989, sponsored by the Canadian Society for Hermeneutics and Postmodern Thought). See, also, *Boundary 2*, (entire issue dealing with symposium on "Engagements: Postmodernism, Marxism, Politics," in Arac, 1982-1983).

3. Thanks to my Ohio State University colleague, Bill Taylor, for helping me work through this section.

4. See Lather (in press).

5. Although impossible to freeze conceptually, deconstruction can be broken down into three steps: (a) Identify the binaries, the oppositions that structure an argument; (b) reverse/displace the dependent term from its negative position to a place that locates it as the very condition of the positive term, and (c) create a more fluid and less coercive conceptual organization of terms that transcends a binary logic by simultaneously being both and neither of the binary terms (Grosz, 1989, p. xv).

[28]

Show-and-Tell
A Response to the Value Issue in
Alternative Paradigms for Inquiry

MADELEINE GRUMET

I am uneasy with the word *value,* especially when it is used to privilege a particular perspective or position from which judgments are made. Values are always the things that older people have and younger people lack, according to older people, of course. Values operate to differentiate class as well as age. "Those people have no values" is the sentence imposed by the bourgeoisie on those richer or poorer than we are. Clutching values to our breasts to compensate us, we imagine that we have relinquished the cultural freedom of poverty and the material freedom of wealth to sustain the life we live in the middle. Values take on the righteous sentimentality of rationalization: We may not have money or fun, but we have values.

In the 1970s we worried about values clarification. Discouraged by Watergate and Vietnam, we recognized that our children were not impressed with the ways we lived and lied. When we could no longer promote the economy of our lives as good for them, we corrected ourselves by projecting our conflicts on to them. Constructing absurd moral dilemmas—There are eight of you in a lifeboat and food enough to sustain only six of you, what would you do?—we ran them through hypothetical situations, much less threatening to us than their analysis of historical situations might have been. Since the 1970s values have been the decoys we deploy to protect us from the real, from the material, bodily, actual consequences of our actions.

The word *value,* Shipley (1984, pp. 422-423) tells us, comes to English from the French word, *valoir,* to be worth. Its earlier Latin form, *valere*, meant power, strength, and health. The association with health came from the root of the Valerian plant, often used as a sedative and a carminative; its comfort lingers in our valium-tranquilized consciousness.

Whereas the root *valere* once referred to both bad and good health, its explicit association with health ultimately collapsed into infirmity (think of invalid and convalescent) while its association with good health became extended to its advantages: valor and power. Note its cognates in some other languages: Lithuanian, *veldeti*, to rule; Old Slavic, *vlasti*, to govern or command; the western dialect of Tocharian, *walo*, king; and Old English, *wield*.

This etymology of value travels a long path that first locates its power in a plant, then lodges it in the body, then displaces it onto the state, and finally misplaces it, lodging it nowhere, suspecting it everywhere. It is estimated, asserted, denied, and mourned. Enter value theory, or axiology.

Now let me remind you that the conference on which this book is based was organized to consider educational research, but this discourse, like our current discussions of values, is stranded in abstraction. Only in Popkewitz's chapter do we hear anything—any thing—that has to do with schools, with children, with curriculum, with learning, with teaching. What ever happened to show-and-tell? I want to pass around things, my pens, my frequent flier coupons. I want to empty my purse on the podium and let lipsticks, old change, keys, and stale pieces of Carefree gum and fuzzy aspirins contaminate the academic altar. I want to be obscene. What that means is that I want to show what goes on behind this scene.

* * *

It is 7:30. Actually it should be 7:30. It's really 7:45. I'm stalling as I walk toward the subway on my way up to Graduate Center. Deans of education are having a breakfast meeting to discuss whether the City University of New York should join the Holmes Group. When a woman gets out at Borough Hall, I get her seat, and then pull out the papers for this conference that I have brought to read on the train. I am halfway through Popkewitz's paper when the man standing in front of me touches my shoulder. He is a Black man, chubby, wearing a blue denim winter jacket, ski gloves, a wool hat, and glasses. He speaks very softly with carefully articulated words.

"Madam, I don't want to startle you. Don't be afraid. I am a homeless person. I am a good Christian. I am well educated. But I have had some trouble finding a job. I hope you will let me speak to you for a moment."

I feel trapped in the deliberate, precisely pronounced introduction. "Tell me what you want to say."

"I would like to ask you to give me 25 cents for a pastrami sandwich." The fellow has good taste. I remember the outrageous sandwiches at the Carnegie Delicatessen, oozing mustard and cole slaw, packed so high with pastrami you have to nibble at them from the sides because you can't open your mouth wide enough to bite them head on without losing control of your face. I wish I were going to the Carnegie Delicatessen instead of to the Holmes meeting, where Cremora and bite-sized danish with pineapple and cherry centers await me. I shove my hand into my pocket and give him one of the dollars I stuck there to buy my way through the city. "I don't have a quarter, here's a dollar."

"Thank you kind madam. You see I am a clean person." He pulls off his gloves and extends his fingers toward me. "Look at my hands, my nails." His hands are almost under my chin.

I nod, "Good luck to you," I say, trying to end the display, looking down again at my paper, retreating to Tom's words.

He moves on.

At 42nd Street I get off and walk, very briskly, through the station. There is wonderful music. Flutes and guitars. An Andean band is playing. "I'd rather be a hammer than a nail, Yes I would, If I could I surely would." The music is marvelous, light, active. I want to stand and listen. But that is dangerous. I reach in and pull out another dollar and drop it in the guitar case and move on.

The way back to Brooklyn is uneventful. That's good. I'm out of dollars. I work on the other papers. The woman across the aisle is reading *El Diario*. She keeps staring at me. I know that because I also stare at her. We take turns reading and staring. And as I read about these paradigms for research in education, I wonder why there is no world that erupts in these texts. I wonder why this world that I am living and working in is *behind* the scene and not the scene itself. Every single paper acknowledges that research is situated, shaped by the lived experience, concerns, and interests of the researchers. Yet all these papers talk about this research hardly mentioning the world that it was, is, might be about.

* * *

Let's face it friends. We do what is called applied research. For those who use knowledge to escape from the world, to separate themselves from their fathers and mothers who earned their livings with their hands and backs, what we do is not classy. The history of political theory, as both Jean Elshtain (1981) and Mary O'Brien (1981) have shown us, is strung from Plato to the present along a route that carries us away from what is tangible, what is mutable, what is domestic and familial. Those practices, knowledge, and language that are credible in the public world are those that leave bodies, babies, life, and death at home. The sense that we are, as Merleau-Ponty (1974) taught us, body-subjects, situated in our bodies in historical time and space, encourages to repudiate the Cartesian project to make thought fundamental. It is not "I think, therefore I am"; rather, it is because I am embodied and situated that I think in particular ways.

I refuse to talk about values only as forms of bias or ideology. I refuse finally to talk about value only in terms of money, even though that is what the alchemy of our culture has substituted for the touch, the texture, and feeling of concrete relations. In our work value is an index to what we care about.

In *Bitter Milk* (1988) I have tried to situate what we do as educators within the relationships that we have had with our own families and transfer to other people's children. I have argued that education is the deliberate and collective effort we make to contradict the limitations that biology and ideology have imposed on our relationships to our children.

Now I understand that it is unusual to mention reproduction, to mention children when we speak about education. For years I went to conferences on educational research when no one ever mentioned knowing a child, having a child, and certainly no one ever admitted ever having been a child. Let me make it clear as well that I do not present reproduction as a norm for human behavior but as a theme in human consciousness that makes us all responsible for the development of the next generation of human beings no matter what our own reproductive histories and projects may be.

The mention of children may seem manipulative, drenched in cuteness or sentimentality. After all, social history teaches us that childhood is a cultural artifact. Or the mention of children may seen sensational, immediately linked to headlines about hotel children,

children with AIDS, children carrying guns, selling drugs. Nevertheless, the work of all of us gathered here at this conference must ultimately refer somewhere, somehow, to children and to the spaces, company, texts, and talk that we provide to fill their days and their dreams.

The issue of value summons us to consider the concrete, visceral, motivated interest we have in what goes on in schools. Nevertheless, we cannot, sorry Husserl, (1962) climb "back to the things, themselves." What the phenomenological reductions reveal to us are never the things themselves but the things to which we are anchored by emotions of hope and dread, fascination and disgust. The objects of our consciousness are just that, the things we think about, and we cannot get to them without encountering ourselves along the way.

We tend to speak of value as a problem, an impediment to knowing, a bias to be dismissed, a history to regard with suspicion, a perspective that occludes our access to other ideas. If we successfully avoid all these traps, we succeed in doing studies that neither we nor anybody else cares about. And then Hirsch (1987) and Bloom (1987) dominate the discourse because they talk about things people do care about: What books shall we read? What language or languages shall we speak? How might we proceed?

In order for our work to have value, it must maintain and acknowledge its vital connection to the world. Phillips (this volume) allows the world to enter his description of postpositivist science in his assertion that method is not as distinct and reliable as we would think. Counterevidence keeps popping up, he reminds us. Lincoln (this volume) lets the world into the constructivist position as she argues for an epistemology that denies subject/object dualisms and seeks situation-based research contexts and hermeneutics. Popkewitz (this volume) welcomes the world to critical theory when he tells us that there is no knowledge that escapes history and interest.

Lather (this volume) extends the discussion of value to feminism's recognition of position and perspective. Feminist critiques of the disciplines began in the effort to shoo fears of relativism out of the house of knowledge. Flapping our aprons and wielding our brooms we got rid of that old ghost, who haunted our research threatening to disqualify it because our studies did not collapse the specificity of women's lives into the generalizations distilled from the lives of the men who had dominated the disciplines of knowledge and public discourse. So inviting the "ex-centrics" into the discussion, Lather celebrates many speakers, situated in many places. Nevertheless, as she lauds postmodernism, Lather herself risks diffusion into the multiple sites she cites. We must be careful not to let ourselves slip through the sieve of poststructuralism's contempt for identity. For we are responsible for what goes on in schools and we bring our names, our histories, and our promises to the report, the evaluation, the vote.

Let me suggest that feminism has had to struggle with the issues Lather raises since the early days of consciousness-raising. Even as the history and ideology of patriarchy became clear and were thematized in feminist critiques of political theory, anthropology, literature, psychology, and so on, women academics continued to tell each other the stories of our daily lives. Holding political theory in one hand and the humiliation of not fitting into last season's bathing suit in another, feminists understood that knowing and being are not identical. Feminists understood that, whether or not it was necessary, desirable, or even fair that we feel a special responsibility for the care of our children or of our aging parents, we could not, would not, repudiate those relations or the responsibility we felt to them and to each other. This doubling of knowing and being keeps us ambivalent, there's that *v* word again, and healthy and sick, and valiant.

When we turn to ambivalence, two ways, or, as Lather prefers, many ways, we work dialectically, moving back and forth from the abstract to the concrete. We work in the middle.

The autobiographical approach to research in education is such a middle way, anchored in the world. Narratives, situated in space and time, take place, say more and other than they intend. Our stories are poorly insulated structures. All kinds of creatures creep in and find refuge under the eaves, building nests in the attic and basement cupboards. Their inevitable hospitality is noted in postmodernism, as Lather has shown us. But our stories, no matter how fanciful, implicate our bodies. There we are, skipping down the pavement, cleaning off the table, and always situated, the eyes and ears for what others see and hear and say and do.

Hermeneutics enters as we and others read what we have written. A critical reading suggests another way, another logic for the tale, for the character, for the plot, for the denouement. Other logics are discovered for the psychology, the sociology, the anthropology, the philosophy, the politics that shape the narrative. After the fact, this method confirms Tom Popkewitz's claim that, although our work cannot control the future, it can help us to think about the meaning of our past. That, in effect, changes the past and then, necessarily, the future too, though not in ways we can describe or predict.

In Dorothy Smith's (1987, p. 89) book, *The Everyday World as Problematic: A Feminist Sociology* we find an analogue drawn from social science:

> Rather than explaining behavior, we begin from where people are in the world, explaining the social relations of the society of which we are part, explaining an organization that is not fully present in any one individual's everyday experience. Since the procedures, methods, and aims of present sociology give primacy to the concepts, relevances, and topics of the discourse, we cannot begin from within that frame. This would be to sustain the hegemony of the discourse over the actualities of the everyday experience of the world. It is precisely that relation that constitutes the break or fault disclosed by the women's movement.

And this is, you may recall, the dialectical movement of Freire's (1981) method of "conscientization" as well, as the encodings that subjects provide of their everyday world are read collectively to reveal limited situations and generative themes that may permit them to act deliberately and effectively in their own interest.

The tension that we need to maintain between the rich, diffuse, complex character of everyday life and the ways our literatures organize and symbolize its buzzing confusions sustains the moral tenor of our work. It is tempting to float in thick description or to concentrate on the careful turns and twists of theory. We must even be wary of the evasions of postmodern literary theory. Designed to reveal all identifications as fictions and all coherence as spurious reductions, this theory leeches intentionality from the teacher who must act now and here to bring the world to sense for these children.

> Deconstruction, a method of interpreting texts, looks for those moments in a text where, despite the writer's intent, the power of the main idea or organizing ideology, opposing ideas and themes emerge. This approach strips the author of the putative power to determine what he says. In this schema we are all Mortimer Snerds perched on the knee of a babbling culture. Society speaks through us. Texts speak through us.... [Deconstruction] divests our political, historical specificity and in so doing erases the constraints that have challenged us to take up the project of determining the character of our own humanity. If our notions of the public world and of knowing are developed in repudiation of the

private, of the domestic, then by relinquishing our anchorage in one harbor the post structuralist hopes to evade our destination in the other. And so we drift.

But human reproduction requires direction. We do not spawn and die. Being human is not something our children pick up, like a toy or an accent. Their lives take place. They and we are located. If we think of education as a linear process designed to create an ideal person we can rightly repudiate its positivism. But if we think of education as an attempt to reconceive our own development and our own relations to our parents and our children, then it is reflexive and not merely adaptive. Education is the act of making ourselves more human. Children serve as projections of our own experience, split off yet connected, our conception of them reveals what we most cherish and dread in ourselves. If deconstruction drains direction from our lives, reflection is itself spurious and we can not educate anyone. (Grumet, 1989, p. 16)

When Lather (this volume) brings a postmodern reading to Yvonna Lincoln's text (this volume), the fascination of identifying contradictions distracts her from sensing its relation to the world, its value. Given the shifting ground of Yvonna Lincoln's constructivism, based on subject-object reciprocity, situation-based research, and hermeneutics, I can understand Lincoln's impulse to hold on to a paradigm for dear life in order to anchor it and herself. Lather objects to universals on postmodern grounds. But the meaning of such a term cannot be literal. It cannot be understood outside of the text in which it speaks.

As we witness Lincoln's very own terms *universal, demand,* and *choice* doing battle in her own paragraph, I recognize the conflict between a commitment to individualism and the longing for community and coherence that the authors of *Habits of the Heart* observed when they studied our stubbornly lonely culture (Bellah, Madsen, Sullivan, Swidler, & Tipton, 1985). The split-off universals are contextualized as Lincoln attempts to portray their evolution through the conversations she has shared with students and colleagues.

As you might guess, I want to know more about the world that spawned these universals. I would want to know whether Lincoln was living in the country or the city. Whether her car was working. I would wonder how often she saw her family, and whether she visited schools now and then. Inappropriate questions? Perhaps, but I am convinced by stories that let in a little more of the world. Conviction is undermined, in my reading, not by Lincoln's assertion that a paradigm is universal so much as by the idea that it is something that can be chosen and adopted.

A paradigm can describe a set of relations in a way that any symbolic representation appears to map a complex phenomena, but it is merely the product of the reflective activity of the paradigm describer, who may try to say how it was but could never promise how it will be. To make a commitment to a paradigm would be to make a commitment to a description of the past. We live values first and describe them later. Our values, our powers, link us to what we can do and what we care about doing in the world.

What, for example, would a decision to join the Holmes Group mean, if anything, to the children of the homeless man and the woman reading *El Diario*? What does a decision to join the Holmes Group mean to the deans of education who have traveled from our respective boroughs to the Graduate Center to eat danish and talk about it?

Paradigms—traditional or alternative—are epistemological systems. As such, they offer us models for coherence that function as preferred substitutes for the complex, quotidian coherence of our everyday lives. Paradigms may satisfy our own needs for mastery and control if we think that they offer us symbolic systems to compare, design, and manipulate. The degree to which these concerns and the culture that surrounds them surround us is the degree to which they distract and separate us from the problems of people we would just as soon forget.

I think that Yvonna Lincoln merely wants her work to be meaningful when she urges us to make a commitment to one paradigm or another in order to escape "paradigmatic perjury" or "psychological disaster." But she needn't worry. There is no escaping coherence. The coherence of our lives is just that, our lives, necessarily linked to each other, through space and time, history, relation, and biography. Coherence doesn't come from a practiced and consistent dogma. It comes from the day that takes us through the 42nd Street subway station on the way to the Holmes meeting at the CUNY Graduate Center. And that information is also available, though not quite as visible, perhaps, all over this country. The coherence of our everyday world demands our recognition as we breathe bad air that has floated toward us from a smokestack in another state, as we find syringes on our beaches, holes in our ozone, bombs on our airplanes, and cyanide in our grapes. If our work will have value, it will acknowledge the coherence of our lives rather than displaying the coherence of our theories. It will reveal our primary, constant, and compulsory attachment to the world.

Merleau-Ponty (1974, p. 456) concludes the *Phenomenology of Perception* with Saint-Exupéry's celebration of value:

> Your abode is your act itself. Your act is you. . . . You give yourself in exchange. . . . Your significance shows itself, effulgent. It is your duty, your hatred, your love, your steadfastness, your ingenuity. . . . Man is but a network of relationships, and these alone matter to him.

Through theoretical work we too give ourselves in exchange. Our significance shows itself, effulgent. It carries us toward or away from the world and anyone who hears us speak or reads our words can figure out which way we are going. Our problem is how to find languages that can link our words to the world so they always refer to that place where our bodies live and die, where we walk down streets, wait on lines, wash our hands, and wish there were milk for our coffee. We must speak languages constantly elaborated with messages from the silence and from those we romantically portray as silent but who are busy sending us messages by land and air and sea.

Starting with paradigms and ending with values, this conference has started in the place where none of us lives and works and has moved from the inside out, from inside our discourse out to the issues it addresses. Like many of my colleagues here, I would like to think of myself as sort of an outsider, outside the paradigm, that is, and so, I work to position myself on the margin of this talk—just close enough to join the conversation, just far enough to stay connected to the man on the subway with clean fingernails and a yen for pastrami.

[29]

Discussion on Values

JOHN P. BECK

United Paperworkers International Union

Let me start with two caveats. Reporting on this group is a lot like Deng Xiaoping's trip to the United States, which he described as viewing flowers from horseback. These notes may obscure more than they quickly illuminate. Second, what I am going to present to you is a paraphrase of what went on including many quotes from the individuals that were a part of that group. In the interest of time, I am not going to note each quotation within my summary. There are four main areas that I would like to cover.

First, regarding the form of the conference, it is unfortunate that the conference did not mirror our desire to be different, to stop us from being subjected again as "victims of knowledge." Changes suggested included early and equal access to papers to ensure that the seminar label is more than just a label; a real commitment to a conversational mode rather than a traditional banking conference mode; and the central use of our own lives and stories and dilemmas as the basis for discussion. As one person said, the conversations are more important than the papers that preceded them. To paraphrase Lenny Bruce, sometimes, in the halls of education, the only education is in the halls.

A second issue is the question of access. We may be in danger of dressing ourselves in the clothes of the emperor we seek to overthrow more than we desire or realize. We may be creating a language that is more elite than the paradigms we seek to replace. It is not anti-intellectual to oppose the opacity of the language. As a participant put it, "I don't speak Foucault at all." "I could have been sitting in the philosophy convention," another put it. Paradigmatic boxes may not be useful ways to see ourselves if we want to take action in the world. The language that frees us also constricts us. Yet, technical language does interrupt commonsense hegemony, and, ultimately, any new language will be accepted like all the other language changes before it. Debates on theory can take us away from the lives going on as we speak. Values can be "decoys," obscuring the real things that need examination. If our research, our language, are only for ourselves, what are they worth?

Third, there was a quite lengthy discussion in the values group surrounding value positions from which researchers work and whether these constitute separate paradigms. The discussion specifically surrounded the issue of gender. The majority of those in the discussion favored the idea that it is impossible to ignore the position of the researcher in looking at the research process in which he or she is involved and that the philosophic assumptions of feminism bring great power to its stance as a separate avenue of new-paradigm, educational research.

Fourth, so what are we doing? We are in a special place in educational research. The special, practice-based life of educational research may get us out of the theoretical cul-de-sacs in which many of the other social science disciplines find themselves. No matter how theoretical our discussions, they ultimately are about real students, real teachers, real schools, and real communities. We do bear responsibility for what happens in schools. Others, who have no trouble answering the question, "Which is the correct interpretation?" will answer if we do not stand up and enter the policy and school life debates. As Madeleine Grumet said in her presentation, "If our work will have value, it will acknowledge the coherence of our lives rather than displaying the coherence of our theories." We can change what happens to our children by reflecting on our own histories and current situations, making choices, and moving on. To meet multiple audiences we must become multilinguists, using diverse languages to talk to colleagues, policymakers, children, parents, and teachers and to change the world. Rather than resolving the problem of individual versus group in both definition and action, the strain between them must be, in effect, the critical tension in our research process.

PART IV

Summation and Projection

Part IV, Summation and Projection, takes a summary look at the conference and projects some next steps that might be taken.

In chapter 30, Alan Peshkin provides a kind of ethnographic view of what the conference was about. His "Postnote: Tales from the Rear" is both informative and entertaining, providing a lighthearted but insightful view of how the conference was experienced by a variety of participants.

Chapter 31, pulled together from eight individual auditor reports by Harbans Bhola, presents next step ideas as expressed by participants in a variety of formal and informal contexts. Both Chapter 30 and Chapter 31 are important precisely because they come in the form of feedback; they are as much a surprise to the conference designers and implementers as they may be to the reader.

In Chapter 32, I identify some major themes that struck me as important, either at the time of the conference or since. I also propose some steps that may keep the momentum of the conference alive and growing. This chapter is quite open-ended, raising more questions than giving answers. Nevertheless, I am hopeful that some professional organizations, and individuals, will see fit to respond to the proposals I make.

[30]

A Postnote
Tales from the Rear

ALAN PESHKIN

A while ago, Egon Guba, Indiana University, and Phi Delta Kappa converged on the prospect of promoting a conference that happened to coincide with Guba's imminent retirement. He was not to go quietly into the soft shade of retirement. The occasion would be marked by an assemblage gathered to explode alternatives to the conventional research paradigm, as Guba often refers to the positivist outlook that had directed his own work for many years. Nowadays, alternative paradigms lie at the heart of Guba's professional life. The conference was not to be his "last hurrah"; no soft shade awaits him at its end, nor, for that matter, at the end of the academic year, which will be his last one at Indiana University. More likely, I thought, the conference would be another milestone in the coming of age of nonconventional research modes and a precursor to more and more and more of the same from a tireless Guba who feeds on intellectual discourse.

Back in March 1988, our conference's convener charged me as "postnoter" to "read and digest the three keynote and eight issue papers," to "become reacquainted with the questions and comments proposed by registrants in response to the abstracts provided to them," and to make a presentation that would become this chapter. Six months later I was encouraged to attend less to substantive and more to emotional, cultural, and social matters. In fact, neither convener nor I knew what a nonsubstantively oriented conference postnoter should say, which left me free—and anxious—to invent my own text.

Reluctant to think I could get started only when the conference registration began at 8:00 a.m., March 25, 1989, I called Egon Guba to get some sense of what his personal antecedents were for a two-day meeting devoted to "alternative paradigms of inquiry." Doing this squares with my sense of conducting qualitative inquiry: get contexts, look broadly, be holistic. Among other things, I learned that Guba had been using the term *paradigm* since the early 1980s. Given the confused conceptions of the term—Kuhn uses it in 21 different ways (see Masterman, 1970)—Guba more often refers to "basic beliefs," which he sees as "a matter of faith" and "what you have left when you can't explain any more." My first, strongest notion of what the proposed conference was to be about derives from Guba's assertion that, as far as he was aware, the only basic belief undergirding the conference is the "moral imperative" to be open to new information, to explore rather than to confirm. He was not "looking for the right version of his own view." I was pleased to learn this because he most definitely has his own view. It is addressed in the keynote paper on constructivism given by his ardent, articulate colleague, Yvonna Lincoln (see Lincoln's chapter in this volume). Though the keynoters and other speakers might possibly express their conceptions in orthodox terms, the conference's focus on three varying paradigms of inquiry ensured that orthodoxy could not prevail overall. This fact was further assured by the number and diversity of issue-paper speakers and their critics, and still further assured by the several hundred conference participants who would be present in varying degrees of irreverence.

Let me put the idea of the conference another way. Egon Guba teaches a course at Indiana University called Y611. He urges students in the course to think of themselves as forever enrolled in Y611, which is to say that they should forever be in the process of exploring, of seeking out. Several hundred conference speakers and participants will shape a conference in personal and unanticipated ways. Nonetheless, this meeting, virtually unprecedented in its length and substantive focus, had a clear thrust: not to settle matters but to further inquiry. We were, so to speak, enrolled in Y611.

Needing to moderate my anticipatory frenzy, I figured that I should begin to accumulate notes, one of several security blankets that fieldworkers hold on to. If a preconference telephone call to Guba was useful, why not a similar call to each of the keynote speakers? I called the three keynote speakers. Among the many things they said, I heard their own independent expression of Guba's moral imperative. (I confess to wondering if in the professional wardrobe of the academic there must hang the garment of self-professed searching inquiry and openness.) The keynoters expressed concern that, as they met their charge to clarify the paradigm of their personal preference, they would contribute to portraying that paradigm as more "discrete," "crystallized," and starkly different from other paradigms than they believe is really true. Their concern anticipated the work of the issue paper on "accommodation"; it suggests to me that perhaps, on another occasion, the practitioners and advocates of the different paradigms would themselves profitably address the concerns of unwarranted discreteness and premature crystallization.

Preconference telephone calls notwithstanding, an "ethnographic" rendering of a two-day meeting could not be prepared before the conference began, much as this possibility appealed to me. I had to be participant, observer, and interviewer in situ, sampling from all the domains of conference activity that were not of a plenary type. My product, as I visualized it, would be several degrees faster than Ray Rist's (1980) "blitzkrieg" ethnography. The product's instantaneous nature cast it as polaroid ethnography, my snippets of prose popping up into ready snapshots, sans time to focus, reflect, and resolve problems of parallax.

Now, of course, I must put aside my thinly disguised appeals for sympathy toward my impossible task and come directly to the conference itself. I begin with some matters of demography. The program contained the names of 48 different persons: 3 in the category of welcomer and stage setter, 3 keynoters, 40 associated in different ways with the 6 issue papers, 1 after-dinner speaker, and 1 postnoter. Of the 48, 22 are female and 26 male; they represent 27 different universities and 7 other professional-type organizations. Approximately 200 other participants attended the conference, most from the United States. Their backgrounds were more diverse than the conference planners anticipated (a fact of some importance that I will refer to later). They were, among other things, graduate students, staff trainers, new Ph.D.s, professors, editors, schoolteachers, soon-to-be retirees, and retirees. Of approximately 15 hours of scheduled meetings, 9 were in plenary sessions and 6 in concurrent sessions, the latter devoted to the issue papers. Participants were encouraged to attend two different issue-paper sessions, one on Saturday afternoon and a second on Sunday morning, when each session was repeated.

When I conduct my own research, I return home from my field of study with a mass of data. I must code before I can place similarly oriented scraps of paper into the clumps that eventually will become chapters. The result, I trust, is a well-ordered, coherent book under a title that captures the story I want my data to tell. Coherence and order of the sort I seek for other "ethnographic" products eludes me here. Thus I present a pastiche, an aggregate of impressions, my own and others, that may suggest the flavor and tone of our two days of formal and informal meetings.

Events that are subsumable by the category "conference" share common attributes and common prospects: some number of people come together for some purpose that has to do with informing and being informed. I'll leave to others what a conference might be in a platonic sense and present the medley of images that the two days conjured up for me, beginning at unplanned, informal, unscheduled levels. As I watched and listened and felt my way through the conference, I saw it as an occasion for varying types of social interaction between and among persons in the roles of friend, acquaintance, antagonist, colleague, publisher, mentor, mentee, admirer, admiree. This is to say that previously defined relationships were played out, though new roles and relationships also had occasion to emerge. When the informal social prospect joined the formal academic prospect, the conference became an occasion for a broad range of behavior. More than occasion, I thought of the conference as stage or platform on which participants acclaimed, affirmed, declaimed, postured, strutted, dismissed, retreated, wondered, wanted, and more. Clearly, mere talking and listening do not begin to capture how conference participants play and transform the shared space they create and occupy.

When considering the formal attributes of the conference, the part shaped by intention, I thought of alpine meadows, those flat areas in mountain heights that in the right season are replete with flowers. Over the years, I've watched hikers reach the point of the alpine meadow too tired to notice its wonders; I've watched hikers descend to the same point hell-bent on reaching their cars parked below—too preoccupied to notice. Which is to say that the perception of an alpine meadow's splendor depends not only on its flowers blooming but also on the readiness of hikers to perceive. During the keynote presentations, I heard some members of the audience ho hum to dismiss what they were hearing, while others were provoked to writing question after question to challenge the speakers. Which is to say again that in some sense there were about as many conferences in progress on March 25 and 26 as there were persons in attendance.

Moreover, I thought of the conference not as an event fixed in time and space but as a journey. Journeys suggest starting points, movement, and arriving somewhere that, once reached, may then lead on to other somewheres. In short, for a conference, there is a beginning, a passage, and a destination that is both shared and more or less idiosyncratic. For some, the conference may live on only in its cream-colored program, a reminder of where we once spent two days. For others, the destination may be the continuing opportunities shaped by contact with promising ideas and persons that hereafter will figure in our lives in different ways. In this instance, the conference may never truly be over. I believe this is Guba's intention.

Finally, I construed the conference as a multisensory kaleidoscope. Each twist of the "tube" offers a changing configuration of sights, sounds, smells, and touches. To be sure, the configurations, like the alpine meadow's flora, were not to everyone's satisfaction. For we come to such academic meetings with personal agendas, allegiances, prejudices, interests, and expectations that dispose us to respond in disparate ways to the occasions and platforms, the journeys and alpine meadows, that a conference affords. So thinking, the adage came to mind that the proof of the pudding is in the eating, whereupon pudding became putting, to which I attached preposition after preposition so that putting became putting in, putting up with, and so on. Accordingly, I then perceived the conference and one's satisfaction with it as related to the many forms that *putting* plus preposition can take, all of them describing one's own conduct and that of all others. For example, there is one's own and other's putting in, out, up with, over, on, by, down, aside, and away (the last three the product of audience contribution). The results of these several actions create one's sense of the conference.

More specifically, I asked participants to give me one-word descriptors of their conference experience, as, when I say "conference," what comes to mind? The results were too uniformly positive to have believably captured the range of prevailing sentiments. If those who funded "Alternative Paradigms for Inquiry" wanted to know if they got their money's worth, they would be cheered by this list:

timely	open	experimental	American
well-organized	personalized	interesting	thought-provoking
friendly	challenging	informal	intellectual
traditional	polite	energetic	exciting

But, clearly, there was more to learn and, accordingly, I asked participants to relate briefly though more generally what to them the conference was about.

The variable responses I heard suggest the impossibility of inferring in advance what a collective experience will signify to the range of persons undergoing it. Noted below is a sample of these responses. (Each is identified by quotation marks, followed immediately by my commentary.) They indicate the breadth of reactions the conference engendered, none of them meant to represent either *a* or *the* theme of the meeting. In fact, I am not able to characterize the conference in terms of themes, which designates something as general, pervasive, and the like. Some of the responses, however, may be indicative of currents, a less emphatic status than a theme.

* * *

"I am looking harder than I ordinarily do at important issues."

The concentration of programmed speakers and discussion, plus unprogrammed talk over several days, focused our attention on research paradigms well beyond the capacity of the ordinary circumstances of our lives to do so.

"I heard ideas that helped crystallize a paper I'm working on."

This possibility is available to those of us with work in progress, which work is the basis for creating a particular type of receptivity to the ideas presented. This person was present in a way that the next respondent was not.

"I've been engaged in a type of mental exercise because I don't have doctoral students."

Neither her work as teacher nor as writer inclined her to have specific interests in the conference talk. She came with a general interest in qualitative research and saw the occasion as a challenge of the sort that mental exercises offer, much as did another person who said of the conference that he feels as if he's "been at a game of intellectual pool." The next two observations capture the feelings of relatively younger participants.

"I see here people in the flesh who have just been names on pages to me."

"I'm getting reassurance that I don't know less than other people."

Small conferences are specially helpful to make people visible to each other, particularly when there may be distinctions that so-called "junior" persons assume regarding so-called "senior" persons. The benefits of junior-senior interaction are too obvious to enumerate, as is the welcome awareness of self that diminishes diffidence and thus enables one to join the scholarly discourse at hand.

The last three observations point to disparate aspects of the conference. They are not a set in any logical sense, neither do they contradict each other. Indeed, the same person could simultaneously believe that the conference promoted a camplike orientation, engaged one in matters of consequence, and provided occasion to vent unease at being a user of nonpositivist research methodologies.

"I hear military music. The sounds from the paradigm camps tell me people are hanging on to their paradigms. They see critiques as threats; they want allies. The conference design facilitated a camp orientation."

"I've been immersed in important ideas."

"I've shared stories of the frustrations of being a practitioner of nonconventional paradigms."

As the last of these three comments intimates, there is a measure of comfort in learning that there is company for one's misery. And it is no doubt true that the "misery" positivist others may inflict upon nonconventional research practitioners can range from mere annoyance to feeling like a pariah who risks not gaining tenure. The very size of the conference—its approximately 250 participants—may comfort those whose paradigm preference contributes at home to their isolation, if not their rejection. (Those who need company should be aware that only $5. stand between them and regular, annual company as a member of AERA's Qualitative Research Special Interest Group.) Even more comfort is derived from the trading of stories as well as from learning that the conference is one of a host of developments—including new professorships, courses, textbooks, research support, and journals—that testify to the national turn to alternative paradigms.

Of the remaining two statements, the one expressing the importance of the conference ideas says succinctly what any conference organizer and sponsor wishes for: that participants judge what is transpiring to be important. "Important" is sufficiently unambiguous to be construed as high praise, as in "that is an important book" or talk or paper or occasion. What is important to us counts as a central event; one, therefore, that will have continuing consequence.

No less unambiguous is the designation of something as camplike, when used in a context marked as military. The spirit of the camp is hostile to the spirit of the moral imperative of openness that Guba espouses. Believers and practitioners of anything can easily sound like advocates. Advocates, when questioned, may cross the line to where a defensive camp mentality prevails. Furthermore, when one's enthusiasm is untempered by an examination of the beliefs of one's paradigmatic detractors, the result may be a presentation that is construable as camplike. This is not to deny the accuracy of the above observer's sense that militancy was afoot among the paradigms but to suggest that the militancy may be open to some relatively innocuous explanations (in addition to some that are not innocuous at all).

* * *

I will add one more point to the above list, marking it as a definite current that emerged in both formal and informal circumstances. It has to do with empowerment, a much-used concept these days. With good reason, people resist feeling silenced and impotent. Powerlessness may arise for different reasons, many of them, again, innocuous, unintended, unavoidable. Nonetheless, the result is disagreeable.

In considerations of literature, culture, and civilization, scholars often identify a *high* and a *low tradition*. By these terms they do not necessarily imply an evaluative judgment or ranking; they are referring to distinctions that usefully differentiate. The language of high and low tradition strikes me as applicable to understanding how the matter of empowerment arose at the conference. Most of the program's papers and some portion of the ensuing discussions were couched in the terms of high tradition: Relatively speaking, their language was abstract and philosophical, their subject matter esoteric, and their speakers, as tenured, established, senior persons, were of high status. Many of the conference participants—more, I believe, than anticipated—were in the low tradition, which strikes a contrast at each point: Its language is the vernacular; its subject matter is ordinary, practical; its speakers greater in number and, by some measures, lower in rank and reputation. Extreme contrasts misrepresent: Neither papers nor people are positioned simply at a single point on a continuum. When, however, there is a perceptible distance between persons in terms of language, content, and rank, unease of varying proportions results.

* * *

Here is how the unease was expressed:

"Without the keynote speaker's papers [in hand], I'm in trouble. I have problems with the vocabulary."

The speakers prepared papers appropriate for a session with peers. We all were not peers. The papers were not available to the nonprogram participants. In fact, except for persons who read broadly in philosophy of science, one might listen knowledgeably to papers that are, so to speak, within one's own paradigm but less meaningfully to papers that are not. Moreover, contexts and terms vary across paradigms, often in formidable ways.

"I need more time to digest ideas at the level of the keynote papers. The afternoon sessions built on the morning sessions and the two were too close together for me to handle."

"If we have problems understanding the paradigms, what terrible problems the practitioners out there will have."

"The conference talk is decontextualized from research about what will make schools work better."

The first voice is that of one who is too unfamiliar with the papers' language and content to receive them at the pace with which they were delivered. The second and third voices capture related but different concerns.

In times past—albeit far from past for all researchers—the practitioners out there were a "they" routinely referred to at best in passing, the great unwashed who failed to follow the best dictates of scholarly research findings. We and they faced each other across unbridgeable chasms. Now, many nonconventional paradigm advocates insist on intimate association with the former "unwashed," their collegial presence a condition for the conduct of sound, ethical inquiry. The moderate consternation expressed above at the problem of understanding the paradigms may be exacerbated for those who are alert to the practitioner's role that some of the alternative paradigms stipulate. Irony at work! The unanticipated presence of low tradition conference participants meant that empowerment would become an issue: What one cannot have access to that is deemed worthy leaves one on the outside with feelings of disappointment, frustration, distress, or impotence.

Other participants felt competent to deal with the paradigms as presented, but their own low tradition orientation toward the world of practice left them dismayed by the dominance of high tradition discourse. They were hard put to see a relationship between work in the avenues of their concern and the abstractions of most papers and subsequent talk.

Another note was struck from the low tradition by a respondent who said, "What I do depends on the situation I'm in. So, I could be interested in one paradigm at one time, and another at another time." Her eclectic orientation leaves her unattached to any paradigm. Untroubled by epistemological and ontological niceties, she feels free to move where she sees fit, neither paradigm purity nor paradigm war darkening the landscape of her research life.

To the contrary, paradigm practitioners whose attachments locate them at some distance from, if not at odds with, those of the usual positivist majority face problems of still another type. They derive from the status differential between themselves and this positivist majority who are gatekeepers to goods the nonpositivists seek. This majority has its counterparts on the editorial staffs of scholarly journals and in the decision-making ranks of funding agencies. Obviously, the goods just referred to are tenure, publications, and fundings. They give rise to the three "will I's":

Will I get funded?
Will I get published?
Will I get promoted?

How these will-I questions get answered gives nonpositivist junior faculty members the willies. In the midst of conference deliberations framed at the level of high tradition, the willies were heard.

While some of us rejoice at the evident indicators of a new paradigmatic age a—dawning, others don't see the age coming so certainly and so soon as to relieve doubts about the security of their future. Is it too glib to reassure: that the market for qualitative researchers has never been better? That the old, established, best education journals (*Harvard Education Review, Teachers College Record, American Journal of Education, Phi Delta Kappan, Educational Researcher,* and the *American Educational Research Journal*) will publish their papers? That the best university presses will publish their books? That the private and public funding agencies will support their proposals?

Promotion is a matter I feel less inclined to be glib about. The politics of tenure and power and opportunity within a given institution can mercilessly squeeze qualitative researchers. They may more readily acquire these goods of the academic life than has ever before been true, but what is true on the average may be far from true in a particular place. Thus our conference, a historic occasion, a genuine moment for exultation, was also a time for some participants to reflect on the unpleasantly contrasting anomalies of their own professional careers.

* * *

I approach the end of my tales from the rear with some random thoughts of a substantive nature, some one-line gleanings that I heard, overheard, or perhaps even imagined.

* * *

"I believe in the dialectical relationship between theory and practice."

Is this a mom-and-pie truism that we must never publicly deny but generally leave to others to worry about? Where can we see a modeling of this dialectic? Is there such a model? Is there such a dialectic?

"There is no queen science."

This reaction, I presume, is engendered by the historic hegemony of positivism, which relegated other paradigms to untouchable status, where one is not just lowly but not even ranked. It may also be a reaction to the aforementioned camplike advocacy, whereby speakers did not so much say of their paradigm, "This is it," but—by verbal acts of omission—implied that it was. By its terseness—"There is no queen science"—we do not learn from the respondent if there can never be a queen science or if, as of now, there is none.

"Paradigms are great as long as you don't believe in them."

Do we have here the musings of profound sense, wags at work, or both? Does the speaker mean "believe" in the sense of "true believer," for whom orthodoxy stiffens and stultifies belief and believer? Is he suggesting that the consideration of paradigms is enlightening until one becomes an advocate of one of them? Are we being invited to play (in its serious sense) with ideas but not to believe in them?

* * *

Perhaps prompted by the fact that the conference coincided with the great occasion of Easter, some participants thought that what they were experiencing had a curiously familiar ring to it. In consideration of paradigms, it wasn't the camp outlook but the old-time religion that they observed at the conference, complete with holy writ, high priests, agnostics, atheists, evangelicals, and conversion experiences. It could be sobering to those of us who feel distant from the world of theological true believers to wonder if we have not borrowed more than one page from their book when we set out to write or talk about what we "believe" in the secular domains of our professional lives. Unless, of course, we have sacralized that domain too.

Here's what I make of two days immersed in alternative paradigms of inquiry. It doesn't mean much to read that nothing grows under a banyan tree, unless you can picture a tree with a canopy so dense and expansive that sunlight cannot penetrate. In the absence of sunlight, photosynthesis will not occur. Though positivism, the uninvited "host" of this conference, has never been able to smother growth in the fashion of a banyan tree, I think that it has been predisposed to do so. Accordingly, I see the conference as one of many steps taken to open up the canopy of positivism's banyan tree so that new growth can occur. Both weeds and wild flowers may spring up in new sun-fed openings. The intent of the conference surely is to nurture the flowers, but what in fact will grow in the gardens of our paradigms will long continue to be a matter of interest and concern. Needless to say, the very considerable remaining canopy of positivism leaves ample scope for more hole pokings.

Finally, what I make of this conference I draw from sociologist Robert Merton's (1957) concept of functional analysis and his reference to Hopi rain dances. On the face of it, the Hopi wanted rain to occur. Similarly, Egon Guba intended that we scrutinize alternatives to the conventional paradigm, in what might eventuate in an ongoing exploration of issues of inquiry. Unlike the Hopi rain dances, the alternative paradigms conference did lead to outcomes congruent with its convener's intentions: Paradigms were presented and explored. All this activity is in the arena of manifest function. As a latent function, the occasion of the Hopi rain dances served the cause of integrating Hopi who otherwise did not ordinarily see each other. Our conference also enhanced affiliation and solidarity. Moreover, it was an occasion for fostering our identity and promoting our legitimation as scholars who define themselves and measure their worth not just in opposition to our unseen, positivist host, but in terms and measures of our own making.

A declaration of independence is a beginning not an ending; it is a series of events, not just one day's announcement. These two days on an Easter weekend in March must be included not as the first but surely among the independence-declaring events of consequence for nonpositivist researchers.

[31]

Next Steps
The Auditors' Report

HARBANS S. BHOLA

The conference auditors had been assigned the task of reading the conference documentation, listening to the presentations made at the conference, monitoring discussions and remarks during the plenary and the special issue sessions, and attending to comments in formal and informal settings to develop a sense of the initiatives and actions that could be undertaken by the conference participants, as individuals and in groups, after the international "Alternative Paradigms Conference" had ended. Envisioning the "next steps" had been seen as a critical task of the conference. Without this collective projection into the future and without individual commitment and action on the part of the participants to actualize that future, there would be no continuity in what had been accomplished during the two days of the conference. The conference would be less than what it could have been.

The picture labeled "next steps" can be painted in three bold strokes, in terms of three overlapping agendas: (a) the intellectual agenda, (b) the agenda for advocacy, and (c) the operational agenda. Some elements of the agenda received greater attention from the conference auditors than did other elements.

AUTHOR'S NOTE: This chapter has been developed on the basis of notes and oral reports supplied by auditors H. S. Bhola, Marie Brennan, Robert B. Donmoyer, Edward S. Halpern, Les McLean, Judith A. Meloy, Rodman B. Webb, and David D. Williams.

The Intellectual Agenda

The participants were strongly of the view that the dialog started at the San Francisco conference be continued; that further conceptual and methodological clarifications be sought on all of the substantive issues identified for the San Francisco conference; and that the conference as an instrument of implementing the intellectual agenda should itself be more effectively used.

The Need for Continuing Dialog

We need to talk more among ourselves to keep the conversation going. In another two years, we need another national conference such as the one just concluded. In the meantime, we need to schedule preconference sessions to go along with some of the largely attended annual meetings of professional associations such as the American Educational Research Association and the International Reading Association. In addition, we need regional conferences for expanding the discussion among a larger number of people; and we also need local conferences so that practitioners from classroom settings can participate to learn and to contribute.

We need to talk to more people and to different people. The new partners in conversation should, of course, include methodologists of the classical positivist paradigm (and of the "reconditioned" positivist paradigm). More important, we should go beyond the "educational types." We must bring into the dialog historians, anthropologists, sociologists, and philosophers of science. We should include teachers, nurses, and artists. Names like R. J. Bernstein (1983), V. Kestenbaum (1982), A. L. Strauss (1973), and R. M. Zaner (1981) should be on the program of a future conference.

Further Discussion of Issues Already Identified

The future conference proposed by the participants, it was suggested, should discuss all the various issues formulated at the San Francisco conference: accommodation among paradigms, ethics of new inquiry, goodness criteria for research and evaluation under the alternative paradigms, implementation, knowledge accumulation, methodology, training, and values implicit in the new alternative paradigms.

Accommodation. A variety of significant questions needed serious attention. Accommodation among the various paradigms may be theoretically possible and paradigmatically desirable, but the nature of various modes of accommodation needed discussion as did the professional and personal implications of those modes of accommodation. Paradigms not discussed at this conference—the Marxist paradigm, for example—merited discussion at a future conference.

Ethics. A multiplicity of ethical concerns had been raised that must be addressed before and during a future conference. For instance, we do not seem to have many models of ethical decision making. We are neither taught nor provided opportunities to acquire experience in ethical decision making. Indeed, we are taught to avoid such decisions. The play between personal ethical decisions and the ethical imperatives embedded in institutions is seldom understood. We need to raise our collective consciousness about ethical questions and should bring a "code of ethics" for discussion at a future conference.

Goodness criteria. Questions regarding the theoretical possibility and the practical necessity of having criteria of goodness for alternative inquiry had remained unanswered. The criteria of goodness, it seemed, had to be based on the regulative ideal of objectivity, not truth, but what would be an elaboration of such criteria? These questions should be on the agenda of a future conference.

Implementation. Two aspects of the issue of implementation had been discussed at the conference: the implementation of research and evaluation studies under the new paradigm and the implementation of findings of such studies. Both required further discussion. Additional work was needed to identify how implementation was confounded by individual motivations and realities of the political culture at a particular historical time.

Knowledge accumulation. A future conference needed to pay attention to such practical questions as these: How do we inherit already existing knowledge most of which is based on positivist assumptions? Can we recontextualize what is already in the libraries and data bases? A future conference needs to continue to raise questions about the relationships between knowledge and power and knowledge and responsibility.

Methodology. It was clear that different methodologies were, in Bernstein's words (1983), different moments of theorizing about social and political life. Yet, a multiparadigm methodology needed discussion at a future conference. The interpenetration of ideology and methodology, and of the inquirer's and the practitioner's worlds, needed to be understood better.

Training. Training should be a crucial issue at a future conference. An alternative model of training seems necessary for an alternative paradigm of inquiry. The dilemmas are many: If methods and designs of alternative paradigms are not first structured and formalized, how can we teach them? On the other hand, would not such formalization do violence to the spirit and the integrity of the alternative paradigms? How can we both train and socialize for the new paradigms? How to teach an approach and not a new dogma? What is the role of self-training and support groups in training in the alternative inquiry? It is important that the history of methodologies be taught to those working with new paradigms who should also be helped to understand that people can and should make personal choices on inquiry paradigms.

Values. Finally, values needed further discussion. The dilemma was that discussing values implicit in the new paradigms was easier than internalizing those values and acting upon them. The San Francisco conference itself, the auditors felt, may not have acted on the values it espoused in the papers and in its rhetoric. A future conference should fully implement the participative values implied in the new paradigms, also inviting inquirers to enter the policy and school-life debates.

Improving the Conference Process

There were several do's and don't's suggested in regard to the holding of a future conference in implementation of the intellectual agenda. The following suggestions were made to the organizers of the next conference:

Drop the word paradigm. One suggestion was that we should drop the word *paradigm* and carry out discussions at the concrete level of the problem of making warranted assertions using appropriate methods and strategies.

Drop the word alternative. There was also the suggestion that, by dropping the word *alternative* from our discourse, we could get out of the mode of confrontation between paradigms and may at least begin to consider the possibility of reconciliation between paradigms.

Ask proponents of paradigms (i.e., the contributors of major papers) to point out implications for the eight conference issues. Ask the proponents of each of the three paradigms to indicate the implications of each paradigm for each of the eight issues discussed in the concurrent sessions of the San Francisco conference. The proponents were experts in their paradigms and could better point out or speculate about the application of paradigms in relation to issues of accommodation, knowledge accumulation, criteria of goodness, ethics and values, training, and so on than a newcomer to the discussion. What the participants were asking for was not to be spoon-fed but to be given the benefit of good thinking that could serve as springboard for further discussion and elaboration.

Do not limit access to knowledge at the conference. In a future conference the participants would like to have prior access to the papers delivered at the conference. They would like to have read the conference papers before coming to the conference. It was regrettable that the publication arrangements for the San Francisco conference had denied the participants the opportunity to obtain conference papers. The suggestion was made to build cycles of discussion and revision into the publication process, for instance, by first issuing proceedings of the conference and selling xeroxed copies to interested participants; and, as an intermediate step, publishing a special issue of a journal based on selected papers before publishing the final report in book form.

Combine theory with story. A future conference, it was suggested, should provide actual case studies, published and unpublished, using alternative paradigms. This will develop a dialectic between theory and practice. To concretize things give people questions, not paradigms.

Let participants participate; let the conferees confer. The sentiment was that there were too many keynote addresses, and because discussion time provided after each keynote was always exhausted by the speaker, it was five presentations, and more than half a day, before participants could say anything at all. The "input glut" kept the participants from participating. The conference program made conferring less possible. This should be avoided at a future conference.

Names for networks. The participants suggested that a list of names and addresses of participants be prepared immediately and distributed for different groups of people with shared interests to begin to develop networks of various kinds.

An act of self-analysis by the conference. Participants were worried about the composition of people attending the international "Alternative Paradigms Conference." They were worried that the basic humanism of the new epistemology undergirding new paradigms was not reflected in the composition of the participants of the conference. They would like to see more women and minorities selected in those attending a future conference.

The Agenda for Advocacy

The conferees were of the opinion that the intellectual agenda delineated above had to be complemented with an agenda of advocacy. Such advocacy, it was suggested, should be undertaken in regard to (a) politicians who allocate resources to research, evaluation, and development, (b) the popular press to reach stakeholders other than scholars and researchers, and (c) classroom teachers who must use the new paradigms of research and evaluation in their day-to-day work.

Suggestions were made about the general tone our advocacy should take. It should be an advocacy of reason, though it need not be devoid of passion. We do need to leave the negative posture of beating up on positivism. In the same vein we need to stop the fraternal war among the various postpositivist or alternative paradigms.

To underscore the positive in our advocacy of the alternative paradigms would mean that we share with others our successes rooted in experience.

The Operational Agenda

The intellectual agenda seeking clarification of issues and the agenda of advocacy to build convictions and solidarity cannot be implemented without activism on the part of all concerned and their ability to make demands on surrounding institutional structures. Individually, those working with alternative paradigms must incorporate the "next steps" into their daily practice; and they must band together to demand that structures of policy, research, development, and evaluation around them do not continue to be organized on the assumptions of the old positivist paradigm but become responsive to alternative paradigms.

Internalization of assumptions, implications for practice. We need to engage in self-learning and self-critiquing. We need to simplify our writing. (Some of the presentations made at the San Francisco conference were unnecessarily mystifying and some of the papers, according to the auditors, were unnecessarily dense and, therefore, less than effective in communicating.) We need to clarify our values. We need to articulate the assumptions of the alternative paradigms and work these seriously into our practice, as we teach classes, design calendars of socializations for our student-researchers and student-evaluators, and develop training curricula and student assessments. The last item, student assessment, under the alternative paradigms was considered to be a particularly promising one as assessment is a form of inquiry and can be informed by a discussion of alternative paradigms. All schools conduct assessments of all their students, and, therefore, this approach is likely to be a most influential one. Finally, it might be an interesting exercise for most of us to reread our own writing and see if our assumptions are still those we attack so glibly at the rhetorical level.

Training for socialization in alternative paradigms. Training in new paradigms is not going to be easy because we do not have the luxury of formulaic assertions and steps to teach. Most of the ideas are offered as something to "think with" rather than as something to be followed as instructions. Socialization of the inquirer using new paradigms is of particular significance. Such socialization must involve the experience of raising and dealing with ethical questions in real-life settings.

Working for institutional responsiveness. In back-home institutional settings, we should work for greater responsiveness from our own institutions. Bias against alternative paradigms, built into course and dissertation requirements, should be identified and squarely faced. Associated groups should be built at our back-home institutions for organizing groups for alternative research. Training exchanges should be established in association with other departments and other institutions.

Institutionalization of initiatives. Appropriate relationships should be built with professional associations and professional journals. As exponents of alternative paradigms to inquiry, we should make our presence felt at professional conferences. Participants should offer to serve on review boards of journals and offer to guest-edit special issues.

Linking with policymakers and funding institutions. As proponents of alternative paradigms, we need to establish linkages with policymakers and funding agencies to earn legitimization and win contracts for evaluation and research. This is something that will have to be done both individually and as organized groups.

A Point of Crystallization

Conference participants at the end of the conference dispersed across America and beyond. For the agenda of actions to be implemented, there had to be a small steering committee to serve as the point of crystallization around which initiatives by individuals, groups, and their institutions could develop and multiply. Because there was no time during the two-day conference in San Francisco to establish such a steering committee, the expectation was that the organizers of the San Francisco conference themselves would provide leadership in establishing such a steering committee using their best judgment already ably demonstrated in organizing the San Francisco conference.

Such a steering committee will act with deliberate haste to

(1) promote the establishment of professional networks on each of the eight substantive issue areas discussed at the San Francisco conference to engage in further dialog and discussion;

(2) seek interested groups and institutions willing to provide leadership in planning for a second international conference on alternative paradigms; and

(3) consider ways and means of giving the steering committee a more formal shape and a more permanent home.

The auditors group sincerely hoped that, as the more formal initiatives and structures took shape and developed, each participant, individually, would plan and act upon his or her own individual agenda and, in the process, implement the agenda of the San Francisco conference.

[32]

Carrying on the Dialog

EGON G. GUBA

In this final chapter it is my intent to do two things: identify some themes that seem to me to have emerged from the "Alternative Paradigms Conference" and outline certain next steps that might be taken to preserve and extend whatever momentum the conference may have generated. The chapter is, accordingly, divided into two sections.

Some Emergent Themes

The themes that I have chosen to discuss are *not* substantive in nature; that is, they do not address any of the conceptual issues that were the focus of the conference itself. These themes could not be so well articulated by me as they already have been by the several presenters. Further, an attempt by me to fashion from those individual presentations something that looked like summaries, "right" interpretations, or, worst of all, final and unproblematic statements, would violate the principles on which the conference was itself based.

I like to think that this book represents an opportunity for you—the reader—to engage in a major hermeneutic exercise focused on the characteristics of inquiry paradigms and on the issues raised by their juxtaposition. Every issue remains open for further discussion; there are no answers, only questions. You will recall my comments in the Foreword about the debate on whether this book should be an "authentic" or a "sanitized" version of what happened at the conference. We chose to make it authentic in the sense that it would demonstrate the ambiguity, confusion, and disagreement that plague but also stimulate and inform paradigm discussions. In this chapter as well, I mean to leave matters unsettled and, hopefully, unsettling.

Having come this far, you will have devised for yourself a tentative construction that, if you take the constructivist's moral imperative seriously, must be continuously challenged and continuously reconstructed. Your initial construction, with its many unresolved questions and conflicts (even as mine), further jostled by the themes that I shall lay out, is now open to a reconstruction that can be considerably aided by a rereading of the entire book. The resulting part/whole interchange, so typical of the hermeneutic process, will lead to a more informed and sophisticated construction, in turn facilitating a more informed rereading, and so on and on. Nothing could be more inhibiting to that process than that I should pretend to have resolved all these matters, providing the authoritative word on what *you* should have gleaned on your own. I may be more familiar with the contents of this book than you, but it would be utterly arrogant of me to suggest that I knew best about the form that your construction should take. My interest is less in pontificating about conclusions than in engaging minds, in *connecting*.

I must also emphasize that the themes I have chosen were not necessarily all in my mind at the time of the conference or even at its close. Rather, they have emerged after some nine months of reflection, of rereading and editing papers, of lengthy conversations with many of the participants, and in other ways. My personal construction changed from beginning to end of the conference, and it has changed a great deal since. Further, I reserve the right to change my construction again and again as my own level of information and sophistication grows. I invite you to assume a similar posture.

A final note: I trust that you will appreciate the fact that space constraints make it impossible for me to document the thematic assertions I am about to make. I hope that supportive examples from the preceding chapters will come to your mind, but, if not, then the themes may at least serve as guides to the hermeneutic rereading that I have urged you to undertake.

Theme 1: Greater openness to alternative paradigm critiques. I noted in Chapter 1 that positivism (which Alan Peshkin referred to as the conference's "uninvited guest") seems to be rejected by nearly everyone but that the mantle of its hegemony has fallen on the shoulders of its intellectual cousin, postpositivism. New ideas that challenge any dominant paradigm seem always to be initially rejected. Darwin despaired of converting any but young and uncommitted naturalists to his theory of evolution. Einstein found Bohr's complementarity theory too radical, for God did not play at dice. More recently, chaos theory was found to be too experimental by mathematicians and too theoretical by physicists. Fuzzy logic is antithetical to Western rationality, although not to oriental philosophy; hence the marked progress being made with its application in Japan while it is virtually overlooked in the United States. Proposed alternatives to the conventional inquiry paradigm have, until recently, been rejected with equal vigor, indeed, often with sarcasm and invective. But I sensed, among those conference participants and registrants who espoused postpositivism, a new spirit of ecumenicism and respect. The early demise of alternative paradigms so frequently predicted by defenders of conventionalism such as Miles and Huberman (1984) has, like the report of Mark Twain's death, been greatly exaggerated.

Theme 2: Decline in confrontationalism by alternative paradigm proponents. Fortunately, the ecumenical spirit is not one-sided. I sense that proponents of nonconventional views feel less embattled than heretofore. The use of military metaphors (attack, defend, camp, struggle, fight, resist, engage, and on and on) is on the decline. It is obvious that these proponents feel at least minimally legitimated and enfranchised. While there are many political skirmishes yet to be fought (see Theme 8 below), universal suffrage is in effect and free speech is not only tolerated but encouraged. Proponents once treated as eccentrics are now recognized as promulgating possibly useful points of view. As Lather (Chapter 27) notes, some critics of conventionalism feel that the time may be right to move beyond the paradigm debate, arguing that, although the concept of *paradigm* may have been transitionally useful, continuing polemic and hypercriticism are counterproductive.

Theme 3: Fruitful dialog is now a possibility. A consequence of Themes 1 and 2 is that it is now possible to open a dialog directed toward a reconstruction of existing paradigms, bringing them into a more ecumenical, if not consensual, posture. Of course, there are forces pushing toward this end other than the desire for conceptual reconciliation. As Gage (1989) points out in his witty analysis of "the great paradigm wars," without an appropriate exchange among various paradigm adherents, "invective and vituperation" will continue to the detriment of all. But ecumenical interchange need not be understood as accommodation; indeed, it is quite probable that the paradigms *cannot* be accommodated because they are basically incommensurable. That is, there probably does not exist some fundamental, rational framework to which all paradigms can be reduced so that conflicts and inconsistencies can be resolved. It is certain that accommodation will not be reached because one paradigm will be found to subsume all others as special cases, because the superior rationality of one will ultimately be acknowledged, or because empirical data will finally support one to a greater extent than the others. What *is* likely, however, is that dialog may lead to the development of an as yet unimaginable paradigm (dare I say, metaparadigm?) that will render the existence of the present competitors irrelevant. This new paradigm will not be any more "true" or "foundational" than those it replaces; it will simply be more informed and sophisticated (at least in my constructivist view). The gain in both information and sophistication is likely to come from an honest and open interchange among proponents, in which the positions of each are respected, examined, and weighed by the others.

It seems to me likely that we are now in a position to begin such a productive dialog. Just a few years ago, Smith and Heshusius (1986) expressed concern over the "closing down of the conversation." That judgment turns out to have been premature. There can be no guarantee, of course, that consensus will *ever* occur; honest persons working from positions of integrity may nevertheless continue to disagree (the incommensurability problem again). Perhaps it may even be most useful if disagreements *continue* to occur, to maintain the problematic character of the paradigm discussion. However those issues may be resolved, it does seem clear to me that the time to begin these discussions is *now*. The most useful aftermath of the "Alternative Paradigms Conference" may be the stimulation and staging of such a dialog.

Theme 4: Confusion remains rampant. Even among those who are most intimately involved with the paradigm dialog, such as the conference participants and even the presenters, there remains a great deal of confusion about just what the paradigm dialog should, or does, encompass. I noted in Chapter 1 that some of this confusion is occasioned by the fact that postpositivists have identified paradigm problems with *imbalances,* believing that redressing these imbalances will correct noted deficiencies. Thus the call for conducting inquiry in *natural* settings, using more *qualitative* methods, *grounding* theory in the inquiry itself rather than specifying it a priori, and recognizing the proper place of *discovery* processes has led many to the conclusion that these steps solve paradigm-level problems, whereas I believe they simply address methodological-level differences. Further, the widespread appropriation of older terms such as *field research, ethnography, case studies,* and the like *as descriptors for the alternative paradigm(s)* confuses the issue by implying that there is nothing new about the "new" paradigms after all. I have also noted the fact that many believe the several proposed alternative paradigms to be fundamentally commensurable (and, therefore, accommodatable), when that issue remains very much in doubt.

But even among those most au courant with the alternative paradigms, and the characteristics that distinguish them, there is a great deal of difference in the way terms are defined and issues are formulated. While united in what they oppose, proponents of the various paradigms differ greatly in what they support. Startling evidence for the existence of such differences can be seen in the list of references appended to this volume. I originally thought that, by combining references from the individual papers, I would save a great deal of space; I was sure that the individual writers would tend to cite the same sources. But I was astonished to discover how little overlap there was, a fact that the reader can verify by simply comparing citations over two or three chapters. Such diversity is probably to the good; keeping everything as problematic as possible just now is vital to the emerging dialog. But it does seem reasonable that, as a first step, participants in the dialog should aim to eliminate as many confusing distractors as possible in order to close quickly and efficiently onto the main issues.

Theme 5: Everything connects. The confusion noted under Theme 4 is exacerbated by the fact that everything connects to everything else. Critic/respondents repeatedly found it difficult to focus *solely* on the papers read by the issue presenters, and the discussion in the eight issue sessions inevitably wandered from the focus of the nominal issue to include others, some of which were not contemplated in the conference format at all. In an insightful introduction to the recorder reports, which, for editorial reasons, could unfortunately not be included in this volume, Tom Gregory, chair of the recorder group, spoke eloquently of the many "wanderings and meanderings" that took place, calling to his mind an apparent "yearning for order" that is probably impossible to satisfy when the phenomena are essentially chaotically structured. Of course, it has become apparent in recent years that chaotic structure itself reflects a kind of order but not one that can be reflected in flowcharts or linear representations. Sorting out these many interrelationships is inordinately difficult, even for the expert.

But the fact of such universal connection should not be taken as an evil; on the contrary, it illustrates that paradigm issues and characteristics cannot be considered independently from others. A holistic approach is essential. Positivism's claim that the universe can be abstracted into variables that can be meaningfully manipulated at the behest of the investigator is rejected by all the emergent paradigms; if that is so, interconnectedness is not only ineluctable but becomes part of the fabric that must be taken into account in building understandings.

Theme 6: Caveat—interpretations are paradigm constrained. A further source of confusion is found in the fact that the interpretations that individuals make of paradigm characteristics and issues are themselves grounded in and constrained by the paradigm to which those individuals are implicitly or explicitly committed. This phenomenon is manifested in a variety of ways. For example, insistence that accommodation among paradigms can be accomplished assumes that they are basically commensurable, a tenet characteristic only of rationalistic paradigms. Goodness criteria such as validity and reliability that assume a real, stable world may not be germane in paradigms that make no such assumptions. The celebration of subjectivity, and the concomitant attack on paradigms that prize objectivity, is meaningful only within a paradigm that assumes a monist epistemology. The claim of value freedom can be meaningful only in light of an assumption that there exists an impermeable barrier between observational and theoretical languages. What I mean to warn against here is the tendency displayed by adherents of *all* paradigms to set challenges for other paradigms in terms that cannot be meaningful to them. It is as though Lutherans posed challenges for Catholics by asking questions that reflected only Lutheran presuppositions. There can be debate, of course, about which set of presuppositions *ought* to be adopted, but, given a paradigm perspective based on a particular set, it is inappropriate to challenge it except on the grounds of internal inconsistency or conflict. It's one thing if Catholics are not consistent with their *own* professed principles, but quite another if they are not consistent with *Lutheran* principles. In any paradigm dialog, care needs to be taken to separate out questions of the appropriateness of particular assumptions from questions about whether paradigm practices are internally consistent.

Theme 7: Contemplating, and possibly adopting, a new paradigmatic posture, is an odyssey. It is almost certainly the case that those of us who practice social/behavioral inquiry in the twentieth century were initially socialized into the positivist paradigm. Even the move into a postpositivist posture implies severe conceptual and value dislocations; other paradigms require even more traumatic shifts. Yvonna Lincoln's remembrance of things past as she traces her own making as a constructivist is the clearest example, but so is Jennifer Greene's discussion of her "stances." Shulamit Reinharz's chapter on training reflects some of the elements that go into the resocialization of students as they learn about alternatives. I could recount my own odyssey over 38 years as an academic, from the time I completed my doctorate in statistics and measurement until today when I stand a committed constructivist. The movement from one paradigm commitment to another cannot be accomplished overnight; there are no counterparts to St. Paul's sudden conversion on the road to Damascus. If the dialog I have urged is to lead anywhere, time and effort will be required, at least as much as one might be willing to invest with a psychotherapist.

Theme 8: Power and politics will play an important role as the paradigm dialog unfolds. When I used the term *hegemony* earlier, in suggesting that power has passed from positivists to postpositivists, I meant to state forcefully that there is a great deal more at stake in the paradigm dialog than simply a debate over a few conceptual issues. *Hegemony* implies *at least* control over appointment, promotion, tenure, publication, legitimation, status, training, accountability, funding, research agendas, and myriad other factors that determine the quality of our professional lives. It is the rare person who, possessing power, is willing to give it up for the greater good. Yet that is exactly what we must expect, indeed, insist on—from our colleagues who presently do enjoy hegemony. I like to think that they will concede out of enlightened self-interest, for, if they do not, Gage's "invective and vituperation" will engulf us all. Society in general is unimpressed with the contributions of social/behavioral inquiry; a pox will soon be called down on all our houses if there is continuing conflict rather than cooperation among the paradigm adherents. It is to everyone's benefit to cooperate.

Theme 9: The conference was useful even if not all of its goals were met. My intent here is not to evaluate goal achievement (and, for that matter, what conference has *ever* achieved all its goals?) but to make the point that participants found the conference useful. It enabled participants to see one another face to face, perhaps for the first time. There were many opportunities in formal sessions and in informal gatherings to exchange opinions, raise questions, and engage in self-affirmation. Feelings of solidarity were formed and firmed. Participants felt both personally and professionally stimulated. Perhaps most important, "closet" alternativists were enabled to emerge into the light of day, recognizing that they had like-minded colleagues (as well as different-minded ones), and feeling more legitimated than they ever had before. The call from the auditors (Chapter 31) for additional conferences—reinforced by on-site comments and later communications from a variety of participants—confirms my judgment that this conference was a success despite a variety of particular shortcomings.

Theme 10: This conference was not successful in reflecting the participatory philosophy espoused by alternative paradigms; subsequent conferences and activities must be certain to remedy that defect. The essential problem was expressed in many ways that reflect an intuited polarization: high versus low tradition, theoreticians versus practitioners, sophisticates versus unsophisticates, priesthood versus laypersons, and, in a follow-up letter I received, *blancos* versus *rojas*. Some persons saw the failure to connect with various subgroups in the audience as a power issue: Controlling language is, after all, one way of exercising power. Some saw it as a form of elitism, with the audience as "victims." Some saw it as a form of distrust, reflecting an implicit judgment that many in the audience did not possess the technical background needed to cope with the issues raised. Almost all agreed that, although differences in information and sophistication needed to be taken into account, the audience should have been given greater opportunity to participate. The very format of the conference reflected traditional values rather than emergent ones, they said. The conference should have modeled the dialectic, the dialog, that seemed to be called for so centrally. We should have lived up to our own assumptions.

They were right. It was a difficult lesson to learn, but a necessary and valuable one.

Next Steps

It is my impression, and that of many of the participants, that a considerable momentum was built up at the conference in support of continuing the dialog that was so auspiciously begun in San

Francisco. Indeed, the auditors' report, as summarized by that group's chair, Harbans Bhola, proposes three "agendas" that might be undertaken. The *intellectual* agenda, most notably in evidence at the conference itself, deals with the problems and issues that confront the inquiry community at this historical point. The recorders proposed that a similar national conference be held every second year (presumably the next in 1991); that there be frequent regional conferences (with perhaps the "qualitative" conference held in January for each of the past several years at the University of Georgia as a prototype); that "local" conferences be held as it may be useful to do so, with universities, school systems, health care systems, juvenile justice systems, and the like, taking the leadership in organizing them; and that persons interested in alternatives should make "their presence felt" at national meetings of professional societies.

The *advocacy* agenda includes systematic contacts with political figures, the media (including, of course, journals and other elements of the professional press), and with practitioners such as teachers, health workers, social workers, government functionaries, and the like. This agenda was least in evidence in San Francisco and is no doubt the least well developed currently.

The *operational* agenda included an exhortation to ourselves to engage in self-learning and self-criticism; to decide on a paradigm, and, if that decision comes down on the side of an alternative, to work at resocializing ourselves and those trainees already in the pipeline or who will soon be entering it; to work for "institutional responsiveness," by which I assume the group meant an institutional willingness to entertain and support those who lean toward an alternative paradigm; to build relationships with professional associations and professional journals; and to build linkages with policymakers and funders.

It is quite apparent that very few of these clearly laudable aims can be accomplished without organization. The auditors recognized this fact of life and called for a "point of crystallization" at which these efforts could be focused and from which subsequent activity might spring. They had two suggestions for such a point of crystallization. The first was that a "steering committee," presumably temporary, be established that would take the responsibility for such immediate tasks as organizing the proposed 1991 conference; establishing contacts with professional organizations, journals, public media, and other means for establishing a "presence"; and seeking funding that would help underwrite the 1991 conference as well as the planning activities of the steering committee itself. The second suggestion was that a "permanent home" be established that would accept long-range responsibility for the three agendas (and any others that might emerge) as well as take over from the temporary steering committee at an appropriate time.

My own predisposition would be to follow up on the steering committee suggestion but leave the matter of a permanent home in abeyance. Setting up a permanent home in the *near* future would, it seems to me, ignore the central message of Theme 10 above calling for greater attention to implementing the *participatory* philosophy that alternative paradigms putatively espouse. Such a move is both premature and politically inopportune.

Given that some sort of steering committee is formed, I nevertheless believe that one of the major planning issues confronting it is precisely what form a permanent home should take and in what context it would most usefully exist. My own inclination would be to think in terms of some kind of consortium or partnership arrangement, whose membership would be formed from among the variety of organizations that have some stake in the paradigm debate. These stakeholders are those most placed at risk by any hasty or ill-considered resolution(s) and who must, therefore, be given a "seat at the table." And because these stakeholders represent a wide variety of existing institutional contexts, it would be inappropriate to house the mechanism in any of those already existing agencies. It is my hope that the steering committee might devise and implement a funding plan that would make it possible to establish this mechanism in some independent setting.

So far as the temporary steering committee itself is concerned, my own preference would be to form a committee, council, or task force whose members would be nominated by a variety of professional organizations that are concerned with paradigm issues. Preeminent among these organizations are the professional societies, but others that represent special interests might also be considered. I have in mind, as a prototype, the recently functioning Joint Committee on Standards for Educational Evaluation (1981), comprising representatives from a number of professional associations representing persons often involved in *doing* educational evaluations (American Psychological Association, American Educational Research Association, and National Council on Measurement in Education), and a number of others representing persons or types of agencies that are often *targets* of evaluations (American Personnel and Guidance Association, American Association of School Administrators, Education Commission of the States, Association for Supervision and Curriculum Development, Council for American Private Education, National Association of Elementary School Principals, National Education Association, National School Boards Association, and the American Federation of Teachers). The joint committee was formed originally on the initiative of the first three societies, acting on a recommendation from an earlier committee that had been set up to establish testing standards. When the representatives of those groups met for the first time, they were (quite properly) sensitive to the fact that target groups were *not* represented and proceeded to invite those others named above (as well as some additional ones that declined to participate). In the end a committee was formed that was both intellectually and politically competent to carry out its task. I might note that, despite the extremely volatile subject matter involved, every one of the committee's finally recommended standards had the *unanimous* consent of all parties. Participatory involvement is not only feasible but works!

I believe it would be possible to duplicate the work of such a joint committee if several of the more centrally involved professional associations would take the initiative to form a nuclear group and to provide support for a few organizational meetings. It would make very little difference what the forming societies were, provided that the nuclear group received a clear mandate to incorporate other stakeholder groups as well. I foresee that in a relatively short period a strong working committee could be formed that would carry out the functions the conference auditors projected as well as any others that might occur to them to undertake. Given the entrée that such a committee would have with its parent professional societies, I believe that many of the political problems would be de facto solved. Further, the cachet such a group would have would make the solicitation of funding from a variety of public and private sources a relatively simple task.

It may or may not be the case that professional societies will wish to undertake such an initiative without some committed agent volunteering to play a leadership role. I invite any of the conference participants, or anyone else interested in the paradigm dialog, to step forward. The rewards will be plentiful and the opportunity for lasting professional impact unsurpassed.

References

Agee, J., & Evans, W. (1941). *Let us now praise famous men.* New York: Houghton Mifflin.

Agger, R., Goldrich, D., & Swanson, B. (1964). *The rulers and the ruled.* New York: John Wiley.

Althusser, L. (1977). *For Marx* (B. Brewster, Trans.). Thetford, Norfolk: New Left. (Original work published 1965)

American Educational Research Journal. (1987). 24(2).

Antonio, R. (1989). The normative foundations of emancipatory theory: Evolutionary versus pragmatic perspectives. *American Journal of Sociology, 94,* 721-748.

Apple, M. (1979). *Ideology and curriculum.* London: Routledge & Kegan Paul.

Apple, M. (1982). *Education and power.* London: Routledge & Kegan Paul.

Arac, J. (1982-1983). Introduction to engagements: Postmodernism, Marxism, politics [special issue]. *Boundary, 2,* 1-4.

Arnheim, R. (1985). The double-edged mind: Intuition and intellect. In E. Eisner (Ed.), *Learning and teaching the ways of knowing* (pp. 77-96). Chicago: University of Chicago Press.

Ary, D., Jacobs, L., & Razavieh, A. (1985). *Introduction to educational research.* New York: Holt, Rinehart & Winston.

Atkin, M. (1973). Practice oriented inquiry: A third approach to research in education. *Educational Researcher, 2,* 3-4.

Atkin, M. (1989). *Curriculum action research: An American perspective.* Paper presented at the meeting of the American Educational Research Association, San Francisco.

Atkinson, P., Delamont, S., & Hammersley, M. (1988). Qualitative research traditions: A British response to Jacob. *Review of Educational Research, 58,* 231-250.

Babbie, E. (1983). *The practice of social research* (3rd ed.). Belmont, CA: Wadsworth.

Bahm, A. (1971). Science is not value-free. *Policy Sciences, 2,* 391-396.

Bakhtin, M. (1984). *Problems of Dostoevsky's poetics* (C. Emerson, Ed. and Trans.). Minneapolis: University of Minnesota Press.

Bargar, R., & Duncan, J. (1982). Cultivating creative endeavor in doctoral research. *Journal of Higher Education, 53,* 1-31.

Barker, R., & Wright, H. (1951). *One boy's day.* New York: Harper.

Barnes, B. (1982). *T. S. Kuhn and social science.* New York: Columbia University Press.

Barnes, J. (1984). Ethical and political compromises in social research. *The Wisconsin Sociologist, 21,* 100-111.

Bauman, Z. (1978). *Hermeneutics and social science.* London: Century Hutchinson.

Baumrind, D. (1979). IRBs and social science research: The costs of deception. *IRB, A Review of Human Subjects Research, 1,* 1-4.

Baumrind, D. (1985). Research using intentional deception: Ethical issues revisited. *American Psychologist, 40,* 165-174.

Bazerman, C. (1987). Codifying the scientific style. In J. Nelson et al. (Eds.), *The rhetoric of the human sciences* (pp. 125-144). Madison: University of Wisconsin Press.

Beardsley, P. (1980). *Redefining rigor: Ideology and statistics in political inquiry: Vol. 104. Sage library of social research.* Beverly Hills, CA: Sage.

Becker, H. (1970). *Sociological work: Method and substance*. Chicago: Aldine. (Reissued by Transaction Books, New Brunswick, NJ, 1977).

Becker, H. (1977). On methodology. In H. Becker (Ed.), *Sociological work: Method and substance* (rev. ed.; pp. 3-24). New Brunswick, NJ: Transaction.

Becker, H., Geer, B., Hughes, E., & Strauss, A. (1961). *Boys in white: Student culture in medical school*. Chicago: University of Chicago Press.

Beechey, V., & Donald, J. (1985). *Subjectivity and social relations*. Philadelphia: Opa University Press, Milton Keyes.

Bellah, R., Madsen, R., Sullivan, W., Swidler, A., & Tipton, S. (1985). *Habits of the heart*. New York: Harper & Row.

Benhabib, S., & Cornell, D. (Eds.). (1987). *Feminism and critique*. Minneapolis: University of Minnesota Press.

Berger, P., & Luckmann, T. (1973). *The social construction of reality*. London: Penguin.

Berger, T. (1977). Max Weber, interpretive sociology, and the sense of historical science: A positivistic conception of verstehen. *Sociological Quarterly, 18*, 165-177.

Berliner, D. (1984). The half-full glass: A review of research in teaching. In P. Hosford (Ed.), *Using what we know about teaching* (pp. 51-77). Alexandria, VA: Association for Supervision and Curriculum Development.

Bernstein, B. (1971). On the classification and framing of educational knowledge. In M. Young (Ed.), *Knowledge and control* (pp. 47-69). London: Collier-Macmillan.

Bernstein, R. (1976). *The restructuring of social and political theory*. Philadelphia: University of Pennsylvania Press.

Bernstein, R. (1983). *Beyond objectivism and relativism: Science, hermeneutics, and praxis*. Philadelphia: University of Pennsylvania Press.

Betti, E. (1980). Hermeneutics as the general methodology of the *Geisteswissenschaften*. In J. Bleicher (Ed.), *Contemporary hermeneutics* (pp. 51-94). London: Routledge & Kegan Paul.

Birnbaum, N. (1988). *The radical renewal*. New York: Pantheon.

Black, M. (1952). *Critical thinking: An introduction to logic and scientific method* (2nd ed.). Englewood Cliffs, NJ: Prentice-Hall.

Blake, R., Ducasse, C., & Madden, E. (1960). *Theories of scientific method: The renaissance through the nineteenth century*. Seattle: University of Washington Press.

Blakemore, S. (1988). *Burke and the fall of language: The French revolution as linguistic event*. Hanover, NH: University Press of New England.

Blau, P. (1964). *Exchange and power in social life*. New York: John Wiley.

Blau, P. (1977). *Inequality and heterogeneity: A primitive theory of social structure*. New York: Free Press.

Bleicher, J. (1980). Contemporary hermeneutics. London: Routledge & Kegan Paul.

Bleier, R. (Ed.). (1986). *Feminist approaches to science*. Oxford: Pergamon.

Bloland, H. (1989). Higher education and high anxiety: Objectivism, relativism, and irony. *Journal of Higher Education, 60*, 519-543.

Bloom, A. (1987). *The closing of the American mind*. New York: Simon & Schuster.

Bloor, M. (1983). Notes on member validation. In R. Emerson (Ed.), *Contemporary field research* (pp. 156-172). Prospect Heights, IL: Waveland.

Bogdan, R., & Biklen, S. (1982). *Qualitative research for education: An introduction to theory and methods*. Boston: Allyn & Bacon.

Boli, J. (1989). *New citizens for a new society: The institutional origins of mass schooling in Sweden*. New York: Pergamon.

Borko, H., & Shavelson, R. (in press). Teacher decision making. In B. Jones & L. Idol (Eds.), *Dimensions of thinking and cognitive instruction.* Hillsdale, NJ: Lawrence Erlbaum.

Boruch, R. (1986). *What we have learned about randomized social experiments over the last decades.* Paper presented at the meeting of the American Evaluation Association, Kansas City, MO.

Bourdieu, P. (1977). *Outline of a theory of practice.* Cambridge, MA: Cambridge University Press.

Bowles, G., & Klein, R. (Eds.). (1983). *Theories of women's studies.* London: Routledge & Kegan Paul.

Brecht, A. (1959). *Political theory.* Princeton, NJ: Princeton University Press.

Bredo, E., & Feinberg, W. (1982a). The critical approach to social and educational research. In E. Bredo & W. Feinberg (Eds.), *Knowledge and values in social and educational research* (pp. 115-128). Philadelphia: Temple University Press.

Bredo, E., & Feinberg, W. (1982b). Conclusion: Action, interaction, and reflection. In E. Bredo & W. Feinberg (Eds.), *Knowledge and values in social and educational research* (pp. 423-442). Philadelphia: Temple University Press.

Bredo, E., & Feinberg, W. (1982c). *Knowledge and values in social and educational research.* Philadelphia: Temple University Press.

Brody, H. (1981). *Ethical dimensions in medicine* (2nd ed.). Boston: Little, Brown.

Bronowski, J. (1975). *Science and human values.* New York: Harper & Row. (Original work published 1956).

Brown, H. (1977). *Perception, theory, and commitment.* Chicago: University of Chicago Press.

Buchler, J. (Ed.). (1940). *The philosophy of Peirce: Selected essays.* London: Routledge & Kegan Paul.

Burrell, G., & Morgan, G. (1979). *Sociological paradigms and organizational analysis.* London: Heinemann.

Bussis, A., Chittenden, E., & Amarel, M. (1976). *Beyond surface curriculum.* Boulder, CO: Westview.

Cahnman, W. (1965). *A sociology of history.* New York: Free Press.

Callahan, R. (1962). *Education and the cult of efficiency.* Chicago: University of Chicago Press.

Campbell, D. (1984). *Can an open society be an experimenting society?* Paper presented at the International Symposium on the Philosophy of Karl Popper, Madrid, Spain.

Campbell, D. (1986). Relabeling internal and external validity for applied social scientists. In W. Trochim (Ed.), *Advances in quasi-experimental design and analysis* (New Directions for Program Evaluation, No. 31, pp. 67-77). San Francisco: Jossey-Bass.

Campbell, D. (1988). A tribal model of the social system vehicle carrying scientific knowledge. In E. Overman (Ed.), *Methodology and epistemology for social science: Selected papers, Donald T. Campbell* (pp. 489-503). Chicago: University of Chicago Press.

Campbell, D., & Fiske, D. (1959). Convergent and discriminant validation by the multitrait-multimethod matrix. *Psychological Bulletin, 56,* 81-105.

Caputo, J. (1987). *Radical hermeneutics: Repetition, deconstruction, and the hermeneutic project.* Bloomington: Indiana University Press.

Carnap, R. (1956). The methodological character of theoretical concepts. In H. Feigl & M. Scriven (Eds.), *Minnesota studies in the philosophy of science, I* (pp. 38-76). Minneapolis: University of Minnesota Press.

Carroll, L. (1915). *Alice's adventures in wonderland*. London: Macmillan.

Cassell, J., & Wax, M. (1980). Editorial introduction: Toward a moral science of human beings. *Social Problems, 27*, 259-264.

Charmaz, K. (1983). The grounded theory method: An explication and interpretation. In R. Emerson (Ed.), *Contemporary field research* (pp. 109-126). Prospect Heights, IL: Waveland.

Cherryholmes, C. (1988). *Power and criticism: Poststructural investigations in education*. New York: Teachers College Press.

Chisholm, R. (1973). *The problem of the criterion*. Milwaukee, WI: Marquette University Press.

Chisholm, R. (1977). *Theory of knowledge*. Englewood Cliffs, NJ: Prentice-Hall.

Chronicle of Higher Education. (1988, November 30). [Conference of the American Anthropological Association].

Clark, C., & Peterson, P. (1986). Teachers' thought processes. In M. Wittrock (Ed.), *Handbook of research on teaching* (pp. 235-296). New York: Macmillan.

Clark, T. (1973). *Prophets and patrons: The French university and the emergence of social science*. Cambridge, MA: Harvard University Press.

Clifford, J. (1988). *The predicament of culture: Twentieth century ethnography, literature, and art*. Cambridge, MA: Harvard University Press.

Cohen, E. (1988). Qualitative sociology in Israel. In S. Reinharz & P. Conrad (Eds.), Qualitative sociology in international perspective [Special issue]. *Qualitative Sociology, 11*, 88-98.

Cole, M. (1985). Mind as a cultural achievement: Implications for I.Q. testing. In E. Eisner (Ed.), *Learning and teaching the ways of knowing* (pp. 218-249). Chicago: University of Chicago Press.

Coleman, J. (1989). Response to SOE section award. *ASA Footnotes, 17*, 4-5.

Coleman, J., Kelly, S., & Moore, J. (1975). *Trends in school segregation*. Washington, DC: Urban Institute.

Collins, J. (1987). Postmodernism and cultural practice: Refining the parameters. *Screen, 28*, 11-26.

Collins, R. (1984). Statistics versus words. In R. Collins (Ed.), *Sociological theory 1984* (pp. 329-362). San Francisco: Jossey-Bass.

Comstock, D. E. (1982). A method for critical research. In E. Bredo & W. Feinberg (Eds.), *Knowledge and values in social and educational research* (pp. 370-390). Philadelphia: Temple University Press.

Cook, T. (1983). Quasi-experimentation: Its ontology, epistemology, and methodology. In G. Morgan (Ed.), *Beyond method: Strategies for social research* (pp. 74-94). Beverly Hills, CA: Sage.

Cook, T. (1985). Postpositivist critical multiplism. In R. Shotland & M. Mark (Eds.), *Social science and social policy* (pp. 21-62). Beverly Hills, CA: Sage.

Cook, T., & Campbell, D. (1979). *Quasi-experimentation: Design and analysis issues for field settings*. Chicago: Rand McNally.

Crandall, D., & Associates (1983). *People, policies, and practices: Examining the chain of school improvement* (Vols. 1-10). Andover, MA: The NETWORK, Inc.

Crane, D. (1976). *Invisible colleges: Diffusion of knowledge in scientific communities*. Chicago: University of Chicago Press.

Cronbach, L. (1957). The two disciplines of scientific psychology. *American Psychologist, 12*, 671-684.

Cronbach, L. (1975). Beyond the two disciplines of scientific psychology. *American Psychologist, 30*, 116-127.

Cronbach, L. (1982). *Designing evaluations of educational and social programs*. San Francisco: Jossey-Bass.

Cronbach, L., & Suppes, P. (1969). *Research for tomorrow's schools: Disciplined inquiry in education*. New York: Macmillan.

Crutchfield, J., Farmer, J., Packard, N., & Shaw, R. (1986). Chaos. *Scientific American, 225*, 46-57.

Dahl, R. (1961). *Who governs democracy and power in an American city?* New Haven, CT: Yale University Press.

Dallmayr, F. (1981). *Beyond dogma and despair*. Notre Dame, IN: University of Notre Dame Press.

Dallmayr, F. (1985). Pragmatism and hermeneutics. *The Review of Politics, 47*, 411-430.

Daly, M. (1978). *Gyn/ecology: The metaethics of radical feminism*. Boston: Beacon.

Danziger, K. (1987). Psychology in twentieth-century thought and society. In M. Ach & W. Woodward (Eds.), *Contemporary history of psychology* (pp. 13-33). New York: Cambridge University Press.

de Beauvoir, S. (1952). *The second sex* (H. Parshley, Ed. and Trans.). New York: Knopf.

Deleuze, G. (1988). *Foucault*. Minneapolis: University of Minnesota Press.

Denzin, N. (1978). *The research act: An introduction to sociological methods*. New York: McGraw-Hill.

Derrida, J. (1978). Structure, sign, and play in the discourse of the human sciences. In *Writing and difference* (A. Bass, Trans.; pp. 278-293). Chicago: University of Chicago Press.

Derrida, J. (1982). *Margins of philosophy* (A. Bass, Trans.). Chicago: University of Chicago Press.

Dewey, J. (1934). *Art as experience*. New York: Minton, Balch.

Dewey, J. (1966). *Logic: The theory of inquiry*. New York: Holt, Rinehart & Winston.

Dewey, J. (1984). The quest for certainty. In J. Boydston (Ed.), *John Dewey: The later works, 1925-1953* (Vol. 4; pp. 3-250). Carbondale: Southern Illinois University Press. (Original work published 1929)

Dews, P. (1987). *The logic of disintegration: Poststructuralist thought and claims of critical theory*. London: Verso.

Diesing, P. (1971). *Patterns of discovery in the social sciences*. Chicago: Aldine.

Douglas, J. (1976). *Investigative social research*. Beverly Hills, CA: Sage.

Dreyfus, H., & Rabinow, P. (1983). *Michel Foucault: Beyond structuralism and hermeneutics* (2nd ed.). Chicago: University of Chicago Press.

Duffy, G., Roehler, L., & Rackliffe, G. (1986). The relationship between explicit verbal explanations during reading skills instruction and student awareness and achievement: A study of reading teacher effects. *Reading Research Quarterly, 21*, 237-252.

Durkheim, É. (1951). *Suicide*. New York: Free Press.

Durkheim, É. (1977). *The evolution of educational thought: Lectures on the formation and development of secondary education in France* (P. Collins, Trans.). London: Routledge & Kegan Paul. (Original work published 1938)

Dyasi, H. (1989). *Report of the science inquiry program (Saturday Academy) for District Five at City College*. New York: City College of the University of New York, City College Workshop Center.

Eash, M. (1985). A reformation of the role of the evaluator. *Educational Evaluation and Policy Analysis, 7*, 249-253.

Easlea, B. (1986). The masculine image of science: How much does gender really matter? In J. Harding (Ed.), *Perspectives on gender and science* (pp. 123-158). London: Falmer.

Easton, D. (1957). *Political systems: An inquiry into the state of political science.* New York: Knopf.

Eckberg, D., & Hill, L., Jr. (1979). The paradigm concept in sociology. *American Sociological Review, 44*, 925-936.

Eckert, J. (1987). Ethnographic research on aging. In S. Reinharz & G. Rowles (Eds.), *Qualitative gerontology* (pp. 241-255). New York: Springer.

Eisenhart, M. (1988). The ethnographic research tradition and mathematics education research. *Journal for Research in Mathematics Education, 19*, 99-114.

Eisner, E. (1982). *Cognition and curriculum: A basis for deciding what to teach.* New York: Longman.

Eisner, E. (1983). The art and craft of teaching. *Educational Leadership, 40*, 4-13.

Eisner, E. (1985). *The educational imagination: On the design and evaluation of educational programs* (2nd ed.). New York: Macmillan.

Eisner, E. (1986). *Action research in classrooms and schools.* London: Allen & Unwin.

Eisner, E. (1988). The primacy of experience and the politics of method. *Educational Researcher, 17*, 15-20.

Eliade, M. (1959). *The sacred and the profane.* New York: Harcourt, Brace, & World.

Elliott, J. (1986). *What is action research?* Paper presented at the CARN Conference, Cambridge, England.

Ellis, J. (1974). *The theory of literary criticism: A logical analysis.* Berkeley: University of California Press.

Ellsworth, E. (1987). *The place of video in social change: At the edge of making sense.* Unpublished manuscript.

Elshtain, J. (1981). *Public man, private woman.* Princeton, NJ: Princeton University Press.

Elzinga, A. (1985). Research, bureaucracy, and the drift of epistemic criteria. In B. Wittrock & A. Elzinga (Eds.), *The university system: The public policies of the Home of Scientists* (pp. 191-220). Stockholm: Almquist & Wiksell International.

Emerson, R. (Ed.). (1983). *Contemporary field research.* Prospect Heights, IL: Waveland.

Emrick, J., Peterson, S., & Agarwala-Rogers, R. (1977). *Evaluation of the National Diffusion Network* (2 vols.). Menlo Park, CA: Stanford Research Institute.

Epstein, T. (1989). *An aesthetic approach to the study of teaching and learning in the social studies.* Unpublished doctoral dissertation, Harvard University, Cambridge, MA.

Erickson, F., & Schultz, J. (1981). When is a context? Some issues and methods in the analysis of social competence. In J. Green & C. Wallat (Eds.), *Ethnography and language in educational settings* (pp. 147-160). Norwood, NJ: Ablex.

Fay, B. (1975). *Social theory and political practice.* London: Allen & Unwin.

Fay, B. (1987). *Critical social science.* Ithaca, NY: Cornell University Press.

Fekete, J. (Ed.). (1987). *Life after postmodernism: Essays on value and culture.* New York: St. Martin's.

Festinger, L., Riecken, H., & Schachter, S. (1964). *When prophecy fails.* New York: Torchbooks. (Original work published by University of Minnesota Press, 1956).

Feyerabend, P. (1968). How to be a good empiricist. In P. Nidditch (Ed.), *The philosophy of science* (pp. 12-39). Oxford: Oxford University Press.

Feyerabend, P. (1970). Against method. In M. Radner & S. Winokur (Eds.), *Minnesota studies in the philosophy of science, IV* (pp. 17-130). Minneapolis: University of Minnesota Press.

Feyerabend, P. (1975). *Against method: Outline of an anarchistic theory of knowledge.* London: NLB.

Feyerabend, P. (1981). *Problems of empiricism.* Cambridge: Cambridge University Press.

Fine, A. (1987). And not anti-realism either. In J. Kourany (Ed.), *Scientific knowledge* (pp. 359-368). Belmont, CA: Wadsworth.

Firestone, W. (1976). Ideology and conflict in parent-run free schools. *Sociology of Education, 49,* 169-175.

Firestone, W. (1980). *Great expectations for small schools: The limitations of federal projects.* New York: Praeger.

Firestone, W. (1987). Meaning in method: The rhetoric of quantitative and qualitative research. *Educational Researcher, 16,* 16-21.

Firestone, W., & Rosenblum, S. (1988). Building commitment in urban high schools. *Educational Evaluation and Policy Analysis, 10,* 285-300.

Firestone, W., & Wilson, B. (1983). Assistance and enforcement as strategies for knowledge transfer and program reform. *Knowledge: Creation, Diffusion, Utilization, 4,* 429-452.

Fischer, F. (1985). Critical evaluation of public policy: A methodological case study. In J. Forester (Ed.), *Critical theory and public life* (pp. 231-257). Cambridge: MIT Press.

Fiske, D., & Shweder, R. (Eds.). (1986). *Metatheory in social science: Pluralisms and subjectivities.* Chicago: University of Chicago Press.

Foucault, M. (1978). Politics and the study of discourse. *Ideology and the Study of Discourse, 3,* 7-26.

Foucault, M. (1980). *Power/knowledge: Selected interviews and other writings* (C. Gordon, Ed., and C. Gordon et al., Trans.). New York: Pantheon.

Fraser, N., & Nicholson, L. (1988). Social criticism without philosophy: An encounter between feminism and postmodernism. In A. Ross (Ed.), *Universal abandon: The politics of postmodernism* (pp. 83-104). Minneapolis: University of Minnesota Press.

Freeman, D. (1983). *Margaret Mead and Samoa: The making and unmaking of an anthropological myth.* Canberra: Australian National University Press.

Freire, P. (1981). *Pedagogy of the oppressed* (M. Ramos, Trans.). New York: Continuum.

Friedrichs, R. (1970). *Sociology of sociology.* New York: Free Press.

Furner, M. (1975). *Advocacy and objectivity: A crisis in the professionalization of American social science, 1865-1905.* Lexington: University of Kentucky Press.

Gadamer, H. (1975). *Truth and method* (G. Barden and J. Cumming, Trans.). New York: Seabury.

Gadamer, H. (1986). On the scope and function of hermeneutical reflection. In B. Wachterhauser (Ed.), *Hermeneutics and modern philosophy* (pp. 277-299). Albany: State University of New York Press.

Gage, N. (1989). The paradigm wars and their aftermath: A "historical" sketch of research on teaching since 1989. *Educational Researcher, 18,* 4-10.

Gardner, H. (1983). *Frames of mind.* New York: Basic Books.

Geertz, C. (1973). *The interpretation of cultures.* New York: Basic Books.

Geertz, C. (1980). Blurred genes: The refiguration of social thought. *American Scholar, 49,* 165-179.

Geertz, C. (1983). *Local knowledge*. New York: Basic Books.

Geertz, C. (1988). *Works and lives: The anthropologist as author*. Stanford, CA: Stanford University Press.

Gergen, K. (1973). Social psychology as history. *Journal of Personality and Social Psychology, 26,* 309-320.

Gergen, K. (1982). *Toward transformation in social knowledge*. New York: Springer-Verlag.

Gerth, H., & Mills, C. (1946). *From Max Weber*. New York: Oxford University Press.

Giarelli, J. (1988). Qualitative inquiry in philosophy and education: Notes on the pragmatic tradition. In R. Sherman & R. Webb (Eds.), *Qualitative research in education* (pp. 22-27). London: Falmer.

Giddens, A. (1976). *New rules of sociological method*. New York: Basic Books.

Giddens, A. (1987). *Social theory and modern sociology*. Stanford, CA: Stanford University Press.

Ginsburg, M. (1988). Educators as workers and political actors in Britain and North America. *British Journal of Sociology of Education, 9,* 359-367.

Giorgi, A. (1970). *Psychology as a human science: A phenomenologically based approach*. New York: Harper & Row.

Giroux, H. (1983). *Theory and resistance in education*. Boston: Bergin & Garvey.

Giroux, H. (1988). Critical theory and the politics of culture and voice: Rethinking the discourse of educational research. In R. Sherman & R. Webb (Eds.), *Qualitative research in education* (pp. 190-210). London: Falmer.

Giroux, H., & McLaren, P. (1986). Teacher education and the politics of engagement: The case for democratic schooling. *Harvard Educational Review, 56,* 213-238.

Glaser, B., & Strauss, A. (1967). *The discovery of grounded theory*. Chicago: Aldine.

Gleick, J. (1987). *Chaos*. New York: Viking.

Goetz, J., & LeCompte, M. (1984). *Ethnography and qualitative design in educational research*. New York: Academic Press.

Gonzalvez, L. (1986). *The new feminist scholarship: Epistemological issues for teacher education*. Unpublished manuscript.

Goodman, N. (1973). *Fact, fiction, and forecast*. Indianapolis, IN: Bobbs-Merrill.

Goodman, N. (1978). *Ways of worldmaking*. Indianapolis, IN: Hackett.

Gouldner, A. (1970). *The coming crisis in Western sociology*. New York: Basic Books.

Gouldner, A. (1979). *The future of the intellectual and the rise of the new class*. New York: Seabury.

Gramsci, A. (1971). *Selections from the prison notebooks of Antonio Gramsci* (Q. Hoare and G. Smith, Eds. and Trans.). New York: International.

Green, J. (1990). *Multiple perspectives: Issues and directions*. Paper presented at the Conference on Multidisciplinary Perspectives on Literacy Research, National Conference on Research in English, Chicago.

Green, J., & Collins, E. (in press). Challenges to qualitative research: An overview. In M. Brown (Ed.), *Qualitative research in education: Proceedings of the Third Qualitative Interest Group Conference*. Athens: University of Georgia.

Green, J., & Harker, J. (Eds.). (1988). *Multiple perspective analysis of classroom discourse*. Norwood, NJ: Ablex.

Greenfield, T. (1985). [Editorial]. *Curriculum Inquiry, 15,* 1-6.

Griffiths, M., & Whitford, M. (Eds.). (1988). *Feminist perspectives in philosophy*. Bloomington: Indiana University Press.

Grossberg, L. (1988). Rockin' with Reagan, or the mainstreaming of postmodernity. *Cultural Critique, 10,* 123-149.

Grosz, E. (1989). *Sexual subversions: Three French feminists.* Sydney, Australia: Allen & Unwin.

Grumet, M. (1988). *Bitter Milk: Women and teaching.* Amherst: University of Massachusetts Press.

Grumet, M. (1989). Knots: Feminist theorizing in the middle. *Resources for Feminist Research, 18,* 13-18.

Guba, E. (1981). Criteria for assessing the trustworthiness of naturalistic inquiries. *Educational Communication and Technology Journal, 29,* 75-92.

Guba, E. (1987). What have we learned about naturalistic evaluation? *Evaluation Practice, 8,* 23-43.

Guba, E. (1988). *Sorting out alternative paradigms for inquiry: Parameters and issues.* Unpublished proposal for the International Conference on Alternative Paradigms for Inquiry, San Francisco.

Guba, E. (1990). *Relativism.* Paper presented at the meeting of the American Educational Research Association, Boston.

Guba, E. (in press). Subjectivity and objectivity. In E. Eisner & A. Peshkin (Eds.), *Qualitative inquiry in education.* New York: Teachers College Press.

Guba, E., & Lincoln, Y. (1981). *Effective evaluation.* San Francisco: Jossey-Bass.

Guba, E., & Lincoln, Y. (1987). The countenances of fourth generation evaluation: Description, judgment, and negotiation. In D. Palumbo (Ed.), *The politics of program evaluation* (pp. 202-234). Newbury Park, CA: Sage.

Guba, E., & Lincoln, Y. (1988a). Do inquiry paradigms imply inquiry methodologies? In D. Fetterman (Ed.), *Qualitative approaches to evaluation in education* (pp. 89-115). New York: Praeger.

Guba, E., & Lincoln, Y. (1988b). The countenances of fourth generation evaluation: Description, judgment, and negotiation. In M. Lipsey & D. Cordray (Eds.), *Evaluation studies review annual* (Vol. 11, pp. 70-88). Newbury Park, CA: Sage.

Guba, E., & Lincoln, Y. (1989). *Fourth generation evaluation.* Newbury Park, CA: Sage.

Gumperz, J. (1982). *Discourse strategies.* New York: Cambridge University Press.

Gusfield, J. (1976). The literary rhetoric of science: Comedy and pathos in drinking driver research. *American Sociological Review, 41,* 16-34.

Habermas, J. (1971). *Knowledge and human interests* (J. Shapiro, Trans.). Boston: Beacon.

Habermas, J. (1980). The hermeneutic claim to universality. In J. Bleicher (Ed.), *Contemporary hermeneutics* (pp. 181-211). London: Routledge & Kegan Paul.

Habermas, J. (1981). Modernity versus postmodernity. *New German Critique, 22,* 3-14.

Habermas, J. (1984). *The theory of communicative action: Vol. 1. Reason and the Rationalization of society* (T. McCarthy, Trans.). Boston: Beacon.

Habermas, J. (1986). A review of Gadamer's *Truth and method.* In B. Wachterhauser (Ed.), *Hermeneutics and modern philosophy* (pp. 243-276). Albany: State University of New York Press.

Habermas, J. (1987). *The theory of communicative action: Vol. 2. Lifeworld and system: A critique of functionalist reason* (T. McCarthy, Trans.). Boston: Beacon.

Hall, S. (1985). Signification, representation, ideology: Althusser and the post-structuralist debates. *Critical Studies in Mass Communication, 2,* 91-114.

Hamilton, D. (1989). *Towards a theory of schooling.* London: Falmer.

Hamilton, D., McDonald, B., King, C., Jenkins, D., & Parlett, M. (Eds.). (1977). *Beyond the numbers game*. Berkeley, CA: McCutchan.

Hammersley, M., & Atkinson, P. (1983). *Ethnography: Principles in practice*. London: Tavistock.

Hanson, N. (1958). *Patterns of discovery*. Cambridge: Cambridge University Press.

Haraway, D. (1988). Situated knowledges: The science question in feminism and the privilege of partial perspective. *Feminist Studies, 14*, 575-599.

Harding, S. (1982). Is gender a variable in conceptions of rationality? *Dialectica, 36*, 225-242.

Harding, S. (1986). *The science question in feminism*. Ithaca, NY: Cornell University Press.

Harding, S. (Ed.). (1987). *Feminism and methodology*. Bloomington: Indiana University Press.

Harding, S., & Hintikka, M. (1983). *Discovering reality: Feminist perspectives on epistemology, meta-physics, methodology, and philosophy of science*. Boston: D. Reidel.

Hare, R. (1964). *The language of morals*. London: Oxford University Press. (Original work published 1952)

Hare, R. (1972). *Applications of moral philosophy*. London: Macmillan.

Harland, R. (1987). *Superstructuralism: The philosophy of structuralism and post-structuralism*. New York: Methuen.

Harre, R. (1981). The positivist-empiricist approach and its alternative. In P. Reason & J. Rowan (Eds.), *Human inquiry: A sourcebook of new paradigm research* (pp. 3-18). New York: John Wiley.

Hartsock, N. (1987). Re-thinking modernism: Minority vs. majority theories. *Cultural Critique, 7*, 187-206.

Hassan, I. (1987). *The postmodern turn: Essays in postmodern theory and culture*. Columbus: Ohio State University Press.

Havelock, R. (1973). *The change agent's guide to innovation in education*. Englewood Cliffs, NJ: Educational Technology Publications.

Heap, J. (1977). Verstehen, language, and warrants. *Sociological Quarterly, 18*, 177-185.

Heap, J. (1987). *The context of presentation*. Unpublished manuscript, Ontario Institute for Studies in Education, Department of Sociology in Education, Toronto, Canada.

Heidegger, M. (1962). *Being and time* (J. Macquarrie & E. Robinson, Trans.). London: SCM.

Hempel, C. (1966). *Philosophy of natural science*. Englewood Cliffs, NJ: Prentice-Hall.

Heron, J. (1981). Philosophical basis for a new paradigm. In P. Reason & J. Rowan (Eds.), *Human inquiry: A sourcebook of new paradigm research* (pp. 19-36). New York: John Wiley.

Hesse, M. (1980). *Revolutions and reconstructions in the philosophy of science*. Bloomington: Indiana University Press.

Hirsch, E. (1967). *Validity in interpretation*. New Haven, CT: Yale University Press.

Hirsch, E. (1987). *Cultural literacy*. Boston: Houghton Mifflin.

Homans, G. (1950). *The human group*. New York: Harcourt, Brace, & World.

Homans, G. (1974). *Social behavior: Its elementary forms* (rev. ed.). New York: Harcourt Brace Jovanovich.

Hooks, B. (1984). *Feminist theory: From margin to center*. Boston: South End.

Horkheimer, M. (1974). *Eclipse of reason*. New York: Seabury. (Original work published 1947)

Horowitz, I. (Ed.). (1974). *The rise and fall of Project Camelot: Studies in the relationship between social science and practical politics.* Cambridge: MIT Press.

House, E. (1980). *Evaluating with validity.* Beverly Hills, CA: Sage.

House, E. (1988). *Jesse Jackson and the politics of charisma: The rise and fall of the PUSH-EXCEL program.* Boulder, CO: Westview.

Howe, K. (1985). Two dogmas of educational research. *Educational Researcher, 17,* 10-16.

Howe, K. (1988). Against the quantitative-qualitative incompatibility thesis or dogmas die hard. *Educational Researcher, 17,* 10-16.

Huberman, M. (1983). Recipes for busy kitchens: A situational analysis of everyday knowledge use in schools. *Knowledge, 4,* 478-510.

Humphreys, L. (1975). *Tearoom trade: Impersonal sex in public places.* Chicago: Aldine.

Husserl, E. (1962). *Ideas* (W. Gibson, Trans.). New York: Collier.

Hutcheon, L. (1988). *A poetics of postmodernism: History, theory, and fiction.* New York: Routledge & Kegan Paul.

Huyssen, A. (1987). Foreword: The return of Diogenes as postmodern intellectual. In P. Sloterdijk (Ed.), *Critique of cynical reason* (pp. ix-xxv). Minneapolis: University of Minnesota Press.

Hymes, D. (1974). *Foundations of sociolinguistics.* Philadelphia: University of Pennsylvania Press.

Ingram, D. (1987). *Habermas and the true dialectic of reason.* New Haven, CT: Yale University Press.

International Reading Association. (n.d.). *Guidelines for application of editing the reading research quarterly.* Typescript.

Jackson, P. (1968). *Life in classrooms.* New York: Holt, Rinehart, & Winston.

Jacob, E. (1987). Qualitative research traditions: A review. *Review of Educational Research, 57,* 1-50.

Jacob, E. (1988). Clarifying qualitative research: A focus on traditions. *Educational Researcher, 17,* 16-24.

Jacobs, S. (1980). Where have we come? *Social Problems, 27,* 371-378.

James, T. (1986). *The social scientist and minority groups in crisis.* Paper presented at the meeting of the American Educational Research Association, San Francisco.

Jay, M. (1973). *The dialectical imagination: A history of the Frankfurt School and the Institute of Social Research, 1923-1950.* Boston: Little, Brown.

Jensen, A. (1969). How much can we boost IQ and scholastic achievement? *Harvard Educational Review, 39,* 1-123.

Jick, T. (1983). Mixing qualitative and quantitative methods. In J. Van Maanen (Ed.), *Qualitative methodology* (pp. 135-148). Beverly Hills, CA: Sage.

Johnson, M. (1987). *The body in the mind.* Chicago: University of Chicago Press.

Joint Committee on Standards for Educational Evaluation. (1981). *Standards for evaluations of educational programs, projects, and materials.* New York: McGraw-Hill.

Jones, B., & Fennimore, T. (1990). *Restructuring to promote learning in America's schools* (Guidebook 1). Elmhurst, IL: North Central Regional Educational Laboratory.

Jones, J. (1987). *Agatha Christie's Miss Marple in The moving finger* [Television presentation]. England: BBC; USA: Arts and Entertainment Network; Australia: The Seven Network.

Kaestle, C. (1983). *Pillars of the republic: Common schools and American society, 1780-1860.* New York: Hill & Wang.

Kanter, R., with Stein, B. (1980). *The tale of "o": On being different in an organization.* New York: Harper & Row.

Kaplan, A. (1964). *The conduct of inquiry.* San Francisco: Chandler.

Katz, J. (1983). A theory of qualitative methodology: The social system of fieldwork. In R. Emerson (Ed.), *Contemporary field research* (pp. 127-148). Prospect Heights, IL: Waveland.

Keiss, H., & Bloomquist, D. (1985). *Psychological research methods: A conceptual approach.* Boston: Allyn & Bacon.

Keller, E. (1985). *Reflections on gender and science.* New Haven, CT: Yale University Press.

Kelman, H. (1968). *A time to speak: On human values and social research.* San Francisco: Jossey-Bass.

Kennedy, M. (1979). Generalizing from single-case studies. *Evaluation Quarterly, 3,* 661-678.

Kennedy, M. (1984). How evidence alters understanding and decisions. *Educational Evaluation and Policy Analysis, 6,* 207-226.

Kerlinger, F. (1979). *Behavioral research: A conceptual approach.* New York: Holt, Rinehart & Winston.

Kestenbaum, V. (Ed.). (1982). *The humanity of the ill: Phenomenological perspectives.* Knoxville: University of Tennessee Press.

Kloppenberg, J. (1986). *Uncertain victory: Social democracy and progressivism in European and American thought, 1870-1920.* New York: Oxford University Press.

Kuhn, T. S. (1962). *The structure of scientific revolutions.* Chicago: University of Chicago Press.

Kuhn, T. S. (1970). *The structure of scientific revolutions* (2nd ed.). Chicago: University of Chicago Press.

Kuhn, T. S. (1977). *The essential tension.* Chicago: University of Chicago Press.

Kuhn, T. S. (1984). Professionalism recollected in tranquility. *Isis, 75,* 29-32.

Lakatos, I. (1972). Falsification and the methodology of scientific research programs. In I. Lakatos & A. Musgrave (Eds.), *Criticism and the growth of knowledge* (pp. 91-196). Cambridge: Cambridge University Press.

Lakoff, G., & Johnson, M. (1980). *Metaphors we live by.* Chicago: University of Chicago Press.

Langer, S. (1957). *Problems of art.* New York: Scribner.

Larmore, C. (1986). Tradition, objectivity, and hermeneutics. In B. Wachterhauser (Ed.), *Hermeneutics and modern philosophy* (pp. 147-167). Albany: State University of New York Press.

Lather, P. (1986a). Issues of validity in openly ideological research: Between a rock and a soft place. *Interchange, 17,* 63-84.

Lather, P. (1986b). Research as praxis. *Harvard Educational Review, 56,* 257-277.

Lather, P. (1988a). *Values in openly ideological research.* Paper presented at the American Educational Research Association, New Orleans.

Lather, P. (1988b). Feminist perspectives on empowering research methodologies. *Women's Studies International Forum, 11,* 569-581.

Lather, P. (1988c). *Educational research and practice in a postmodern era.* Paper presented at the meeting of the American Educational Research Association, New Orleans.

Lather, P. (1989a). *Deconstructing/deconstructive inquiry: The politics of knowing and being known.* Paper presented at the meeting of the American Educational Research Association, San Francisco.

Lather, P. (1989b). Postmodernism and the politics of enlightenment. *Educational Foundations, 3*, 7-28.

Lather, P. (in press). *Getting smart: Empowering approaches to research and pedagogy.* London: Routledge & Chapman Hall.

Laudan, L. (1977). *Progress and its problems.* Berkeley: University of California Press.

Leach, E. (1969). *Genesis as myth and other essays.* London: Jonathan Cape.

LeCompte, M. (1972). The uneasy alliance between community action and research. *The School Review, 79*, 123-132.

Lecourt, D. (1975). *Marxism and epistemology, Bachelard, Canguilhem, Foucault* (B. Brewster, Trans.). London: New Left.

Leinhardt, G. (1986). Expertise in mathematics teaching. *Educational Leadership, 43*, 23-27.

Leplin, J. (1984). *Scientific realism.* Berkeley: University of California Press.

Lewis, O. (1930). *Life in a Mexican village: Tepoztlan revisited.* Urbana: University of Illinois Press.

Liebow, E. (1967). *Tally's corner.* Boston: Little, Brown.

Lightfoot, S. (1983). *The good high school.* New York: Basic Books.

Lincoln, Y. (Ed.). (1985). *Organizational theory and inquiry: The paradigm revolution.* Beverly Hills, CA: Sage.

Lincoln, Y. (1988). *The role of ideology in naturalistic research.* Paper presented at the meeting of the American Educational Research Association, New Orleans.

Lincoln, Y. (1989). Trouble in the land: The paradigm revolution in the academic disciplines. In E. Pascarella & J. Smart (Eds.), *Higher education: Handbook of theory and research* (Vol. 5, pp. 57-133). New York: Agathon.

Lincoln, Y. (in press). Toward a categorical imperative for qualitative research. In E. Eisner & A. Peshkin (Eds.), *Qualitative research in education.* New York: Teachers College Press.

Lincoln, Y., & Guba, E. (1985). *Naturalistic inquiry.* Beverly Hills, CA: Sage.

Lincoln, Y., & Guba, E. (1986a). But is it rigorous? Trustworthiness and authenticity in naturalistic evaluation. In D. Williams (Ed.), *Naturalistic evaluation* (New Directions for Program Evaluation, No. 30, pp. 73-84). San Francisco: Jossey-Bass.

Lincoln, Y., & Guba, E. (1986b). Research, evaluation, and policy analysis: Heuristics for disciplined inquiry. *Policy Studies Review, 5*, 546-565.

Lincoln, Y., & Guba, E. (1986c). *The development of intrinsic criteria for authenticity: A model for trust in naturalistic research.* Paper presented at the meeting of the American Educational Research Association, San Francisco.

Lincoln, Y., & Guba, E. (1987). *Ethics: The failure of positivist science.* Paper presented at the meeting of the American Educational Research Association, Washington, DC.

Lincoln, Y., & Guba, E. (1988). *Criteria for assessing naturalistic inquiries as reports.* Paper presented at the meeting of the American Educational Research Association, New Orleans.

Lincoln, Y., & Guba, E. (1989). Ethics: The failure of positivist science. *Review of Higher Education, 12*, 221-240.

Lindblom, C., & Cohen, D. (1979). *Useable knowledge: Social science and social problem solving.* New Haven, CT: Yale University Press.

Long, N. (1958). Local community as an ecology of games. *American Sociological Review, 64*, 251-261.

Longino, H. (1988). Science, objectivity, and feminist values (A review essay). *Feminist Studies, 14,* 561-574.

Loucks-Horsley, S., & Hergert, L. (1985). *An action guide to school improvement.* Alexandria, VA: Association for Supervision and Curriculum Development, and Andover, MA: The NETWORK, Inc.

Louis, K., Kell, D., Dentler, R., Corwin, R., & Herriott, R. (1984). *Exchanging ideas: The communication and use of knowledge in education.* Boston: Abt Associates, Inc., and Amherst, MA: The Center for Survey Research, University of Massachusetts.

Louis, K., & Rosenblum, S. (1981). *Linking R&D with local schools: A summary of implications for dissemination and school improvement programs.* Washington, DC: National Institute of Education.

Lybarger, M. (1987). Need as ideology: A look at the early social studies. In T. Popkewitz (Ed.), *The formation of school subjects: The struggle for creating an American institution* (pp. 176-189). London: Falmer.

Lyotard, J. (1984). *The postmodern condition: A report on knowledge* (G. Bennington & B. Massumi, Trans.). Minneapolis: University of Minnesota Press.

MacIntyre, A. (1973). Ideology, social science, and revolution. *Comparative Politics, 5,* 321-342.

MacIntyre, A. (1984). *After virtue* (2nd ed.). Notre Dame, IN: University of Notre Dame Press.

MacKenzie, D. (1981). *Statistics in Great Britain: 1865-1930.* Edinburgh: Edinburgh University Press.

Malinowski, B. (1967). *A diary in the strict sense of the word.* New York: Harcourt Brace.

Manicas, P. (1987). *A history and philosophy of the social sciences.* Oxford: Basil Blackwell.

Manicas, P., & Rosenberg, A. (1985). Naturalism, epistemological individualism, and "The Strong Programme" in the sociology of knowledge. *Journal for the Theory of Social Behavior, 15,* 76-101.

Mannheim, K. (1936). *Ideology and utopian* (L. Wirth & E. Shils, Trans.). New York: International Library of Psychology, Philosophy of Scientific Method.

Maquet, J. (1964). Objectivity in anthropology. *Current Anthropology, 5,* 47-55.

Marcus, G., & Fischer, R. (1986). *Anthropology as cultural critique: An experimental moment in the human sciences.* Chicago: University of Chicago Press.

Marshall C. (1985a). Field studies and educational administration and policy: The fit, the challenge, the benefits and costs. *Urban Education, 20,* 61-80.

Marshall C. (1985b). Appropriate criteria of trustworthiness and goodness in qualitative research on education or organizations. *Quality and Quantity, 19,* 353-373.

Marshall C., Mitchell, D., & Wirt, F. (1986). The context of state level policy formulation. *Educational Evaluation and Policy Analysis, 84,* 347-378.

Marshall C., Mitchell, D., & Wirt, F. (1989). *Culture and education policy in the American states.* Hampshire, England: Falmer.

Martin, L., Gutman, H., & Hutton, P. (1988). *Technologies of the self, a seminar with Michel Foucault.* Amherst: University of Massachusetts.

Martineau, H. (1988). *How to observe morals and manners* (M. Hill, Ed.). New Brunswick, NJ: Transaction. (Original work published 1838)

Masterman, M. (1970). The nature of a paradigm. In I. Lakatos & A. Musgrave (Eds.), *Criticism and the growth of knowledge* (pp. 59-89). Cambridge: Cambridge University Press.

Maxwell, G. (1962). The ontological status of theoretical entities. In H. Feigl & G. Maxwell (Eds.), *Minnesota studies in the philosophy of science, III* (pp. 3-27). Minneapolis: University of Minnesota Press.

May, W. (1980). Doing ethics: The bearing of ethical theories on fieldwork. *Social Problems, 27*, 358-370.

McCann, H. (1978). *Chemistry transformed: The paradigmatic shift from phlogiston to oxygen.* Norwood, NJ: Ablex.

McCloskey, D. (1983). The rhetoric of economics. *Journal of Economic Literature, 21*, 481-517.

McCutcheon, G. (1979). Beyond the raspberry bushes. *Journal of Curriculum Theorizing, 1*, 18-25.

McCutcheon, G. (1980). How do elementary teachers plan their courses? *Elementary School Journal, 81*, 4-23.

McCutcheon, G. (1981). On the interpretation of classroom observations. *Educational Researcher, 10*, 5-10.

McGrath, J. (1982). Dilemmatics: The study of research choices and dilemmas. In J. McGrath, J. Martin, & R. Kulka (Eds.). *Judgment calls in research* (pp. 69-102). Beverly Hills, CA: Sage.

McKeon, R. (1941). *The basic works of Aristotle.* New York: Random House.

Mead, G. (1967). *Mind, self, and society* (C. Morris, Ed.). Chicago: University of Chicago Press. (Original work published 1934)

Mead, M. (1961). *Coming of age in Samoa.* Harmondsworth, England: Penguin.

Melville, H. (1959). *The complete short stories of Nathaniel Hawthorne.* Garden City, NY: Hanover House.

Merleau-Ponty, M. (1974). *Phenomenology of perception* (C. Smith, Trans.). New York: Humanities.

Merquior, J. (1986). *A critique of structuralist and poststructuralist thought.* London: Verso.

Merton, R. (1957). *Social theory and social structure.* New York: Free Press.

Miles, M., & Huberman, A. (1984). *Qualitative data analysis.* Beverly Hills, CA: Sage.

Mills, C. (1956). *The power elite.* New York: Oxford University Press.

Miner, H. (1952). The folk-urban continuum. *American Sociological Review, 17*, 529-537.

Mischler, E. (1979). Meaning in context: Is there any other kind? *Harvard Educational Review, 49*, 279-305.

Mischler, E. (1984). *The discourse of medicine: Dialectics of medical interviews.* Norwood, NJ: Ablex.

Mitchell, B., & Green, J. (1986). Of searchers, solons, and soldiers. In J. Niles & R. Kalik (Eds.), *Solving problems: Learners, teachers, and researchers* (pp. 395-405) (35th Yearbook). National Reading Conference, Rochester, New York.

Morgan, G. (1983a). *Beyond method: Strategies for social research.* Beverly Hills, CA: Sage.

Morgan, G. (1983b). Toward a more reflective social science. In G. Morgan (Ed.), *Beyond method: Strategies for social research* (pp. 368-376). Beverly Hills, CA: Sage.

Morgan, G. (1983c). Exploring choice: Reframing the process of evaluation. In G. Morgan (Ed.), *Beyond method: Strategies for social research* (pp. 392-404). Beverly Hills, CA: Sage.

Nagel, E. (1961). *The structure of science.* New York: Harcourt Brace Jovanovich.

Namenwirth, M. (1986). Science through a feminist prism. In R. Blier (Ed.), *Feminist approaches to science* (pp. 18-41). New York: Pergamon.

Napoli, D. (1981). *Architects of adjustment: The history of the psychological profession in the United States*. Port Washington, KY: Kennikat.

Newton-Smith, W. (1981). *The rationality of science*. London: Routledge & Kegan Paul.

Noblit, G. (1984). The prospects of an applied ethnography of education: A sociology of knowledge interpretation. *Educational Evaluation and Policy Analysis, 6*, 95-101.

O'Brien, M. (1981). *The politics of reproduction*. Boston: Routledge & Kegan Paul.

O'Donnell, J. (1985). *The origins of behaviorism: American psychology, 1976-1920*. New York: University of New York Press.

Ortony, A. (1979). *Metaphor and thought*. New York: Cambridge University Press.

Overman, E. (1988). Introduction: Social science and Donald T. Campbell. In E. Overman (Ed.), *Methodology and epistemology for social science, selected papers, Donald T. Campbell* (pp. vii-xix). Chicago: University of Chicago Press.

Palmer, R. (1969). *Hermeneutics*. Evanston, IL: Northwestern University Press.

Pannanberg, W. (1986). Hermeneutics and universal history. In B. Wachterhauser (Ed.), *Hermeneutics and modern philosophy* (pp. 111-146). Albany: State University of New York Press.

Parlett, M., & Hamilton, D. (1977). *Introduction to illuminative evaluation*. Cardiff-by-the-Sea, CA: Pacific Soundings.

Patai, D. (1988). Constructing a self: A Brazilian life story. *Feminist Studies, 14*, 143-166.

Pateman, C. (1988a). The patriarchal welfare state. In A. Gutman (Ed.), *Democracy and the welfare state*. Princeton, NJ: Princeton University Press.

Pateman, C. (1988b). *The sexual contract*. Stanford, CA: Stanford University Press.

Patience, A., & Smith, J. (1986). Derek Freeman and Samoa: The making and unmaking of a biobehavioral myth. *American Anthropologist, 88*, 157-167.

Patton, M. (1975). *Alternative evaluation research paradigms*. Grand Forks, ND: University of North Dakota Press.

Patton, M. (1980). *Qualitative evaluation methods*. Beverly Hills, CA: Sage.

Peirce, C. (1878). How to make our ideas clear. In V. Tomas (Ed.), *Charles S. Peirce: Essays in the philosophy of science* (pp. 31-56). New York: Liberal Arts.

Peirce, C. (1896). Lessons from the history of science. In V. Tomas (Ed.), *Charles S. Peirce: Essays in the philosophy of science* (pp. 195-234). New York: Liberal Arts.

Peirce, C. (1931-1935). *Collected papers of Charles Sanders Peirce* (C. Hartshorne & P. Wiess, Eds.). Cambridge, MA: Harvard University Press.

Peshkin, A. (1986). *God's choice*. Chicago: University of Chicago Press.

Peters, R. (1965). Education as initiation. In R. Archambault (Ed.), *Philosophical analysis and education* (pp. 87-112). London: Routledge & Kegan Paul.

Phillips, D. (1983). After the wake. *Educational Researcher, 12*, 4-12.

Phillips, D. (1987a). On what scientists know and how they know it. In W. Shadish, Jr., & C. Reichardt (Eds.), *Evaluation studies review annual* (Vol. 12; pp. 377-399). Newbury Park, CA: Sage.

Phillips, D. (1987b). *Philosophy, science, and social inquiry*. Oxford: Pergamon.

Phillips, D. (1987c). Validity in qualitative research: Why the worry about warrant will not wane. *Education and Urban Society, 20*, 9-24.

Phillips, D. (in press). Subjectivity and objectivity: An objective inquiry. In E. Eisner & A. Peshkin (Eds.), *Qualitative inquiry in education*. New York: Teachers College Press.

Pillemer, K. (1987). Combining qualitative and quantitative data in the study of elder abuse. In S. Reinharz & G. Rowles (Eds.), *Qualitative gerontology* (pp. 256-273). New York: Springer.

Pinar, W. (1988). Whole, bright, deep with understanding: Issues in qualitative research and autobiography. In W. Pinar (Ed.), *Contemporary curriculum discourses* (pp. 134-153). Scottsdale, AZ: Gorsuch Scarisbrick.

Polanyi, M. (1962). *Personal knowledge.* Chicago: University of Chicago Press.

Popkewitz, T. (1984). *Paradigm and ideology in educational research: The social functions of the intellectual.* London: Falmer.

Popper, K. (1961). *The poverty of historicism.* London: Routledge & Kegan Paul.

Popper, K. (1968a). *Conjectures and refutations.* New York: Harper & Row.

Popper, K. (1968b). *The logic of scientific discovery* (2nd ed.). New York: Harper & Row.

Popper, K. (1976). The logic of the social sciences. In T. Adorno et al. (Eds.), *The positivist dispute in German sociology* (pp. 87-104). New York: Harper Torchbooks.

Putnam, H. (1981). *Reason, truth, and history.* Cambridge: Cambridge University Press.

Putnam, H. (1987). *The many faces of realism.* LaSalle, IL: Open Court.

Rabine, L. (1988). A feminist politics of non-identity. *Feminist Studies, 14,* 11-31.

Rabinow, P. (1983). Humanism as nihilism. In N. Haan, R. Bellah, P. Rabinow, & W. Sullivan (Eds.), *Social science as moral inquiry* (pp. 52-75). New York: Columbia University Press.

Rajchman, J. (1985). *Michel Foucault: The freedom of philosophy.* New York: Columbia University Press.

Ralston, A. (1986). Discrete mathematics: The new mathematics of science. *American Scientist, 74,* 611-618.

Rappaport, R. (1986). Desecrating the holy woman: Derek Freeman's attack on Margaret Mead. *American Scholar, 55,* 313-347.

Ravetz, J. (1971). *Scientific knowledge and its social problems.* Oxford: Clarendon.

Rawls, J. (1971). *A theory of justice.* Cambridge, MA: Belknap.

Read, H. (1943). *Education through art.* New York: Pantheon.

Reason, P., & Rowan, J. (Eds.). (1981). *Human inquiry: A sourcebook of new paradigm research.* New York: John Wiley.

Redfield, R. (1941). *The folk culture of Yucatan.* Chicago: University of Chicago Press.

Reinharz, S. (1978). *On becoming a social scientist.* San Francisco: Jossey-Bass.

Reinharz, S. (1981). Implementing new paradigm research: A model for training and practice. In P. Reason & J. Rowan (Eds.), *Human inquiry: A sourcebook of new paradigm research* (pp. 415-436). New York: John Wiley.

Reinharz, S. (1984a). *On becoming a social scientist* (rev. ed.). New Brunswick, NJ: Transaction.

Reinharz, S. (1984b). Feminist research methodology groups: Origins, forms, and functions. In L. Tilly & V. Petraka (Eds.), *Feminist visions and re-visions* (pp. 197-228). Ann Arbor: University of Michigan, Women's Studies.

Reinharz, S. (1987). Feminist distrust: Problems of content and context in sociological work. In D. Berg & K. Smith (Eds.), *The self in social inquiry* (pp. 153-172). Newbury Park, CA: Sage.

Reinharz, S. (1989). Sociologists working in Israel. *ASA Footnotes, 17,* 3-4.

Reinharz, S., with Davidman, L. (in press). *Social research methods, feminist voices.* New York: Pergamon.

Ricoeur, P. (1981). *Hermeneutics and the social sciences* (J. Thompson, Ed. and Trans.). Cambridge: Cambridge University Press.

Riley, D. (1988). *"Am I that name?" Feminism and the category of "women" in history.* Minneapolis: University of Minnesota Press.

Rist, R. (1980). Blitzkrieg ethnography: On the transformation of a method into a movement. *Educational Researcher, 9,* 8-10.

Ritzer, G. (1980). *Sociology: A multiple paradigm science.* Boston: Allyn & Bacon.

Rorty, R. (1979). *Philosophy and the mirror of nature.* Princeton, NJ: Princeton University Press.

Rorty, R. (1982a). *Consequences of pragmatism.* Minneapolis: University of Minnesota Press.

Rorty, R. (1982b). Method, social science, and social hope. In *Consequences of pragmatism* (pp. 191-210). Minneapolis: University of Minnesota Press.

Rorty, R. (1985). Solidarity or objectivity? In J. Rajchman & C. West (Eds.), *Post-analytic philosophy* (pp. 3-19). New York: Columbia University Press.

Rossman, G., Corbett, H., & Firestone, W. (1988). *Change and effectiveness in schools: A cultural perspective.* Albany: State University of New York Press.

Rossman, G., & Wilson, B. (1985). Numbers and words: Combining quantitative and qualitative methods in a single large-scale evaluation study. *Evaluation Review, 9,* 627-643.

Sacks, O. (1986). *The man who mistook his wife for a hat.* London: Pan.

Said, E. (1986). Orientalism reconsidered. In F. Barker et al. (Eds.), *Literature, politics, and theory* (pp. 210-229). London & New York: Methuen.

Said, E. (1989). Representing the colonized: Anthropology's interlocutors. *Critical Inquiry, 15,* 205-225.

Savage, M. (1988). Can ethnographic narrative be a neighborly act? *Anthropology and Education Quarterly, 19,* 3-19.

Schaefer, R. (1967). *The school as a center of inquiry.* New York: Harper & Row.

Schaff, A. (1973). *Language and cognition* (R. Cohen, Ed.). New York: McGraw-Hill.

Schatzman, L., & Strauss, A. (1973). *Field research.* Englewood Cliffs, NJ: Prentice-Hall.

Scheffler, I. (1967). *Science and subjectivity.* New York: Bobbs-Merrill.

Scheffler, I. (1974). *Four pragmatists: A critical introduction to Peirce, James, Mead, and Dewey.* New York: Humanities.

Schoen, D. (1983). *The reflective practitioner.* New York: Basic Books.

Schoen, D. (1987). *Educating the reflective practitioner.* San Francisco: Jossey-Bass.

Schoenfeld, A. (1985). *Mathematical problem solving.* New York: Academic Press.

Schutz, A. (1967). *The phenomenology of the social world.* Evanston, IL: Northwestern University Press. (Original work published 1932)

Schwandt, T. (1989a). Solutions to the paradigm conflict: Coping with uncertainty. *Journal of Contemporary Ethnography, 17,* 379-407.

Schwandt, T. (1989b). Recapturing moral discourse in evaluation. *Educational Researcher, 18,* 11-16.

Schwandt, T., & Halpern, E. (1988). *Linking auditing and metaevaluation: Enhancing quality in applied research.* Newbury Park, CA: Sage.

Schwartz, P., & Ogilvy, J. (1979). *The emergent paradigm: Changing patterns of thought and belief* (Analytic Report no. 7, Values and Lifestyle Program). Menlo Park, CA: SRI International.

Scott, J. (1987). Critical tensions. Review of Teresa de Lauretis, Feminist studies/critical studies. *Women's Review of Books, 5,* 17-18.

Scott, J. (1988). Deconstructing equality-versus-difference: Or, the uses of post-structuralist theory for feminism. *Feminist Studies, 14,* 33-50.

Scriven, M. (1956). A possible distinction between traditional scientific disciplines and the study of human behavior. In H. Feigl & M. Scriven (Eds.), *Minnesota studies in the philosophy of science, I* (pp. 330-339). Minneapolis: University of Minnesota Press.

Scriven, M. (1958). Definitions, explanations, and theories. In H. Feigl et al. (Eds.), *Minnesota studies in the philosophy of science, II* (pp. 99-195). Minneapolis: University of Minnesota Press.

Scriven, M. (1959). Truisms as the grounds for historical explanations. In P. Gardiner (Ed.), *Theories of history* (pp. 443-475). New York: Free Press.

Scriven, M. (1966). *Primary philosophy*. New York: McGraw-Hill.

Scriven, M. (1969). Logical positivism and the behavioral sciences. In P. Achinstein & S. Barker (Eds.), *The legacy of logical positivism* (pp. 195-210). Baltimore, MD; Johns Hopkins University Press.

Sellar, A. (1988). Realism vs. relativism: Towards a politically adequate epistemology. In M. Griffiths & M. Whitford (Eds.), *Feminist perspectives in philosophy* (pp. 169-186). Bloomington: Indiana University Press.

Sergiovanni, T. (1983). *Supervision* (3rd ed.). New York: McGraw-Hill.

Shadish, W. Jr., Cook, T., & Houts, A. (1986). Quasi-experimentation in a critical multiplist mode. In W. Trochim (Ed.), *Advances in quasi-experimental design and analysis* (pp. 29-46). San Francisco: Jossey-Bass.

Shavelson, R. (1983). Review of research on teachers' pedagogical judgments, plans, and decisions. *Elementary School Journal, 83*, 392-415.

Sherman, R., & Webb, R. (1988). Qualitative research in education: A focus. In R. Sherman & R. Webb (Eds.), *Qualitative research in education* (pp. 2-21). London: Falmer.

Shils, E. (1968). The concept and function of ideology. In D. Sills (Ed.), *International encyclopedia of social science*. New York: Macmillan.

Shimony, A. (1981). Integral epistemology. In M. Brewer & B. Collins (Eds.), *Scientific inquiry and the social sciences* (pp. 98-123). San Francisco: Jossey-Bass.

Shipley, J. (1984). *The origins of English words*. Baltimore, MD: Johns Hopkins University Press.

Shulman, L. (1987). Knowledge and teaching: Foundations of the new reform. *Harvard Educational Review, 57*, 1-22.

Siegel, H. (1987). *Relativism refuted*. Dordrecht, the Netherlands: Reidel.

Silva, E., & Slaughter, S. (1984). *Serving power: The making of the academic social science expert*. Westport, CT: Greenwood.

Simmel, G. (1950). *The sociology of Georg Simmel* (K. Wolff, Ed. and Trans.). New York: Free Press.

Simons, H. (1987). *Getting to know schools in a democracy*. London: Falmer.

Sirotnik, K., & Oakes, J. (in press). *Evaluation and social justice: Issues in public education* (New Directions for Program Evaluation). San Francisco: Jossey-Bass.

Smith, A., & Louis, K. (1982). Multi-method policy research: Issues and applications. *American Behavioral Scientist, 26*, 1-144.

Smith, D. (1987). *The everyday world as problematic: A feminist sociology*. Toronto: University of Toronto Press.

Smith, J. (1983). Quantitative vs. interpretive: The problem of conducting social inquiry. In E. House (Ed.), *Philosophy of evaluation* (New Directions for Program Evaluation, No. 19, pp. 27-51). San Francisco: Jossey-Bass.

Smith, J. (1984). The problem of criteria for judging interpretive inquiry. *Educational Evaluation and Policy Analysis, 6*, 379-391.

Smith, J., & Heshusius, L. (1986). Closing down the conversation: The end of the quantitative-qualitative debate among educational inquirers. *Educational Researcher, 15*, 4-12.

Smith, L. (1979). An evolving logic of participant observation, educational ethnography, and other case studies. In L. Shulman (Ed.), *Review of research in education* (pp. 316-377). Chicago: Peacock.

Smith, L. (in press). Ethics in qualitative research and individual perspective. In E. Eisner & A. Peshkin (Eds.), *Qualitative research in education*. New York: Teachers College Press.

Smith, L., & Geoffrey, W. (1968). *The complexities of an urban classroom*. New York: Holt, Rinehart & Winston.

Smith, L., Kleine, P., Prunty, J., & Dwyer, D. (1986). *Educational innovators: Then and now*. London: Falmer.

Smith, L., & Pohland, P. (1974). Education, technology, and the rural highlands. In D. Sjogren (Ed.), *Four evaluation examples: Anthropological economic, narrative, and portrayal* (pp. 5-54) (AERA Monograph Series on Curriculum Evaluation, No. 7). Chicago: Rand McNally.

Smith, M. (1987). Publishing qualitative research. *American Educational Research Journal, 24*, 173-183.

Soltis, J. (1984). On the nature of educational research. *Educational Researcher, 13*, 5-10.

Spindler, G., & Spindler, L. (1989). Comments on the future of anthropology and education. *Anthropology Newsletter, 30*, 9 (Council on Anthropology and Education Section).

Spiro, M. (1966). Religion: Problems of definition and explanation. In M. Banton (Ed.), *Anthropological approaches to the study of religion* (pp. 85-125). London: Tavistock.

Spivak, G. (1987). *In other words: Essays in cultural politics*. New York: Methuen.

Spradley, J. (1979). *The ethnographic interview*. New York: Holt, Rinehart & Winston.

Stake, R. (1975). *Evaluating the arts in education*. Columbus, OH: Charles E. Merrill.

Stake, R. (1978). The case study method in social inquiry. *Educational Researcher, 7*, 5-8.

Stake, R. (1983). The case study method in social inquiry. In G. Madaus, M. Scriven, & D. Stufflebeam (Eds.), *Evaluation models* (pp. 279-286). Boston: Kluwer-Nijhoff.

Stake, R. (1985). Evaluation: Retrospect and prospect—a personal interpretation. *Educational Evaluation and Policy Analysis, 7*, 243-244.

Stanic, G. (1987). Mathematics education in the United States at the beginning of the 20th century. In T. Popkewitz (Ed.), *The formation of school subjects: The struggle for creating an American institution* (pp. 145-175). London: Falmer.

Statt, D. (1981). *Dictionary of psychology* (1st ed.). New York: Barnes & Noble.

Strauss, A. (1973). *Field research: Strategies for a natural sociology*. Englewood Cliffs, NJ: Prentice-Hall.

Strauss, A. (1987). *Qualitative analysis for social scientists*. Cambridge: Cambridge University Press.

Strauss, A., Schatzman, A., Ehrlich, D., Bucher, R., & Sabshin, M. (1963). The hospital and its negotiated order. In E. Friedson (Ed.), *The hospital in modern society* (pp. 147-169). New York: Macmillan.

Sullivan, W. (1986). *Reconstructing public philosophy*. Berkeley: University of California Press.

Taylor, C. (1985). *Human agency and language.* Cambridge: Cambridge University Press.

Tiles, M. (1984). *Bachelard: Science and objectivity.* Cambridge: Cambridge University Press.

Toennies, F. (1957). *Community and society.* New York: Harper.

Tom, A. (1984). *Teaching as a moral craft.* New York: Longman.

Toulmin, A. (1970a). Does the distinction between normal and revolutionary science hold water? In I. Lakatos & A. Musgrave (Eds.), *Criticism and the growth of knowledge* (pp. 39-48). Cambridge: Cambridge University Press.

Toulmin, A. (1970b). Reasons and causes. In R. Borger & F. Cioffi (Eds.), *Explanation in the behavioral sciences* (pp. 1-26). Cambridge: Cambridge University Press.

Toulmin, S. (1972). *Human understanding.* Princeton, NJ: Princeton University Press.

Toulmin, S. (1983). The construal of reality: Criticism in modern and postmodern science. In W. Mitchell (Ed.), *The politics of interpretation* (pp. 99-117). Chicago: University of Chicago Press.

Toulmin, S., & Goodfield, J. (1961). *The fabric of the heavens.* London: Hutchinson & Co.

Toulmin, S., & Goodfield, J. (1965). *The discovery of time.* London: Hutchinson & Co.

Trigg, R. (1985). *Understanding social science.* Oxford: Basil Blackwell.

Turner, J., & Beeghley, L. (1981). *The emergence of sociological theory.* Homewood, IL: Dorsey.

Turner, S. (1980). *Sociological explanation as translation.* Cambridge: Cambridge University Press.

Tyler, S. (1987). *The unspeakable: Discourse, dialogue, and rhetoric in the postmodern world.* Madison: University of Wisconsin Press.

Udehn, L. (1987). *Methodological individualism: A critical appraisal.* Uppsala, Sweden: Uppsala Universitet Reprocentralen HSC, Sociologiska Institutionen.

U.S. Department of Education. (1986). *What works: Research about teaching and learning.* Washington, DC: Author.

Valle, R., & King, M. (Eds.). (1978). *Existential phenomenological alternatives for psychology.* New York: Oxford University Press.

van Fraassen, B. (1980). *The scientific image.* Oxford: Oxford University Press.

Van Maanen, J. (Ed.). (1979). The seminar. *Administrative Science Quarterly, 24,* 519.

Van Maanen, J. (1988). *Tales of the field: On writing ethnography.* Chicago: University of Chicago Press.

Wallace, A. (1970). *Culture and personality* (2nd ed.). New York: Holt, Rinehart & Winston.

Warshay, L. (1962). The breadth of perspective. In A. Rose (Ed.), *Human behavior and social process: An interactional approach* (pp. 148-176). New York: Houghton Mifflin.

Wax, M. (1980). Paradoxes on "consent" to the practice of fieldwork. *Social Problems, 27,* 272-283.

Wax, R. (1971). *Doing fieldwork.* Chicago: University of Chicago press.

Webb, E., Campbell, D., Schwartz, R., & Sechrest, L. (1966). *Unobtrusive measures.* Chicago: Rand McNally.

Weber, M. (1962). Science as a vocation. In B. Barber & W. Hirsch (Eds.), *The sociology of science* (pp. 569-589). New York: Free Press.

Weber, M. (1968). *Economy and society.* New York: Bedminster.

Webster's Seventh New Collegiate Dictionary. (1972). Springfield, MA: G. & C. Merriam Co.

Weedon, C. (1987). *Feminist practice and poststructuralist theory*. Oxford, England: Basil Blackwell.

Weiss, C. (1980). *Social science research and decision making*. New York: Columbia.

West, C. (1987). Postmodernism and black America. *Zeta Magazine, 1*, 27-29.

Whyte, W. (1955). *Street corner society: The social structure of an Italian slum* (3rd ed.). Chicago: University of Chicago Press.

Williams, R. (1977). *Marxism and literature*. Oxford: Oxford University Press.

Willis, P. (1980). Notes on method. In S. Hall et al. (Eds.), *Culture, media, language* (pp. 88-95). London: Hutchinson.

Wilson, E. (1971). *Sociology: Rules, roles, and relationships*. Homewood, IL: Dorsey.

Wolcott, H. (1973). *The man in the principal's office*. New York: Holt, Rinehart & Winston.

Wolcott, H. (1988). Ethnographic research in education. In R. Jaeger (Ed.), *Complementary methods for research in education*. Washington, DC: American Educational Research Association.

Woolf, V. (1979). Professions for women. In M. Barrett (Ed.), *Women and writing* (pp. 57-63). New York: Harcourt Brace Jovanovich. (First American edition, 1980)

Wright, E. (1978). *Class, crisis, and the state*. London: New Left.

Yin, R. (1984). *Case study research: Design and methods*. Beverly Hills, CA: Sage.

Yinger, R. (1988). *Community, place, and the conversation of teaching*. Paper presented at the Reflective Inquiry Conference, Orlando, FL.

Zaharlick, A. & Green, J. (in press). Ethnography and education. In J. Squires, J. Jensen, & J. Flood (Eds.), *Handbook of research in English language arts*. New York: Macmillan.

Zaner, R. (1981). *The context of self: A phenomenological inquiry using medicine as a clue*. Athens: Ohio University Press.

Zeller, N. (1987). *A rhetoric for naturalistic inquiry*. Unpublished doctoral dissertation, Indiana University.

Zukav, G. (1979). *The dancing Wu-Li masters*. New York: Bantam.

Author Index

Subject Index

About the Contributors

Harbans S. Bhola is Professor of Education, Indiana University, where he teaches comparative education, educational policy analysis, and planning and management of educational change. His evaluation work for UNESCO, Paris, and the German Foundation for International Development, Bonn, West Germany, in various Third World countries has made of him a methodological pragmatist if not a complete naturalistic evaluator. His interests are well reflected in his recent work: "The CLER Model of Innovation Diffusion, Planned Change and Development: A Conceptual Update and Applications," *Knowledge in Society: The International Journal of Knowledge Transfer, 4* (1989), 56-66; "Training of Evaluators in the Third World: Implementation of the Action Training Model (ATM) in Kenya," *Evaluation and Program Planning, 12* (1989), 249-258; and *World Trends and Issues in Adult Education* (International Bureau of Education Science Series), Paris: UNESCO, London: Jessica Kingsley Publishers.

Susanne Chandler is a doctoral candidate at The Ohio State University involved in exploring factors that support and/or constrain learning in the everyday contexts of schooling. She examines the nature of curriculum as a product and process in classroom life. She is concerned with articulating qualitative research perspectives and has written on the purposes of educational research. Central to her work (as well as that of her coauthor, Judith Green) is a concern for understanding the purposes and goals of educational research; theory-method relationships; the nature of research as a process for exploring educational issues, processes, and institutions; and the relationships among theory, research, and practice.

David P. Crandall is Executive Director of the Regional Laboratory for Educational Improvement of the Northeast and Islands located in Andover, Massachusetts. In 1969 he founded THE NETWORK, Inc., a research and training organization that promotes a research-driven, school-based approach to educational improvement. He was principal investigator of the last large-scale empirical investigation of federal school improvement initiatives, "The Study of Dissemination

Efforts Supporting School Improvement" (DESSI). As Coordinator of the External Support Group of the OECD-sponsored International School Improvement Project (ISIP), he was involved with ministry representatives from 14 countries exploring how to fashion support mechanisms needed for school improvement policies to be successfully implemented. Publications include the award-winning "Strategic Planning Issues That Bear on the Success of School Improvement Efforts," "External Support Systems for School Improvement," and *People, Policies, and Practices: Examining the Chain of School Improvement.*

Elliot W. Eisner is Professor of Education and Art, Stanford University. He was trained as a painter at the Art Institute of Chicago and afterward in the social sciences at the University of Chicago. He has devoted a major portion of his career to studying the contributions of the arts to education and the use of methods from the arts for understanding and improving educational practice. His publications on these topics include *The Art of Educational Evaluation, The Educational Imagination, Cognition and Curriculum,* and, forthcoming, *The Enlightened Eye: Qualitative Inquiry and the Enhancement of Educational Practice.*

William A. Firestone is Senior Fellow in the Center for Policy Research in Education, Rutgers University. He spent most of his career working in applied research settings at Abt Associates, Inc., and Research for Better Schools. He has used both qualitative and quantitative methods to study such issues as change and implementation, school cultures, alienation and commitment, knowledge dissemination and use, and linkages in educational systems. A particular scholarly interest is the comparison of the rhetoric used in qualitative and quantitative research studies. He has written three books, the most recent of which is *Change and Effectiveness in Schools: A Cultural Perspective* (with Gretchen Rossman and H. Dickson Corbett). His articles have appeared in *Human Organization, Sociology of Education, Educational Researcher, Evaluation Review, American Journal of Education, Educational Evaluation and Policy Analysis,* and *Educational Administration Quarterly.*

Judith L. Green is Professor at The Ohio State University and is involved in exploring factors that support and/or constrain learning in the everyday contexts of schooling. She explores learning and knowledge construction in classrooms and other educational settings

from an interactional sociolinguistic perspective that combines ethnography with discourse analysis. She has written extensively on
research methodology (e.g., ethnography and sociolinguistics in education) and on factors involved in multiple perspective research
approaches.

Jennifer C. Greene is Associate Professor of human service studies at
Cornell University. As an applied methodologist, she works primarily
within an HSS graduate-level program in program evaluation and
planning. Her research interests emphasize improving the quality of
the social-political impact of applied social science, including specific
interests in qualitative, participatory, and mixed-method approaches
to social inquiry.

Thomas B. Gregory teaches at Indiana University, Bloomington,
where he conducts research and writes on alternative education. He
is author or coauthor of three books, including *High Schools as Communities: The Small School Reconsidered* (with Gerald R. Smith). He
spent the 1987-1988 school year as a Lilly Fellow, conducting a naturalistic study at Mountain Open High School. Mountain Open is a
most unusual public alternative school that was, at that time, located
in Evergreen, Colorado. He is now finishing a book, titled *A Real
Logical Way*, that is a chronicle of that experience.

Madeleine Grumet is Dean of the School of Education of Brooklyn
College/City University of New York. A curriculum theorist and
teacher educator, she specializes in humanities education. Bringing
literary and philosophical research methods to education, her research involves the analysis of autobiographical accounts of educational experience. She is currently working with Brooklyn College
faculty in education and the liberal arts to develop new programs for
teacher education that integrate studies of the academic disciplines
with studies in education. She is the author of *Bitter Milk: Women and
Teaching*, published by the University of Massachusetts Press, and
editor of a series of books on feminist theory in education for the State
University of New York Press.

Egon G. Guba is Professor Emeritus of Education, Indiana University.
Trained as a statistician, he practiced conventional inquiry for more
than 25 years of his 38-year academic career but became increasingly

dissatisfied with that approach as a model for *human* inquiry. Beginning with the publication of a monograph applying "naturalistic inquiry" to evaluation in 1978, he has devoted himself to the refinement and development of that new paradigm, recently renamed "constructivist." Three resulting books, all written with Yvonna S. Lincoln, *Effective Evaluation* (1981), *Naturalistic Inquiry* (1985), and *Fourth Generation Evaluation* (1989), have been well received. He regards the present volume, reporting on the "Alternative Paradigms Conference," which he developed and directed, as his major contribution to what he hopes will be a continuing paradigm dialectic.

Ernest R. House is Professor of Education and Director of the Laboratory for Policy Studies, School of Education, University of Colorado at Boulder. He has written extensively on the topics of evaluation, innovation, and policy. His latest book is *Jesse Jackson and the Politics of Charisma: The Rise and Fall of the PUSH/Excel Program* (Westview, 1988). He is the recipient, with William Madura, of the Fifth Annual Harold D. Lasswell Prize in the policy sciences.

Patti A. Lather is Assistant Professor in the Department of Educational Leadership of The Ohio State University. She teaches a three-course sequence in postpositivist research. Her publications have dealt with the methodological implications of critical theories, specifically, feminism, neo-Marxism, and poststructuralism. Her most recent project is *Getting Smart: Empowering Approaches to Research and Pedagogy*, forthcoming from Routledge.

Margaret D. LeCompte is Associate Professor at the University of Colorado at Boulder. She received her doctorate from the University of Chicago in 1974. Her research includes studies of dropouts, school and community organization, classroom interaction and socialization, and qualitative research methods. Her books include *Ethnography and Qualitative Design in Educational Research*, with Judith Goetz; *How Schools Work: A Sociological Analysis of Education*, with Kathleen Bennett; and *Giving Up in School: Teacher Burnout and Student Dropout in America*, with A. Gary Dworkin. She serves on the editorial board of *Education and Urban Society*, has been president of the Council on Anthropology and Education of the American Anthropological Association, and is active in Divisions D, G, and H of the American Educational Research Association.

Yvonna S. Lincoln is Associate Professor of Educational Leadership at Vanderbilt University. She has been in the forefront of criticism of the dominant paradigm for educational research for more than a decade. Her research interests have been in the history of academic thought and discourse for research, and she has pursued this by proposing a phenomenological approach to social science research. She has explored the paradigm shift in evaluation, in organizational theory, and the history of science generally, coauthoring (with Egon Guba) *Effective Evaluation, Naturalistic Inquiry,* and *Fourth Generation Evaluation* and editing *Organizational Theory and Inquiry: The Paradigm Revolution.* She is currently working on a book tracing the paradigm shift and debates about the shift throughout the academic disciplines. She is currently president of the American Evaluation Association, vice president elect of Division J (Post-Secondary Education) of the American Educational Research Association, and the 1990 recipient of Division J's Young Researcher of the Year award.

Catherine Marshall is Associate Professor in the Department of Educational Leadership at Vanderbilt University. The ongoing goal of her teaching and research has been to use an interdisciplinary approach to analyze cultures—of schools, state policy systems, and other organizations. She is editor of the *Peabody Journal of Education* and has published extensively on the politics of education, qualitative methodology, and women's access to careers and on socialization, language, and values in educational administration. Of special interest here are her papers "Appropriate Criteria of Trustworthiness and Goodness for Qualitative Research on Education Organizations" (*Quality and Quantity,* 1985); "Field Studies and Educational Administration and Policy: The Fit, the Challenge, the Benefits, and the Costs" (*Urban Education,* 1985); and "Analyzing the Culture of School Leadership" (*Education and Urban Society,* 1988) and two books *Culture and Education Policy in the American States* and *Designing Qualitative Research* .

Gail McCutcheon is Associate Professor at The Ohio State University, where she does qualitative research about curriculum studies and teacher courses and writes about both topics. Of primary concern for her is the nature of teachers' thinking about the curriculum and what students actually have opportunities to learn. She is currently writing a book about relationships between curriculum development and practice.

Jeri R. Nowakowski is Executive Director, North Central Regional Educational Laboratory, Elmhurst, Illinois. She coauthored *Program Evaluation: A Practitioner's Guide for Trainers and Evaluators* and *A Handbook of Educational Variables* and edited *The Client's Perspective on Evaluation*. She is the author of a number of articles on educational evaluation, including recent work studying school boards' responses to mandated reform through analysis of school board minutes. She was Associate Professor, Leadership and Educational Policy Studies, Northern Illinois University, prior to assuming her current position. She has been president of the Evaluation Network and Interim President of the American Evaluation Association.

Alan Peshkin is Professor of Education at the University of Illinois, Urbana-Champaign, and studies American high schools within the context of their host communities. To date, his work has been in rural, fundamentalist Christian, and multiethnic schools. This research is conducted by means of qualitative inquiry, including long-term participant observation and interviewing. His experiences as researcher have led to an interest in subjectivity as an aspect of all phases of the research process.

Denis C. Phillips is Professor of Education and, by courtesy, of Philosophy, Stanford University. An Australian by birth who came to Stanford in 1974, he has as his main research interests the philosophy of social science and educational and social science research methodology. He retains a strong interest in the history of ideas, especially nineteenth- and twentieth-century educational and psychological thought. He is author or coauthor of seven books, including *Philosophy, Science, and Social Inquiry* (1987), *Visions of Childhood* (1986), and *Toward Reform of Program Evaluation* (1980). He has published extensively in journals, including the *Psychological Review, The Monist, Inquiry, Harvard Educational Review,* and *Educational Theory*. He is president of the Philosophy of Education Society (1990-1991).

Thomas S. Popkewitz is Professor in the Department of Curriculum and Instruction at the University of Wisconsin—Madison. His work is concerned with the social and political implications of educational research, reform, and teacher education. He is currently writing a book on issues of power and knowledge in educational reform.

Shulamit Reinharz is Associate Professor of Sociology at Brandeis University. Her first book, *On Becoming a Social Scientist: From Survey Research and Participant Observation to Experiential Analysis*, was reissued in 1984 in paperback by Transaction Books. She coauthored *Psychology and Community Change* and coedited *Qualitative Gerontology*. She is currently finishing a monograph, *Social Research Methods, Feminist Voices* with former graduate student Lynn Davidman. Her next project is a field study, *Aging on the Kibbutz*. Between 1982 and 1987 she coedited the journal *Qualitative Sociology*. She has published about 50 articles on a wide range of topics, including females in the history of sociology, females in the history of the kibbutz, miscarriage, gerontological theory, feminist theory, and alternative education. At Brandeis she teaches the graduate research seminar in field methods and undergraduate courses on the history of women's contributions to sociology, group dynamics, and social gerontology.

Thomas R. Schwandt is Associate Professor in the program in Educational Inquiry Methodology, School of Education, Indiana University. He teaches courses in interpretive-qualitative methodology, program evaluation, and philosophy of social science and has published books in the fields of both evaluation and research methodology. His current research focuses on the role of moral discourse in shaping conceptions and practices of inquiry. He is committed to the view that social science inquiry is not simply a set of procedures for conceptualizing and investigating problems but a cultural practice grounded in the sociohistorical and political dynamics of human judgment and argument. He believes that *debate* among paradigms is meaningless but that *conversation* about consequences of our beliefs and practices must continue.

Thomas M. Skrtic is Professor of Special Education at the University of Kansas. In addition to his work in special education, he teaches courses and directs research in the areas of educational inquiry, curriculum and instruction, and educational policy and administration. Initially trained in traditional large- and small-group research, his interests in school organization, educational change, and policy analysis and implementation led him to pursue alternative modes of inquiry, including naturalistic inquiry and critical theory. His current research interest is critical pragmatism, the incorporation of a number of antifoundational methodologies under the guiding philosophical orientation of American pragmatism, and its implications for school renewal and cultural transformation. His most recent book, *Behind Special Education*, is an application of critical pragmatism to the problem of school failure.

John K. Smith is Professor of Education at the University of Northern Iowa. He is the author of numerous articles and a book, *The Nature of Social and Educational Inquiry: Empiricism vs. Interpretation*, devoted to examining alternative paradigms and their implications for research practices. His most recent work, including a forthcoming book titled, *After the Demise of Empiricism: The Problem of Judging Social and Educational Research*, focuses on the importance of hermeneutics for understanding the nature of inquiry.

Louis M. Smith is Professor in the Department of Education at Washington University, St. Louis, and holds the Ph.D. degree in psychology from the University of Minnesota. His interests evolved from measurement to the qualitative study of classrooms, curricula, schools, and school districts and, now, to history and biography. His publications include *Educational Psychology* (1964, with B. B. Hudgens), *The Complexities of an Urban Classroom* (1968, with W. Geoffrey), *Anatomy of Educational Innovation* (1971, with P. Keiter), the Kensington Revisited trilogy (with D. Dwyer, P. Kleine, and J. Prunty) *Educational Innovators: Then and Now* (1986), *The Fate of an Innovative School* (1987), and *Innovation and Change in Schooling* (1988).

CPSIA information can be obtained
at www.ICGtesting.com
Printed in the USA
BVHW051717151022
649212BV00001BA/3

9 780803 938236